America's
SECRET
Recreation Areas

Your Travel Guide to the
Forgotten Wild Lands of the
Bureau of Land Management

by **Michael Hodgson**

Foghorn Press
BOOKS BUILDING COMMUNITY
San Francisco

Foghorn Press, Inc.
555 De Haro Street
The Boiler Room #220
San Francisco, CA 94107
(415) 241-9550

Library of Congress Cataloging-in-Publication Data

Hodgson, Michael.

America's Secret Recreation Areas: your guide to the forgotten wild lands of the Bureau of Land Management/Michael Hodgson.
p. cm.

Includes bibliographical references and index.
ISBN 0-935701-60-5: $15.95
1. Recreation areas—West (U.S.)—Directories. 2. Wilderness areas—West (U.S.)—Recreational use—Directories. I. United States. Bureau of Land Management. II. Title.
GV191.42.W47H63   1993
790'.02578—dc20

92-21179
CIP

Printed in the United States of America

America's
SECRET
Recreation Areas

**Your Travel Guide to the
Forgotten Wild Lands of the
Bureau of Land Management**

by Michael Hodgson

BOOKS BUILDING COMMUNITY

San Francisco

Book Credits

Managing Editor/Book Design—**Ann Marie Brown**
Assistant Editor—**Samantha Trautman**

Photographs

Front Cover: Colorado Bureau of Land Management

Color Section (in order of pages):
1) C. W. Telford
2) C. W. Telford (upper)
   James Thomson (lower)
3) Colorado Bureau of Land Management (upper and lower)
4) Glade Walker
5) Glade Walker (upper)
   Bureau of Land Management (lower)
6) James Thomson (upper)
   Glade Walker (lower)
7) Idaho Bureau of Land Management (upper)
   Bureau of Land Management (lower)
8) Ed Bovy

This book is dedicated to Bill Smith,
my Muncie Northside High School English teacher,
who showed me that a passion for the outdoors
and a love for the written word
are a perfect match.

DISCLAIMER

Foghorn Press, Inc. and Michael Hodgson assume no responsibility for the safey of any users of this guidebook. You alone are responsible for determining your level of fitness and ability to wander into Bureau of Land Management lands. Foghorn Press, Michael Hodgson and the BLM are in no way responsible for personal injury, damage to property, or violation of law in connection with the use of this book. Before heading out to any area described in this book, we recommend that you first check with the administering BLM office for updated information regarding the region.

Foghorn Press, Inc. and Michael Hodgson are not responsible for erroneous information, if any, contained within this book, nor for changes made in roads, trails and other features by agencies private or public, nor for changes brought about by weather conditions or acts of God. Further, nothing in this book implies the right to use private property. Public lands may be completely surrounded by private land, which restricts access. Private inholdings may exist within the boundaries of public land. Any and all landowner restrictions must be respected—it's the law and common courtesy.

ADVISORY

A few words about roads: It's true, much of our nation is crisscrossed with fascinating roads that aren't on highway maps at all. You will need BLM surface maps or Forest Service maps to find them. In fact, the National Forest Service alone has more miles of road than all the paved state and federal highways. Add to them the BLM roads and an infinite number of ranch roads, mining roads and timber company roads, and our land begins to look rather like a tangled mess of twine that a cat has scattered all over the living room floor.

Although you will read on Forest Service and BLM maps and hear from officials terms such as "improved," "graded," "primitive," "jeep," "unimproved," and "graveled," treat all ratings with skepticism. While the road you wish to travel on may indeed have earned an "improved" rating several months ago, rains and other weather may have turned it into a rutted, soupy quagmire. When in doubt, check with the locals—they travel and hunt on the roads and will be able to give you accurate and up-to-date information. Many BLM roads are passable when dry in an ordinary automobile, although I never venture out without my four-wheel-drive no matter what the road conditions state. As a rule, don't drive in farther than you are willing to walk out. Always pack along extra food and water in the vehicle just in case.

Regarding directions: While I have tried to be as specific as possible about how to get to destinations, please don't rely completely on my written directions. You will need BLM or Forest Service maps to be sure. The maps in this book are for representation only and are not drawn exactly to scale, nor do they show every back road and trail.

It is wise and heartily recommended that before heading out, you call the BLM office with jurisdiction over the area you're going to and ask for specific and detailed instructions. These will guide you through local road names (which can change), road conditions (which are guaranteed to vary), and access points (which given the state of public/private easement conflicts are sure to vary in some instances).

One other word of advice: If you are somewhat confused as to which way to go and end up asking directions at the local gas station, find no comfort in the smiling assurance "Heck, you can't miss it!" Hearing those words means only one thing—ask someone else for directions!

I have done my level best to ensure accuracy within this book, but as time and weather changes, so do the facts. If you discover something that has changed, facts that need revising, comments that need clarifying or know of another area that should be listed, please write to me at Foghorn Press, 555 De Haro Street, Suite #220, San Francisco, CA 94107, and I will add your comments to the next edition. I am committed to making *America's Secret Recreation Areas* the most accurate, detailed, helpful and enjoyable outdoor book of its kind. Many thanks—

Michael Hodgson

Contents

•

Introduction

Although many people have heard of the Bureau of Land Management (BLM), most do not realize the vastness of the lands it administers for the American public. The BLM is in charge of what remains of the nation's once vast land holdings—the public domain. This immense public domain originally stretched from the Appalachian Mountains to the Pacific Ocean. Of the 1.8 billion acres of public land first acquired by the United States, two-thirds went to private individuals, industries and states. Much of the remaining land was set aside for national forests, wildlife refuges, national parks and monuments, as well as other public purposes. The BLM was left to manage 272 million acres—approximately one-eighth of the United States. Most of these lands are located in twelve Western states, including Alaska, although small parcels are scattered across the eastern United States.

Although the BLM's mandate is one of multiple-use management, including logging, rangeland and minerals leasing, an increasing amount of energy is being directed towards recreation management. This includes National Conservation Areas, National Recreation Areas, approximately 2,000 miles of the Wild and Scenic River system and approximately 1,700 miles of national trails. In addition, the BLM oversees nearly 85,000 miles of streams containing trout, salmon and other sport fish (enough streams to circle the Earth three and one-half times, to put it in perspective), more than four million acres of lakes and reservoirs, more than 470 developed recreation sites, and many other recreational areas. The entire BLM public recreation area is larger than the National Forest and National Park systems—combined.

Couple the BLM's recreational use mandate with the fact that the BLM protects the U.S. government's largest and most varied body of cultural resources, from campsites of the hemisphere's earliest human inhabitants to physical reminders of the historic settings of the old West, plus a vast wildlife and botanical resource, and you have a recipe for unlimited adventure.

Much of the land you will find under BLM jurisdiction is wild—very wild. Many areas are no place for the uninitiated, the tenderfoot or the unprepared. It is exactly this wildness and ruggedness that is the primary attraction. With few restrictions you can wander and camp where you will—almost like when the west was known as the Wild West. Whether by boat, foot, horse or mountain bike, traveling through BLM lands will take you through time and across tundra, coastline, alpine meadows, sand dunes, slickrock canyons, dry lakes, scenic rivers and even subterranean caves.

These lands exist for you, and I hope that with this book in hand, you will experience the joy of discovering an untapped gold mine of recreational opportunity. Let common sense and courtesy be your traveling companion as a world of adventure spreads open at your feet. There is plenty of elbow room out there, so grab your pack, paddle, saddle or rope, and maybe, just maybe, I'll see you in the backcountry.

HOW TO USE THIS BOOK

The book is divided into an introductory chapter ("A User's Guide to the Lands of the BLM"), 12 state chapters, several appendices and an index. The state chapters are arranged in the following order:

1) Maps: State maps with complete listings of BLM trails, recreation areas, available activities and campgrounds. Each listing has a page number next to it to help you quickly find the corresponding description within the chapter. BLM campgrounds are indicated by a tent symbol on each map, with a corresponding listing of the name of the campground and where to call for information or reservations.

2) Best of the State: A listing that includes five to ten sites within each state that are must-sees or ideal recreation destinations. Each Best of the State listing includes the phone number and address of the administering BLM office, the area's general location and directions to it, camping information, permit requirements, suggested maps (USGS, BLM or other maps that cover the area), and the best season to visit.

3) State by Region: Following Best of the State, each state is divided into geographical sections. Every geographical listing is presented as follows: site name, activities most appropriate in that site (wildlife observation, hiking, backpacking, fishing, horseback riding, camping, mountain biking, spelunking, canoeing, rafting, etc.), area description, directions, a listing of available maps by name and publisher (BLM, USGS, Trails Illustrated, etc.), and BLM address and phone number for the office directly responsible for administration of the site.

4) State Information Overview: This listing gives all of the addresses and phone numbers for the various BLM offices throughout the state.

You can look for your ideal recreation site in several ways. You can simply read the Best of the State for the state you wish to visit to find out all the must-see destinations. Or, if you are planning to travel in a certain area of a state, you can look in the State by Region section for that area of the state to see what sites are close by.

You can also look in the appendix under "Recreational Activities by State" on page 524 to see where on BLM land you can partake in your favorite outdoor recreation. Or just look up your favorite trail, recreation area or activity in the easy-to-use index on page 503.

A User's Guide

to the

Lands of the BLM

1

BACKCOUNTRY SAFETY & OTHER WISDOM

WEATHER

Just when you were counting on it being sunny, it rains or snows. But guess what—this is not a problem unless you make it one. Check your attitude. Rain, snow, hail and ice are all just another scene in a marvelous outdoor set. How you view the occasion is up to you. Some of my best times outdoors have been during a rainstorm and the moments just following, as the clouds break and the sunbeams come streaming through like so many warming fingers. Of course, I was properly prepared and you should be too if you are going to enjoy everything Mother Nature may toss at you. Sunscreen, a hat, extra warm clothing, and rain gear are all requisite items to carry with you for even a basic hike.

WINTER TRAVEL

Heading out in the winter is a wonderful time, but be warned—the backcountry is an unforgiving hostess for the unprepared and uninitiated. It is essential for anyone heading into the snowy wilderness to have at least a basic grasp of avalanche safety and to know the current avalanche conditions in the area you plan on exploring. Know how to dress properly to prevent overheating or freezing and how to identify and prevent frost nip and frost bite.

HYPOTHERMIA

Even in temperatures above freezing, hypothermia is possible. If it goes untreated, it can kill. Anyone exposed to wet, cool and windy conditions can suffer hypothermia. It is caused when the body starts losing heat faster than it is being produced, causing a decline in internal body temperature. A person who is shivering, slurring their speech, showing signs of clumsiness or awkwardness, and feeling drowsy may lapse into unconsciousness and could quite possibly die. If you suspect hypothermia (and the victim is always the last to recognize a problem), get the victim dry and warm immediately (pitch a tent, start a fire, make a warm drink). Remove all wet clothing, replacing wet clothes with dry ones. Put the victim in a sleeping bag and give them something warm to drink. Keep in mind that if the victim has lost too much body heat, they may not be able to sufficiently rewarm themselves without assistance, even in a sleeping bag. It this case, climbing in the bag with the victim is required, helping to heat both the bag and the victim with your body.

DON'T DRINK THE WATER

Well, okay, maybe that is a bit severe. Actually, don't drink the water anywhere without first treating it. Crystal clear rivers, streams and mountain lakes may give the impression of purity, but that is far from the truth. Water clarity is not an indication of the presence or absence of bacteria or parasites. Giardia may in fact be present in all wilderness water sources. The only safe solution is to filter, chemically treat or boil all water before drinking it.

ALTITUDE

Many mountainous areas within BLM lands lie above 8,000 feet—an altitude which can cause difficulty for city dwellers who are acclimated to far lower levels. Unless you take the time to acclimate slowly to higher elevations, you risk experiencing various forms of altitude sickness—shortness of breath, headaches, nausea, fatigue, and swelling of the extremities. Should these symptoms occur, check your ascent and rest for a while, overnight if necessary. Once your body adjusts to the different levels of oxygen concentration, you can safely climb higher.

Although rare in elevations below 10,000 feet, a more serious and possibly fatal form of altitude sickness, High Altitude Pulmonary Edema (HAPE) or Cerebral Edema (HACE) can occur. This results in fluid accumulating in the lungs (pulmonary) or brain (cerebral) and can cause death if not treated. If you suspect HAPE or HACE, evacuate the victim to the nearest hospital.

IF YOU GET LOST

Careful route finding and use of a map and compass should keep you on the right track, but in the event of misdirection, it is possible to feel lost—even if you aren't really. If this happens, stop! Realize that you aren't lost, you are right here. Instead, the trail or car is lost because that is what you are trying to find. Study the area and the map and use your compass and awareness to identify surrounding landmarks. If you can carefully retrace your route, do so until you recognize a familiar point. In an emergency, follow a drainage downstream, because drainages almost always lead you to a road, a town or a trail. Keep in mind, however, that if you choose to hike away from your last known point of reference, you may in fact be making it that much more difficult for rescuers to find you.

Carrying and knowing how to use a whistle and signal mirror may be of some help in an emergency situation. A series of three flashes or sharp blasts of the whistle are a universal signal that someone is in distress and can help to summon help—providing someone is watching or listening.

GENERAL TIPS

Be careful with fires—woe be the tenderfoot who lets a fire get out of hand and burn down a forest.

Keep a weather eye skyward. You don't want to be caught on a ridge during a lightening storm, in a canyon bottom during a rainstorm, or on a mountain top during a snow storm.

Stay on trails unless you are an experienced hiker well versed in orienteering skills and map reading knowledge.

Learn a few basic survival skills.

Don't hike alone.

Learn as much about the area you are going to be traveling in as possible.

Keep your trips simple and uncomplicated and don't try to travel too far, too fast. Always travel according to the needs of the slowest and least strong member of your group.

File a travel plan with someone you trust and then stick to the plan. That way, if you get into trouble and don't check in, your chances of help being sent are greatly increased.

Don't play amateur naturalist and begin foraging for wild foods unless you can positively identify what you are gathering. Many wild food eaters have succumbed to poisonous mushrooms, berries and the like.

DESERT TRAVEL TIPS

Avoid heading out in the summer. In most cases, spring and fall are the best seasons to visit.

Know what the water conditions are and where you might be able to find water. Don't count on finding water, however, as a spring that is said to be running and of good quality may have dried up since the last field check. In general, carry one gallon of water per person per day.

Keep a weather eye skyward. Thunderstorms in the distance may mean flash flooding in a canyon through which you had planned on hiking.

Biting flies can be bothersome. Carry insect repellent.

The sun is usually intense. Wear a hat with a visor and light, loose, long-sleeve shirts and long pants. Apply sunscreen to all skin that is exposed. Remember to reapply sunscreen periodically, especially to bare legs after a stream crossing.

FISHING SAFETY

Use caution when fishing on riverbanks. An unstable bank may decide to suddenly drop you into swirling waters below. Ditto the advice when wading, as swift currents and slippery rocks may send you tumbling through the water like just so much bait. Always wear a personal flotation device when fishing from a boat—or anywhere around deep water.

DRUG LAB WASTE

I hate to say it, especially in a book about discovering the joys of wild places, but it's true. An increasing number of drug-manufacturing yahoos have decided that public lands were intended for garbage disposal sites for their manufacturing waste. If you come across a site that has large five-gallon buckets, gallon plastic jugs, large garbage bags, and pieces of lab equipment (beakers, tubes, etc.) get the hell out of Dodge, as both the site and the chemicals are dangerous. Report the siting to the BLM or local law enforcement authorities.

LYME DISEASE

Lyme disease-carrying ticks may be found on public lands in some areas of the country. In the Western United States, the ixodes tick carries the disease and can be identified by its size (tiny) and its color (black and reddish brown). The best prevention for avoiding tick bites is to tuck your shirt into your pants and your pant legs into your socks. Wear light-colored clothing so ticks are easier to spot. Use a tick repellent on your clothing—a number of good repellents can be purchased at most sporting goods stores or specialty outdoor outfitters.

Perform tick checks at least once a day, being especially careful to inspect armpits, behind the ears, and in the navel and groin areas. Prompt removal of the tick lessens the chance of disease transmission. Authorities state that a tick must be attached to the skin for 12 to 24 hours before the disease is transmitted. Lyme disease symptoms include a rash or lesion, flu-like symptoms, headache, stiff neck, fever, muscle ache and general malaise. If you suspect you have lyme disease, see your doctor immediately. If it is left untreated, it can become quite severe.

2

MINIMIZING IMPACTS

Environmental impact problems associated with overuse or individual carelessness are visible in any wilderness or park setting. All you have to do is look—and not very hard at times. Scattered campfire rings, eroding gullies and trails, toilet paper and human waste littering a meadow, girdled trees from improperly tethered horses, food scraps and trash dotting a campsite, graffiti carved on trail signs or trees, vandalized park facilities—sadly, the list goes on.

Land use and impact guidelines are established by land managers for the protection of the wilderness and to enhance each visitor's experience. Before any hiking, boating, mountain biking, camping trip, or other recreational activity, check with the local BLM office for minimum impact recommendations specific to the area you will be traveling in.

Listed below are some general minimum impact guidelines that are appropriate nearly 100% of the time. These "rules to recreate by," when coupled with a dose of common sense, will help to keep the wilderness we love pure and pristine.

HIKING/BACKPACKING

Plan your wilderness trips to avoid major holiday rushes. Trailheads and campgrounds can become so packed with humanity that the water, air and noise impacts become severe. Travel only in small groups—four or less is ideal.

When hiking on a trail, hike in a single file and in the center of the trail. Resist the urge to take a shortcut across a meadow or down a switchback. Doing so will only result in encouraging severe erosion and trail damage.

Take your rest stops only in areas where your presence will not damage the vegetation. Be careful to replace all gear in your pack—the most common time to forget gear or inadvertently litter is during a rest break.

The perfect campsite is never made—it is discovered. Trenching, cutting branches, leveling or removing vegetation are inappropriate camping techniques. Look for a level site that has naturally adequate drainage and is not in a sensitive area that will be irreparably damaged by your presence.

Whenever possible, select campsites that have already been used. This will eliminate the creation or expansion of unnecessary camping areas. Always camp out of sight of others and the trail. Practice no-trace camping.

Use a stove whenever possible. Campfires have romantic appeal, but they have extreme impacts on the environment. Beyond the obvious impacts, keep in mind that the dancing light all but destroys your night vision, obscuring the larger world outside the boundaries of the flame.

Carry out all that you carry in—this includes fishing line, lures, spent cartridges and cigarette butts. Pick up litter as you find it (although sometimes this is difficult because of weight considerations).

Never bury food scraps. They will get dug up and scattered. Burn or pack out all leftover food. Fish entrails must be burned or packed out. Left-over food around campsites is an attraction to animals and a danger to other campers if the attracted animal is a bear.

Use established latrines when they are available. Otherwise, dig a hole six inches deep and at least 200 feet away from the nearest water. Toilet paper does not break down readily so it must be either packed out or burned. Use caution in areas of high fire-risk.

All washing must be done at least 200 feet away from the nearest water source. Use hot water and a minimum amount of soap (avoid using soap if at all possible). Boiling water will serve to sterilize dishes and utensils. Soap residue can cause more harm than the odd speck of grease.

MOUNTAIN BIKING

The following rules of the trail are provided courtesy of the International Mountain Biking Association:

Ride on open trails only. Please respect and abide by all trail closures, private property notices and fences, and all requirements for use permits and authorization. All designated wilderness areas are closed to mountain bikes.

Leave no trace. Do not skid your tires or ride on ground that is rain-soaked and easily scarred. Stick to established trails.

Control your bicycle. Save your "need for speed" for a race. Stay alert at all times. Speed and an out-of-control mountain biker lead to trouble and often injury to other trail users. Always expect that others may be just around a blind corner.

Always yield the right-of-way. When encountering other trail users (hikers, equestrians or fellow bikers), a friendly greeting to announce your presence is considerate and appreciated. Slow to a walk or stop your bike, especially when encountering horses.

Never spook animals. Leave ranch and farm gates as you find them. Disturbing livestock or wild animals can cause serious harm and is considered a major offense. Give plenty of room.

Plan ahead. Know your equipment, know your ability, know the requirements of the area you are riding in, and then plan accordingly. Be self-sufficient at all times.

CLIMBING

Reduce chalk use whenever possible. Climb when it is cooler, chalk up less frequently, use dirt as an alternative agent. There is a new product which looks promising, called X-factor, which dries the hands for a better grip but leaves no unsightly residue behind on the rocks.

If you use tape on your hands, pack it out. Little bits of tape lying around the base of a climb are ugly.

If a path exists to a climbing site, use it. Don't make your own!

Breaking off branches and vegetation that may be in the way on a climb may seem innocent enough, but the practice is indefensible. Work carefully around vegetation or choose another route. It is never acceptable to alter the natural process or balance merely because something is in the way of your climb.

Never modify the rock to create handholds or to improve a hold. If you can't climb the rock face as it exists, then it wasn't meant to be climbed by you.

MOTOR VEHICLES

Off-terrain vehicle use is encouraged and supported on many of the BLM's vast acreages of wild land. Some people use four-wheel-drive or off-road vehicles to obtain access to trailheads and remote river put-ins or other recreational sites. Others use off-road vehicles wholly as a toy for fun-hogging through dunes, across desert lands and through mountain byways. Whatever your use, off-road vehicles are only appropriate if used with responsibility and care for the land—in some cases, this means not using them, even if it is legal. Before you head out with your vehicle, think about your responsibility to the land and the next visitor and tread lightly.

Obtain a travel map from the BLM office or U.S. Forest Service that shows legal routes and passages for vehicles and lists the specific rules and regulations for that area.

Do not run over young trees, shrubs or delicate grasses—it will damage and kill them.

Stay off wet, soft roads and trails that will be readily torn up by a vehicle's churning wheels—this is especially true during hunting season!

Skirt the edges of meadows, steep hillsides and streambanks or lakeshores. These areas are very fragile and traveling on them will irreparably scar them.

Stay on established routes and avoid the urge to venture out and pioneer your own path.

Stay away from wild animals, especially those that are raising young or appear to be suffering from a food shortage (in winter months especially). Human contact can alarm animals and cause them to use vital energy reserves that may kill them.

Obey all gate closures and regulatory signs. Vandalism is on the rise—there is no excuse!

Stay out of all wilderness areas. They are closed to all vehicles for good reason.

Stay off private lands unless you have first obtained the landowner's permission.

Respect the rights of hikers, skiers, campers and others to enjoy their activities undisturbed by roaring engines and spinning tires.

RIVER RUNNING

A river corridor is a thin strip of land and water where use impacts become highly concentrated. For that reason, minimum impact techniques are of utmost importance to keep riverways looking pristine.

All solid human waste must be carried out. The typical method is to make a river toilet using an ammo can, heavy duty plastic bags, a toilet seat, chlorine bleach and toilet paper. Although carrying out all human waste may seem unpleasant, it is far less unpleasant than mounds of human waste scattered all along the river bank.

Pack out everything that you pack in.

Place a large tarp under your eating area to catch food scraps, so beach areas do not become feeding grounds for rodents and massive communities of insects.

Use a fire pan at all times for campfires and only use downed wood. Better yet, bring your own charcoal. Fire pans should always be elevated so heat from the pan does not scorch the soil. All ashes, once cooled and doused, must be carried out. A five-gallon slush bucket is the easiest method.

Camp on beaches, sandbars or a non-vegetated site below the high water line. When the river floods, your passing will be washed away and the site will appear pristine to river runners who follow.

Washing or bathing with soap must be done at least 200 feet away from the nearest water source.

Waste water from cooking should be filtered through a fine-mesh screen to remove food solids and then poured directly into the river. Do not scatter waste water on the beach as it will attract flies and other animals.

ARCHAEOLOGICAL SITES

The single biggest problem for archaeological land managers and cultural resource persons is dealing with the unintentional damage caused by visitors. Even with extreme caution, impacts can and do occur. It is imperative that extreme caution and respect be used when visiting and traveling near archaeological and historical sites.

Viewing a site from a distance and not entering it will reduce the impacts a site receives. Although there may only be one or two of you, there are literally thousands of the same "one or two" visiting a site each year, and that's a lot of traffic.

Stop, look and think before entering a cultural site. Identify the midden area (trash pile) so you can avoid walking on it—middens contain important and fragile bits of archaeological information.

Stay on a trail if it has been built through a site.

Looking at artifacts is fine, picking them up and taking them is not! Leave all potsherds and other artifacts where they lie for others to enjoy.

Camping is not allowed in or around ruins.

Move nothing, including branches or rocks, when scrambling around a site. Avoid touching plaster walls. Climbing on the roofs and walls of a site can lead to an immediate collapse of a cultural site that has stood for hundreds of years.

Enjoy rock art by viewing, sketching or photographing. Never chalk, trace or otherwise touch rock art as any kind of contact will cause the ancient figures to disintegrate.

Never build fires in or around cultural sites.

Finally, some cultural sites are places of ancestral importance to Native Americans and demand to be treated with the respect and reverence they deserve.

WATCHING WILDLIFE

You can harm wildlife unintentionally by getting too close! Most wild animals react with alarm when approached by humans on foot or by vehicle. A panic reaction is stressful and causes the animal to use energy and food reserves that are needed for other activities. Repeated disturbances can cause animals and birds to avoid an area—even if that area offers the best food and habitat. Learn animal behavior patterns that will warn you if you are getting too close. You will get your closest peeks at wildlife if you let them come to you. Never, ever use food to attract animals!

Quality binoculars (7 x 35 magnification as a minimum) or a spotting scope will help you to observe wildlife from a safe distance. Use a telephoto lens (300mm) and tripod to get close-up photos.

Rushing around is no way to watch wildlife! The more time that you take, the greater your chances for seeing wildlife that would otherwise be missed. Set up a base camp and spend a few days in a given area. Wild animals are most often spotted at or around dawn and dusk.

Wear muted colors, sit quietly and leave pets at home. Refrain from using scented soaps or perfumes.

Spend time at local museums of natural history to learn about the wildlife in the area you are visiting. Natural history museums and organizations typically have books, brochures, maps and displays that will be of assistance to you. Learn to recognize an animal by its tracks, droppings and sounds.

There are many field guides on the market today that are area-specific pertaining to birds, mammals, animal tracks, edible plants, wildflowers, trees, rocks and gems, and more. Most major bookstores should carry a selection that will prove helpful.

You are too close to a bird if it:
- seems skittish
- raises its head to watch you
- preens excessively, pecks at dirt or feet, or wipes its bill repeatedly
- gives alarm calls
- flushes repeatedly
- gives distraction displays, such as feigning a broken wing.

You are too close to a mammal if it:
- raises its head high, ears pointed in your direction with raised hairs on the neck and shoulders
- exhibits signs of skittishness, such as jumping at sounds or movements
- lowers its head, ears back in preparation for a charge
- moves away
- displays aggressive or nervous behavior

3

MAP AND COMPASS

Staring in bewilderment at a splotch of ink on a map, trying to determine whether or not that splotch is the mountain you are looking at, is not the time to wish you had a better grasp of map and compass skills. Take the time to learn how to use a map and compass before heading out. One excellent way to become proficient with a map and compass is to join a local orienteering club. Check with your nearest outdoor or backpacking store for information about clubs. I also recommend the *Outward Bound Map & Compass Handbook* by Glenn Randall, published by Lyons and Burford, as an excellent source of practical and instructional reading.

WATERPROOFING A MAP

There is nothing fun about trying to navigate while clinging to a soggy map in a downpour. Right before your eyes, the route home turns into a greenish-brown papier-mache clump. When this happens, your only hope is that your memory of the route didn't wash out like the map did.

Making a see-through, waterproof cover for your maps is an easy way to prevent soggy map syndrome. All you need is a large, freezer-weight Zip-loc bag and a few sections of sturdy, waterproof tape like duct or packing tape.

Simply cut the tape into a strip long enough to completely adhere to one edge of the bag from top to bottom. Press one-half of the tape, lengthwise, onto the bag, leaving the other half of the tape hanging over the edge. Now flip the bag over, and fold the tape down on itself and the other side of the bag. Repeat each step two more times, once for the bottom and once for the remaining side. You now have a wonderful waterproof map container that is reinforced on three edges.

Several other ways to waterproof a map are:

•Cover it with clear contact paper (this makes the map waterproof but very stiff and there is no way to write on the map).

•Paint on a product called "Stormproof," available at most

---

map and outdoor specialty stores. The clear chemical coating renders the map waterproof, flexible, and the map can still be written on.

• Apply a coating of "Thompson Water Seal" or other brick and masonry sealant. It will make a map water-repellent, but not waterproof.

FOLDING A MAP

Map folding is an acquired skill. With a blowing wind, a little rain and a sprinkling of fatigue, you can get an irresistible desire to jam or crumple your trail map into the nearest pocket and forget the idea of folding.

Believe it or not, there is a better way—a map-folding technique that results in a very easy-to-use accordion-style configuration that is taught to British Boy Scouts. My cousin from England can fold a map like this in his sleep.

This method allows you to look at any portion of the map without having to fully open it, which is ideal in windy or wet weather. Further, the accordion configuration collapses to pocket-size with ease. Once you've established the creases, any map will fold up and down almost without effort.

Step 1—Lay the map flat, printed side up. Fold it in half vertically, with the face inside the first fold to establish the first crease. Make this and every subsequent crease clean and sharp.

Step 2—Working with only the right half of the map, fold the right side in half towards the center, resulting in quarter-folds.

Step 3—Fold the outside quarter-fold back to the edge, producing an eighth-fold. Use this fold as a guide and fold the other quarter the same way. Trust me, it's easier than it sounds.

Step 4—Half the map should now have four accordion-style folds.

Step 5—Repeat steps 2 and 3 on the map's other half so that you end up with a full accordion of eight folds in a long ruler-like shape.

Step 6—Finally, fold the map in the shape of a Z so it's in thirds. Voila! Now you can look at any section without having to completely unfold the map and it snaps into place almost by itself.

4

BEARS & OTHER FURRY NOCTURNAL VISITORS

Snuffle, snuffle, slurp...It's a nocturnal sound that when heard outside your tent flap means one of two things—either your camping partner has developed a case of the sniffles while secretly gorging on your personal stash of sweets, or *Ursus americanus* is rototilling his way through your pack in search of anything remotely edible.

Before going camping, you will want to know which animals may or may not frequent your campsite. From kangaroo rats to bears, animals are an inquisitive lot that like to take advantage of each and every opportunity for free food. A kangaroo rat gnawing through a pack to reach some nuts inside is not an immediate threat to nearby humans, but the damage to your pack could create real problems.

A bear, on the other hand, rummaging through camp because it smells food, is going to be very surprised when it encounters humans as well as chocolate or fish. The surprise and resulting screaming and growling can, and has, led to very unfortunate consequences. In a conflict between bears and unarmed humans, bears usually cause the most immediate damage. This is not to say that bears should automatically invoke panic among humans, but that they should be respected and proper precautions taken to protect them and us.

The first step to take to avoid unpleasant encounters is to learn to bearproof your camp. Hang all food well away from camp, leaving no food in packs, and never take food or clothing that smells of food into tents. In general, if you keep your camp clean, you should experience no serious bear problems.

A bear may still periodically wander through just because you are on his selected route for the evening. If a bear should approach your camp, yell, wave your arms, bang pots—do anything to alert the bear to your presence, which should encourage it to retreat. If it chooses not to retreat, *you* should—slowly and methodically with your eyes to the ground and making no outward appearance of being aggressive. Speak to the bear in calm but firm tones to help it recognize that you are human and not a threat. If the bear attacks, don't run! Ball up and protect your vitals and lie still.

When traveling through bear country, your best defense is good ears and alert senses. Some people have taken to wearing bells or clapping hands or whatnot to alert bears to their presence. In theory, this sounds good. If the bear knows you are there, you are less likely to surprise him and he will more likely move out of the way. On the other hand, aside from the fact that some areas of our wilderness are beginning to sound like a bad rendition of Jingle Bells, there is evidence to support the idea that bears are learning to identify bells and other human noises like clapping as meaning "dinner's on!" Not exactly the approach you want.

A better idea is to travel quietly and learn to anticipate bear country. Look for signs. Listen frequently for noises. Try to see a bear before it sees you. If you are traveling in bear country that is managed by a BLM office, each district has its own rules and guidelines for you to follow. Be sure to check in and find out what they are.

If there is no bear hazard and you choose not to hang your food, at the very least you should leave your pack pockets open. An eager rodent will gnaw through fabric to get to food, but if an invitation is left via an open zipper or flap, it will usually take the easy route. To ensure you receive no unwanted visitors in your tent, leave all food outside of your sleeping area.

5

REPELLING BITING NASTIES

It smells bad, it melts plastic, and don't even think of getting any on your nylon jacket. So why are millions of people liberally applying Deet-based (N, N-Diethyl-Meta Tolumide) insect repellents to their skin? Because they work, that's why. But, are standard levels of 100% Deet, previously considered essential to combat biting nasties, now considered potentially risky and basically overkill?

The answer is yes, with a qualification since the EPA has yet to offer any official position on new percentage recommendations and still maintains that Deet is safe for human use. Still, it is hard to ignore the fact that Deet is a chemical solvent and easily absorbed through the skin. Which leaves you wondering about its potential toxicity to the human body.

A number of holistic repellents, made increasingly popular with the fears regarding Deet, rely on Citronella (a chemical derived from a grass native to India) as well as a whole host of other herbs to keep insects from alighting.

Avon's *Skin So Soft,* not advertised as a repellent (to do that, they would have to register their product with the EPA), has achieved almost cult-like distinction as a repellent among outdoorsmen and women. In fact, some say that *Skin So Soft* accounts for nearly 20% of repellent sales in this country.

But, like holistic remedies, studies have shown that *Skin So Soft* can't hold a candle to the repelling effectiveness enjoyed by Deet. Chemically, Deet does three things: masks body odor, creates a smell that insects do not like, and offers a surface insects do not like to be on. Frankly, given the choice, I wouldn't want to stand on something that melts dashboards either.

So if the chemical Deet is so bad for you, why keep using it? Because the alternative of being "meat on the hoof" for a myriad of insects is not only unpleasant, in certain circumstances it may be more dangerous than the chemical itself. (Lyme disease, Rocky Mountain spotted fever, malaria, yellow fever and many more debilitating illnesses are all transmitted by insect bites.)

There is, however, a growing resistance to the use of Deet in heavy concentrations, especially by children and those individuals who require frequent applications over a prolonged period, such as backpackers on an extended journey.

And what of the ongoing debate regarding Deet toxicity or safety? It's not likely that any clear answers will be offered soon, but unless you are inclined to stay home, hide in the tent, or bury yourself in mud, Deet remains the best alternative to slap, duck and run. Just apply it as you would a drug—with common sense—and only in concentrations of 30% or less.

For those of you still inclined to stay away from Deet and go with an alternative repellent, I dug up an old backwoods recipe for "fly-dope," although it comes with no guarantee of success: Mix one-half ounce of citronella, one-quarter ounce of cedarwood oil, one ounce of heated Vaseline for softening, and one-quarter ounce of camphor spirits. Cool and use.

Barring using repellent, what else can you do? Your best bet is to wear light-colored, long-sleeved shirts and long pants tucked into your boots. A good hat and a bandana around your neck helps. For extra protection, spray insect repellent on your clothing, not on your skin. There is also a mosquito netting product that drapes over your head and seals around your neck, but I find that it feels a little claustrophobic.

If you do get bitten, calamine lotion or a mixture of baking soda and water will help to relieve the itching.

6

OUTDOORS WITH CHILDREN

Children and the wilderness go together like peanut butter and jelly. The wilderness becomes a natural teacher, educating your children about themselves and their world in an unhurried setting. Memories of a child gazing intently at a ladybug crawling on her finger, and the uncontrolled giggling of youngsters searching for crawfish in a stream, make camping with children so enjoyable for me. Given the opportunity, I think you will find the same happiness.

Camping with children is not without effort. Constant vigilance on an adult's part is necessary. Care must be taken to ensure the safety of children at all times. Additionally, care must be taken to teach children that the wilderness is fragile and must be protected.

The following is a brief summary to aid in planning your family's camping experience:

•Always maintain a high level of flexibility.

•Begin with backyard camping, progressing to organized campgrounds and then to a simple backpacking experience.

•When hiking, keep elevation gain and loss to a minimum. Five hundred feet is about right.

•Plan your routes well within the hiking abilities of all adults and children.

•Let the children dictate the hiking pace.

•Plan rest breaks frequently and before children get tired.

•Include favorite foods for snacks and mealtimes.

•When planning, packing and hiking, let your children help so they become part of the entire adventure.

•Be clear about safety procedures and rules with your children.

•Always purify water.

•Pick campsites that are away from dangerous obstacles and that will minimize your impact upon the environment.

•Don't relegate yourself to the role of distant observer. Get down and dirty with your children.

•Have your children drink plenty of water and eat plenty of

snacks—keep your children well fueled.

•Allow for lots of time to explore, romp and splash along the way.

•Keep smiling and make the best of every situation. Be prepared for anything!

7

AMPHIBIOUS CANYONEERING

Standing waist-deep in water while staring up at a 1,000-pound log wedged in the narrow canyon walls above your head may not give you the impression of traveling through a fragile and irreplaceable environment. On the contrary, the rugged nature of and difficulty presented by traveling through remote riparian canyons in Utah, Arizona and other states presents a picture of a magnificent yet unforgiving and potentially violent offering. Still, these amphibious canyons demand the highest level of wilderness ethic. Once polluted or vandalized, their resources and beauty are irreplaceable.

Some of your travel through canyons of this nature will be in the form of raftpacking—floating your pack along the streambed and pulling or pushing it. The rest of the time will be spent hiking through wet and lush canyon floors, often wading knee-deep in water. Only travel in small groups. Any group larger than four is really too large and the resulting impacts will be severe.

Do not bring pets along. Although some will argue that properly controlled dogs have a place in the wilderness, canyoneering is not one of those places. The intensity of swimming, jumping, climbing and rough scrambling will not be a pleasure for either your canine friend or yourself.

Always stay in the streambed unless circumstances force you out. Bushwhacking along the lush edges of these canyon-bottom, riparian environments will cause permanent damage both to the delicate soil structure (cryptogamic soil for you naturalists) and the vegetation. Do not pick or even touch the flowers.

On occasion, traveling through certain sections of a canyon will require you to use climbing ropes, slings and anchors. It is not a reasonable practice to leave behind an anchor, rope or sling. If you cannot take your equipment with you, then do not use it. Find an alternate method or route.

It is a difficult process, but do your best to refrain from

sending wastewater directly into the stream. It is virtually impossible to practice washing and urination 200 feet from many canyon bottom streams. At least attempt to provide as much filtration opportunity as possible by dumping wastewater in the soil, rocks and sandy environs away from the immediate stream edge. Periodic flash flooding will flush the canyons clean. Adequately filter all waste water through a bandana so that all food and particulate matter is removed before dumping it. Pack out all solid waste.

Boaters rules should apply regarding defecation. Create a miniature river-runner's toilet using a coffee can lined with multiple plastic bags. Add small amounts of chlorine bleach to prevent odor and gas production. Do not urinate in the bags. Squeeze out all air when packing, seal the bags, and then replace the coffee can lid to secure the contents.

Camp only on sand banks, gravel washes or rocky ledges. Never set up camp in vegetated areas. Campfires are not acceptable, even with significant amounts of driftwood littering the canyon. The resulting blackening of rocks and ash/charcoal production leaves behind permanent reminders of your visit. Stoves are the only environmentally sound way of cooking.

8

CAVING ON PUBLIC LAND

CAVE CONSERVATION

Leave no trace. Pack out what you brought in. The pristine and fragile cave environment is no place to leave spent carbide, graffiti, trash or human waste. Leave nothing but footprints on established or designated trails.

Avoid sensitive areas. Examine each cave and cave passage for delicate features and sensitive formations. Be careful not to touch formations. Stay on established trails to avoid trampling areas needlessly. Be cautious to protect irreplaceable archaeological or paleontological artifacts. Collecting specimens or removing any materials from caves is strictly prohibited.

Respect cave life. Some caves have insect and bat populations that are easily disturbed. In the precariously balanced cave environment, any disruption could conceivably lessen a creature's survivability. Polluting pools and waking bats are two unacceptable examples of disturbing cave biological features.

CAVE SAFETY

Consider individual fitness levels and caving experience. The recommended minimum group size is three people, the maximum is eight.

Be informed of cave-specific conditions including physical and legal access, cave map availability, temperature, dust conditions, the presence of water, vertical drops, radon levels, and rock fall hazards.

Include as a minimum three reliable light sources, a helmet, sturdy boots, vertical gear and the knowledge for its proper and safe use, a first aid kit, food, water, and a container for wastes.

Let others know your specific caving plans, secure appropriate use authorizations, and be informed as to weather conditions and the possibility of flash floods. In the event of an emergency, know where the nearest phone is and dial 911.

9

LAND ACCESS CONCERNS

Recently, the Department of the Interior acknowledged that public access to public lands is not satisfactory—the understatement of the year. A recent investigation by the General Accounting Office has revealed that access was inadequate to nearly 50.4 million acres of public land managed by the U.S. Forest Service and the Bureau of Land Management. According to both the U.S. Forest Service and the BLM, private landowners' unwillingness to grant public easement access across their land is on the increase—while the public's use of federal land is also on the rise.

Private landowners cite concerns pertaining to vandalism and possible liability—understandable to be sure. What isn't so forgivable is the fact that some landowners won't grant access because of a desire for exclusive personal use and gain—such as pay-to-hunt privileges. "Want to hunt on the public land? Well then, you have to pay to cross mine." One friend, an outdoors editor of a major city newspaper, even reports being threatened and run off the land by a pick-up load of cowboys—this while looking for a place to camp on public land in Wyoming. Reminiscent of the range wars in the late 1800s, don't you think?

Much of the problem stems from inadequate or removed signs—especially in Wyoming, where the mingled federal, state and private lands represent a confusing mosaic. How are you to know if a road is public or private if it is not properly signed? That's anyone's guess. Fortunately, unsigned roads are becoming less common due to diligent efforts by the BLM and other public agencies. You can be sure that most private land in states other than Wyoming will carry obvious signage— sometimes to visual excess. Wyoming has no such sign requirement, leaving you, the visitor, with the responsibility of knowing when and if you are crossing onto private property.

Want to know what is open and what is closed? Your best bet is to contact the local BLM office that holds jurisdiction over the region and they will be more than happy to fill you in on the pertinent details. The BLM also publishes maps that show private and public land ownership. If you cannot contact the BLM for some reason, then the following guide should keep you out of trouble with the law and in the good graces of private land owners:

Just because there is public land lying over the rise and surrounded by private land does not mean the landowner must grant access. Obtain permission before attempting to cross private lands. Plying the owner's good favor with a bottle of wine or other favorite treat is a trick many hunters and fishermen have used to gain access to private lands owned by farmers—amazing what a little show of respect and gratitude does for opening gates, isn't it? If an owner denies access for any reason, don't rant and rave. Anger won't open the gates for you or any future visitor. Click your heels and return the way you came.

If you feel you are on public land but are hassled by a landowner or a group of cowboys, as in my friend's case, your best bet is to pack up quietly and quickly and then head to the nearest BLM office to sort things out. Chances are, although it doesn't happen too frequently thank goodness, the problem lies with a rancher who has leased BLM land for years and has come to think of it as his own.

The last thing to remember is this: Most landowners who I have come in contact with (ranchers, farmers, homesteaders) are wonderful people who are only concerned about protecting their land and livestock—and who can blame them. If you convey the fact that you only want to enjoy the land they love, it is more than likely that access will be granted with a smile—and often with a secret tip to a secluded swimming hole or great fishing area too.

10

ADVENTURES IN THE PAST

Tucked in among the nearly 270 million acres of public lands the BLM administers across the U.S. lies a virtually unparalleled resource of cultural wealth—Indian ruins, historic ghost towns, cross-country wagon trails, old forts, and prehistoric sites (some more than 10,000 years old). Perhaps what is most remarkable is that many of these sites are accessible while enjoying a backcountry adventure by either foot, bicycle or boat. There is, however, a problem with the accessibility—vandalism! Many sites are being looted and damaged beyond repair. Sometimes even innocent visitors commit unintentional vandalism simply by treading where they shouldn't tread, touching what they shouldn't touch. If you see any signs of vandalism or suspicious activity, report it as soon as possible to the nearest BLM office. As for your own travels? Look, but don't touch. Revel in the history before you that stands as a silent testimony to another time, another place. Listen quietly to the lessons and messages that are there for all.

SITES AT A GLANCE

Many of these sites are referred to in the chapters that follow. Many are not since they do not lie within the identified wilderness or recreation sites which are the primary focus of this book. I have given the state in which the site lies and more specific information is available simply by contacting each state's district BLM office.

Historic Gold and Silver Mining Camps

Coldfoot Gold Camp, Alaska
Rochester Gold Camp, Nevada
South Pass City Historic Mining District, Wyoming
Spanish Gulch Mining District, Oregon
Alpine Loop National Backcountry Byway, Colorado
Garnet Ghost Town, Montana

Prehistoric Rock Carvings and Figures

Three Rivers Petroglyph Site, New Mexico
Rochester Muddy Creek Petroglyph Site, Arizona
Little Black Mountain Petroglyph Site, Arizona
Hickison Summit Petroglyph Site, Nevada
Wees Bar Petroglyph Site, Birds of Prey Conservation
    Area, Idaho
Whoopup Canyon Petroglyph Site, Wyoming
Blythe Intaglios, California
Carrizo Plain Pictograph Site, California
Canon Pintado Historic District, Colorado

Ancient Caves and Campsites

Hidden Cave and Grimes Point Sites, Nevada
Tangle Lakes Archaeological District, Alaska
Hogup Cave, Utah
Catlow Cave, Oregon

Frontier Trails

Flagstaff Hill and Keeney Pass Trail Sites, Oregon
Iditarod National Historic Trail, Alaska
Pony Express Trail, Utah and Nevada
Spanish Trail / Old Mormon Road, Nevada
Honeymoon Trail and Beale Wagon Road, Arizona
Central Pacific Railroad Grade, Utah
Emigrant Trails of Southern Idaho, Idaho
Oregon National Historic Trail, Wyoming
Bizz Johnson Logging Railroad Trail, California
Lewis and Clark Trail, Montana

Cabins and Homesteads

Ward Ranch Site, New Mexico
Black Pine Valley Homesteads, Idaho
Rogue River Ranch and Whiskey Creek Cabin, Oregon
Fort Benton to James Kipp Recreation Area Float Trip,
    Montana
Riddle Brothers Historic Ranch District, Oregon
John Jarvie of Brown's Park, Utah

Indian Pueblos

Anasazi Heritage Center Escalante Ruins Complex,
    Colorado
Grand Gulch Archaeological District, Utah

Chama Gateway Pueblos, New Mexico
Perry Mesa Pueblo Sites, Arizona
Lowry Ruins National Historic Landmark, Colorado

Military Sites
Fort Egbert National Historic Landmark, Alaska
Patton's Camps, California
Boots and Saddles Forts, New Mexico
Santa Cruz de Terrentate Spanish Presidio, Arizona
Cantonment Reno, Wyoming

Prehistoric Campsites
Red Rocks Recreation Site, Nevada
Mack Canyon Archaeological District, Oregon
Murray Springs Clovis Site, Arizona
Baker Femont Site, Nevada
Fossil Falls Area of Critical Environmental Concern,
   California
Lower Salmon River Sites, Idaho
Hanson Folsom Site, Wyoming
Shelter Cove, California
Henry Smith Buffalo Jump Site, Montana
Warner Wetlands Area, Oregon

ARCHAEOLOGICAL RESOURCES—THE LAW

When hiking through many areas of BLM land, it is common to stumble across archaeological sites and artifacts—pottery, dwellings, ruins, arrowheads, grinding stones, etc. These discoveries can inspire a sense of intrigue and excitement and afford us a unique peek into a past lived by former cultures very different from our own. However, the opportunity to enjoy these discoveries without also seeing some form of violation is becoming more and more difficult. Ruins are being destroyed by eager hikers clambering all over them, graffiti scars the walls of many pictograph and petroglyph sites, and wholesale removal and vandalizing of artifacts has and continues to occur by amateur and professional trophy hunters.

Two federal laws, the Antiquities Act of 1906 and the Archaeological Resources Protection Act of 1979, forbid the removal or destruction of archaeological resources on public lands. Stiff fines and imprisonment can result from failure to abide by the law. This includes pocketing an arrowhead—a simple enough act by itself, but the person pocketing the arrowhead now prevents anyone else from enjoying a similar discovery of that arrowhead.

Besides operating under a "look but don't take" creed, you can help the authorities by reporting any and all signs of vandalism or theft you see occurring. In many instances, there are rewards offered for information that leads to an arrest and conviction.

11

ADVENTURER'S CHECKLIST

The following checklist will help you to plan your next adventure. Not all items listed will be needed on every trip. Pack only what you need and leave the rest at home; remember, you've got to carry what you pack.

PACKS
Backpack (external or internal frame)
Waterproof pack cover
Child carrier (if camping with a child under four who has difficulty walking long distances)
Day pack or fanny pack

SHELTER
Lightweight tent (including poles, stakes and guy lines)
Mosquito netting (for around your head when sleeping under the stars)
9-foot by 12-foot nylon tarp with grommets

SLEEPING
Sleeping bag (down or synthetic)
Sleeping pad
Pillow
Ground cloth

TEN-PLUS ESSENTIALS
Sunglasses
Water bottle (carry two quarts per person per day in the mountains when water is available; one gallon per person per day in desert environments)
Water purification
Nylon cord (50 feet)
Waterproof/windproof matches
Flashlight (extra bulb and batteries)
Fire starter
Pocket knife

Toilet paper
Topographic map
Compass
Emergency blanket
Whistle
Signal mirror
Emergency snacks

KITCHEN
Stove
Fuel/fuel bottle
Primer paste
Lighter or matches
Windscreen
Cook set
Frying pan
Water bag (collapsible)
Storage containers for food
Zip-loc bags (freezer variety)
Large spoon
Knife
Spatula
Can opener (GI folding variety)
Small whisk
Small grater
Pot grips
Knife, fork, spoon
Plate
Cup
Bowl
Cutting board (small nylon variety)
Ice chest
Scrub pads
Biodegradable soap
Paper towels
Aluminum foil
Spice kit

FIRST AID
Antibiotics
Antiseptics
Tylenol

Benadryl
Tincture of benzoin
Sterile gauze pads
Roller gauze
Nonadherent dressing
One-inch adhesive tape
Steri-strips
Ace wrap
Large compress
Moleskin
Second Skin
Tweezers
Bandage scissors
Irrigation syringe
Low-reading thermometer
SAM splint
Space blanket
Sawyer snakebite kit
Emergency report form
Pencil
Emergency phone numbers and money for a phone call

HYGIENE
Comb/brush
Toothbrush/toothpaste
Dental floss
Deodorant
Small towel
Shaving kit
Biodegradable skin and hair soap
Moisturizing lotion
Towlettes
Sunscreen (15 SPF or better)
Lip balm
Tampons

CLOTHING
First Layer:
    Underwear
    Long underwear (tops and bottoms)
    Liner socks
    Wool outer socks
    T-shirt

Second Layer:
  Wool shirt
  Synchilla, Polartec or wool sweater
  Shorts
  Long pants

Protective Layer:
  Wool, A16 Bomber, or Synchilla hat
  Sun hat
  Bunting, Polartec, or Synchilla jacket
  Parka (synthetic fill or down)
  Wool mittens
  Rain suit (jacket and pants)
  Gaiters
  Windbreaker
  Hiking boots
  Camp shoes or sneakers

MISCELLANEOUS GEAR
Butane or candle lantern
Fishing gear and license
Trowel
Thermometer
Bandana
Note pad and pencil
Camera, film, lenses
Binoculars
Plastic trash bags

FUN AND GAMES
Frisbee
Nerf ball
Hacky sack
Miniature games (backgammon, checkers, chess, etc.)
Harmonica
Kazoo
Paperback books
Coloring books
Star guide
Mini microscope
Magnifying glass
Small plastic collection containers
Aquarium net

Sketch pad
Pencils
Crayons
Colored felt-tip pens
Gold pan and mineral book

MOUNTAIN BIKING
Cycling shorts
Cycling gloves
Cycling shoes
Helmet
Tire-patch kit
Spare parts
Mini tool kit
Panniers

CROSS-COUNTRY SKIING
Skis (waxless for convenience, waxable for performance)
Boots
Bindings
Poles
Extra ski tip
Basic repair parts

CANOEING
Canoe
Paddles
Life jackets
Waterproof duffles
Waterproof containers for camera gear
Rope to secure duffles and contents in boat

INFANT NEEDS
Bottles and extra nipples
Rubber or plastic pants
Diapers
Sleep suits
Extra clothing
Warm snuggle suit
Rain suit
Baby food
Baby wipes
Baby powder or corn starch

ALASKA

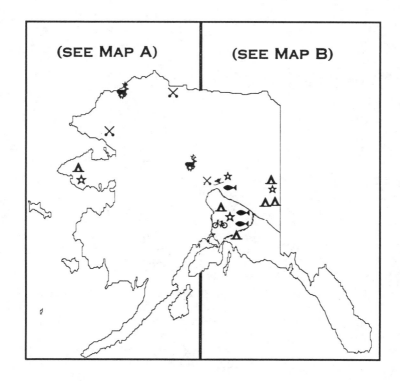

Map A—Alaska

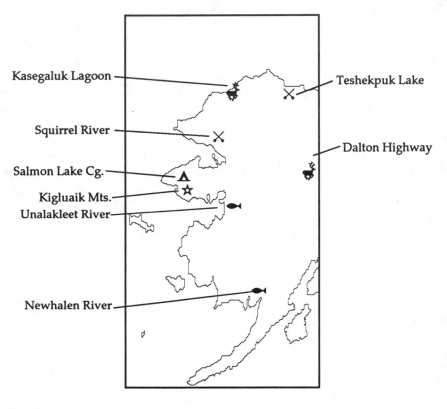

Kasegaluk Lagoon

Teshekpuk Lake

Squirrel River

Dalton Highway

Salmon Lake Cg.

Kigluaik Mts.

Unalakleet River

Newhalen River

▲ campsite
☆ best of state
🚶 hiking
🚲 mountain biking
⛷ winter recreation
🦃 wildlife viewing
🐟 fishing
🛶 whitewater
⚑ general recreation
⊕ caves or spelunking
⚲ cultural/historical site
✕ canoeing
✕ rock climbing

MAP REFERENCES

Dalton Highway—p. 70
Kasegaluk Lagoon—p. 80-81
Kigluaik Mountains—p. 59-61
Newhalen River—p. 68-69
Squirrel River—p. 82
Teshekpuk Lake—p. 81-82
Unalakleet River—p. 69

CAMPGROUNDS

The following campground is found in this area of Alaska. Please call the BLM office (listed following each campground's name) for reservations and information. Contact information for each BLM office is on pages 83-84 of Alaska.

Salmon Lake Campground, Kigluaik Mountains, Kobuk District Office

MAP B—ALASKA

Pinnell Mtn. Rec. Trail
White Mtns. Nat. Rec. Area
Beaver Creek

Birch Creek
Tangle Lakes/Tangle River Cgs.
Tangle Lakes Arch. District
Denali Highway

Eagle Cg.
Fortymile River
Walker Fork Cg.
West Fork Cg.
Gulkana River
Delta River
Sourdough Cg.

▲ campsite
☆ best of state
𝟰𝟰 hiking
𝜎𝜎 mountain biking
🛷 winter recreation
🦆 wildlife viewing
🎣 fishing
🚣 whitewater
⭣ general recreation
⊕ caves or spelunking
🎋 cultural/historical site
✕ canoeing
✗ rock climbing

MAP REFERENCES

Beaver Creek—p. 78
Birch Creek—p. 79
Delta River—p. 65-66
Denali Highway—p. 64-65
Fortymile River—p. 56-58
Gulkana River—p. 66-67
Pinnell Mountain National Recreation Trail—p. 54-56
Tangle Lakes Region—p. 61-63
Tangle Lakes Archaeological District—p. 65
White Mountains National Recreation Area—p. 70-72

CAMPGROUNDS

The following campgrounds are found in this area of Alaska. Please call the BLM office listed following each campground's name for reservations and information. Contact information for each BLM office is on pages 83-84 of Alaska.

Eagle Campground, Steese/White Mountains District Office
Sourdough Campground, Glennallen District Office
Tangle Lake Campground, Glennallen District Office
Tangle River Campground, Glennallen District Office
Walker Fork Campground, Steese/White Mountains District Office
West Fork Campground, Steese/White Mountains District Office

Alaska

1

PINNELL MOUNTAIN NATIONAL RECREATION TRAIL

Established within the one-million-acre White Mountains National Recreation Area, the only National Recreation Area in Alaska, the Pinnell Mountain National Recreation Trail offers rugged alpine-style backpacking along its 27.3-mile length. It is the first National Recreation Trail established in the state.

Sweeping vistas of surrounding mountains and a profusion of summer wildflowers are the standard fare. Moss campion, alpine azalea, frigid shooting star, arctic forget-me-not and Lapland cassiope are some of the more common varieties you'll see. Dominant woody plants include dwarf birch, alpine bearberry and blueberry. Wolves, grizzly bear and wolverines may occasionally be spotted from the trail by those who keep a sharp lookout. Small herds of caribou are also sometimes seen. In addition to a wide variety of migratory birds, the rock and willow ptarmigan, gyrfalcon and raven are year-round residents.

Amateur geologists will thrill to the fact that some of the oldest rocks in the state may be viewed along the trail—formations made of sediments deposited over a billion years ago and then compressed into rock 500 million years ago.

HIKING

The Pinnell Mountain National Recreation Trail follows a somewhat serpentine route along mountain ridges and through high passes mostly above a 3,500-foot elevation. Vantage points along the trail offer excellent views of the surrounding landscape including the White Mountains, Tanana Hills, the Brooks Range, and the Alaska Range.

The trail is clearly marked with rock cairns and mile markers. Plan on three days to navigate the trail's entire length. Bad weather may occur at any time and force you to wait out a storm, so some flexibility in scheduling is advised (low clouds and fog can obscure the trail, making hiking difficult or dangerous). The trail itself is very steep and rugged, crossing talus slopes and alpine tundra—backpackers must be physically prepared!

MANAGEMENT
BLM Steese/White Mountains District Office, 1150 University Avenue, Fairbanks, AK 99708-3844; (907) 474-2350

LOCATION
Approximately 30 miles north of Fairbanks off the Steese Highway.

GETTING THERE
From Fairbanks, drive northeast on the Steese Highway. The road is paved to mile 42; the remainder of the road is gravel. Trailheads are located at Twelvemile Summit (milepost 85.6) or Eagle Summit (milepost 107.1). Parking is available at both trailheads. Register at the trailhead before entering and leaving the trail.

CAMPING
Camping is possible anywhere along the trail. There are two permanent emergency shelters spaced eight miles apart, each approximately 10 miles from their respective trailhead. There is no wood along the entire trail, so bring a backpacking stove. Winds are sometimes fierce, making a windscreen a necessity. Be careful with matches and any open flame as tundra burns very easily. Overnight accommodations may be found in Fairbanks or at several campgrounds located along the Steese Highway. Contact the Alaska Public Lands Information Center in Fairbanks for current campground information at (907) 451-7352.

PERMITS
No permits are necessary.

MAPS
USGS topographic maps: Circle B-3, B-4, C-3 and C-4

ADDITIONAL INFORMATION
• *The Alaska Wilderness Milepost,* published by Alaska Northwest Books, 22026 20th Avenue Southeast, Bothell, WA 98021; (800) 331-3510.
• *Alaska Atlas and Gazetteer,* published by DeLorme Mapping, P.O. Box 298, Freeport, ME 04032; (207) 865-4171.

SEASON
June through September is the best time to visit, although the trail is accessible year round. Temperatures will vary from 20°F to 80°F with snow possible at any time. Since the ridge is exposed, wind can become a problem. Winter temperatures of minus 60°F to minus 70°F are not unusual. June 18 to June 25 is an especially popular time as hikers can experience the midnight sun from many of the high points along the trail. June is also the month when many of the wildflowers are at their peak.

---

*TIP: Pack out all that you pack in—
and a little extra if you find it.*

BEST OF THE STATE

2

FORTYMILE RIVER

Located in east central Alaska, this Wild and Scenic River is fed by numerous streams and drainages as it flows east, dumping into the Yukon River in Canada. Its 392 miles of waterway, including the main river and its numerous forks, comprise the longest nationally designated river of its kind in the United States. The fall foliage is absolutely outstanding. Rapids vary from Class II to Class V. The region is an historically significant gold mining area with remnants of cabins and mines visible along the river banks. Float trips from one day to one week are available.

FLOAT TRIPS

There are many options available to the river runner, including trips that offer anywhere from Class I to Class V water. In general, the further downstream you head, the more difficult the rapids become. All are easily scouted on foot and portaged if needed. The river and its various forks follow a wonderful, yet utterly confusing, serpentine route through rugged and mountainous countryside. No signs mark rapids or portages, so it is vital that you carry adequate maps and a good compass, and that you are consistently tracking and verifying your position on the river. Should an accident happen on the river, a cross-country trek may be necessary. Carry sufficient supplies and maps of the surrounding terrain. Those running the river in canoes or kayaks are advised to wear wetsuits as the water is very cold and hypothermia is a real threat. For those planning on floating the Fortymile River to the Yukon River, you will need to check in with Canadian customs upon arrival in Clinton in the Yukon Territories. Phone (403) 667-6471 for further information from the Whitehorse Customs Office. After re-entry into the U.S. on the Yukon River, check in with U.S. customs at Eagle.

MANAGEMENT
General information: Contact the BLM Steese/White Mountains District Office, 1150 University Avenue, Fairbanks, AK 99709; (907) 474-2350.
Specific information: Contact the BLM Tok Field Office, P.O. Box 309, Tok, AK 99780; (907) 883-5121.
Up-to-date river information (summer only): Contact the BLM Chicken Field Station, Mile 68.2, Taylor Highway, Chicken, AK 99732.

LOCATION
In southeastern Alaska off the Taylor Highway, northeast of Anchorage and adjacent to the Alaska/Canada border.

GETTING THERE
If you are contemplating a trip on the Fortymile River, you have many starting and stopping point-options. The trip can be lengthy, involving an air-taxi service from Tok to the Joseph Airstrip in the Middle Fork drainage, followed by a 7 to 10-day float out to Eagle. Or your trip could be an afternoon float

---

from Mosquito Fork Bridge to the South Fork Bridge. Whatever your fancy, access is the key to success, which means that you should get the BLM brochure *The Fortymile River— Access Points and Float Times*.

CAMPING

You can camp anywhere along the river, but stay away from posted mining claims! Bear precautions are a must—cook and store food well away from sleeping areas. All drinking water must be treated for Giardia.

PERMITS

No permits are necessary.

MAPS

USGS topographic maps:
•Joseph to Fortymile Bridge: Eagle A-2, B-1, B-2, B-3, B-4, B-5
•South Fork Bridge to Fortymile Bridge: Eagle A-2, B-1, B-2
•Fortymile Bridge to Eagle: Eagle C-1, C-2 and Canadian maps Fortymile 116C/7, Cassiar 116C/8, Shell Creek 116C/9, Mount Gladman 116C/10
•Mosquito Fork Bridge to South Fork Bridge: Eagle A-2
•West Fork Campground to South Fork Bridge: Eagle A-2, Tanacross D-2, D-3
•Walker Fork Campground to Fortymile Bridge: Eagle A-2, B-1, B-2.

ADDITIONAL INFORMATION

•BLM brochures: *The Fortymile River—Rapids, The Fortymile River—Access Points and Float Times, The Taylor Highway— Tetlin Junction to Boundary, Eagle to Fort Egbert*
•*Alaska Atlas and Gazetteer,* published by DeLorme Mapping, P.O. Box 298, Freeport, ME 04032; (207) 865-4171.

SEASON

High water can be expected from late May to mid-June. Generally, flows drop to low levels by September. However, the river level can fluctuate dramatically at any time, due to sudden storms. Be prepared for high waters during any month. July and August are the best months to float the river if you desire calmer waters and a safer but slower river trip.

> TIP: *Never leave a campfire unattended,*
> *even for a few moments.*

BEST OF THE STATE

3

KIGLUAIK MOUNTAINS

This mountain range is attractive and inviting because of its ruggedness and awesome beauty. Visitors will find superb recreational opportunities from fishing, hiking, backpacking, mountaineering, and backcountry skiing to snowmobiling, dog mushing and photographing wildlife. There is evidence of early gold seekers, who entered this region at the turn of the century, throughout the spectacular and changing panorama of mountain passes and glacial valleys.

FISHING

Sport fishing for Arctic grayling and Dolly Varden is excellent in Canyon Creek as well as the Sinuk, Grand Central and Cobblestone Rivers. Chum and pink salmon may also be caught from early July to mid-August.

HIKING

There are no established trails within the mountain range, and the lack of trails is the main attraction to the area—travel is spectacular, rugged and remote. All travel by foot requires more than basic backcountry skills. Navigational skills are at a premium. Drinking water must be purified. Bear precautions are a must—no food should be kept in or around sleeping areas.

It is possible that while backpacking or mountaineering, you may encounter private lands or private structures. The local residents use much of this range to make their living and it is imperative that their privacy is respected. There are a large number of cultural resources that may be discovered within the mountain range, including old cabins. Artifacts are protected by law from removal, excavation or vandalism. Take only pictures and help preserve our heritage.

One point of outstanding interest and relatively easy accessibility is the Mosquito Pass area. Hike in from Windy Creek to the Cobblestone River through Mosquito Pass to view spectacular side canyons, steep and sharp peaks and cirque lakes—and don't forget your camera! During the summer, it is possible to hike into the area by exiting the Nome-Taylor Highway near the confluence of Hudson Creek and Nome River.

MANAGEMENT
•BLM Kobuk District Office, 1150 University Avenue, Fairbanks, AK 99709; (907) 474-2330
•BLM Nome Field Office, P.O. Box 952, Nome, AK 99762; (907) 443-2177

LOCATION
Fifty miles north of Nome on the Seward Peninsula, 100 miles south of the Arctic Circle.

GETTING THERE
Anchorage has daily jet service to Nome. From Nome, you can rent a car and drive to either the west or east end of the range. The Kougarok Road provides perhaps the most central access, with the Salmon Lake Campground being an ideal starting point. There are numerous landing sites within the range and arranging for an air charter for drop-off and pick-up is yet another alternative. If you are visiting in the winter, and many Alaskans prefer this option, travel is best achieved by a snowmachine out of Nome, offering access to areas that are not ordinarily accessible during the rest of the year.

CAMPING
The BLM administers one campground, the Salmon Lake Campground, located at the eastern end of the Kigluaik Mountains on Salmon Lake, near milepost 40 on the Kougarok Road. The city of Nome also maintains a public emergency shelter in the Mosquito Pass area. All other camping is primitive and is allowed anywhere within the mountain range.

PERMITS
No permits are necessary.

MAPS
USGS topographic maps: Nome D-1, D-2, D-3; Teller A-1, A-2, A-3; Bendeleben A-6; Solomon A-6

ADDITIONAL INFORMATION
• *The Alaska Wilderness Milepost,* published by Alaska Northwest Books, 22026 20th Avenue Southeast, Bothell, WA 98021; (800) 331-3510.
• *Alaska Atlas and Gazetteer,* published by DeLorme Mapping, P.O. Box 298, Freeport, ME 04032; (207) 865-4171.

SEASON
You can visit this area all year. "Summer" runs from mid-June to mid-August but temperatures may vary from 20°F to 80°F. Wind and rain are common. Winter temperatures in the minus 10°F to minus 20°F range are commonplace. Avalanches become a major hazard in the winter and early spring months—do not travel in this region unless you know how to read the country for avalanche dangers.

> *TIP: Stay on the main trail even if it is wet or snow-covered. Leaving the trail to skirt these areas only creates another trail and another point of erosion.*

BEST OF THE STATE

4

TANGLE LAKES REGION

Tangle Lakes has a rich archaeological history. Studies have documented more than 400 archaeological sites in this area and findings indicate that ancient peoples inhabited this area over 10,000 years ago. Collecting or damaging any artifacts or sites is prohibited by law. This subarctic region features a rich natural diversity as well, with visitors likely to spot grizzly bear, caribou, moose, wolf, coyote, ptarmigan and fox. At any time of the year, be prepared for all types of weather which can sweep in over the glaciers, lakes and tundra without warning. Tangle Lakes is an area ideally suited for cross-country exploration as the brush is low and the terrain is relatively open. Cross-country travel should never be attempted without adequate navigational skills. There are at least eight side roads and trails in the immediate area that are suitable for mountain biking and hiking.

HIKING

There are several super hiking and backpacking trails in the area—inquire at the BLM office for details. The Maclaren River Road trail begins and ends at milepost 43.5 on the Denali Highway. The trail is in good condition and runs approximately 13 miles each way from the highway to the Maclaren Glacier and back. There is a potential deep ford of the West Fork of the Maclaren River at the four-mile mark. The river is a glacial stream that can force a very cold, waist-deep crossing depending on the time of year. After the crossing, the trail continues for five miles before petering out through one-half mile of willow thicket. Watch out for grizzlies! Following the willow thicket, the trail returns to a good condition for the remaining three miles to the glacier. Return the way you came.

MOUNTAIN BIKING

There are several ideal mountain bike trails in the area—inquire at the BLM office for details. Landmark Gap Trail South begins and ends at milepost 24.8 on the Denali Highway. Two miles from the trailhead, the trail forks. Bear to the right and head toward Osar Lake. The trail peters out after approximately five miles. The surrounding hills are an excellent place to spot caribou, grizzly, wolf and ptarmigan.

MANAGEMENT
BLM Glennallen District Office, P.O. Box 147, Glennallen, AK 99588; (907) 822-3217

LOCATION
In south central Alaska, located between mileposts 15 and 45 along the Denali Highway, approximately 21 miles west of Paxson.

GETTING THERE

From Anchorage, take State Highway 1 to State Highway 4. Head north toward Fairbanks. After approximately 71 miles, turn left on Highway 8, the Denali Highway.

CAMPING

There are two BLM campgrounds in the area. Tangle River Campground and Tangle Lake Campground both have water and toilet facilities. There is no camping fee, but stays are limited to 14 days. Both these campsites make an excellent base of operations from which to enjoy a rich mountain biking or hiking experience. Wood is scarce along the river, so bring in your own or use a backpacking stove.

PERMITS

No permits are necessary.

MAPS

USGS topographic maps: Mount Hayes A-4, A-5

ADDITIONAL INFORMATION

• *Alaska's Parklands, The Complete Guide,* by Nancy Lange Simmerman, published by The Mountaineers, Seattle, WA.
• *The Alaska Wilderness Milepost,* Alaska Northwest Books, 22026 20th Avenue Southeast, Bothell, WA 98021; (800) 331-3510.
• *Alaska Atlas and Gazetteer,* published by DeLorme Mapping, P.O. Box 298, Freeport, ME 04032; (207) 865-4171.

SEASON

Mid-May to mid-September is the best time to visit. All roads and trails in the area are open to off-road vehicle travel, but visitors should find relative solitude free from traffic, except during hunting season which begins in mid-August. Expect the summer weather to be cool, moist and often overcast. Once October arrives, snow and bitter cold make this an unattractive area to casual visitors.

TIP: Never cut trees or live wood for campfires or any other reason.

1

SOUTH CENTRAL ALASKA

This is the most populated region of Alaska, chiefly because Anchorage is within this geographical area. Mud flats of the coast give way to the up-and-down and abrupt topography of high mountains and broad river valleys. The variable terrain means variable and lush vegetation. The climate is maritime in nature along the coastal reaches—foggy and rainy with mild temperature fluctuations. Temperature changes become more extreme and weather fluctuations more abrupt the more inland you go. Wildlife is abundant, from brown bear and moose to deer and wolf. Lynx, marten, weasel, beaver, red fox, land otter, porcupine, and wolverine are also seen.

DENALI HIGHWAY
car camping/day hiking combination, mountain bike touring, fishing, wildlife observation

Once the primary travel route to Denali National Park, the Denali Highway is now bypassed by many visitors. It's too bad, because the scenic qualities of this route are outstanding! Grab your mountain bike and head on out. Generally open for access from mid-May to October 1, the Denali Highway is only paved for the first 21 miles west of Paxson and the Richardson Highway. The remaining 112 miles to Cantwell and the George Parks Highway are gravel. Vehicles traveling this route must be sure that they are carrying necessary spare parts and tires. Extra water and provisions are advised.

There are five inns or roadhouses along the route offering services (food and lodging, sometimes gas) as well as three BLM-administered campgrounds. Primitive camping is allowed anywhere along the highway on BLM land. The highway offers superb opportunities to view wildlife, including caribou, moose, black and grizzly bear, ptarmigan, trumpeter swan and more. Fishing is best for lake trout and grayling. Salmon may be found, but only in the upper Gulkana River near Paxson.

Bring your canoe along to enjoy floating opportunities on the Tangle Lakes, upper Nenana River, Delta River, and Gulkana River.

Resources: *Alaska Atlas and Gazetteer,* published by DeLorme Mapping, P.O. Box 298, Freeport, ME 04032; (207) 865-4171.
For more information: Contact the BLM Glennallen District Office, P.O. Box 147, Glennallen, AK 99588; (907) 822-3217.

TANGLE LAKES ARCHAEOLOGICAL DISTRICT
biking, camping, mountain biking, canoeing, rafting, kayaking, hunting, fishing, historic sites, wildlife observation

Between mileposts 15 and 45 along the Denali Highway lies the Tangle Lakes Archaeological District—tucked in among the jagged upthrusts of nearby mountains and the sweeping grandeur of glaciers. Over 400 archaeological sites representing cultures that are over 10,000 years old are found here. This area is recognized as having one of the densest concentrations of archaeological resources in the North American Subarctic. Due to the sensitive nature of the area, BLM rangers are on patrol. Violators of off-road regulations and vandals in violation of the Archaeological Resources Protection Act will be fined and forced to surrender their equipment to the government. This is a spectacular area—please help to preserve it!
•**See also Tangle Lakes in Best of the State, page 61**•
For more information: Contact the BLM Glennallen District Office, P.O. Box 147, Glennallen, AK 99588; (907) 822-3217.

DELTA RIVER
canoeing, kayaking, rafting, fishing, wildlife observation

Flowing north out of Tangle Lakes, the Delta River, a National Wild and Scenic River, is a clear and silt-free waterway until its confluence with Eureka Creek. At the creek, the Delta River mixes with cold, silty glacial runoff and is filled with debris. The first 35 miles of the river, from Tangle Lakes Campground to the Richardson Highway, are rated Class I to II. From the highway to Black Rapids, a distance of 17 miles, the river is rated Class II. One of the longest fault zones in the state of Alaska, the Denali Fault, will be crossed during a mandatory portage located two miles after the last lake. Beware of rocks during the several miles following re-entry to the river after the portage, as the river annually claims a number of canoes. It's a long trek out on foot.

If it is a river float you seek, then rafts are the perfect choice. For a little more excitement and involvement with the river, canoes and kayaks are recommended.

Fish in season for lake trout, Arctic grayling, whitefish, and burbot. Wildlife viewing includes moose, brown and black bear, Dall sheep, caribou, beaver, muskrat, golden eagle, bald eagle, and a multitude of waterfowl.

Resources: *Alaska Atlas and Gazetteer,* published by DeLorme Mapping, P.O. Box 298, Freeport, ME 04032; (207) 865-4171.
For more information: Contact the BLM Glennallen District Office, P.O. Box 147, Glennallen, AK 99588; (907) 822-3217.
USGS topographic maps: Mount Hayes A-4, B-4, C-4

GULKANA RIVER
canoeing, kayaking, rafting, fishing, wildlife observation

This nationally designated Wild and Scenic River offers several outstanding trip options with excellent wildlife viewing. Beginning at the Denali Highway in the Tangle Lakes area, the route heads south, nine miles by paddle and portage through the Tangle Lakes canoe trail. The Middle Fork Gulkana flows out of Dickey Lake, and while the first several miles are runnable, it is not recommended that you run them as they are extremely shallow and negotiating them is time consuming and difficult. Following the shallows, there are approximately three miles of swift, shallow and very rocky water that are not recommended for floating. The section ends by dropping steeply through a narrow rock canyon which requires careful and skillful lining. Most boaters prefer to begin their trip at Paxson Lake and float the main section of the Gulkana down to Sourdough Campground. That run is 50 miles and requires approximately three to four days of travel.

Once you're on the main Gulkana, you'll find that the river meanders, churning its way through sweepers and logjams in some sections and quiet floats in others. Watch out for the rougher section between Swede Lake and Hungry Hollow Creek.

There is one Class III section named Canyon Rapids that should only be run by experienced boaters. There is a sign

that marks a quarter-mile portage around the rapids if needed.
Just after the portage, there is a trail on the left bank that leads
to Canyon Lake, one mile away. Superb grayling fishing may
be enjoyed. From the Canyon Rapids, the river drops in
intensity to Class II for eight miles and then to Class I for the
remainder of the trip.

Canoes or kayaks are ideal on this river, as are rafts,
although crossing the nine miles of Tangle Lakes Canoe Trail
with rafts on the first day will be arduous at best. For a more
remote journey, float the West Fork of the Gulkana which puts
in at Lake Louise and continues through Susitna Lake and the
Tyone River. The entire route travels through lake-dotted
country that is ideal wildlife viewing habitat. There are a
number of portages that are not too difficult. The West Fork is
one of the most remote and least visited areas of the Gulkana
watershed. The entire West Fork is a 110-mile adventure that
takes approximately 12 to 20 days to complete.

Fish in season for rainbow trout, whitefish, Arctic grayling,
red and king salmon, lake trout, and burbot.

Wildlife viewing includes moose, brown and black bear,
wolf, fox, caribou, muskrat, beaver, golden eagle, bald eagle, a
variety of hawk, and a multitude of waterfowl.

Resources: *Alaska Atlas and Gazetteer,* published by DeLorme
Mapping, P.O. Box 298, Freeport, ME 04032; (207) 865-4171.
For more information: Contact the BLM Glennallen District Office,
P.O. Box 147, Glennallen, AK 99588; (907) 822-3217.
USGS topographic maps: Mount Hayes A-5; Gulkana B-3, B-4, C-4,
D-4 and D-5

---

*TIP: Always use a river-runner's toilet when boating,
and never bury human waste around river camps. Human
waste, including toilet paper, must be packed out.*

2

WESTERN ALASKA

Fish-rich deltas and vast tracts of tundra, broken periodically by dense forest and knife-edged mountain ranges, make up this region. Temperatures range from the low forties to the mid-sixties during the summer months and plunge sharply to between minus 5°F and plus 20°F during the winter. Big game is predominant here, including brown bear, moose, caribou, wolf, and Dall sheep. Musk ox may also be seen.

NEWHALEN RIVER
kayaking, rafting, fishing, wildlife observation

Sixmile Lake is the headwaters and put-in for this large and turquoise-colored whitewater river. From Sixmile, the river calmly floats for eight miles to Upper Landing, reached by road from Iliamna airport. Class I and II water follows until the river erupts for the last seven miles in a Class V churner followed by a series of seven Class IV rapids. A ledge that crosses the width of the river announces the beginning of the rapids as the river bears right and turns white and frothy. Contact the BLM for specific river running information.

Fish in season for salmon, grayling, Arctic char, rainbow trout, and lake trout. Lake Iliamna helps to support what some call the world's largest red salmon run. Wildlife viewing includes bear, moose, eagles, and beavers.

This river is suitable for experienced whitewater kayakers and rafters only. Kayakers and rafters will need to portage a Class V section unless superbly trained and experienced.

Important Note: Boaters must be aware that all of the land bordering the Newhalen is owned by Native Corporations. Write or call the BLM, 222 West Seventh Avenue #13, Anchorage, AK 99513, (907) 271-5960, for updated information and specific locations of public easements. Access to the area is by float plane from the airport at Lake Iliamna to the put-in at Sixmile Lake.

Resources: *Alaska Atlas and Gazetteer,* published by DeLorme Mapping, P.O. Box 298, Freeport, ME 04032; (207) 865-4171.

For more information: Contact the BLM Anchorage District Office,

6881 Abbott Loop Road, Anchorage, AK 99507; (907) 267-1246.
USGS topographic maps: Iliamna C-6, D-5, D-6

UNALAKLEET RIVER
canoeing, rafting, fishing, wildlife observation

With crystal clear waters free of waterfalls or rapids, this six-day, 76-mile journey is an ideal family float along a very scenic river. Ideal wildlife viewing opportunities exist at various places along the river, although at times the vegetation is so dense that it obscures views of the surrounding countryside. Fishing is excellent for chinook, coho, chum, and pink salmon. Arctic grayling and Arctic char may also be fished here. The only drawback is the possibility of encountering power boats on the lower reaches of the river. Put-in is at the confluence with Tenmile Creek and is reached by air taxi. Take-out is at Unalakleet.

Resources: *Alaska Atlas and Gazetteer,* published by DeLorme Mapping, P.O. Box 298, Freeport, ME 04032; (207) 865-4171.
For more information: Contact the BLM Anchorage District Office, 6881 Abbott Loop Road, Anchorage, AK 99507; (907) 267-1246.
USGS topographic maps: Norton Sound A-1, A-2; Unalakleet D-2, D-3, D-4

KIGLUAIK MOUNTAINS
backpacking, mountaineering, cross-country skiing, dog mushing, snowmobiling

This area is located 50 miles north (as the crow flies) of Nome on the Seward Peninsula and approximately 100 miles south of the Arctic Circle. Cirque lakes, abrupt peaks, spectacular canyons and superb wildlife viewing, especially for birds, make this mountain range a must-visit proposition. Access is relatively easy by Alaskan standards.

•**See also Best of the State, page 59**•
For more information: Contact the BLM Kobuk District Office, 1150 University Avenue, Fairbanks, AK 99709; (907) 474-2330.

> *TIP: Travel or camp in small groups.*

3

ALASKAN INTERIOR

Say Mount McKinley and you have to say no more. This entire region is made up of mountains and valleys that spark the imagination and inspire superlatives. One third of the state, most of it wilderness, lies within this region. Winter lows of minus 50°F give way to summer highs of 80°F. Wildlife and bird life are abundant.

DALTON HIGHWAY
car camping, wildlife observation, mountain biking

This road is listed because it is the only road that crosses the Arctic Circle, and because car camping and wildlife viewing are favored activities. Watch out for truckers, as they seem almost ballistic at times in their haste to haul materials to and from Prudhoe Bay. Mountain biking is a suitable activity but can be periodically frustrating because of vehicle traffic stirring up dust and throwing gravel. Wildlife viewing is considered superb—keep your eyes on the lookout for muskox and grizzly. Services are minimal. Carry extra food, fuel and a CB for contact with truckers should you experience difficulties.

Resources: *Alaska Atlas and Gazetteer,* published by DeLorme Mapping, P.O. Box 298, Freeport, ME 04032; (207) 865-4171.
For more information: Contact the BLM Arctic District Office, 1150 University Avenue, Fairbanks, AK 99709; (907) 474-2301.

WHITE MOUNTAINS
NATIONAL RECREATION AREA
cross-country skiing, snowmobiling, snowshoeing, gold panning, hiking, backpacking

Located between Elliott and Steese Highways approximately 30 miles northeast of Fairbanks, this one-million-acre recreation area features nearly 175 miles of winter recreation trails appropriate for snowshoeing, cross-country skiing or snowmobiling, and approximately 50 miles of trail dedicated to summer use, including the Pinnell Mountain National Recreation Trail. Significant sections of Beaver Creek, a National Wild and Scenic River, may be enjoyed within the area. Of special interest is the opportunity to participate in recreational gold panning within the Nome Creek Valley—an historic, as well as, active placer gold-mining site. From milepost 57.3 on the Steese Highway, follow U.S. Creek Road north for approximately six miles to the Nome Creek gold-panning site. There is one stream crossing that is appropriate for most vehicles with high clearance, but keep a sharp lookout for submerged rocks which are just waiting to relieve unwary drivers of miscellaneous car parts.

Be warned that gold panning is limited to only the four-mile designated area. Panning out of bounds may mean illegally encroaching on surrounding established mine claims—not something you want to do if you wish to depart the area with all your fingers and toes in working order. Gold panning is limited to hand tools and basic equipment including gold pans, picks, shovels, and rocker boxes.

Resources: *Alaska Atlas and Gazetteer,* published by DeLorme Mapping, P.O. Box 298, Freeport, ME 04032; (207) 865-4171
For more information: Contact the BLM Steese/White Mountain District Office, 1150 University Avenue, Fairbanks, AK 99709; (907) 474-2350.

WHITE MOUNTAINS NATIONAL RECREATION AREA— BACKCOUNTRY CABINS

There are ten recreational cabins available for rent through the BLM and one additional shelter cabin, the Wickersham Creek Trail cabin, for which no fee is charged and no reservations are necessary. Reservations are accepted by the BLM up to 30 days in advance with complete payment. You cannot stay in the cabins without a reservation. The fee is currently listed as $20 per night and the stay is limited to three consecutive nights (check with the BLM for current fees as they may change at any time). Phone reservations are accepted, but payment must be received by the BLM within 48 hours or the reservation will be cancelled. Of course, this precludes most people in the lower 48 from making a phone-in reservation. A receipt is issued and must be carried with you as proof of reservation.

Cabins come completely outfitted with wood stoves, a Coleman lantern, white-gas cookstove (bring your own gas), ax, bowsaw, and an outhouse. Garbage must be carried out. Cut firewood is available. Always restock the firewood for the next visitor. Dead or downed wood is the only wood legally foraged for a fire.

Resources: *Alaska Atlas and Gazetteer,* published by DeLorme Mapping, P.O. Box 298, Freeport, ME 04032; (207) 865-4171.

For more information: Contact the BLM Steese/White Mountain District Office. Ask specifically for the brochure *White Mountains National Recreation Area Winter Trails and Cabins.*

For reservations: By mail or in person, contact BLM Land Information Office, 1150 University Avenue, Fairbanks, AK 99709; (907) 474-2250.

Cabin facts:

•Borealis-Lefevre Cabin (near the junction with Wickersham and Big Bend Trails): sleeps five, has boat access, trail access, good fishing.

•Colorado Creek Cabin (located at mile 14 on Colorado Creek Trail): sleeps five, trail access.

•Cripple Creek Cabin (summer-use cabin, off mile 60 on the Steese Highway): sleeps three, trail access, fishing.

•Cache Mountain Cabin (located at mile 6 on O'Brien Creek Trail): sleeps six, hunting.

•Moose Creek Cabin (located near junction of Moose Creek and Trail Creek Trail): sleeps three, trail access.

•Windy Gap Cabin (located at mile 22 on Lower Fossil Creek Trail): sleeps four, trail access, fishing.

•Wolf Run (located at mile 1.5 on Windy Creek Trail): sleeps six, trail access.

•Wickersham Creek Trail Shelter (located near the junction of Wickersham Creek and Moose Creek Trails): sleeps two, trail access, no reservations or fee.

•Crowberry Cabin (located on Trail Creek Trail): sleeps four, trail access.

•Caribou Bluff (located on a side trail off Fossil Gap near the junction with Lower Fossil Creek Trail): sleeps four, trail access.

BIG BEND TRAIL
backpacking, hiking, cross-country skiing, snowshoeing, dog mushing, snowmobiling

Located in the White Mountains National Recreation Area, the Big Bend Trail is 15 miles in length and begins at mile 14.5 on the Colorado Creek Trail. The trail is of moderate difficulty and ends at mile 19.5 on the Wickersham Creek Trail. Because of several wet and very muddy sections in the lowlands during the summer months, winter is perhaps the best time to navigate this trail. From the Colorado Creek Trail junction, head past the Colorado Creek Cabin and through a large, open meadow for three miles. After a steep one-mile climb to the top of a ridge, follow the ridgeline in a southerly direction for three miles (highest elevation is reached at 2,675 feet). Descend approximately three miles to a bridge crossing over Beaver Creek. Five more miles of wandering over relatively level terrain through meadows and black spruce forests will find you at the junction with Wickersham Creek Trail.

For more information: Contact the BLM Steese/White Mountain District, 1150 University Avenue, Fairbanks, AK 99709; (907) 474-2350.

USGS topographic maps: Livengood B-2

COLORADO CREEK TRAIL
backpacking, hiking, cross-country skiing, snowshoeing, dog mushing, snowmobiling

This 23-mile trail is located in the White Mountains National Recreation Area and is of moderate difficulty. Wet and muddy conditions in the lowlands make summer travel difficult at times. Winter is the best season to traverse the trail although use caution as blowing snow in some areas can make navigation difficult. The trail begins at milepost 57 on the Elliott Highway and climbs easily for approximately 14 miles to the top of the ridge. In the last three miles the elevation gain becomes more pronounced. Approximately one-half mile beyond the ridge, the trail junctions with the left trail branching towards Beaver Creek, nine miles away, and the right trail heads one-half mile to Colorado Creek Cabin. Bear left towards Beaver Creek where the trail will take you through old burn and then through spruce forests and open meadows, some of which offer superb views of the White Mountains. It is in this section that caution must be used during the winter, as the wind can drift snow in open areas, obscuring the trail. Once you reach Beaver Creek, continue for one-half mile to reach a sign designating the Windy Creek Trail.

For more information: Contact the BLM Steese/White Mountain District, 1150 University Avenue, Fairbanks, AK 99709; (907) 474-2350.

USGS topographic maps: Livengood B-2, B-3, C-2, C-3

LOWER FOSSIL CREEK TRAIL
cross-country skiing, snowshoeing, dog mushing, snowmobiling

Recommended only for winter use since the trail crosses two frozen lakes, this 23-mile-long route is of moderate difficulty. Beginning at Beaver Creek and mile 20 of the Wickersham Creek Trail, winter travelers are advised to watch for open water and water flow-over during the first seven miles—both lakes are crossed during this section. From mile 13 on, the trail parallels Fossil Creek to the trail's termination at Windy Gap Cabin/Windy Creek Trail Junction.

For more information: Contact the BLM Steese/White Mountain District, 1150 University Avenue, Fairbanks, AK 99709; (907) 474-2350.

USGS topographic maps: Livengood B-1, B-2, C-1

MOOSE CREEK TRAIL
hiking, cross-country skiing, snowshoeing, dog mushing, snowmobiling

This relatively flat, 10-mile-long trail is best experienced in the winter due to wet and muddy sections during the summer. Beginning at mile 11.2 on the Wickersham Creek Trail, the Moose Creek Trail winds its way through spruce forest and open burn and meadow areas before ending and meeting up with mile 10 of the Trail Creek Trail. Moose Creek Cabin is located just beyond the trail junction and at the eastern part of the meadow.

For more information: Contact the BLM Steese/White Mountain District, 1150 University Avenue, Fairbanks, AK 99709; (907) 474-2350.

USGS topographic maps: Livengood A-2, B-2

O'BRIEN CREEK TRAIL

hiking, cross-country skiing, snowshoeing, dog mushing, snowmobiling

The 19-mile-long O'Brien Creek Trail is most suitable for winter travel, due to wet and muddy sections in the summer months. Beginning at Beaver Creek, mile 20 of the Wickersham Creek Trail, the route heads northeast for approximately three miles through open areas and spruce forest. At O'Brien Creek, the trail heads north and parallels the creek for the next nine miles. O'Brien Creek Cabin is located at approximately mile 6, and a tiny trapper cabin located at mile 12 may be used in emergency situations. Several miles past the trapper cabin the trail bears left and climbs, at times steeply, up a drainage to a high alpine meadow, 3.5 miles away. The trail ends at the junction with Upper Fossil Creek Trail and the Cache Mountain Divide.

For more information: Contact the BLM Steese/White Mountain District, 1150 University Avenue, Fairbanks, AK 99709; (907) 474-2350.
USGS topographic maps: Livengood B-1, C-1

PINNELL MOUNTAIN NATIONAL RECREATION TRAIL

backpacking, mountaineering, backcountry skiing

This is a 27.3-mile trail that traverses talus slopes and alpine tundra. It features spectacular scenery, earned by the challenging hiking conditions.

•See also Best of the State, page 54•
For more information: Contact the BLM Steese/White Mountain District, 1150 University Avenue, Fairbanks, AK 99709; (907) 474-2350.

SKI LOOP TRAIL

hiking, cross-country skiing, snowshoeing, dog mushing

Because of its accessibility from the Elliott Highway, this trail is an ideal day-hiking or cross-country skiing destination. Beginning at milepost 27.8 on the Elliott Highway, the easy five-mile loop follows 1.5 miles of the Wickersham Creek Trail and approximately two miles of the Summit Trail. Views of the

Alaska

Alaska Range can be enjoyed when the weather is clear.

For more information: Contact the BLM Steese/White Mountain District, (907) 474-2350.

USGS topographic maps: Livengood A-3

SUMMIT TRAIL
backpacking, hiking, cross-country skiing, snowshoeing, dog mushing

Beginning at milepost 27.8 on the Elliott Highway, this is the only trail besides the Pinnell Mountain National Recreation Trail that is designed for summer use within the White Mountains National Recreation Area. A boardwalk has been installed over many of the wet and boggy areas to make hiking easier and to minimize the environmental impact of foot traffic. From the highway, the trail takes seven miles, heading up and over Wickersham Dome. Two miles of fairly level trail through spruce forest prepare the hiker for the next four miles of steep up and down. The last seven miles are downhill, much of the time back to the highway. The last two miles are on Wickersham Creek Trail, following a crossing of Beaver Creek that can be hazardous during high water. LeFevre Cabin may be found on the north side of the creek.

For more information: Contact the BLM Steese/White Mountain District, 1150 University Avenue, Fairbanks, AK 99709; (907) 474-2350.

USGS topographic maps: Livengood A-3, B-2, B-3

TRAIL CREEK TRAIL
hiking, cross-country skiing, snowshoeing, dog mushing, snowmobiling

Best used during the winter months due to exceptionally wet and muddy sections in the summer, this 27-mile-long trail begins at mile 6 of the Wickersham Creek Trail and follows a forested ridge for four miles. After climbing steadily, the trail joins up with Moose Creek Trail and the Moose Creek Cabin at mile 10. At approximately mile 12, the trail reaches its highest point—2,387 feet. The final 15 miles descend, at times steeply, to Beaver Creek and the O'Brien Creek Trail. Caution must be used when crossing Beaver Creek as ice here is notoriously thin and hazardous.

For more information: Contact the BLM Steese/White Mountain District, 1150 University Avenue, Fairbanks, AK 99709; (907) 474-2350.

USGS topographic maps: Livengood A-2, B-1, B-2

UPPER FOSSIL CREEK TRAIL

cross-country skiing, snowshoeing, dog mushing, snowmobiling

This 14-mile-long trail is best used in the winter due to wet and muddy conditions prevailing during the summer. Beginning at mile 23 on the Windy Creek Trail, the trail follows Fossil Creek for virtually its entire route until a final steep climb out of the drainage to the top of Cache Mountain Divide and the O'Brien Creek Trail. Use extreme caution on overflow ice as it is very easy to break through. Windy Gap Cabin may be reached near the Windy Creek Trail junction.

For more information: Contact the BLM Steese/White Mountain District, 1150 University Avenue, Fairbanks, AK 99709; (907) 474-2350.

USGS topographic maps: Livengood C-1

WICKERSHAM CREEK TRAIL

hiking, cross-country skiing, snowshoeing, dog mushing, snowmobiling

Recommended for winter use only for much of the trail, the route begins at milepost 27.8 on the Elliott Highway. The trail serves as a main artery of sorts, connecting the many trails within the region. The Wickersham Creek Trail junctions with Trail Creek Trail at mile 6, Moose Creek Trail at mile 11, O'Brien Creek at mile 20, and serves as an access point for both the Summit and Ski Loop Trail. The Wickersham Creek Trail Shelter is found at mile 11.2. This small two-person cabin is the only cabin in the BLM cabin system that needs not be reserved.

For more information: Contact the BLM Steese/White Mountain District, 1150 University Avenue, Fairbanks, AK 99709; (907) 474-2350.

USGS topographic maps: Livengood A-2, A-3, B-2

WINDY CREEK TRAIL
hiking, cross-country skiing, snowshoeing, dog mushing, snowmobiling

This ten-mile trail, beginning at mile 23 on the Colorado Creek Trail and ending at Fossil Creek, is recommended for winter use only due to very wet conditions during the summer months. At mile 1.5, the Wolf Run Cabin is encountered. From here, the trail parallels Windy Creek five miles up the valley through black spruce and open meadows. After a steep two-mile climb, the trail breaks through Windy Gap and crests on a plateau overlooking the Fossil Creek drainage. Views of the White Mountains, Limestone Gulch and Windy Arch are superb. From the plateau, descend rapidly one mile to Windy Gap Cabin and Fossil Creek.

For more information: Contact the BLM Steese/White Mountain District, 1150 University Avenue, Fairbanks, AK 99709; (907) 474-2350.
USGS topographic maps: Livengood C-1, C-2

BEAVER CREEK
canoeing, kayaking, rafting

Rated a Class I waterway, this clear-water stream is a National Wild and Scenic River, originating within the White Mountain National Recreation Area and flowing north through Yukon Flats National Wildlife Refuge before dumping into the Yukon River. The headwaters may be accessed by vehicle from milepost 57.3 on the Steese Highway via U.S. Creek Road to Nome. The distance from the headwaters to Victoria Creek is 127 miles, and usually takes eight to ten days. Float planes are able to fly in and out of Victoria Creek. From here to the next possible take-out, 268 miles away at the Yukon River Bridge on the Dalton Highway, takes an additional 8 to 14 days. Fishing in Beaver Creek is good for grayling, burbot, whitefish and northern pike.

Resources: *Alaska Atlas and Gazetteer,* published by DeLorme Mapping, P.O. Box 298, Freeport, ME 04032; (207) 865-4171.
For more information: Contact the BLM Steese/White Mountain District, 1150 University Avenue, Fairbanks, AK 99709; (907) 474-2350; or the BLM Fairbanks Support Center, 1541 Gaffney Road, Fairbanks, AK 99703; (907) 356-2025.
USGS topographic maps: Circle B-6, C-6, D-5, D-6; Livengood B-1, B-2, C-1, C-2, D-1

BIRCH CREEK
canoeing, kayaking, rafting

This Wild and Scenic River originates nearly 70 miles northeast of Fairbanks and flows predominantly east and north to the Yukon River—most of the way within the Steese National Conservation Area. The river meanders through low, rolling hills with occasional cliffs and outcroppings of bedrock. Remnants of mining and trapping cabins add flavor to the float. Much of the waterway is rated Class I or II, although there are several Class III rapids just above the confluence with Wolf Creek. These may be portaged. Access to the river at both ends is via the Steese Highway, with the put-in located near milepost 94 (there is a dirt road and parking area), and the take-out located at milepost 147.1 (Steese Highway Bridge). The boatable section of the river is approximately 126 miles long and takes between 7 and 10 days. Fishing is for grayling, northern pike and whitefish. A word of caution—there are several actively mined areas along the river. These are private claims and trespassing is illegal.

Resources: *Alaska Atlas and Gazetteer,* published by DeLorme Mapping, P.O. Box 298, Freeport, ME 04032; (207) 865-4171.
For more information: Contact the BLM Steese/White Mountain District, 1150 University Avenue, Fairbanks, AK 99709; (907) 474-2350; or the BLM Fairbanks Support Center, 1541 Gaffney Road, Fairbanks, AK 99703; (907) 356-2025.
USGS topographic maps: Circle A-3, A-4, B-1, B-2, B-3, B-4, C-1

FORTYMILE RIVER
canoeing, kayaking, rafting

Located in east central Alaska, this Wild and Scenic River is fed by numerous streams and drainages as it flows east, dumping into the Yukon River in Canada. Its 392 miles of waterway, including the main river and its numerous forks, comprise the longest nationally designated river of its kind in the United States. Fall foliage is considered absolutely outstanding. Rapids vary from Class II to Class V. The area is an historically significant gold mining area with remnants of cabins and mines visible along the river banks. Float trips from one day to one week are available.

•**See also Best of the State, page 56**•

Resources: *Alaska Atlas and Gazetteer,* published by DeLorme Mapping, P.O. Box 298, Freeport, ME 04032; (207) 865-4171. **For more information:** Contact the BLM Steese/White Mountain District, 1150 University Avenue, Fairbanks, AK 99709; (907) 474-2350 or the BLM Fairbanks Support Center, 1541 Gaffney Road, Fairbanks, AK 99703;(907) 356-2025.

TIP: Apply a no-trace ethic everyday, everywhere.

ALASKA BY REGION

4

ARCTIC CIRCLE

The Arctic is known as the last great wilderness on earth, perhaps most recognized for its vast mountain range, the Brooks, and also for its massive as-far-as-the-eye-can-see coastal plains stretching across the top of the world. Summer, July and August, is short with temperatures in the thirties and forties. Winters are long and harsh with temperatures frequently as low as minus 60°F. Polar bears, walruses, beluga whales, and a variety of seals make their coastal home here, as do many migratory birds. Further inland, brown bear, Dall sheep, wolf, moose and caribou wander.

KASEGALUK LAGOON
wildlife observation, sea kayaking

With shallow waters only three to six feet deep and protected from ocean waves, this largest barrier island-lagoon system in North America offers fantastic ocean kayaking opportunities coupled with excellent wildlife viewing. Located along a 120-mile stretch of the Chukchi Sea coast, from south of Wainwright to just beyond Point Lay, Kasegaluk Lagoon is considered an important and extremely productive habitat by the Alaska Department of Fish and Game.

There are no facilities at the lagoon. Wilderness camping is the order of the day and visitors should be adequately prepared for high winds and cold, often biting weather year-

---

round. The only access to the site is by chartered plane from Barrow or Kotzebue. Weather rules here, so it is critical that campers pack extra food in the event that weather socks in and flying is prevented.

Wildlife viewing is super all year long. Between July and September, hundreds of thousands of migrating eiders and thousands of terns, gulls, jaegers, loons, brants and more can be seen. Beluga whales frequent the area in June. Arctic fox, lemming, caribou, brown bear, seal and gray whale are frequently seen in the area at other times of the year.

An historic site, the abandoned Eskimo village of Tolegeak, is marked by remains of sod huts and exists near the mouth of the Utukok River. Wildlife in the area is protected by law and must not be harassed. Subsistence hunting is conducted in the area by local residents. At the north end of the lagoon is private land owned by the village of Wainwright—respect their privacy!

Resources: *Alaska Atlas and Gazetteer,* published by DeLorme Mapping, P.O. Box 298, Freeport, ME 04032; (207) 865-4171.
For more information: Contact the BLM Arctic District Office, 1150 University Avenue, Fairbanks, AK 99709; (907) 474-2300.

TESHEKPUK LAKE
canoeing, wildlife observation, wildlife photography

Teshekpuk Lake lies just a few miles from the Arctic Ocean, tucked in among the wet tundra lowlands southeast of Barrow. The 22-mile-wide lake and its many smaller sister lakes are considered vital waterfowl and caribou habitats. Wildlife viewing and photographic opportunities are excellent. Migratory brants, greater white-fronted geese, and Canada geese arrive in July and August. The lake system protects them from predators while they molt and regrow wing feathers. Plovers, sandpipers, phalaropes, dunlins, loons, old-squaws, jaegers, gulls and snowy owls nest in the lake region. Caribou, Arctic fox and lemming may also be seen. Access to the area is by charter plane from Barrow or Prudhoe Bay. No facilities exist at the lake—wilderness camping only. Use restrictions are in effect during the summer months of July and August to minimize wildlife disturbance—check with the BLM for updated regulations.

Resources: *Alaska Atlas and Gazetteer,* published by DeLorme
Mapping, P.O. Box 298, Freeport, ME 04032; (207) 865-4171.
For more information: Contact the BLM Arctic District Office, 1150
University Avenue, Fairbanks, AK 99709; (907) 474-2300.

SQUIRREL RIVER
kayaking, fishing

Originating in the Baird Mountains and flowing southeast
to the Kobuk River near Kiana, this 53-mile river float rewards
paddlers with a sampling of the geography and scenery
characteristic of classic northwest Alaska. All but the upper
reaches of the river are rated Class I. The river is under consid-
eration for inclusion in the National Wild and Scenic Rivers
System. Arctic grayling, northern pike, and chum and pink
salmon may be fished on the river.

Resources: *Alaska Atlas and Gazetteer,* published by DeLorme
Mapping, P.O. Box 298, Freeport, ME 04032; (207) 865-4171.
For more information: Contact the BLM Kobuk District Office, 1150
University Avenue, Fairbanks, AK 99709; (907) 474-2330.
USGS topographic maps: Baird Mountains A-3, A-4, A-5, B-5;
Selawik D-3

---

*TIP: Only gather firewood well away from more popular
camping areas. Removing all downed wood from an area
severely impacts the ecological balance of the region and
removes vital nutrients that the soil and animals need.*

State Information Overview

Alaska State Office
222 West Seventh Avenue #13, Anchorage, AK 99513; (907) 271-5960

Anchorage District Office
6881 Abbott Loop Road, Anchorage, AK 99507; (907) 267-1246

Arctic District Office
1150 University Avenue, Fairbanks, AK 99709; (907) 474-2300

Glennallen District Office
P.O. Box 147, Glennallen, AK 99588; (907) 822-3217

Kobuk District Office
1150 University Avenue, Fairbanks, AK 99709; (907) 474-2330

Kotzebue Field Station, P.O. Box 1049, Kotzebue, AK 99752; (907) 442-3430

Nome Field Station, P.O. Box 952, Nome, AK 99762; (907) 443-2177

Kigluiak Mountains, P.O. Box 952, Nome, AK 99762; (907) 443-2177

Steese/White Mountain District Office
1150 University Avenue, Fairbanks, AK 99709; (907) 474-2350

Steese National Conservation Area, 1150 University Avenue, Fairbanks, AK 99709; (907) 474-2352

White Mountains National Recreation Area, 1150 University Avenue, Fairbanks, AK 99709; (907) 474-2350

TOK FIELD STATION
P.O. Box 309, Tok, AK 99780; (907) 883-5121

Fort Egbert/Eagle Historic District, P.O. Box 309, Tok, AK 99780; (907) 883-5121. Near Eagle—open seasonally

CHAPTER

3

ARIZONA

Maps—p. 86
Best of the State—p. 90
Arizona by Region—p. 102
Information Resources—p. 125

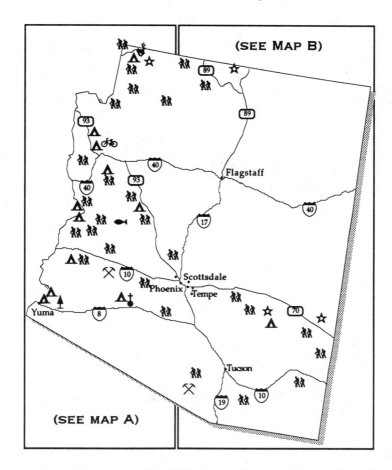

MAP A—ARIZONA

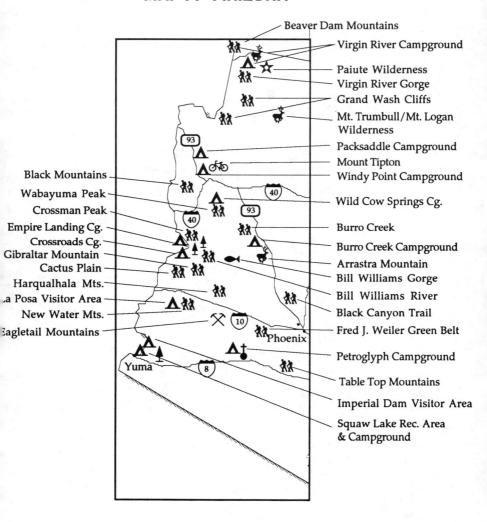

Beaver Dam Mountains
Virgin River Campground
Paiute Wilderness
Virgin River Gorge
Grand Wash Cliffs
Mt. Trumbull/Mt. Logan Wilderness
Packsaddle Campground
Mount Tipton
Windy Point Campground
Wild Cow Springs Cg.
Burro Creek
Burro Creek Campground
Arrastra Mountain
Bill Williams Gorge
Bill Williams River
Black Canyon Trail
Fred J. Weiler Green Belt
Petroglyph Campground
Table Top Mountains
Imperial Dam Visitor Area
Squaw Lake Rec. Area & Campground

Black Mountains
Wabayuma Peak
Crossman Peak
Empire Landing Cg.
Crossroads Cg.
Gibraltar Mountain
Cactus Plain
Harqualhala Mts.
La Posa Visitor Area
New Water Mts.
Eagletail Mountains

Phoenix
Yuma

△ campsite
☆ best of state
🐾 hiking
🚲 mountain biking
⛷ winter recreation
🦌 wildlife viewing

◄ fishing
≈ whitewater
↕ general recreation
⊕ caves or spelunking
↕ cultural/historical site
✕ canoeing
✗ rock climbing

MAP REFERENCES

CAMPGROUNDS

The following campgrounds are found in this area of Arizona. Please call the BLM office (listed following each campground's name) for reservations and information. Contact information for each BLM office is on pages 125-126 for Arizona.

Burro Creek Campground; Kingman Resource Area
Crossroads Campground; Havasu Resource Area
Empire Landing Campground; Havasu Resource Area
Imperial Dam Visitor Area; Yuma Resource Area
La Posa Vistor Area; Yuma Resource Area
Packsaddle Campground; Kingman Resource Area
Petroglyph Campground; Lower Gila Resource Area
Squaw Lake Campground; Yuma Resource Area
Virgin River Campground; Shivwitz Resource Area
Wild Cow Spring Campground; Kingman Resource Area
Windy Point Campground; Kingman Resource Area

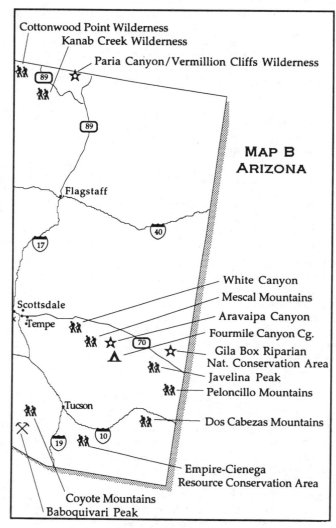

Cottonwood Point Wilderness
Kanab Creek Wilderness
Paria Canyon/Vermillion Cliffs Wilderness

89

89

MAP B
ARIZONA

Flagstaff

17

40

Scottsdale
·Tempe

White Canyon
Mescal Mountains
Aravaipa Canyon
Fourmile Canyon Cg.
Gila Box Riparian
Nat. Conservation Area
Javelina Peak
Peloncillo Mountains

70

Tucson

Dos Cabezas Mountains

19

10

Empire-Cienega
Resource Conservation Area

Coyote Mountains
Baboquivari Peak

▲ campsite
☆ best of state
🏃 hiking
🚵 mountain biking
⛷ winter recreation
🦌 wildlife viewing
🐟 fishing
🛶 whitewater
⚐ general recreation
⊕ caves or spelunking
♦ cultural/historical site
✕ canoeing
⚒ rock climbing

Map References

Aravaipa Canyon—p. 90-92
Baboquivari Peak—p. 122-123
Black Hills Bike Trail—p. 96-97
Cottonwood Point Wilderness—p. 102
Coyote Mountains—p. 123
Empire-Cienega Resource Conservation Area—p. 119
Gila Box Riparian National Conservation Area—p. 94-96
Javelina Peak—p. 120
Kanab Creek Wilderness—p. 102-103
Mescal Mountains—p. 121
Paria Canyon/Vermillion Cliffs Wilderness—p. 98-101
Peloncillo Mountains—p. 121-122
Safford-Morenci Trail—p. 97-98
White Canyon—p. 122

Campgrounds

The following campgrounds are found in this area of Arizona. Please call the BLM office (listed following each campground's name) for reservations and information. Contact information for each BLM office is on pages 125-126 of Arizona.

Fourmile Canyon Campground, Safford District Office

1

ARAVAIPA CANYON

This is the natural area that former U.S. Interior Secretary James Watt referred to as "a gem of the southwestern desert." Journalists and outdoors writers also speak glowingly of the canyon as a unique, special and wonderful place. Colorful 1,000-foot walls make this area "one of the most scenic places in Arizona," according to the BLM. Fortunately, the BLM has taken steps to ensure that its pristine state is preserved by strictly limiting use.

BACKPACKING

The canyon is approximately 11 miles long. There are no marked trails, although history and use have established relatively clear routes. This is a wilderness area, so mountain bikes are prohibited! The hiking routes ford Aravaipa Creek numerous times so it is essential to have sturdy footgear that can get wet. Flash floods are always a possibility—stay alert and stay safe. All water must be treated prior to drinking. Hiking is considered easy. Elevations range from 2,600 feet to 3,100 feet.

MANAGEMENT

BLM Safford District Office 711 14th Avenue, Safford, AZ 85546; (602) 428-4040

LOCATION

In the southeastern part of Arizona, approximately 45 miles west of Safford.

GETTING THERE

To reach the west entrance, take State Highway 177 south from Superior through Kearny, Hayden and Winkelman. At Winkelman, turn south on State Highway 77 for 11 miles to the Aravaipa Road. The turnoff is well marked. The last 12 miles are a combination of paved and gravel road suitable for all vehicles.

To reach the east entrance, drive approximately 15 miles northwest of Safford on US Highway 70. Turn west on Klondyke Road and drive approximately 45 miles to the entrance. Klondyke Road is graded dirt, and although it fords Aravaipa Creek six times, it is suitable for all vehicles except following occasional washouts during July and August rains. Call the BLM for conditions in these months before heading out.

CAMPING

Fourmile Canyon Campground is an excellent base camp for hiking excursions into the Aravaipa Canyon. From Safford, travel 15 miles northwest on US Highway 70 to Aravaipa-Klondyke Road. Proceed 45 miles southwest to Klondyke; go left at Klondyke for one-quarter of a mile to the campground. There are 10 tent or RV sites. Flush toilets, fire grills, picnic tables, and drinking water are all available. No fee is charged. Within Aravaipa Canyon, overnight primitive camping is allowed, providing you have a permit.

PERMITS

Permits are required! No one can use this region without a permit, which allows a maximum stay of three days and two nights in the area. No more than 50 people are allowed within the canyon per day. A fee of $1.50 per person per day is required and may be paid at the self-service fee station at each trailhead. No pets are allowed. Group size is limited to a maximum of 10 people. Day-use horseback riding is allowed but party size is limited to five horses. Reservations for permits may be made up to 13 weeks in advance of your planned entry date.

ADDITIONAL INFORMATION

BLM brochure: *Aravaipa Canyon Wilderness*

MAPS

USGS topographic maps: Brandenburg Mountain, Booger Canyon
BLM surface maps: Mammoth

SEASON

Fall to spring is the best time to visit, although the canyon is open all year.

> *TIP: Travel responsibly to protect the environment*
> *and preserve opportunities*
> *to enjoy recreation in wilderness areas.*

BEST OF THE STATE

PAIUTE WILDERNESS

Within this 55-square-mile wilderness, there is an immense variety of wildlife. Visitors typically see lizards, desert tortoise, Chuckwallas, gila monsters, chipmunks, blacktail jackrabbits, mountain lion, and mule deer. The rugged nature of the area is its primary attraction, inviting challenge and solitude.

BACKPACKING

The Virgin Ridge Loop Trail is the best developed hike in the area with adequate trailhead parking. The eight-mile-long trail is very steep and rugged, requiring excellent physical condition and very sturdy boots. A good working knowledge of a compass and topographic map-reading skills are essential. Carry at least two quarts of water in reserve; one gallon per person is best. The trail takes you up into a ponderosa forest on a ridge, more than a mile above the Mojave Desert to the west. The views are spectacular. Three miles from the trailhead, a second trail plunges down off the ridge through manzanita-clad slopes to Atkin Spring. With a short hike from Atkin Spring, visitors can wander through limestone cliffs and into a natural gateway to Sullivans Canyon. This canyon contains wild natural ecosystems ranging from the Mojave Desert to pinyon-juniper forests to ponderosa pine and Douglas fir stands.

NATURE WALK

Just north of the Paiute Wilderness, in the Virgin River Canyon Recreation Area and near the Virgin River Campground, is the Virgin River Interpretive Trail. This quarter-mile hike each way is well worth the time to get acquainted with the natural surroundings and the geology and history of the Virgin River Gorge. Signs along the way give the common names of plants native to the area. This trail is wheelchair accessible as long as assistance is provided.

MANAGEMENT

BLM Shivwits Resource Area, 225 North Bluff Street, St. George, UT 84770; (801) 628-4491

LOCATION

In the northwestern corner of Arizona near the Utah and Nevada borders.

GETTING THERE

Parking and the trailhead are near Cougar Spring. On Interstate 15 east of Littlefield, take Quail Hill Road to Wolfhole Valley. From there, follow Black Rock Mountain Road to the junction with Elbow Canyon. Bear right on Elbow Canyon to Cougar Spring. Undeveloped vehicle parking is located approximately one-half mile north of Spring at the trailhead.

CAMPING

There are no developed camping areas within the Paiute Wilderness, however the Virgin River Campground, located in the spectacular Virgin River Gorge, is a super base camp for both the Paiute Wilderness and the Beaver Dam Wilderness. To get there, drive 20 miles southwest of St. George, Utah or 16 miles north of Littlefield, Arizona on Interstate 15. The campground is located near the Cedar Pockets interchange. There is a fee charged for overnight camping. The campground is open year-round and facilities include 115 camping sites, flush toilets, drinking water, picnic areas, and RV sites. No showers are available at this campground.

PERMITS

No permits are necessary.

ADDITIONAL INFORMATION
•*Arizona Traveler's Handbook,* by Bill Weir, published by
Moon Publications, 722 Wall Street, Chico, CA 95928; (916)
345-5473.
•BLM brochure: *Paiute and Beaver Dam Mountains Wilderness
Areas*

MAPS
USGS topographic maps: Littlefield, Mountain Sheep Spring
BLM surface maps: Littlefield
Additional maps: A visitor map is available from the Arizona
Strip District Office.

SEASON
Fall to spring is the best time of year to visit here.

---

*TIP: Always walk single file in the center of a trail.
Resist the urge to spread out or walk two abreast.*

BEST OF THE STATE

3

GILA BOX RIPARIAN NATIONAL CONSERVATION AREA

This area is very special, primarily because desert rivers are
exceedingly rare. The backpacker will wander through an
oasis where Rocky Mountain bighorn sheep, mule deer,
mountain lion, javelina, numerous song birds, and raptors
survive. The Gila River winds along a buff-colored canyon in
which 1,000-foot slopes provide a striking contrast against the
mesquite woodland on the river banks. Slopes are covered
with creosote bush, ocotillo, prickly pear, and desert grasses.
Spires and notch canyons are but a few of the numerous
geological features along the canyon. There is an historic cabin
located at Bonita Creek.

HIKING

There is no established trail. The hiking is cross-country through the canyon for 20 miles, along uneven terrain over river cobbles and sandy beaches. There are several thigh-deep river fords. Elevation loss and gain is not noticeable. Hiking is only recommended when the river flow is at or below 250 cubic feet per second. The river is floatable at various other water flows depending on the watercraft used. Sandy beaches make for excellent camping and the natural Gillard Hot Spring is available for soaking in at low water levels.

MANAGEMENT
BLM Safford District Office, 711 14th Avenue, Safford, AZ 85546; (602) 428-4040

LOCATION
In a desert river canyon 20 miles northeast of Safford.

GETTING THERE
Best access is at the downstream end at Bonita Creek. Take Sanchez Road north at Solomon. Beyond Sanchez, follow the signs to Bonita Creek. Trail access is also available at the upstream end at Old Safford Bridge Picnic Area. Take US Highway 70 east to US Highway 191. Follow US Highway 191 to the north end of Old Safford-Clifton Road. Follow the road four miles to Old Bridge. High-clearance vehicles are recommended for access to each end of the National Conservation Area.

CAMPING
Camping is allowed anywhere within the canyon.

PERMITS
No permits are necessary.

MAPS
USGS topographic maps: Gila Box, Guthrie, Lone Star Mountain, Bonita Spring, San Jose
BLM surface maps: Safford, Clifton

SEASON

Fall to spring is the best time to visit; summer temperatures are extreme.

> *TIP: Ride only on open roads and trails.*
> *Riding cross-country is destructive and leaves an*
> *obvious path that tempts others to follow.*

BEST OF THE STATE

BLACK HILLS BIKE TRAIL

This route follows the historic road from Safford to Clifton, passing by active rock hounding and mining areas. The Gila and San Francisco River canyons, an historic Civilian Conservation Corps camp, and a river picnic site can be enjoyed along the bike trail.

MOUNTAIN BIKING

The Black Hills Bike Trail is approximately 20 miles long. The road is dirt and winds towards the foothills and mountains with sweeping views of the Gila Box Riparian National Conservation Area.

MANAGEMENT

BLM Safford District Office, 711 14th Avenue, Safford, AZ 85546; (602) 428-4040

LOCATION

Approximately 20 miles east of Safford, Arizona, near the New Mexico border.

GETTING THERE

From Safford, drive 10 miles east on US Highway 70 to US Highway 191. Go north on Highway 191 to either Black Hills Rockhound Area (eight miles), or the Old Safford Bridge Picnic Area (34 miles) along the Old Safford-Clifton Road.

*Old growth forest along the North Umpqua River Trail
in Douglas County, Oregon*

Above: *The North Umpqua River at Tioga Falls in Oregon is a Bureau of Land Management National Wild and Scenic River*

Below: *Sunset at the Tangle Lakes along the Denali Highway in Alaska*

Above: Morning catch at Hidden Lake, Colorado
Below: Bicyclist on the Midland Trail in Colorado

Autumn in BLM-managed land in Eastern Idaho

Above: *Area near the Owyhee Dam Project in Oregon*

Below: *Kayaker in BLM-managed land in southwestern Idaho*

Above: *Riding the Canyon Rapids on the Gulkana River in Alaska*

Below: *Looking out from a cave in Three Fingers Gulch, Oregon*

Above: The North Fork of the Owyhee River in Idaho
Below: Rock climber in Southwest Idaho
Following page: Gold panning at Jack Wade Dredge, Alaska

PERMITS

No permits are necessary.

MAPS

USGS topographic maps: Guthrie, Clifton, Gila Box, Tollgate Tank
BLM surface maps: Safford, Clifton

SEASON

From fall to spring is the best time to visit here.

TIP: Leave behind your "need for speed" mentality. It has no place in the wildlands of our country.

BEST OF THE STATE

5

SAFFORD-MORENCI TRAIL

This trail winds through the rugged canyons of the Gila and Turtle Mountains. Prehistoric Indian cliff dwellings, remnants of early homesteads, incredible rock outcroppings, and sweeping views of Bonita Creek in the Gila Box Riparian National Conservation Area may be enjoyed.

HIKING / HORSEBACK RIDING

The Safford-Morenci Trail is maintained by volunteers and links the Gila Mountains, Bonita Creek, Turtle Mountain, and Eagle Creek together. It is 15 miles each way. Streams and springs are scarce, but water can normally be found about halfway into Bonita Creek. Any water that is found must be purified. Elevations range from 3,700 feet to 6,000 feet. Hiking difficulty is considered moderate.

MANAGEMENT

BLM Safford District Office, 711 14th Avenue, Safford, AZ 85546; (602) 428-4040

LOCATION
Approximately 12 miles northeast of Safford.

GETTING THERE
From Safford, take the San Juan Road northeast about eight miles. At the fork, bear left and head for Walnut Springs and West Ranch. In wet weather, this road is considered impassable for two-wheel-drive vehicles.

PERMITS
No permits are necessary.

MAPS
USGS topographic maps: Lone Star Mountain, Bonita Spring, Copper Plate Gulch
BLM surface maps: Safford, Clifton

ADDITIONAL INFORMATION
BLM brochure: *Safford-Morenci Trail*

SEASON
Fall to spring is the best time to visit.

TIP: Avoid planning your backcountry vacation during normally crowded times.

6

PARIA CANYON/ VERMILLION CLIFFS WILDERNESS

Tom Wharton, outdoors editor for the *Salt Lake Tribune,* calls Paria Canyon one of the best backpacking locations in the West. Few who have traveled the trail dispute the claim, and you won't either if it is desert and canyon hiking you prefer.

The thoroughly wild and twisting canyon is part Eden, with its hanging gardens of ferns and orchids, and part sandstone sculpture, offering miles of colorful, swirling patterns in cliff walls that at times are so close together that they virtually block out the sky above. Ancient petroglyphs seen on the canyon walls are evidence that the Pueblo Indians used the canyon over 700 years ago for hunting and raising corn, beans and squash. In later years, when prospectors ventured into the surrounding terrain searching for gold and uranium, Paria Canyon remained virtually unblemished. In 1984, following a recommendation by the BLM, the Arizona Wilderness Act designated Paria Canyon a protected wilderness area.

HIKING

Plan on four to six days to hike the canyon in comfort. Typically, hikes begin at the Paria Canyon Ranger Station as that is where the closure of the canyon due to weather conditions is regulated. Be forewarned—the river can rush through the upper narrows at a depth of 40 feet during extreme weather. Your feet will be wet much of the time as wading through ankle-deep, silty water is standard fare. Wear old sneakers or sturdy all-terrain sandals, ones you can hike in, or boots that are comfortable even when wet. Pack plenty of sock changes or wear neoprene socks.

The backpack is 37 miles in length and is considered moderately difficult—chiefly because of all the river crossings and loose terrain. While springs are generally flowing with sufficient frequency along the route, it is recommended that you carry a container that can hold one gallon of water, just in case. Check on current water conditions at the Paria Canyon Ranger Station. Water is available at the station. Due to possible chemical contamination from farms and ranches upstream, drinking directly from the river is not suggested.

By the way, there is quicksand along the route, but it is generally not more than knee deep and certainly not the variety made famous by Hollywood. A good hiking staff will allow you to probe the murky waters before stepping out into uncharted territory.

MANAGEMENT
•BLM Vermillion Resource Area, 225 North Bluff, St. George, UT 84770; (801) 628-4491

Arizona

•BLM Kanab Resource Area, 320 North First East, Kanab, UT
84741; (801) 644-2672

LOCATION
Approximately 40 miles east of Kanab, Utah near the Utah/
Arizona border.

GETTING THERE
From Page, follow US Highway 89 west for 30 miles to the
ranger station near milepost 21. From Kanab, drive 40 miles
east on US Highway 89. The ranger station is located just off
the south side of the highway. The trailhead for Paria Canyon
is two miles south of the station. You will need to plan on a
car shuttle for this trip. Most trips begin at White House
Canyon because of flash-flood dangers. Leave a second vehicle
at Lees Ferry (a 145-mile trip from the trailhead to Paria
Canyon) or arrange for your car to be shuttled. Page is your
last stop for supplies and the traditional place to arrange for
someone to shuttle your vehicle. Costs for a shuttle typically
range from $55 and up if you use your car and $150 and up if
you use a driver's.

CAMPING
There are two organized car campgrounds at either end of the
trail. White House Campground is at the beginning and Lees
Ferry is at the end. Primitive camping is allowed anywhere
along the trail itself, but no campfires are permitted within the
canyon. Minimum impact regulations are stressed within the
canyon. No latrines are allowed within 100 feet of the river or
campsite locations and always pack out your toilet paper.

PERMITS
Registration is required for traveling within the Paria Canyon.
Recommended group size is three to four. Organized groups
must contact the Kanab BLM Office for permit information at
(801) 644-2672.

MAPS
USGS topographic maps:
Utah/Arizona: West Clark Bench, Bridger Point
Arizona: Wrather Arch, Water Pockets, Ferry Swale, Lees Ferry
BLM surface maps: Smokey Mountain, Glen Canyon Dam

Additional maps: A visitor map is available from the Arizona Strip District Office.

ADDITIONAL INFORMATION
• *Hiking the Southwest's Canyon Country,* by Sandra Hinchman, published by The Mountaineers, 1011 Southwest Klickitat Way, Suite 107, Seattle, WA 98134; (800) 553-4453.
• *Arizona Traveler's Handbook,* by Bill Weir, published by Moon Publications, 722 Wall Street, Chico, CA 95928; (916) 345-5473.
• BLM brochure: *The Hiker's Guide to Paria Canyon*

SEASON
Spring, early summer and fall are the times to go. Temperatures can become exceedingly hot during July and August. Flash floods, which are always a threat in the canyon, are most prevalent during the months of July through September. May and June are the busiest months, with the Easter holiday being notorious for "campsite competition derbies." Winter is the least crowded, but also the chilliest—hikers frequently complain of cold feet.

TIP: Camp 200 feet or more from the nearest water source—more if regulations indicate. Only camp in established or previously used sites if available.

1

NORTHWESTERN ARIZONA

COTTONWOOD POINT WILDERNESS
backpacking, horseback riding

Access is very difficult, but this convoluted plateau is worth a peek—check in with the BLM office for updated access information. It's located east of Colorado City on the Arizona/Utah border. Many say that the rugged scenery is very much like Zion National Park but in miniature. Indeed, the high cliffs and plateau, dissected by deep and narrow canyons with dense riparian vegetation, does remind one of Zion in some respects.

For more information: Contact the BLM Vermillion Resource Area, 225 North Bluff Street, St. George, UT 84770; (801) 628-4491.
USGS topographic maps: Colorado City, Hildale, Moccasin

GRAND WASH CLIFFS WILDERNESS
backpacking, horseback riding

Located along the Colorado River, the Grand Canyon and 15 miles east of the Arizona/Nevada border, the Cliffs are relatively accessible by seasonal service roads. Check in with the BLM office to determine the best access route at your time of visit. The Cliffs are like giant 1000-foot steps up to the Shivwits Plateau area. A number of picturesque canyons cut through the Cliffs, making for interesting scrambling opportunities.

For more information: Contact the BLM Shivwits Resource Area, 225 North Bluff Street, St. George, UT 84770; (801) 628-4491.
USGS topographic maps: Cane Springs Southeast, St. George Canyon, Olaf Knolls, Last Chance Canyon, Grand Gulch Bench

KANAB CREEK WILDERNESS
backpacking, canyoneering

Running south from the town of Fredonia, the Kanab

Creek crosses the Kaibab Indian Reservation, cuts deeper into the plateau as it crosses BLM lands, winds for about ten miles through the bottom of a canyon in the Kaibab National Forest, and finally ends up dumping into the Colorado River and Grand Canyon National Park. While it is possible to backpack down Kanab Creek to the Grand Canyon—and then out via any number of alternate routes—the backpacking is considered very strenuous and should not be taken lightly. Fall is the best time to head out. Check with the BLM office for specific access and backpacking information.

For more information: Contact the BLM Vermillion Resource Area, 225 North Bluff Street, St. George, UT 84770, (801) 628-4491; or the Kaibab National Forest, Williams, AZ; (602) 635-2681.
USGS topographic maps: Heaton Knolls, Jumpup Canyon, Kanab Point

MOUNT TRUMBULL WILDERNESS AND MOUNT LOGAN WILDERNESS
backpacking, camping, wildlife observation

With an elevation of 8,028 feet, Mount Trumbull is the highest point for miles around. Nearby Mount Logan (hard to find on maps even though the BLM recognizes it as a designated wilderness) sits slightly lower at 7,966 feet. Virgin timber and ponderosa pine cover the upper reaches of both peaks. Slopes are steep and rocky, an ideal habitat for the pinyon-juniper woodlands that cling to them. In addition to the usual high desert rodent population (mice, gophers, chipmunks, jackrabbits and such), the wilderness areas support porcupine, coyote, spotted skunk, mountain lion, bobcat, and mule deer. On the west slope of Mount Logan, the Hells Hole, a giant rock amphitheater, provides a curious and colorful attraction.

The Mount Trumbull Trail, two and a half miles each way, is a good introduction to the area. To get to the trailhead, take the Toroweap Road (County Road 109) that branches off Arizona 389, eight miles west of Fredonia. Follow the dirt road about 46 miles to County Road 5, a major fork. Bear right, heading west toward Mount Trumbull. After approximately six miles, you will reach an area known as Nixon Flat. A sign marks the trailhead. The trail disappears within one mile of the summit, but the summit is accessible to those with strong map reading and compass skills. Follow the northern edge of the basalt flow.

For more information: Contact the BLM Vermillion Resource Area, 225 North Bluff, St. George, UT 84770; (801) 628-4491.
USGS topographic maps: Mount Trumbull, Northwest
BLM surface map: Mount Trumbull
Additional maps: A visitor map is available from the Arizona Strip District Office.

VIRGIN RIVER CAMPGROUND
camping, hiking, picnicking, rock hounding, wildlife/nature photography

The Virgin River Campground, located in the spectacular Virgin River Gorge, is a super base of operations for both the Paiute Wilderness and the Beaver Dam Wilderness. To get there, drive 20 miles southwest of St. George, Utah, or 16 miles north of Littlefield, Arizona on Interstate 15. The campground is located near the Cedar Pockets interchange. There is a fee charged for overnight camping. The campground is open year-round and facilities include 115 camping sites, flush toilets, drinking water, picnic areas, and RV sites. No showers are available at this campground. A nearby primitive trail will take you into the Paiute Wilderness for a day of hiking.

For more information: Contact the BLM Shivwits Resource Area, 225 North Bluff Street, St. George, UT 84770; (801) 628-4491.

PAIUTE WILDERNESS
backpacking, camping, hiking, wildlife observation, horseback riding

Located just south of Interstate 15 in the northwestern corner of the state, the Paiute Wilderness, best known for the Virgin Mountains within, is a rugged, geologically and ecologically complex environment. This is one of Arizona's hidden gems, although more and more people are discovering the beauty and adventure to be experienced here.

•**See also Best of the State, page 92**•
For more information: Contact the BLM Shivwits Resource Area, 225 North Bluff Street, St. George, UT 84770; (801) 628-4491.

BEAVER DAM MOUNTAINS
backpacking, camping, hiking, wildlife observation

Located just north of Interstate 15, this wilderness area is wonderfully rugged and encompasses the alluvial plains and mountains of far northwestern Arizona and parts of Utah. Desert bighorn sheep, desert tortoise, numerous species of raptors and an endangered fish—the woundfin minnow—may be found here. There are no trails. All hiking and exploration is cross-country. Hikers must be extremely proficient at reading a map and compass. Of special note is the pretty Joshua tree forest in the lower elevations.

For more information: Contact the BLM Shivwits Resource Area, 225 North Bluff Street, St. George, UT 84770; (801) 628-4491.
USGS topographic maps: Littlefield
BLM surface maps: Littlefield

VIRGIN RIVER GORGE
backpacking, picnicking, camping, hiking, wildlife observation

BLM insiders say that this is one of the "most spectacular river canyons in the southwest, bar none." Located just off Interstate 15 and northeast of US 91, the Virgin River Gorge lies within the Virgin River Scenic Area, created in 1973. Backpacking trips into the Paiute Wilderness, south of the Gorge, are possible from here.

For more information: Contact the BLM Shivwits Resource Area, 225 North Bluff Street, St. George, UT 84770; (801) 628-4491.
USGS topographic maps: Mountain Sheep Spring, Purgatory Canyon

PARIA CANYON / VERMILLION CLIFFS WILDERNESS
backpacking, canyoneering, wildlife observation

The Paria Canyon area is classic canyoneering at its best. Take a four to six-day, 35-mile journey from Kanab, Utah down to Lees Ferry, Arizona. Numerous side canyons beckon to be explored, but use caution because flash flooding is a real danger. Desert bighorn have been reintroduced to a canyon wildlife population that includes raccoon, fox, beaver, bobcat, and mule deer.

•**See also Best of the State, page 98**•

For more information: Contact the BLM Shivwits Resource Area, 225 North Bluff Street, St. George, UT 84770; (801) 628-4491.

BLACK MOUNTAINS
backpacking, hiking, camping, horseback riding, wildlife observation

This is a lightly visited area, yet it is undeservedly ignored. It's located just west of Kingman and bordered by the Colorado River, Interstate 40 and US 93. Formed by volcanic flows, the mountains and canyons are rugged and steep with seasonal springs that flow well into April, during wet years. The best time to visit is between January and April. There are three wilderness areas within the Black Mountains: Mount Nutt, Warm Springs and Mount Wilson. Juniper, yucca, catclaw, creosote, and in riparian areas, willow, nettle (ouch!) and watercress are the most common plants. Besides the assortment of bats, reptiles and rodents, wildlife residents include coyote, gray fox, badger, spotted skunk, bobcat, bighorn sheep, and mule deer. Camping is allowed anywhere. A number of unmaintained unsigned roadways provide super access for informal base camps from which to day-hike. There are no maintained trails. Travel is cross-country. Be sure of your map reading skills.

For more information: Contact the BLM Kingman Resource Area, 2475 Beverly Avenue, Kingman, AZ 86401; (602) 757-3161.
USGS topographic maps: Union Pass, Secret Pass, Oatman, Mount Nutt, Kingman Southwest, Boundary Cone, Warm Springs, Yucca Northwest, Warm Springs Southwest, Warm Springs Southeast, Yucca

GRAND WASH CLIFFS
backpacking, camping

To get there, take US 93 northwest from Kingman approximately 27 miles. Turn northeast towards Pearce Ferry for 20 miles to the Pearce Ferry Road. The Grand Wash Cliffs form an escarpment that is 4,000 feet high in places—a colorful and spectacular contrast between the forested land above and the dry, desert plain below. Though no hiking trails exist, it is relatively easy to get to the top of the cliffs from the north. Bighorn sheep may be spotted in the area.

For more information: Contact the BLM Kingman Resource Area, 2475 Beverly Avenue, Kingman, AZ 86401; (602) 757-3161.

MOUNT TIPTON
camping, backpacking, hiking, wildlife observation, rock bounding, mountain biking

Part of the Cerbat Mountain Range, 7,148-foot-high Mount Tipton affords the visitor superb views of the surrounding peaks and ridges. It is located north of Kingman off US 93. Unpaved Big Wash Road is the main access into the Cerbat range.

The BLM maintains both the Packsaddle Campground and Windy Point Campground, open May 1 to November 1. Both sites serve as an excellent base from which to explore. From Kingman, travel 23 miles northwest on Highway 93. Turn right on BLM's dirt Chloride/Big Wash Road and drive nine miles to the Packsaddle Campground or 11 miles to the Windy Point Campground. There is no water, so bring your own. Facilities include seven tent sites (10 at Windy), vault toilets, fire grills, and picnic areas. No fee is charged.

Mountain bikes are permitted on old mining roads and trails outside of the designated wilderness area—use caution as off-highway vehicles use these trails too.

There are hundreds of old mines in the area which the BLM states are "ripe for exploration." As with any old site exploration, do it strictly at your own risk (there are extreme hazards possible when entering an old mine). The sites are protected—no removing artifacts.

Spectacular views of the nearby ridges may be enjoyed from the campgrounds. The shallow valleys and bowls and pinyon pine-vegetated slopes provide good habitat for kit fox, bobcat and mule deer. If you like to observe raptors, this is a good site. Numerous hawks and other raptors often play the thermals during the day.

For more information: Contact the BLM Kingman Resource Area, 2475 Beverly Avenue, Kingman, AZ 86401; (607) 757-3161.
USGS topographic maps: Dolan Springs, Mount Tipton, Mount Tipton 3 Southeast, Grasshopper Junction

TIP: Constantly stay alert for signs of your passing and erase them if possible.

2

SOUTHWESTERN ARIZONA

ARRASTRA MOUNTAIN
backpacking, hiking, wildlife observation

Located just south of Burro Creek and northeast of Alamo Lake, the Arrastra Mountain Wilderness Area is a vast acreage of rugged terrain, granite outcrops, volcanic hills, washes, and serpentine canyons. The presence of vegetation and available water attracts a wide variety of birds, making the area an outstanding destination for birders. Washes make the best hiking routes, as do old jeep tracks, used to service now abandoned mines. The Santa Maria River flows through this area.

For more information: Contact the BLM Lower Gila Resource Area, 2015 West Deer Valley Road, Phoenix, AZ 85027; (602) 780-8090. **USGS topographic maps:** Malpais Mesa Southwest, Arrastra Mountain Northeast, Artillery Peak, Palmerita Ranch, Arrastra Mountain Southeast, Arrastra Mountain, Thorn Peak, and many others.

EMPIRE LANDING CAMPGROUND
swimming, fishing, jet-skiing, off-road vehicle use

This campground is located approximately nine miles north of Parker on the California side of the Colorado River. Cross the river at Parker and drive north. The campground is a destination area for those interested in recreational boating, fishing and rock hounding. Off-highway vehicle use is also a popular activity in designated areas. An overnight camping fee is charged. Facilities include 26 tent sites, 50 RV sites, flush toilets, picnic areas, and cold showers. Coyotes are the most probable wildlife sightings, although bobcats, gray foxes and badgers are known to reside in the area. Fishing is for crappie, bluegill, bass, and catfish. Migratory birds in the winter include numerous species of duck and geese.

Don't feel like paying a fee and want to look for more primitive camping? Crossroads is your alternative, although it is probably just as crowded.

For more information: Contact the BLM Havasu Resource Area, 3189 Sweetwater Avenue, Lake Havasu City, AZ 86403; (602) 855-8017.

CROSSROADS CAMPGROUND
swimming, fishing, jet-skiing, off-road vehicle use

Located approximately eight miles north of Parker on the California side of the Colorado River. Cross the river at Parker and drive north on Parker Dam Road. The campground is a destination area dedicated primarily to water sports, with eight tent or RV sites available. No fee is charged. There are pit toilets, picnic areas and fire grills—no showers. The campsites are shaded by cottonwood, tamarisk and palm that grow down by the river's edge. Sightings of roadrunners, mallards, cottontail rabbits, as well as a variety of snakes, lizards and bullfrogs are common. Numerous species of birds may also be enjoyed. For a more wilderness type setting, escape to the Bill Williams River Area.

For more information: Contact the BLM Havasu Resource Area, 3189 Sweetwater Avenue, Lake Havasu City, AZ 86403; (602) 855-8017.

BILL WILLIAMS RIVER
backpacking, horseback riding

Intersected by State Road 95, north of Parker Dam, this area is bounded by a national forest and wildlife refuge and by private land, making access difficult. Inquire at the BLM office before entering to get advice as to the best point of access. There are no designated hiking trails. Hiking is along the river's edge. Side canyons may be explored and offer some interesting routes into the nearby mountains. One thing is for sure—you will probably have the area much to yourself as most visitors to the area bypass the surrounding BLM lands in favor of the Colorado River and Lake Havasu.

For more information: Contact the BLM Havasu Resource Area, 3189 Sweetwater Avenue, Lake Havasu City, AZ 86403; (602) 855-8017.
USGS topographic maps: Monkeys Head, Casteneda Hills Southwest, Centennial Wash

BILL WILLIAMS GORGE
backpacking, hiking, fishing (in the river below the dam),
wildlife observation

Downstream of Alamo Lake, the Bill Williams River meanders through a deep canyon, the Bill Williams Gorge.
Bounded on the southeast by the Rawhide Mountains (a
designated BLM Wilderness Area), a relatively low-lying range,
and on the west by the Buckskin Range, a more dramatic
mountain range, the Bill Williams Gorge features a perennial
stream, colorful bluffs and riparian vegetation of cottonwood
and willow.

For more information: Contact the BLM Havasu Resource Area, 3189
Sweetwater Avenue, Lake Havasu City, AZ 86403; (602) 855-8017.
USGS topographic maps: Swansea, Reid Valley, Alamo Dam

BURRO CREEK
camping, backpacking, hiking, wildlife observation, rock
hounding

Burro Creek is located near the town of Wikieup, off US 93
and approximately 60 miles northwest of Wickenburg. Fall,
winter and spring are the best seasons to visit. Summer is too
hot for outdoor recreation, although the occasional thunder-
storm does offer a unique hiking opportunity and a cooling
respite—if your timing is good.

The scenery is very dramatic with vertical rock faces,
spires, buttes, rugged canyons, springs, and perennial streams.
The numerous microhabitats created by the unique geography,
coupled with plant diversity and available water, attract and
support a wide variety of birds and wildlife. Raptors are fully
represented, including bald eagles, osprey, kestrels, Cooper's
and red-tails. Beavers, raccoons, ringtails, gray foxes, a variety
of skunks, javelinas, bobcats, mountain lions, mule deer and
pronghorn antelope round out the wildlife population. Bird
watching is reportedly superb (150 identified species).

Camping is available at the Burro Creek Campground (fee
charged). It's very scenic and features a desert garden. There
are no formal trails. Hiking and backpacking are best along the
canyons. Uplands are laced with several jeep tracks, but travel
is challenging and navigational skills are at a premium. If you
can't use a map and compass, stick to the canyons. Stream and
spring water must be treated before drinking.

For more information: Contact the BLM Kingman Resource Area,
2475 Beverly Avenue, Kingman, AZ 86401; (602) 757-3161.
BLM brochures: *Burro Creek Recreation Site, Burro Creek Desert
Garden*
USGS topographic maps: Kaiser Springs

CACTUS PLAIN
hiking, horseback riding, plant study

An immense, undulating area made up predominantly of
sand dunes—some stable, some not. It's like walking through
snow. Sound is muffled, giving the visitor a feeling of complete and total isolation from the outside world. Hiking in the
early morning or late afternoon as the sun is setting offers the
most spectacular lighting and rewarding moments. Located
near State Road 72, approximately 10 miles southeast of
Parker. A botanist friend tells me that the plants of primary
interest in the area are woolly heads, Death Valley Mormon
tea, and sand flat milkvetch. Although extremely hard to spot,
the elf owl also resides here, as does the flat-tailed horned
lizard.

For more information: Contact the BLM Havasu Resource Area, 3189
Sweetwater Avenue, Lake Havasu City, AZ 86403; (602) 757-4011.
USGS topographic maps: Crossroads, Black Peak Southwest, Black
Peak Southeast, Buckskin Mountains West/Southwest, Linskey
Northwest, Linskey Northeast, Bouse Hills Northwest

CROSSMAN PEAK
camping, hiking, backpacking, horseback riding

Approximately 10 miles northeast of Havasu City, this area
is best appreciated up close, because from a distance it looks
barren and foreboding. Once within the area, however, you
discover a number of hidden springs and a remarkable variety
of desert plant life—all tucked within the numerous canyons
and drainages.

For more information: Contact the BLM Havasu Resource Area, 3189
Sweetwater Avenue, Lake Havasu City, AZ 86403; (602) 757-4011.
USGS topographic maps: Crossman Peak

EAGLETAIL MOUNTAINS
camping, backpacking, hiking, climbing, horseback riding

This area is truly spectacular because of the many arches, giant spires, monoliths and jagged ridges that rise above the surrounding flatlands. Courthouse Rock, a huge granite monolith just north of Eagle Peak, rises 1,274 feet toward the sky, making it an attractive hangout for rock climbers. Located south of Interstate 10 and west of Phoenix, the best access to the region is from the east via Harquahala Valley or Courthouse Rock roads. Summer temperatures are abominable— 100°F is normal. Late fall, winter and early spring are the best times to visit. Desert vegetation predominates and includes: ocotillo, cholla, creosote, ironwood, saguaro, Mormon tea, barrel cactus, and mesquite. With the heat-generated updrafts and a large population of desert rodents, expect to see numerous raptors as well as the great horned owl and coyote.

For more information: Contact the BLM Yuma Resource Area, 3150 Winsor Avenue, Yuma, AZ 85365; (602) 726-6300.
USGS topographic maps: Lone Mountain, Little Horn Mountains Northeast, Eagletail Mountains West, Nott Busch Butte, Columbus Peak

GIBRALTAR MOUNTAIN
hiking, horseback riding

Gibraltar Mountain is a gem for those seeking unique photography and sightseeing opportunities. Panoramas are constantly changing, leading the adventurous hiker or equestrian through an always varying landscape. The surrounding area has been heavily used by off-highway vehicles, but not enough to detract from the beauty of the site. Adjacent Buckskin Mountain State Park offers additional recreational opportunities.

For more information: Contact the BLM Havasu Resource Area, 3189 Sweetwater Avenue, Lake Havasu City, AZ 86403; (602) 757-4011.

FRED J. WEILER GREEN BELT
camping, backpacking, hiking, birdwatching

This area consists of a single, dense 100-mile strip of vegetation alongside the Gila River, stretching from just west of

Phoenix to just above Date Palm. Although the river has limited flow year-round, numerous potholes in the sandy wash continue to hold water after the surface flow subsides, attracting many waterfowl and other wildlife. Dove and quail hunters know this area well.

The strip is best accessed from State Road 85 or Interstate 85. A few local access routes require the use of a four-wheel-drive vehicle. Pack plenty of water along—as much extra as you can carry or load in your vehicle. Spring, fall and winter are the best seasons to visit.

Arizona state law prohibits camping anywhere within 440 yards of a watering hole—this is so wildlife is not driven away from the few watering places that sustain life. Seasonal waterfowl include mallards, pintails, teals, red-heads, canvasbacks, and Canada geese. Songbirds include pyrrhuloxias, cardinals, and a variety of finches, orioles, tanagers, woodpeckers, and hummingbirds. Roadrunners and phainopeplas can also be seen in this area. Herons, egrets, yellowlegs and snipe also frequent the watering holes. Foxes, coyotes, raccoons, bobcats, mule deer and javelinas round out the "expect-to-see" wildlife listing.

For more information: Contact the BLM Phoenix Resource Area, 2015 West Deer Valley Road, Phoenix, AZ 85027; (602) 780-8090. **USGS topographic maps:** Hassayampa, Arlington, Cotton Center, Cotton Center Northwest

PETROGLYPH CAMPGROUND
Indian petroglyphs, historic sites, birdwatching, hiking, rock bounding, rock climbing

Located southwest of Phoenix near the Gila River, the top of Painted Rock Mountain offers panoramic vistas of the Dendora Valley and Sentinal Plain stretching out below. The Gila River winds through this convoluted and rugged volcanic region. Ancient Indian rock drawings and carvings gave this site its name, and visitors to the region will still marvel at the extensive historical canal networks and numerous petroglyphs. To get to the campground, take Highway 8 west from Gila Bend 20 miles to Painted Rocks Road. Head north on Painted Rocks approximately 11 miles to the campground.

The campground is open year round. No fee is charged. Facilities include 30 tent or RV sites, vault toilets, picnic areas, shade ramadas, fire grills, and an RV disposal station.

For more information: Contact the BLM Lower Gila Resource Area, 2015 West Deer Valley Road, Phoenix, AZ 85027; (602) 780-8090.

HARQUALHALA MOUNTAINS
camping, backpacking, hiking, horseback riding

"Running water up high" is the literal translation of the Native American name "Harqualhala," which bodes well for the backpacker, except in the summer when temperatures are so hot you could boil water on a rock. November to April are the best times to visit, when perennial springs, seeps and the occasional seasonal waterfall may be enjoyed.

Located approximately 15.5 miles west of Aquila and 39.5 miles west of Wickenburg, Harqualhala Peak, at 5,681 feet, is the tallest peak around, which is why the Smithsonian Institute built an observatory here in the 1920s, now a National Register Historic Site. From on top of the peak, Table Top, you can spot 100 miles or so to the southeast, and Chemehuevis, just under 100 miles to the northwest. Evidence of mining activity may be found throughout the area. The combination of a rugged desert mountain range with available water and lush, green campsites make this area worth checking out.

Numerous raptors may be spotted in the skies overhead. Brown's Canyon is a protected desert tortoise habitat. Expect to see mule deer, coyotes, and an abundance of desert rodents. The BLM recommends the Harqualhala Mountain Pack Trail, a 5.4-mile one-way historic trail used by the Smithsonian Institute in the 1920s to haul supplies to the mountain top. The trail is rugged and obscure; follow the rock cairns.

To get to the trailhead, take US Highway 60 west from Aquila for 14 miles to the rest area on the south side of the highway. Turn south on the dirt road and follow it to the wilderness boundary—be sure to close the gate behind you. At the wilderness boundary, begin hiking on the old jeep trail, evident from the parking area.

For more information: Contact the BLM Lower Gila Resource Area, 2015 West Deer Valley Road, Phoenix, AZ 85027; (602) 780-8090.
USGS topographic maps: Harqualhala Mountain, Socorro Peak, Webber Canyon, Gladden.
BLM surface maps: Salome

BLACK CANYON TRAIL
backpacking, hiking, horseback riding, wheelchair accessible

As this book goes to press, this trail is 13 miles in length each way. When the trail is completed (sometime in the next several years), it will be 62 miles long. It will provide an all-important link within the Arizona Trail System by effectively tying into the 110-mile-long Sun Circle Trail at the southern end and the trail network within the Prescott National Forest at the northern end. Talk about backpacking nirvana!

Lower elevations of this trail segment are wheelchair accessible. The entire trail has an historic origin as it has been used for livestock since pioneer times. Located 35 miles north of Phoenix, take Highway 17 to the New River exit. Go west for approximately three miles. The trailhead is marked by a picnic area, ramadas and restrooms on the north side of the road. The best time to visit is between fall and spring. Hiking difficulty is rated as moderate with elevations ranging from 1,500 feet to 4,500 feet.

For more information: Contact the BLM Phoenix Resource Area, 2015 West Deer Valley Road, Phoenix, AZ 85027; (602) 780-8090.
USGS topographic maps: New River, Black Canyon City, Bumble Bee, Cleator
BLM surface maps: Phoenix North, Bradshaw Mountains

NEW WATER MOUNTAINS
camping, backpacking, rock hounding

Located between Interstate 10 and the Kofa National Wildlife Refuge, this region of crags, spires, jagged ridges, steep smooth-walled canyons, and big rock outcrops offers good backpacking and hiking opportunities. Nearly 20 miles worth of old vehicle byways make travel within the area easier. Vegetation is sparse. Pack all the water you will need; finding it in this area is next to impossible. Bighorn sheep and mule deer roam the mountains.

For more information: Contact the BLM Yuma District Office, 3150 Winsor Avenue, Yuma, AZ 85365; (602) 726-6300.
USGS topographic maps: Crystal Hill, New Water Mountains, New Water Well

WABAYUMA PEAK
backpacking, camping, hiking, horseback riding, mountain biking

Tucked into the Hualapai Mountains, approximately 30 miles southeast of Kingman and east of Interstate 40, lies Wabayuma Peak, a relatively large roadless area recovering from past abuse by cattle and mining. Many of the old road tracks are still evident, although they are growing over with vegetation. It can get a bit confusing in here unless you are proficient with a compass and topographic map.

Wabayuma Peak is 7,601 feet high, making it appropriate for recreational use all year, even when the temperatures in the lower elevations are downright hot and miserable. There are quite a number of springs, and most show past development for cattle use. Be sure to purify all water. Despite the springs, it is recommended that you carry a day's supply of water with you at all times.

Hiking can be strenuous on the steep slopes of the peak and surrounding range. There are many roads in the Hualapai available for mountain biking, but no mountain biking is allowed in the Wabayuma Peak Wilderness Area—or any other wilderness area for that matter. Wildflowers are spectacular during the late spring and early summer.

The BLM recommends hiking the Wabayuma Peak Trail, which is three miles each way. The difficulty of the trail is rated as moderate. At times, the trail becomes hard to see, but if you follow the blaze marks on large Ponderosa pines you will get to the top with little difficulty.

Camping is available at the Wild Cow Springs Campground, open May 1 to November 1. To get there, take Hualapai Mountain Road out of Kingman. After passing through Hualapai Mountain County Park, turn right onto the dirt road marked with signs for Flag Mine Road and Wild Cow Springs. This road will also take you to the trailhead for Wabayuma Peak, 13.5 miles past the campground. No fee is charged for camping. Facilities at Wild Cow Springs include 22 tent or trailer sites, vault toilets, fire grills, and picnic areas. No water is available, so you must bring your own. Summer temperatures have been known to dip into the thirties, so pack warmly.

For more information: Contact the BLM Kingman Resource Area, 2475 Beverly Avenue, Kingman, AZ 86401; (602) 757-3161.

USGS topographic maps: Wabayuma Peak
BLM surface map: Valentine

TABLE TOP MOUNTAIN
hiking, wildlife observation

If you happen to be in the Phoenix area, then Table Top is worth a visit. Primarily a day-hiking proposition, the views from the top are spectacular and the mountain itself is a well-recognized landmark. The top is unique in that it is a 40-acre plateau (hence the name table-top) covered with desert grasses. The area around the mountain and the mountain itself is an important desert bighorn and desert tortoise habitat. Coyote and javelina round out the most-often-seen category.

For more information: Contact the BLM Lower Gila Resource Area, 2015 West Deer Valley Road, Phoenix, AZ 85027; (602) 780-8090. **USGS topographic maps:** Antelope Peak, Little Table Top, Vekol Mountains Northeast, Indian Bottle

SQUAW LAKE RECREATION SITE
boating, canoeing, fishing, jet-skiing, swimming, camping

Located near Yuma, Arizona across the California border, this campground is a popular destination for RVers and is open year-round. If it is solitude you seek, avoid this site. There is no wilderness value to be experienced here. However, if you want watersport recreation and a campground atmosphere, this is a good destination. Expect temperatures to be HOT. On average, over 100 days a year exceed the 100°F mark.

Fishing is for largemouth bass and bluegill on nearby Squaw Lake. Campground facilities include 115 tent or RV sites, flush toilets, drinking water, fire grills, picnic areas, a beach area, boat ramp, and cold showers. A fee is charged for overnight camping.

One main redeeming feature in this area, besides the Colorado River, is Betty's Kitchen, a one-half-mile-long interpretive trail that is a must-see if you are in the area, or even if you are just passing through. Hiking it takes only about 30 minutes—time well spent. To get there, take Highway 95 seven miles east from Yuma. Turn north on Avenue 7E and follow the road for nine miles until the paved road turns to gravel just past Laguna Dam. Turn left at the sign for Betty's Kitchen Wildlife and Interpretive Area on the right side of the road. The loop nature trail is maintained by the Betty's Kitchen Protective Association, (602) 627-2773, and is part of an old access road to the small cafe that the area is named after. There are outstanding birdwatching opportunities here. Be sure to pick up the Betty's Kitchen Interpretive Trail brochure for your self-guided walk.

If you like to fish, the fishing is good, too—bluegill, largemouth bass, carp, flathead, and channel catfish are all plentiful. The best season to visit the trail is from September to May.

For more information: Contact the BLM Yuma Resource Area, 3150 Winsor Avenue, Yuma, AZ 85365; (602) 726-6300.
USGS topographic maps: Laguna Dam

TIP: The most serious damage to a cultural site occurs from innocent visitation. Staying on the trail will minimize the damage.

ARIZONA BY REGION

3

SOUTHEASTERN ARIZONA

ARAVAIPA CANYON
backpacking, horseback riding

This is the natural area that former U.S. Interior Secretary James Watt referred to as "a gem of the southwestern desert." Journalists and outdoors writers also speak glowingly of the canyon as a unique, special and wonderful place. Fortunately, the BLM has taken steps to ensure that its pristine state is preserved by strictly limiting use. No one can enter the area without a permit, which allows a maximum stay of three days and two nights in the area. No more than 50 people are allowed within the canyon per day.

• **See also Best of the State, page 90** •
For more information: Contact the BLM Safford District Office, 711
14th Avenue, Safford, AZ 85546; (602) 428-4040.

EMPIRE-CIENEGA RESOURCE
CONSERVATION AREA

hiking, camping, horseback riding, mountain biking, wildlife
observation

Relatively new 1988 acquisitions of the BLM, the Empire
and Cienega ranches, along with portions of the adjacent Rose
Tree Ranch, create a 45,000-acre playground of rolling grasslands and woodlands. Tall lush grass, six feet high in some
places, is the dominant feature of the region. Sitting at an
elevation of 4,500 feet with 15 inches of annual rainfall, the
high-desert basin setting supports some of the best examples
of native grasslands in Arizona. In a state where most stream-
beds remain bone-dry throughout much of the year, the
perennial flow of Cienega Creek makes it a highly valuable
resource.

Giant cottonwoods hug the banks of the creek and are
interspersed with willows and ash. Oak and juniper trees
thrive on the hillsides. Birdwatching is considered quite good
with over 200 species of birds identified by members of the
Audubon Society and other volunteers.

The BLM's Empire Ranch headquarters and field station are
46 miles southeast of Tucson and 10 miles north of Sonoita.
One entrance is seven miles north of Sonoita on the east side
of Arizona Route 93, near mile marker 40. The other entrance
is five miles east of Sonoita on the north side of Arizona Route
82, near mile marker 36.

For more information: Contact the BLM Tucson Resource Area,
12661 East Broadway, Tucson, AZ 85748; (602) 722-4289.
BLM surface maps: Tucson, Fort Huachuca

GILA BOX RIPARIAN NATIONAL
CONSERVATION AREA

canoeing, rafting, camping, backpacking, hiking, fishing,
horseback riding, mountain biking, wildlife observation

This area is very special, primarily because desert rivers are
exceedingly rare. The visitor will wander through an oasis

---

where Rocky Mountain bighorn sheep, mule deer, mountain lions, javelinas, numerous song birds, and raptors survive. The Gila River winds along a buff-colored canyon in which 1,000-foot slopes provide a striking contrast against the mesquite woodland on the river banks. Slopes are covered with creosote bush, ocotillo, prickly pear, and desert grasses. Spires and notch canyons are but a few of the numerous geologic features along the canyon. One 15-mile-long trail, the Safford-Morenci Trail, crosses the National Conservation Area and links the Gila Mountains, Bonita Creek, Turtle Mountain and Eagle Creek.

Another trail, the Black Hills Bike Trail, is approximately 20 miles long and ideal for mountain bikes. It follows the Black Hills Backcountry Byway and winds toward the foothills and mountains with sweeping views of the Gila Box Riparian National Conservation Area.

•**See also Best of the State on page 94**•
For more information: Contact the BLM Safford District Office, 711 14th Avenue, Safford, AZ 85546; (602) 428-4040.

JAVELINA PEAK
camping, backpacking, hiking, horseback riding

This area is located southeast of Safford off US Highway 70. Access is via Haekel Road. Javelina Peak lies among the Whitlock Mountain Range, tucked between the San Simon and Whitlock valleys. The mountains rise steeply from the valley floor. A small area of badlands and a sand dune area, located just south of the mountain range, are used heavily by off-highway vehicles and lie within the BLM region. Of great interest are the possible birdwatching opportunities to be had during the drive along Haekel Road near the San Simon River. The river, which flows only after heavy rains, and a large number of ponds that exist in the area, attract a good population of waterfowl during the fall and winter season. Since traffic is typically light, birding is considered good for waterfowl, songbirds and raptors.

For more information: Contact the BLM Safford District Office, 711 14th Avenue, Safford, AZ 85546; (602) 428-4040
BLM surface maps: Safford

MESCAL MOUNTAINS
camping, backpacking, hiking

Part of the Gila River Canyon slices through the Mescal Mountains, which are located near Coolidge Dam and San Carlos Lake, adjacent to the San Carlos Indian Reservation. If you like your land rough and isolated, then this is the place. Access is strictly limited to four-wheel-drive vehicles and even then it's dicey! Stay out of the Indian Reservation, which is not open for public use. Call the BLM office for detailed access instructions. The Gila River Canyon is quite deep, very narrow, serpentine, and in most places, inaccessible from above.

Grapevine and Dick Spring are two side canyons worth a peek and also viable routes into the canyon itself. Once inside the canyon, it is river scrambling only—expect to get your feet wet. This river is NOT for boating. Fences, overhanging branches, widow makers, and sweepers create hazards that at best are deadly—I don't even want to think about worst!

Visiting in the summer months is no fun, unless you enjoy feeling like an egg being pan-fried. Fall through spring is the best time of year. Along the canyon bottom, you will scramble through dense vegetation consisting of cottonwood, mesquite, sycamore, velvet ash, willow, and salt cedar. Away from the canyon, the vegetation is more desert-like; you'll find barrel cactus, acacia, jojoba, and saguaro. Raptors are the most frequently seen birds. Bald eagles nest here in the winter.

For more information: Contact the BLM Phoenix District Office, 2015 West Deer Valley Road, Phoenix, AZ 85027; (602) 863-4464.
USGS topographic maps: El Capitan Mountain, Mescal Warm Spring, Coolidge Dam, Christmas

PELONCILLO MOUNTAINS
camping, backpacking, hiking, horseback riding

Like the Mescal Mountains, this area is rugged with a capital "R." Created from volcanic upheaval and eruptions, the Peloncillo Mountains feature a virtual maze of oak-lined canyons draining in every which way. There are enough private holdings in the area that make access difficult.

This area is located near the New Mexico and Arizona state boundary, north of San Simon on Interstate 10 and south of Duncan on State Road 75. Call the BLM prior to heading out to determine the best points of access. Fall through spring is the best time to visit.

For more information: Contact the BLM Safford District Office, 711 14th Avenue, Safford, AZ 85546; (602) 428-4040.

USGS topographic maps: Doubtful Canyon, Engine Mountain (Arizona / New Mexico); San Simon, Orange Butte (Arizona)

WHITE CANYON
backpacking, camping, hiking, wildlife observation, horseback riding

Located just southeast of Superior, off State Road 177 and south of Tonto National Forest, White Canyon's proximity to the national forest makes this site ideal for longer backpacking trips. The sculptured rocky terrain holds pools of water, even after the stream has dried up. Seasonal rains create picturesque waterfalls that cascade from the canyon rim. White Canyon, part of the Mineral Mountain Range, is narrow in places, with walls that extend as high as 800 feet. An area known as the Rincon is a large rock amphitheater, spectacular in its enormity. Since water is often available here when it is scarce elsewhere, a wide variety of wildlife and bird life is attracted to the canyon. Both black bears and mountain lions are known to frequent the region.

For more information: Contact the BLM Phoenix Resource Area, 2015 West Deer Valley Road, Phoenix, AZ 85027; (602) 780-8090.

USGS topographic maps: Mineral Mountain, Tea Pot Mountain

BABOQUIVARI PEAK
rock climbing, hiking

Note: This mountain area has no legal access at this time. To reach the mountains, you must cross private land, which requires landowner permission.

This peak is well known to climbers as the only Grade 6 (multi-day) and Class 6 (requires aid) climb in all of Arizona. It's a massive granite monolith that rises to 7,734 feet, towering 1,000 feet above the surrounding Baboquivari Mountains and over 4,000 feet above the Altar Valley floor. It is possible to hike to the mountain crest, although it is a strenuous route.

Access to the peak is across private land through Thomas Canyon, previously owned by The Nature Conservancy but sold with a condition that an easement be provided to hikers visiting the BLM-managed Baboquivari Peak. But here's the problem: Currently, private lands ringing the peak are not subject to the easement, so although the peak is open to the public, you still must cross private land to get to it, which requires landowner permission.

The area is located along the eastern edge of the Tohono O'odham Indian Reservation and south of State Highway 86. Fall through spring is the best time to visit.

For more information: Contact the BLM Tucson Resource Area, 12661 East Broadway, Tucson, AZ 85748; (602) 722-4289.

COYOTE MOUNTAINS
backpacking, hiking, wildlife observation

Note: This mountain area has no legal access at this time. To reach the mountains, you must cross private land, which requires landowner permission.

Some consider this to be the little Yosemite of the Southwest, presumably because of the sheer cliffs and wide canyons. Although others see little resemblance to Yosemite, all agree that this area is highly scenic and only a fool wouldn't want to visit here. There are several miles of hiking trails within the mountain area, attracting hikers, artists, rock hounds, wildlife watchers and hunters from all over.

Located southwest of Tucson, south of State Highway 86 and east of State Highway 386, these mountains are in close proximity to the Baboquivari Range.

For more information: Contact the BLM Tucson Resource Area, 12661 East Broadway, Tucson, AZ 85748; (602) 722-4289.

DOS CABEZAS MOUNTAINS
camping, picnicking, hiking, backpacking, horseback riding, wildlife observation

These mountains are located south of Interstate 10 and due east of Willcox in the southeastern corner of the state. A road south of the town of Bowie provides access into an area known as Happy Camp Canyon, where the BLM maintains a picnic area. The 11,700 acres of wilderness are predominantly roadless and worthy of exploration. There are three peaks over 7,000 feet within this area, as well as a number of pretty canyons. Howell Canyon, accessible from the picnic area, has vestiges of old road and housing foundations from turn-of-the-century mining operations. Government Peak, perhaps the most noteworthy of all the area's peaks, stands at a proud 7,587 feet high and is spectacular with boulders, rock outcrops, seasonal pools and waterfalls. Fall through spring is the best time to visit.

For more information: Contact the BLM Safford District Office, 425 East Fourth Street, Safford, AZ 85546; (602) 428-4040.
BLM surface maps: Willcox, Chiricahua Peak

TIP: Stay on the main trail even if it is wet or snow-covered. Leaving the trail to skirt these areas only creates another trail and point of erosion.

STATE INFORMATION OVERVIEW

ARIZONA STATE OFFICE
3707 North Seventh Street, P.O. Box 16563, Phoenix, AZ 85014; (602) 640-5501

ARIZONA STRIP DISTRICT OFFICE
390 North, 3050 East, St. George, UT 84770; (801) 673-3545

Shivwits Resource Area, 225 North Bluff Street, St. George, UT 84770; (801) 628-4491

Vermillion Resource Area, 225 North Bluff Street, St. George, UT 84770; (801) 628-4491

PHOENIX DISTRICT OFFICE
2015 West Deer Valley Road, Phoenix, AZ 85027; (602) 780-8090

Kingman Resource Area, 2475 Beverly Avenue, Kingman, AZ 86401; (602) 757-3161

Lower Gila Resource Area, 2015 West Deer Valley Road, Phoenix, AZ 85027; (602) 780-8090

Phoenix Resource Area, 2015 West Deer Valley Road, Phoenix, AZ 85027; (602) 780-8090

SAFFORD DISTRICT OFFICE
711 14th Avenue, Safford, AZ 85546; (602) 428-4040

Gila Resource Area, 711 14th Avenue, Safford, AZ 85546; (602) 428-4040

San Simon Resource Area, 711 14th Avenue, Safford, AZ 85546; (602) 428-4040

San Pedro Conservation Area Office, P.O. Box 9853, RR1, Huachuca City, AZ 85616; (602) 457-2265

Tucson Resource Area, 12661 East Broadway, Tucson, AZ 85748; (602) 722-4289

YUMA DISTRICT OFFICE
3150 Winsor Avenue, Yuma, AZ 85365; (602) 726-6300

Havasu Resource Area, 3189 Sweetwater Avenue, P.O. Box 685, Lake Havasu City, AZ 86403; (602) 855-8017

Imperial Dam Long-Term Visitor Area, approximately 25 miles north of Yuma, AZ; (602) 726-6300

Empire Landing State Recreation Area, located near Lake Havasu, AZ; (602) 855-8017

Parker State Recreation Management Area, located near Parker, AZ; (602) 855-8017

Squaw Lake Recreation Site, located 22 miles north of Yuma, AZ; (602) 726-6300

Yuma Resource Area, 3150 Winsor Avenue, Yuma, AZ 85365; (602) 726-6300

CHAPTER

4

CALIFORNIA

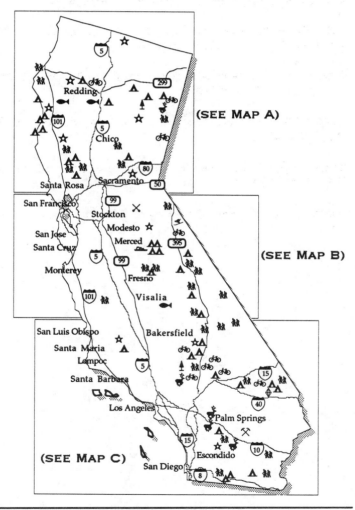

MAP A—CALIFORNIA

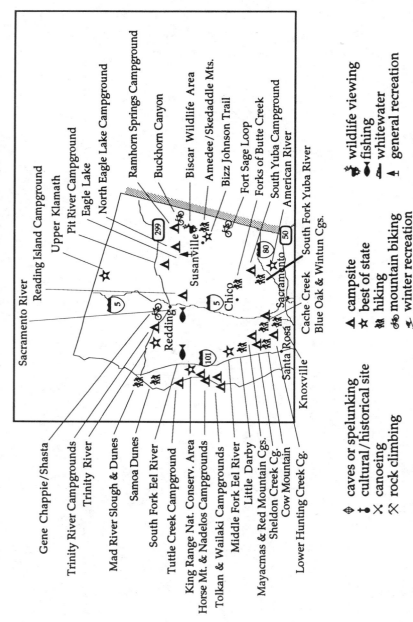

Sacramento River
Reading Island Campground
Upper Klamath
Pit River Campground
Eagle Lake
North Eagle Lake Campground
Ramhorn Springs Campground
Buckhorn Canyon
Biscar Wildlife Area
Amedee/Skedaddle Mts.
Bizz Johnson Trail
Fort Sage Loop
Forks of Butte Creek
South Yuba Campground
American River

Gene Chappie/Shasta
Trinity River Campgrounds
Trinity River
Mad River Slough & Dunes
Samoa Dunes
South Fork Eel River
Tuttle Creek Campground
King Range Nat. Conserv. Area
Horse Mt. & Nadelos Campgrounds
Tolkan & Wailaki Campgrounds
Middle Fork Eel River
Little Darby
Mayacmas & Red Mountain Cgs.
Sheldon Creek Cg.
Cow Mountain
Lower Hunting Creek Cg.

Redding
Susanville
Chico
Sacramento
Santa Rosa
Knoxville

Cache Creek
Blue Oak & Wintun Cgs.
South Fork Yuba River

△ campsite
★ best of state
🦌 hiking
🚲 mountain biking
✦ winter recreation

🦌 wildlife viewing
🎣 fishing
🚣 whitewater
♦ general recreation

✧ caves or spelunking
• cultural/historical site
✕ canoeing
✗ rock climbing

MAP REFERENCES

Amedee/Skedaddle Mountains—p. 154
American River, South Fork—p. 142-144
Biscar Wildlife Area—p. 154
Bizz Johnson Trail—p. 136-137
Buckhorn Canyon—p. 155
Cache Creek—p. 155-156
Cow Mountain—p. 156
Eagle Lake—p. 156
Forks of the Butte Creek—p. 156-157
Fort Sage Loop—p. 157
Gene Chappie/Shasta—p. 157
King Range National Conservation Area—p. 138-140
Knoxville—p. 158
Little Darby—p. 158-159
Mad River Slough & Dunes—p. 159
Middle Fork Eel River—p. 144-145
Sacramento River—p. 160
Samoa Dunes—p. 160
South Fork Eel River—p. 160
South Fork Yuba River—p. 168
Trinity River—p. 146-147
Upper Klamath River—p. 148-149

CAMPGROUNDS

The following campgrounds are found in this area of California.
Please call the BLM office (listed following each campground's name)
for reservations and information. Contact information for each BLM
office is on pages 179-180 for California.

Blue Oak Campground; Clear Lake Resource Area
Horse Mountain Campground; Arcata Resource Area
Lower Hunting Creek Campground; Clear Lake Resource Area
Mayacmas Campground; Clear Lake Resource Area
Nadelos Campground; Arcata Resource Area
North Eagle Lake Campground; Eagle Lake Resource Area
Pit River Campground; Alturas Resource Area
Ramhorn Springs Campground; Eagle Lake Resource Area
Reading Island Campground; Redding Resource Area
Red Mountain Campground; Clear Lake Resource Area
Sheldon Creek Campground; Clear Lake Resource Area
South Yuba Campground; Folsom Resource Area
Tolkan Campground; Arcata Resource Area
Trinity Campgrounds; Redding Resource Area
Tuttle Creek Campground; Bishop Resource Area
Wailaki Campground; Arcata Resource Area
Wintun Campground; Clear Lake Resource Area

MAP B—CALIFORNIA

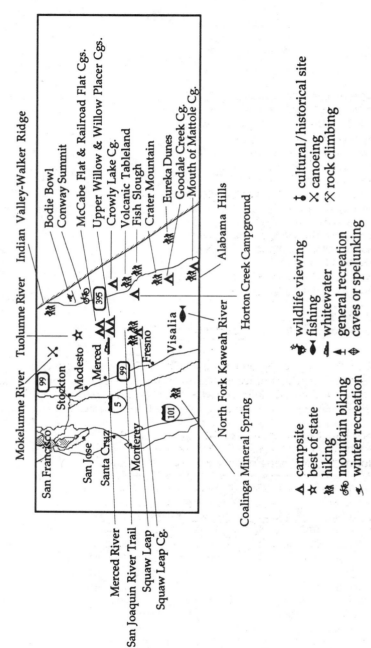

△ campsite
☆ best of state
🏃 hiking
🚲 mountain biking
❄ winter recreation

🦌 wildlife viewing
🐟 fishing
🌊 whitewater
△ general recreation
⊕ caves or spelunking

† cultural/historical site
✕ canoeing
☇ rock climbing

MAP REFERENCES

Alabama Hills—p. 161-162
Bodie Bowl—p. 162-163
Coalinga Mineral Spring—p. 164
Conway Summit—p. 164
Crater Mountain—p. 164
Eureka Dunes—p. 173
Fish Slough—p. 164-165
Indian Valley-Walker Ridge—p. 157-158
Merced River—p. 165
Mokelumne River—p. 166
North Fork Kaweah River—p. 166
San Joaquin River Trail—p. 167
Squaw Leap—p. 168
Tuolumne River—p. 150-151
Volcanic Tableland—p. 169

CAMPGROUNDS

The following campgrounds are found in this area of California.
Please call the BLM office (listed following each campground's name)
for reservations and information. Contact information for each BLM
office is on pages 179-180 for California.

Crowley Lake Campground, Bishop Resource Area
Goodale Creek Campground, Bishop Resource Area
Horton Creek Campground, Bishop Resource Area
McCabe Flat Campground, Folsom Resource Area
Mouth of the Mattole Campground, Arcata Resource Area
Railroad Flat Campground, Folsom Resource Area
Squaw Leap Campground, Hollister Resource Area
Upper Willow Campground, Folsom Resource Area
Willow Placer Campground, Folsom Resource Area

MAP C-CALIFORNIA

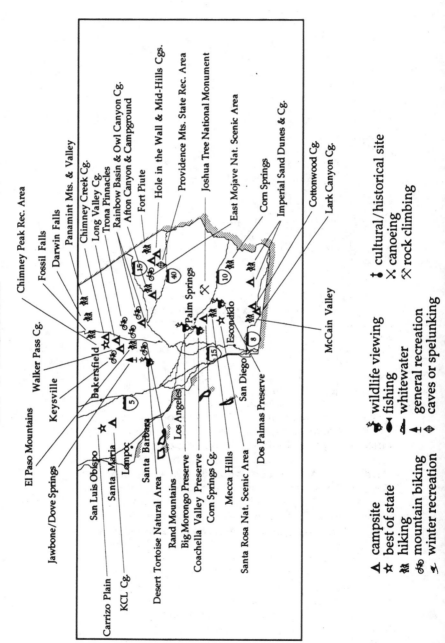

Chimney Peak Rec. Area
Fossil Falls
Darwin Falls
Panamint Mts. & Valley
Chimney Creek Cg.
Long Valley Cg.
Trona Pinnacles
Rainbow Basin & Owl Canyon Cg.
Afton Canyon & Campground
Fort Piute
Hole in the Wall & Mid-Hills Cgs.
Providence Mts. State Rec. Area
Joshua Tree National Monument
East Mojave Nat. Scenic Area
Corn Springs
Imperial Sand Dunes & Cg.
Cottonwood Cg.
Lark Canyon Cg.

El Paso Mountains
Walker Pass Cg.
Keysville
Jawbone/Dove Springs

San Luis Obispo
Santa Maria
Lompoc
Santa Barbara
Carrizo Plain
KCL Cg.
Desert Tortoise Natural Area
Rand Mountains
Big Morongo Preserve
Coachella Valley Preserve
Corn Springs Cg.
Mecca Hills
Santa Rosa Nat. Scenic Area
Dos Palmas Preserve

Bakersfield
Los Angeles
Palm Springs
Escondido
San Diego
McCain Valley

△ campsite
☆ best of state
🏃 hiking
⚲ mountain biking
⚘ winter recreation

🐾 wildlife viewing
🐟 fishing
🌊 whitewater
🚣 general recreation
⬦ caves or spelunking

† cultural/historical site
✕ canoeing
⚔ rock climbing

MAP REFERENCES

Afton Canyon—p. 169-170
Big Morongo Preserve—p. 170
Carrizo Plain Natural Area—p. 140-141
Chimney Peak Recreation Area—p. 163
Coachella Valley Preserve—p. 170
Corn Springs—p. 171
Darwin Falls—p. 171
Desert Tortoise Natural Area—p. 171-172
Dos Palmas Preserve—p. 172
East Mojave National Scenic Area—p. 172
El Paso Mountains—p. 172-173
Fort Piute—p. 173
Fossil Falls—p. 174
Imperial Sand Dunes—p. 174
Jawbone/Dove Springs—p. 174-175
Joshua Tree National Monument—p. 175
Keysville—p. 165
McCain Valley—p. 176
Mecca Hills—p. 176
Panamint Mountains & Valley—p. 166-167
Providence Mountains State Recreation Area—p. 176-177
Rand Mountains—p. 177
Santa Rosa National Scenic Area—p. 152-153
Trona Pinnacles—p. 178

CAMPGROUNDS

The following campgrounds are found in this area of California.
Please call the BLM office (listed following each campground's name)
for reservations and information. Contact information for each BLM
office is on pages 179-180 for California.

Afton Canyon Campground, Barstow Resource Area
Chimney Creek Campground, Caliente Resource Area
Corn Springs Campground, Palm Springs/South Coast Resource Area
Cottonwood Campground, El Centro Resource Area
Hole-In-The-Wall Campground, Needles Resource Area
Imperial Sand Dunes Campground, El Centro Resource Area
KCL Campground, Caliente Resource Area
Lark Canyon Campground, El Centro Resource Area
Long Valley Campground, Caliente Resource Area
Mid-Hills Campground, Needles Resource Area
Owl Canyon Campground, Barstow Resource Area
Rainbow Basin Campground, Barstow Resource Area
Walker Pass Campground, Caliente Resource Area

1

OWENS PEAK WILDERNESS STUDY AREA

Traveling through this area on the Pacific Crest Trail offers the visitor a delightful combination of rocky, steep slopes, rolling terrain, golden meadowlands and juniper, Joshua tree and pine forests. Views of the Domelands Wilderness Area and the Sierra Nevada can be enjoyed from a number of outstanding vista points.

HIKING

Hiking here follows the Pacific Crest Trail. The hike begins just south of Walker Pass Campground and across Highway 178. Water sources along the route are infrequent, although adequate. Just be sure to carry at least one gallon per person as a reserve at all times. The hike terminates approximately 40 miles from Walker Pass in Rockhouse Basin, the boundary for the Domelands Wilderness Area. Rockhouse Basin is worth exploring if you have the time. No permits other than a campfire permit are needed there. Bears are not a major problem near Owens Peak, but bear precautions should be the rule, not the exception.

MANAGEMENT
BLM Bakersfield District Office, 800 Truxtun Avenue, Bakersfield, CA 93301; (805) 861-4191

LOCATION
The southernmost reaches of the Sierra Nevada, just east of Bakersfield and west of Death Valley.

GETTING THERE
Take Highway 178 west from Highway 14 (just west of US 395) to Walker Pass Trailhead Facility. You will need to arrange for your own shuttle or hike back. The most scenic portions of the trail are the upper 20 miles or so—I would

---

recommend beginning an out-and-back hike at Chimney Creek Campground. To get to Chimney Creek, from the town of Brown on Highway 14 drive four miles north. Bear left on Nine Mile Canyon Road and drive 11 miles to the BLM ranger station. Bear left at the dirt road opposite the station. The campground is three miles from the station.

CAMPING
Camp anywhere along the trail. Two maintained campgrounds, Walker Pass Trailhead Facility and Chimney Creek Campground, provide water, toilets, parking and fire grates.

PERMITS
No permits are needed for backpacking. Campfire permits are required.

MAPS
USGS topographic maps: Walker Pass, Owens Peak, Lamont Peak, White Dome, Rockhouse Basin
BLM surface maps: Isabella, Ridgecrest

ADDITIONAL INFORMATION
The Pacific Crest Trail, Vol. 1, by Jeffrey Schaffer, published by Wilderness Press, 2440 Bancroft Way, Berkeley, CA 94704.

SEASON
Travel is best from May to mid-November. Snow is possible in the higher elevations the rest of the year. July and August may be uncomfortably hot in the lower elevations.

TIP: If you must use a campfire, collect only dead and downed wood. Standing dead wood is an important part of the ecological balance of the area and may, in fact, already be in use as a home for a wild animal.

2

BIZZ JOHNSON TRAIL

The trail takes the traveler through several different ecological zones, beginning with Ponderosa pine forests at 5,500 feet near Westwood and ending up in the desert at 4,400 feet near Susanville. Geology fans will enjoy the area because the Susan River establishes an approximate boundary between the southern reaches of the Cascade Mountains and the northern reaches of the Sierra Nevada. Sierra granite mingles magnificently with the igneous basalt cliffs and spires of agglomerate.

The historical significance of the trail is quite fascinating as well. The railroad was used from 1914 to 1956 to connect Westwood with Fernley, Nevada. In 1956, a flood destroyed a bridge and since the lumber company that had been using the rail line had closed, the bridge was never repaired and the rails abandoned. In 1978, Southern Pacific received official permission to abandon the route. Recreational planners from the U.S. Forest Service and the BLM, with assistance from congressman Harold T. "Bizz" Johnson, purchased the right-of-way and the trail was born.

HIKING/MOUNTAIN BIKING

The Bizz Johnson Trail is an outstanding example of the success enjoyed by the Rails to Trails Conservancy. Extending from Mason Station to Susanville, the approximately 25-mile-long trail is ideal for horseback riding, mountain biking and backpacking. In snowy months, the trail can be used for cross-country skiing. The 18-mile segment along the Susan River from Westwood Junction to Susanville is considered the most scenic because of the adjacent river and canyon. The trail is at a gentle 3% grade along the route. Caution should be used when crossing the planking on decked bridges and when proceeding through the unlighted tunnels. There are trails that skirt the tunnels if you don't want to go inside. Fishing is also possible along the Susan River.

MANAGEMENT
This trail is jointly managed by the BLM and the U.S. Forest Service. BLM Eagle Lake Resource Area, 2545 Riverside Drive, Susanville, CA 96130; (916) 257-5381.

LOCATION
Northeastern California at the town of Susanville.

GETTING THERE
The trail is best accessed at Mason Station near Westwood, Highway 44 near Hog Flat Reservoir, Highway 36 near Devils Corral, and Hobo Camp near Susanville. The ideal mountain bike ride (almost all downhill!) can be had by using a shuttle. Leave one car at Hobo Camp. From Susanville, drive west on Highway 36 to County Road A-21, just before Westwood. Turn right and drive three miles to County Road 101. Turn right again and drive one-half mile to the Mason Station Trailhead.

CAMPING
There is a seven-day limit to camping anywhere along the trail. No camping is allowed at the trailheads.

PERMITS
Campfire permits are required. Seasonal fire restrictions apply.

MAPS
USGS topographic maps: Westwood East, Fredonyer Pass, Roop Mountain, Susanville
Additional maps: Bizz Johnson Trail Map, published by the BLM and U.S. Forest Service; and Lassen National Forest Map, published by the U.S. Forest Service.

ADDITIONAL INFORMATION
Cycling the California Outback, published by Bodfish Books, Chico, CA.

SEASON
Go hiking and biking in the spring, summer and fall, and cross-country skiing in the winter.

TIP: *Take the time to animal-proof your campsite for the protection of your gear, yourself and the animals.*

3

KING RANGE NATIONAL CONSERVATION AREA

Sinkyone and Mattole Indians used these beaches and the surrounding area for 2,500 years, up until about 100 years ago. Shell mounds remain as evidence of their presence and are protected by federal legislation against being disturbed. The King Range rises abruptly from sea level to 4,087 feet, the summit of King Peak, in less than three miles. Steep streams cascade into the ocean and the eroding cliffs create huge rock slides and talus piles. Wildlife is abundant. Offshore, expect to see seals, sea lions and a variety of shore birds playing in the kelp beds and tidal areas. In the Douglas fir and chaparral-covered coastline, black-tailed deer, river otter, and black bear make their homes. There are also several threatened species supported here, including the spotted owl and peregrine falcon.

HIKING

The Lost Coast Trail is a beautiful 24-mile trek through one of the most pristine areas on the Pacific Coast. Bounded by the ocean and steep mountains and cliffs, the trail follows the beach most of the way, crossing numerous streams and grassy flats. The trip requires a shuttle, unless you desire a 48-mile round-trip. The terrain varies from fine-grained sand to large boulders. The walking is fairly level as it follows the beach most of the time. There are occasions when the trail wanders onto grassy flats above the beach and through Douglas fir, cypress, chemise, and possibly poison oak. Two areas, Sea Lion Gulch and Shipman Creek, will require the use of a

---

tidetable as the trail is completely cut off by the incoming tide at times. Good camping areas may be found at Cooskie Creek, Spanish Flat and Shipman Creek. Driftwood is readily available for campfires, but a campfire permit must be obtained prior to the trip. Also, watch out for rattlesnakes when collecting wood!

MANAGEMENT
BLM Arcata Resource Area, 1125 16th Street, P.O. Box 1112, Arcata, CA 95521; (707) 822-7648

LOCATION
Located just off US Highway 101 at Garberville, 70 miles south of Eureka in northern California.

GETTING THERE
The best route to travel when hiking is from north to south. Leave a car at one end to facilitate a shuttle unless a round trip is desired. The northern trailhead is located at Mouth of the Mattole Recreation Site. The southern trailhead is located at Black Sands Beach near Shelter Cove. The principal access is from US 101 to within 20 miles of the King Range. Once there, paved mountain roads originating in Ferndale, Humboldt Redwoods State Park and Redway provide trailhead and campground access.

CAMPING
Camping is allowed anywhere within the wilderness.

PERMITS
Campfire permits are required.

MAPS
USGS topographic maps: Point Delgada, Cape Mendocino, Honeydew, Shelter Cove, Shubrick Peak, Bear Harbor, Briceland, Cooskie Creek, Petrolia, Buckeye Mountain

ADDITIONAL INFORMATION
•*King Range National Conservation Area Recreation Guide,* available from the BLM.
• There are mountain biking opportunities in this area as well. See *Cycling the California Outback,* published by Bodfish, Chico, CA.

SEASON

You can visit here year round. This region is typically the wettest area on the Pacific Coast, with an average of 100 inches of rainfall annually.

TIP: Travel responsibly to protect the environment and preserve opportunities to enjoy recreation in wildlands.

BEST OF THE STATE

4

CARRIZO PLAIN NATURAL AREA

Recently, this place was referred to as the "next Serengeti Plain" by an enthusiastic BLM official during a press conference. Press conferences can be prone to exaggeration, but not in this case. Carrizo Plain is indeed spectacular, partly because of its enormity—at 60 miles long, it is the largest wildlife preserve in the state. Nearly 5,000 sandhill cranes are known to winter here, attracted by a 3,000-acre alkali wetland. Surrounding grasslands are home to San Joaquin antelope squirrels, blunt-nosed lizards, San Joaquin kit fox, giant kangaroo rats, western bluebirds, horned larks, tule elk and pronghorn antelope. There are also heavy concentrations of wintering birds of prey, including the short-eared owl, ferruginous hawk, northern harrier, and bald eagle. Hiking and mountain biking are possibilities.

MANAGEMENT

• BLM Caliente Resource Area, 4301 Rosedale Highway, Bakersfield, CA 93308; (805) 861-4236
• The Nature Conservancy, Carrizo Plain Natural Area, P. O. Box 3098, California Valley, CA 93453
• California Department of Fish and Game, Region 3, P.O. Box 47, Yountville, CA 94599

LOCATION

Near the towns of Maricopa and Atascadero in the San Joaquin Valley.

GETTING THERE

From Buttonwillow on Interstate 5, take Highway 58 west for approximately 45 miles to Soda Lake Road. Turn south and drive approximately 14 miles to the signed entrance for the Painted Rock Visitor Center.

CAMPING

Primitive camping within the area is allowed only at the KCL Campground, located on Soda Lake Road, south of the Painted Rock Visitor Center. Water is not available, so you will need to bring all your supplies with you. The nearest town offering predictable services is Buttonwillow, approximately 50 minutes driving time to the east.

PERMITS

No permits are necessary.

MAPS

USGS topographic maps: McKittrick Summit, Painted Rock, Panorama Hills

ADDITIONAL INFORMATION

• BLM brochure: *Carrizo Plain Natural Area*
• *California Wildlife Viewing Guide,* by Jeanne Clark, published by Falcon Press, P.O. Box 1718, Helena, MT 59624; (800) 582-2665.

SEASON

You can visit here year round, although the summer can be very hot.

TIP: Never dig holes, trenches or otherwise alter the campsite for convenience. The perfect campsite is found, not made.

5

AMERICAN RIVER— SOUTH FORK

Encompassing the North, Middle and South Forks of the American River, this region of popular whitewater runs slices right through the very heart and soul of the Mother Lode. Scenic canyons and oak woodlands surround the river, which offers rides ranging from the mildly tame on the South Fork to the wild and woolly on the Middle and North Fork. Despite the crowds that gather here on weekends, many visitors return again and again because of the scenic value of the South Fork. Unlike most Sierra rivers that carve through deep canyons, the South Fork of the American winds through golden foothills sprinkled with oaks and digger pines. Low rock walls of the final "canyon" section increase the whitewater excitement. Expect to see blue herons and golden eagles and, if you visit early enough in the spring, you will enjoy hills covered with California poppy, lilac, shooting star, lupine and more. The fishing isn't great, but expect to reel in the odd trout, bass or catfish. An historic site, Sutters Mill, sits along the river route, just upstream from Marshall State Park. Sutters Mill was the site of the first California gold discovery.

WHITEWATER RAFTING

It's Class III+ water in normal flows, increasing to Class IV when the water flows above 2,500 cubic feet per second. Water level is dam-controlled at the Chili Bar Powerhouse, just upriver from the put-in site. The best time to raft is mid-week. This is a very heavily used river due to its proximity to San Francisco, Sacramento and Lake Tahoe. While you can run the river from your private raft, it is recommended that you go with a commercial outfit since enough people are congesting the waterways already. Water is cold in the spring and wetsuits should be worn.

MANAGEMENT
BLM Folsom Resource Area, 63 Natoma Street, Folsom, CA 95630; (916) 985-4474

LOCATION
Located near Placerville off Highway 50.

GETTING THERE
From Sacramento and Interstate 5, head east on Highway 50 to Placerville. To get to Chili Bar, head north from Placerville on Highway 49 and then take Highway 193.

CAMPING
There are several campgrounds around the Placerville and Coloma area. For updated and accurate campground information, get a copy of Tom Stienstra's book, *California Camping,* published by Foghorn Press, 555 DeHaro Street, San Francisco, CA 94107; (800) 842-7477.

PERMITS
Permits are required. There are numerous commercial outfitters who run trips on the river.

MAPS
USGS topographic maps: Coloma, Garden Valley

ADDITIONAL INFORMATION
•Call the California Outfitter Hotline at (800) 552-3635 for access to 45 California whitewater outfitters. You will receive a directory of licensed outfitters listing individual 800 numbers. The directory also offers basic information regarding what rivers are run and each outfitter's specialty: gourmet food, trips for singles, packages with mountain biking or hot air ballooning, trips for families, women, men or disabled people, fishing trips, wilderness luxury trips and more.
•You can also pick up a copy of *Western Whitewater, From the Rockies to the Pacific,* by Jim Cassady, Bill Cross and Fryar Calhoun, published by North Fork Press, Berkeley, CA; (800) 243-5522.

SEASON

April through August or September is the whitewater season, depending on water flow. The California Department of Water Resources provides water flow information for most California rivers. To determine the best time to go, call (916) 322-3327.

> *TIP: Always use a river runner's toilet when boating and never bury human waste around river camps. Human waste, including toilet paper, must be packed out.*

BEST OF THE STATE

6

MIDDLE FORK
EEL RIVER

This wild, rugged country of dense forests, lush meadows, rolling hills and steep-walled gorges makes for a thrilling river adventure. The area provides a truly unique opportunity to experience a remote wilderness in a river setting. For the first 26 miles or so, the Middle Fork of the Eel rolls steadily through a wide valley filled with firs and pines. Wildflowers are common, and at times appear to carpet all the open area. Resident wildlife includes deer, black bear, otter and coyote. The last four miles, the most difficult to paddle, channel into a narrow gorge where tributary streams create colorful waterfalls off both sides of the canyon.

WHITEWATER RAFTING

The river is rated Class IV overall with a blend of Class II to Class IV+ along its length. This is a 30-mile paddle, recommended for a three-day venture, rather than two. The Middle Fork is entirely dependent on snow-melt and rainwater: a storm can dramatically raise the water level and change the character of the river. There is a possibility that one challenging portage may be required during the final four miles of the run, where the most difficult whitewater is encountered.

MANAGEMENT
BLM Arcata Resource Area, 1125 16th Street, Room 219, Arcata, CA 95521; (707) 822-7648

LOCATION
East of Highway 101 and north of Ukiah.

GETTING THERE
From Highway 101, exit at Highway 162 to the Eel River Ranger Station.

CAMPING
Camping is allowed anywhere along the river. Fire pans and porta-potties are recommended.

PERMITS
No permits are necessary. There are a few commercial outfitters who run trips on the river.

MAPS
USGS topographic maps: Ukiah, Redwood Valley, Willits

ADDITIONAL INFORMATION
•Call the California Outfitter Hotline at (800) 552-3635 for access to 45 California whitewater outfitters. You will receive a directory of licensed outfitters listing individual 800 numbers. The directory also offers basic information regarding what rivers are run and each outfitter's specialty: gourmet food, trips for singles, packages with mountain biking or hot air ballooning, trips for families, women, men or disabled people, fishing trips, wilderness luxury trips and more.
•You can also pick up a copy of *Western Whitewater, From the Rockies to the Pacific,* by Jim Cassady, Bill Cross and Fryar Calhoun, published by North Fork Press, Berkeley, CA; (800) 243-5522.

SEASON
April 1 to May 31 is the whitewater season on the Eel, depending on water flow. The California Department of Water Resources provides water flow information for most California rivers. To determine the best time to go, call (916) 322-3327.

> *TIP: Use a portable stove whenever possible and minimize fire impacts which can leave unsightly scars.*

BEST OF THE STATE

TRINITY RIVER

The Trinity is ideal for a two-day canoe or raft trip through steep canyons and rustic meadows. This river offers a ringside seat for a glimpse into the surrounding region's gold rush legacy and spectacular views of the nearby and often snow-capped Trinity Alps. A wide variety of terrain from forest to canyons to flower-carpeted meadows will be experienced along the way. Wildlife includes black-tailed deer, otter, black bear, egrets, kingfishers, and blue heron.

WHITEWATER RAFTING

The Trinity is an ideal river for the more adventurous to try paddling in inflatable kayaks. Rated at Class III, the river is dam-controlled, and consequently has good paddling water throughout the summer. Along the way, boaters will enjoy visiting modern and historic mining operations. Gold panning is allowed along the river as long as you are not intruding on someone's claim.

FISHING

Fishing is excellent for steelhead, king and silver salmon, rainbow and brown trout.

MANAGEMENT
BLM Redding Resource Area, 355 Hemsted Drive, Redding, CA 96002; (916) 224-2100

LOCATION
West of Redding, north of Highway 299, and east of Arcata.

GETTING THERE
There are several access points along Highway 299. Put-ins are located at Bucktail Hole, Rush Creek, Steelbridge, Douglas City, and North Fork. Take-outs are available all along the river south of the first put-in, Bucktail Hole.

CAMPING
You can camp anywhere along the river. Organized camping is available at Trinity River Campgrounds: 19 improved sites at Douglas City on Highway 199; 21 improved sites at Junction City on Highway 299; eight improved sites east of Douglas City off Highway 299 and near the Steelbridge river access.

PERMITS
No permits are necessary. There are a number of commercial outfitters who run trips on the river.

MAPS
USGS topographic maps: Weaverville, Junction City, Dedrick, Helena, Del Loma

ADDITIONAL INFORMATION
•Call the California Outfitter Hotline at (800) 552-3635 for access to 45 California whitewater outfitters. You will receive a directory of licensed outfitters listing individual 800 numbers. The directory also offers basic information regarding what rivers are run and each outfitter's specialty: gourmet food, trips for singles, packages with mountain biking or hot air ballooning, trips for families, women, men or disabled people, fishing trips, wilderness luxury trips and more.
•You can also pick up a copy of *Western Whitewater, From the Rockies to the Pacific,* by Jim Cassady, Bill Cross and Fryar Calhoun, published by North Fork Press, Berkeley, CA; (800) 243-5522.

SEASON
The California Department of Water Resources provides water flow information for most California rivers. To determine the best time to go, call (916) 322-3327.

> *TIP: Only camp in established or previously used sites if available.*

8

UPPER KLAMATH RIVER

Fishing and whitewater are the popular calling cards for this well-known river. California's second longest river, the Klamath provides excellent salmon and steelhead fishing in the winter and super trout angling (catch and release only) during the summer. Through Oregon, the Klamath rolls and roils along canyons green with pine, cedar, oak and juniper. Once across the border into California, the terrain flattens out into golden hills dotted with oak and littered with the remains of mines, ranches, mills and an historic 19th century health spa. If you stretch your imagination, you can almost see a stagecoach rolling through the hillside off in the distance. Wildlife that inhabit the region include deer, falcon, black bear, osprey, blue heron and bald eagle.

WHITEWATER RAFTING

From just below the dam through Hell's Corner and Satan's Gate rapids, electrifying whitewater is what you'll find here. This is Class IV+ water with one gut-wrencher after another and little time to recover. Boaters must have previous rafting experience and be ready for this. From Rainbow Rock on down, the river subsides to a more relaxing series of Class III and II whitewater with periodic stretches of tranquil water.

MANAGEMENT

BLM Redding Resource Area, 355 Hemsted Drive, Redding, CA 96002; (916) 224-2100

LOCATION

Along the California/Oregon border near Interstate 5.

GETTING THERE

Take Interstate 5 to Oregon State Highway 66 and then west to John Boyle Powerhouse.

CAMPING
Camp anywhere along the river. Fire pans and porta-potties are required.

PERMITS
Permits are required. There are numerous commercial outfitters who run trips on the river.

MAPS
USGS topographic maps: Parker Mountain in Oregon; Hawkinsville, Iron Gate Reservoir and Copco in California

ADDITIONAL INFORMATION
•Call the California Outfitter Hotline at (800) 552-3635 for access to 45 California whitewater outfitters. You will receive a directory of licensed outfitters listing individual 800 numbers. The directory also offers basic information regarding what rivers are run and each outfitter's specialty: gourmet food, trips for singles, packages with mountain biking or hot air ballooning, trips for families, women, men or disabled people, fishing trips, wilderness luxury trips and more.
•You can also pick up a copy of *Western Whitewater, From the Rockies to the Pacific,* by Jim Cassady, Bill Cross and Fryar Calhoun, published by North Fork Press, Berkeley, CA; (800) 243-5522.

SEASON
To find out the best time to go, call the John Boyle Powerhouse at (800) 547-1501 to obtain river flow information.

TIP: Avoid planning your vacation during normally crowded times and places.

TUOLUMNE RIVER

California's premier whitewater river is a slalom course of boulders of escalating intensity. Staircase rapids, chutes and pools by the score and the close proximity of Yosemite National Park help to create the ultimate wilderness river adventure—a journey that is both exhilarating and pristine. Fishing is available for trout. Wildflowers paint the hills during the spring; especially common are paintbrush, shooting star and lupine.

WHITEWATER RAFTING

The river is rated Class IV to V. It is dam controlled and water releases, although scheduled and easy to anticipate, drastically affect the quality of the run. In some cases, lack of water or too much water will make the river unrunnable. Wetsuits are needed until the summer months. Two-day trips are the norm. The only access to the river is at put-in and take-out.

MANAGEMENT

BLM Folsom Resource Area, 63 Natoma Street, Folsom, CA 95630; (916) 985-4474

LOCATION

Near Yosemite National Park in the Sierra Nevada.

GETTING THERE

Take Highway 49 south from Sonora to Highway 120. Head east on Highway 120 past Groveland about 7.5 miles (one-half mile past the turn for County Road J20). Turn left (north) and drive one mile. Turn right onto a dirt road and drive six miles to Lumsden campground and the put-in.

CAMPING

Camp anywhere along the river.

PERMITS

Permits are required. There are numerous commercial outfitters
who run trips on the river.

MAPS

USGS topographic maps: Tuolumne, Standard Hull Creek

ADDITIONAL INFORMATION

•Call the California Outfitter Hotline at (800) 552-3635 for
access to 45 California whitewater outfitters. You will receive a
directory of licensed outfitters listing individual 800 numbers.
The directory also offers basic information regarding what
rivers are run and each outfitter's specialty: gourmet food, trips
for singles, packages with mountain biking or hot air ballooning, trips for families, women, men or disabled people, fishing
trips, wilderness luxury trips and more.
•You can also pick up a copy of *Western Whitewater, From
the Rockies to the Pacific,* by Jim Cassady, Bill Cross and Fryar
Calhoun, published by North Fork Press, Berkeley, CA; (800)
243-5522.

SEASON

April through October is the time to run this river. The California Department of Water Resources provides water flow
information for most California rivers. To find out the best time
to go, call (916) 322-3327.

> *TIP: Pack out all that you bring in—
> and a little extra if you find it.*

10

SANTA ROSA
NATIONAL SCENIC AREA

Jolting skyward 7,000 feet in a spectacularly abrupt fashion from the surrounding Coachella Valley, the Santa Rosa Mountains offer the adventurer a playground landscape that varies from desert shrubbery to hidden palm canyons to conifer-capped peaks. This rugged desert wilderness of boulder-strewn mountains and twisted, eroded canyons is, at times, desolate in appearance. There are few places in southern California where you can truly feel as if you have gotten away from it all, and this is one of the few. America's largest remaining population of Peninsular bighorn sheep roam the rocky crags. Golden eagles, red-tailed hawks and other raptors soar overhead. Coyote, mule deer and bobcat as well as two wild horse herds romp among the canyon and desert floors.

HIKING/BACKPACKING

Few roads cross the Santa Rosa Mountains, but the range is accessible using a number of foot or horseback trails. Notable trails are Cactus Springs Trail, Coyote Creek Trail, Palms to Pines Trail, Palm Canyon Trail, Martinez Mountain Indian Trail, Rabbit Peak Trail and the Mirage Trail. Many of these and other existing trails connect a network of aboriginal and wildlife trails that have existed for eons.

MANAGEMENT
BLM Palm Springs-South Central Coast Resource Area, 63-500 Garnet Avenue, P.O. Box 2000, North Palm Springs, CA 92258; (619) 251-0812

LOCATION
Bounded on the south by the Anza Borrego Desert and on the north by Interstate 10.

GETTING THERE

To get into the Santa Rosa National Scenic Area, you will need a road map. From Interstate 8 out of San Diego, head north on Highway 79 and then east on Highway 74. From Interstate 10, head south through Palm Springs on Highway 111 and then south on Highway 74.

CAMPING

There are a few campgrounds in the area. Once inside the boundaries of the Santa Rosa National Scenic Area, camping is allowed anywhere. Water is scarce. Be sure to carry all that you will need.

PERMITS

No permits are necessary.

MAPS

USGS topographic maps: Clark Lake Northeast, Fonts Point, Rabbit Peak, Seventeen Palms

ADDITIONAL INFORMATION

•*The Guide to Hiking, Biking and Equestrian Trails of the Coachella Valley,* published by the City of Rancho Mirage, available through the BLM.

•*Afoot and Afield in San Diego County,* by Jerry Schad, published by Wilderness Press, Berkeley, CA.

SEASON

November through April is the best time to visit.

TIP: Camp 200 feet or more from the nearest water source—more if regulations dictate.

NORTHERN CALIFORNIA

AMEDEE / SKEDADDLE MOUNTAINS
hiking, backpacking, camping

Rugged peaks, vertical cliffs and steep canyons are the geological recipe here. The higher elevations support scattered aspen groves. Patches of riparian vegetation and small meadows dot the canyon bottoms. There are numerous springs throughout the area, but all water must be treated. The BLM recommends visiting Wendel Canyon for its unique scenic value. Mule deer, pronghorn antelope and mountain lion call the ranges home.

From Susanville, drive east on Highway 395 for 18 miles, then head east on Wendel which bounds the southwest edge of the range. Park off the road and head in.

For more information: Contact the BLM Susanville District Office, 705 Hall Street, P.O. Box 1090, Susanville, CA 96130; (916) 257-5381.
USGS topographic maps: Spencer Creek, Wendel, Bull Flat, Little Mud Flat

BISCAR WILDLIFE AREA
canoeing, wildlife observation

This area has a very small lake, tucked in an arid, high desert rimrock canyon. It is notable for all of its wildlife, including white pelican, osprey, muskrat, marsh wren, sage grouse, mule deer, and pronghorn antelope. Located near the town of Litchfield. Drive approximately 20 miles north on Highway 395. Head west at Karlo Road. Parking for the site is just across a set of railroad tracks—approximately six miles from the highway.

For more information: Contact the BLM Eagle Lake Resource Area, 2545 Riverside Drive, Susanville, CA 96130; (916) 257-5381.
USGS topographic maps: Litchfield

Bizz Johnson Trail
backpacking, hiking, horseback riding, mountain biking

The Bizz Johnson Trail traces the old Fernley and Lassen Railroad from Susanville to Westwood with spectacular views of the surrounding mountains. Enjoy seeing relics of railroad and logging heydays along the route. For much of the 25-mile trip, the trail winds through the rugged Susan River Canyon, crossing the river 11 times on bridges and trestles as well as passing through two tunnels.

•**See also Best of the State, page 136**•

For more information: Contact the BLM Eagle Lake Resource Area, 2545 Riverside Drive, Susanville, CA 96130; (916) 257-5381.

Buckhorn Canyon
mountain biking

Officially recognized as a Backcountry Byway, suitable for two-wheel-drive, high-clearance vehicles, this route is also super for mountain biking. The 28-mile road passes through sagebrush country on the California/Nevada border.

For more information: Contact the BLM Eagle Lake Resource Area, 2545 Riverside Drive, Susanville, CA 96130; (916) 257-5381.
USGS topographic maps: Buckhorn Canyon, Observation Peak, Buckhorn Lake, Dodge Reservoir.

Cache Creek
camping, backpacking, hiking, horseback riding, wildflowers, rafting (when the stream is flowing at high levels during spring runoff)

In the Cache Creek area, valleys abound with spring wildflowers and streams that are filled with fish. There is a seven-mile-long hiking trail that will take you into the heartland of this pastoral recreation area. Tule elk and bald eagle inhabit the area, but Cache Creek is well known for other species as well, including wild turkey, blue heron, belted kingfisher, river otter, golden eagle, and black bear. To get there from Clear Lake Oaks, head east eight miles on Highway 20 to the site entrance.

For more information: Contact the BLM Clear Lake Resource Area, 555 Leslie Street, Ukiah, CA 95482; (707) 462-3873.

USGS topographic maps: Lower Lake, Wilson Valley, Wilbur
Springs, Glascock Mountain, Knoxville

COW MOUNTAIN
*camping, backpacking, hiking, horseback riding, mountain
biking, off-road vehicle use*

The chaparral-covered slopes, peppered with pine and
oak, are very steep and intertwined with miles of trails and fire
roads—ideal for hiking, horseback riding and mountain biking.
Off-highway vehicle use is restricted to the South Cow Mountain. From US 101 at Ukiah, head east on Talmage Road, turn
south on Eastside Road, then east on Mill Creek to Cow
Mountain Access Road.

For more information: Contact the BLM Clear Lake Resource Area,
555 Leslie Street, Ukiah, CA 95482; (707) 462-3873.
USGS topographic maps: Cow Mountain, Purdy's Garden, Lakeport

EAGLE LAKE
*camping, backpacking, hiking, mountain biking, canoeing,
boating, fishing, picnicking, wildlife observation*

This 28,000-acre lake provides for every kind of watersport
imaginable—in addition to a slew of shoreline activities. Eagle
Lake is well known for game fish, including the Eagle Lake
rainbow trout—unique to this lake. Wildlife is abundant and
includes cormorants, terns, osprey, bald eagle, white pelican,
cinnamon teal, egrets, muskrat, and deer. From Susanville,
drive north on Highway 139 for approximately 25 miles to
Eagle Lake.

For more information: Contact the BLM Eagle Lake Resource Area,
2545 Riverside Drive, Susanville, CA 96130; (916) 257-5381.
USGS topographic maps: Spalding Tract, Troxel Point, Gallatin Peak,
Pikes Point

FORKS OF BUTTE CREEK
hiking, fishing, inner-tubing

Rugged canyons invite exploration while the waters of
Butte Creek provide a cooling respite from the nearby Sacramento Valley heat. Fishing for pan-sized trout is good. Bring

an inner tube and float sections of the creek. From Chico and east of Interstate 5, follow Highway 99 to the town of Megalia, above Paradise, and then turn onto Understock Road to Butte Creek. Watch for signs.

For more information: Contact the BLM Redding Resource Area, 355 Hemsted Drive, Redding, CA 96002; (916) 224-2100.
USGS topographic maps: Pulga, Paradise East, Kimshew Point, Stirling City

FORT SAGE LOOP
biking, mountain biking, off-road vehicle use

This 18-mile trail is open to both mountain biking and all-terrain vehicles and provides an easy to moderate trek across sagebrush and tumbleweed country. It's a slice of the Old West. From US 395 south of Susanville, exit at Laver Crossing and follow the signs to the trail.

For more information: Contact the BLM Eagle Lake Resource Area, 2545 Riverside Drive, Susanville, CA 96130; (916) 257-5381.
USGS topographic maps: Doyle, Calneva

GENE CHAPPIE/SHASTA
backpacking, biking, mountain biking, off-road vehicle use

Over 200 miles of fire roads and trails crisscross through this 50,000-acre site, making it a virtual treasure trove for mountain bikers and off-road vehicle use. From Interstate 5, exit at Shasta Dam. The road that crosses the dam leads to the recreation area.

For more information: Contact the BLM Redding Resource Area, 355 Hemsted Drive, Redding, CA 96002; (916) 224-2100.
USGS topographic maps: Shasta Dam

INDIAN VALLEY—WALKER RIDGE
camping, backpacking, biking, horseback riding, mountain biking

This area includes two established hiking trails, two campgrounds and a network of primitive roads for exploring the diverse, mountainous area surrounding Indian Valley Reservoir.

California

For more information: Contact the BLM Clear Lake Resource Area, 555 Leslie Street, Ukiah, CA 95482; (707) 462-3873.
USGS topographic maps: Hough Springs, Benmore Canyon, Leesville, Wilbur Springs

KING RANGE NATIONAL CONSERVATION AREA
camping, backpacking, hiking, horseback riding, mountain biking, wildlife observation

This National Conservation Area protects one of the last areas of coastal wilderness. Rugged topography and heavy rainfall create a desolate grandeur marked with mountains, streams, forests and beaches—ideal for backpackers, hikers, fishermen, mountain bikers or anyone desiring a rugged wilderness experience.

•**See also Best of the State, page 138**•
For more information: Contact the BLM Arcata Resource Area, 1125 16th Street, Room 219, Arcata, CA 95521; (707) 822-7648.

KNOXVILLE
hiking, off-road vehicle use, rock hounding, rare plant observation

Steep chaparral hills are ideal for off-road use, which this area sees a lot of. Still, it is a pleasant destination for others seeking a more sedentary way of life. At Lower Lake Road where Highways 29 and 53 merge, take Morgan Valley Road. Go south to McLaughlin Mine. Follow the road past the tunnel to the Knoxville signs.

For more information: Contact the BLM Clear Lake Resource Area, 555 Leslie Street, Ukiah, CA 95482; (707) 462-3873.
USGS topographic maps: Jericho Valley, Knoxville

LITTLE DARBY
hiking

The Little Darby is a super interpretive trail winding through a mini-preserve of virgin Douglas fir. From US 101 at Willetts, head east on Commercial Street to Hearst-Willetts Road. From there, follow the Berry Canyon Road to the Little Darby parking area.

For more information: Contact the BLM Clear Lake Resource Area, 555 Leslie Street, Ukiah, CA 95482; (707) 462-3873.
USGS topographic maps: Willits

MAD RIVER SLOUGH AND DUNES
hiking, canoeing, picnicking

Hikers will enjoy the diverse ecosystems and trails of this region. There are lofty Sitka pine forests and pockets of wet, verdant woodlands rarely experienced outside of the Olympia Peninsula. These manage to co-exist with intertidal mudflats and salt water marshes. This unique combination supports a remarkable diversity of flora and fauna which include grosbeaks, crossbills, egrets, gray fox, salamanders, and Pacific tree frogs. To get there, take Highway 255 off of Highway 101 and head west. Drive approximately three miles to Young Street and turn right. The site is closed Tuesday through Thursday each week.

For more information: Contact the BLM Arcata Resource Area, 1125 16th Street, Room 219, Arcata, CA 95521; (707) 822-7648
USGS topographic maps: Tyee City

MIDDLE FORK EEL RIVER
kayaking, canoeing, rafting, fishing

This wild, rugged country of dense forests, lush meadows, rolling hills and steep-walled gorges makes for a thrilling river adventure. This is a truly unique opportunity to experience remote wilderness in a river setting. For the first 26 miles or so, the Middle Fork of the Eel rolls steadily through a wide valley filled with firs and pines. Wildflowers are common, and at times appear to carpet all the open area. Wildlife include deer, black bear, otter and coyote. The last four miles, the most difficult of the paddle, channel into a narrow gorge where tributary streams create colorful waterfalls off both sides of the canyon.

•**See also Best of the State, page 144**•
For more information: Contact the BLM Arcata Resource Area, 1125 16th Street, Room 219, Arcata, CA 95521; (707) 822-7648.

SACRAMENTO RIVER
camping, hiking, canoeing, rafting, fishing, horseback riding

California's longest river attracts many visitors because of
its easy access for swimming and boating. Canoes, rafts,
kayaks and power boats all ply the tranquil waterways in
seeming harmony. Shoreline fishing for salmon, steelhead and
trout is fair to good. Located south of Redding and near
Interstate 5.

For more information: Contact the BLM Redding Resource Area, 355
Hemsted Drive, Redding, CA 96002; (916) 224-2100.
BLM surface maps: Redding, Red Bluff

SAMOA DUNES
hiking, horseback riding, mountain biking, off-road vehicle use

This 300-acre dunescape is worth a peek. It is a great place
to kick back, fly a kite or let your toes play in the nearby surf.
Scrounging for driftwood is a popular activity. Seagrasses and
numerous species of wildflowers keep the dune fairly stable
and prevent rapid wind erosion.

From US 101 in Eureka follow the Samoa Bridge to Highway 255 and then go south to the end of Samoa Spit.

For more information: Contact the BLM Arcata Resource Area, 1125
16th Street, Room 219, Arcata, CA 95521; (707) 822-7648.
USGS topographic maps: Eureka

SOUTH FORK EEL RIVER
*kayaking, canoeing, rafting, fishing, hiking, horseback riding,
mountain biking*

A number of Class IV rapids within this river section help
to keep the whitewater enthusiast grinning. Located along
Highway 101 north of Garberville. Put-in and take-out points
are all along Highway 101.

For more information: Contact the BLM Arcata Resource Area, 1125
16th Street, Room 219, Arcata, CA 95521; (707) 822-7648.
USGS topographic maps: Garberville, Mirancla, Myers Flat

TRINITY RIVER
kayaking, canoeing, rafting, camping, hiking, backpacking, mountain biking, horseback riding

Ideal for a two-day canoe or raft trip through steep canyons and rustic meadows. This river offers a ringside seat for a glimpse into the surrounding region's gold rush legacy and spectacular views of the nearby and often snow-capped Trinity Alps.

•**See also Best of the State, page 146**•
For more information: Contact the BLM Redding Resource Area, 355 Hemsted Drive, Redding, CA 96002; (916) 224-2100.

UPPER KLAMATH
kayaking, canoeing, rafting, camping, hiking, backpacking, mountain biking, horseback riding

Fishing and whitewater are the popular calling cards for this well-known river. California's second longest river, the Klamath provides excellent salmon and steelhead fishing in the winter and super trout angling during the summer.

•**See also Best of the State, page 148**•
For more information: Contact the BLM Redding Resource Area, 355 Hemsted Drive, Redding, CA 96002; (916) 224-2100.

CALIFORNIA BY REGION

2

CENTRAL CALIFORNIA

ALABAMA HILLS
camping, hiking, backpacking, horseback riding, mountain biking

The Alabama Hills' weathered granite boulder piles and rounded terrain colored in old southwestern hues have been used as a backdrop for countless western classics. Remember Hopalong Cassidy? This is the pass where he rounded up all those bad guys. Now you can play here too. Time your visit right and you can take in some film nostalgia during the annual Lone Pine Film Festival. Located west of Highway 395 at Lone Pine.

For more information: Contact the BLM Bishop Resource Area, 787 North Main, Suite P, Bishop, CA 93514; (619) 872-4881.

USGS topographic maps: Lone Pine

AMERICAN RIVER
canoeing, rafting, kayaking, backpacking, hiking, horseback riding

Encompassing the North, Middle and South Forks of the American River, this region of popular whitewater runs slices right through the very heart and soul of the Mother Lode. Scenic canyons and oak woodlands surround the river, which offers rides ranging from the mildly tame on the South Fork to the wild and woolly on the Middle and North Fork. Despite the crowds that flock here on weekends, many visitors return again and again because of the scenic value of the South Fork. Unlike most Sierra rivers that carve through deep canyons, the South Fork of the American winds through golden foothills sprinkled with oaks and digger pines. Low rock walls of the final "canyon" section increase the whitewater excitement. Expect to see blue herons and golden eagles and, if you time your visit early enough in the spring, you will enjoy viewing hills covered with California poppy, lilac, shooting star, lupine and more. The fishing isn't great, but expect to reel in the odd trout, bass or catfish. Sutters Mill, an historic site, sits along the river route, within Marshall Gold Discovery State Park. Sutters Mill was the site of the first California gold discovery.

•**See also Best of the State, page 142**•
For more information: Contact the BLM Folsom Resource Area, 63 Natoma Street, Folsom, CA 95630; (916) 985-4474.

BODIE BOWL
hiking, off-road vehicle use, cross-country skiing, mountain biking

The ghost town of Bodie, a living example of a boomtown gone bust, is a California State Park. The area surrounding the town is all BLM land and offers a tremendous opportunity to observe nature, photograph wildlife or naturescapes, or tour on a mountain bike. Quaking aspen in the drainages turn bright yellow and gold in fall. The adventurous explorer will revel in discovering the many enclosed canyons, interior valleys and springs tucked in among the pinyon-covered hills.

From Bridgeport on Highway 395, head east on Aurora Canyon Road and then southeast on Bodie/Masonic Road. Mountain biking can be enjoyed on the several unpaved roads that enter the Bodie Hills through narrow canyons such as Aurora, Clearwater, Cottonwood and Bridgeport. Views of Mono Lake and the Sierra can be enjoyed from on top of some of the higher points.

For more information: Contact the BLM Bishop Resource Area, 787 North Main, Suite P, Bishop, CA 93514; (619) 872-4881.
USGS topographic maps: Bodie, Trench Canyon, Bridgeport, Aurora

CARRIZO PLAIN
wildlife observation, hiking, mountain biking, horseback riding

This place was referred to as the "next Serengeti Plain" by an enthusiastic BLM official during a press conference. Press conferences can be prone to exaggeration, but not in this case. Carrizo Plain is indeed spectacular, partly because of its enormity—it is one of the largest natural areas in the state.

•**See also Best of the State, page 140**•
For more information: Contact the BLM Caliente Resource Area, 4301 Rosedale Highway, Bakersfield, CA 93308; (805) 861-4236.

CHIMNEY PEAK RECREATION AREA
camping, hiking, backpacking, horseback riding

Set among the pinyon pines of the rugged Sierra Nevada foothills, Chimney Creek affords the avid angler an opportunity to fish for trout. This area also serves as a hub of activity for backpackers, hikers and equestrians entering into the wilds via the Pacific Crest Trail. It adjoins the Domelands Wilderness Area, creating possibilities for semi-loop backpacking and horsepacking trips. Permits are required to enter into the wilderness areas. From Lake Isabella, take Highway 178 east to Canebreak Road.

•**See also Owens Peak Wilderness Study Area in Best of the State, page 134**•
For more information: Contact the BLM Caliente Resource Area, 4301 Rosedale Highway, Bakersfield, CA 93308; (805) 861-4236.

COALINGA MINERAL SPRING
hiking

If you are looking for solitude, then this is your spot. Few visit here, yet the hiking is marvelous and quiet along a two-mile trail to the mountain peak. From Coalinga, drive 10 miles west on Highway 198 to Coalinga Mineral Springs Road.

For more information: Contact the BLM Hollister Resource Area, 20 Hamilton Court, Hollister, CA 95023; (408) 637-8183.
USGS topographic maps: Sherman Peak

CONWAY SUMMIT
camping, mountain biking

From the top of the summit, you can see for miles—truly an on-top-of-the-world feeling. Virginia Creek is super for trout fishing and the Virginia Creek Canyon provides an excellent opportunity for primitive camping.

For more information: Contact the BLM Bishop Resource Area, 787 North Main, Suite P, Bishop, CA 93514; (619) 872-4881.
USGS topographic maps: Lundy, Dunberg Peak

CRATER MOUNTAIN
hiking, mountain biking

You can have wonderful fun exploring the cinder cone, lava flows and tube caves from volcanic activity thousands of years ago.

For more information: Contact the BLM Bishop Resource Area, 787 North Main, Suite P, Bishop, CA 93514; (619) 872-4881.
USGS topographic maps: Fish Springs

FISH SLOUGH
hiking, mountain biking, wildlife observation

Three natural springs flow from volcanic cliffs, creating a slough that has been turned into a cooperatively managed wildlife sanctuary overseen by the BLM, the California Department of Fish and Game and the Los Angeles Department of Water and Power. Two endangered fish, the Owen's pupfish and the Owen's tui chub may be viewed within the six acres of clear ponds. Other wildlife that can be seen include: yellow-headed blackbird, prairie falcon, green-winged teal, black-crowned night heron, and a multitude of shorebirds, songbirds and waterfowl.

From Bishop, take Highway 395 north to Highway 6. Go north for 1.5 miles and turn west on Five Bridges Road. Drive approximately 2.5 miles to Fish Slough Road, a right turn just after a sand and gravel plant. After approximately 6.5 miles, you will come to a fenced pond and Fish Slough.

For more information: Contact the BLM Bishop Resource Area, 787 No. Main, Suite P, Bishop, CA 93514; (619) 872-4881.
USGS topographic maps: Bishop, White Mountain Peak

KEYSVILLE
mountain biking, rafting, kayaking

Located near the town of Lake Isabella, this area can become a bit crowded at times. Still, it serves as a good base from which to enjoy whitewater activities on the nearby Kern River as well as fishing, camping and exploring old mine ruins.

For more information: Contact the BLM Caliente Resource Area, 4301 Rosedale Highway, Bakersfield, CA 93308; (805) 861-4236.
USGS topographic maps: Lake Isabella, Miracle Hot Springs, Alta Sierra, Lake Isabella South

MERCED RIVER
kayaking, rafting, camping, hiking, backpacking, horseback riding, mountain biking

The Merced is a hard-charging and highly seasonal whitewater run. To get there, take Highway 141 to Forest Bridge and then Forest Bridge Road to Incline Road. The river is rated Class III to IV.

For more information: Contact the BLM Folsom Resource Area, 63 Natoma Street, Folsom, CA 95630; (916) 985-4474.
USGS topographic maps: Bear Valley, Buckhorn Peak, Feliciana Mountain, El Portal, Kinsley

MOKELUMNE RIVER
kayaking, canoeing, inner-tubing

A short three-mile jaunt past the Gold Rush towns of Jackson and Mokelumne Hill offers easy access and a brief section of whitewater ideal for the novice or whitewater kayaker in training for more difficult runs. The river is rated Class I to II. Take Highway 49 to Jackson and then to Electra Road. The put-in is at the Electra Power House.

For more information: Contact the BLM Folsom Resource Area, 63 Natoma Street, Folsom, CA 95630; (916) 985-4474.
USGS topographic maps: Jackson, Mokelumne Hill

NORTH FORK KAWEAH RIVER
hiking, fishing, swimming

The rustic ambience of this scenic section of the river offers excellent opportunities for fishing, swimming, sunbathing, hiking and primitive camping.

For more information: Contact the BLM Caliente Resource Area, 4301 Rosedale Highway, Bakersfield, CA 93308; (805) 861-4236.
USGS topographic maps: Mount Kaweah, General Grant Grove

PANAMINT MOUNTAINS AND VALLEY
camping, hiking, backpacking

This is an expansive 210,000-acre area along the western boundary of Death Valley National Monument, bisected by State Road 190. A number of maintained roads provide decent access into the region and its four pristine wilderness study areas—Hunter Mountain, Panamint Dunes, Wildrose Canyon, and Surprise Canyon. For the best mobility and access, as well as all-weather safety, a four-wheel-drive vehicle is highly recommended.

Hunter Mountain rises 7,454 feet above the valley floor. The road up and over its back is very hazardous in anything but sunny weather. Grapevine Canyon, which parallels the road, has an abundance of water from numerous springs originating high up on the slopes. Wildlife includes mule deer and bighorn sheep. The area is well regarded for birding opportunities.

Panamint Dunes are a six-square-mile area of developed and developing sand dunes rising above a dry flat lakebed. Some of the dunes rise up to 250 feet above the valley floor. Vegetation varies from scrub in low-lying areas to pinyon pine and juniper in the higher and more rocky reaches. Bighorn sheep and mule deer along with chipmunk and golden eagle are the main fare for wildlife viewing.

Wildrose Canyon Area is deeply cut by canyons from which gently sloping alluvial fans emerge out and onto the valley floor. Creosote bush and desert holly are the predominant vegetation.

Surprise Canyon is an area of outstanding scenic quality and has been designated an Area of Critical Environmental Concern. County-maintained Indian Ranch Road provides access into the area. Telescope Peak sits as a towering monarch over the area at 11,045 feet of elevation. The surrounding terrain is mostly rugged mountains and deeply cut canyons. There is a small badlands area to the northwest. The area has had a history of mining, which explains a number of roads that disappear into the mountainous terrain. Several of the canyons in the area sport flowing springs. Flower displays are seasonal and very colorful on the alluvial fans that extend out from many of the canyons.

For more information: Contact the BLM California Desert District Office, 6221 Box Springs Boulevard, Riverside, CA 92507; (714) 697-5217.

USGS topographic maps: Harris Hill, Jackass Canyon, Wildrose Peak, Emigrant Pass, Maturango Peak Northeast, Panamint, Ballaraf, The Dunes

SAN JOAQUIN RIVER TRAIL
hiking, horseback riding

This 2.5-mile BLM section of the 11-mile trail from the Sierra National Forest to Millerton Lake State Recreation Area offers breathtaking views of the San Joaquin River Gorge. Wildflowers will leave you wide-eyed in the spring. To get there, travel east from Fresno on Highway 168 to Prather and follow the signs to Auberry. Access is via Power House Road to Smalley Road.

For more information: Contact the BLM Hollister Resource Area, 20 Hamilton Court, Hollister, CA 95023; (408) 637-8183.
USGS topographic maps: Millerton Lake East

SOUTH FORK YUBA RIVER
camping, hiking, fishing, swimming, backpacking, mountain biking

History, scenic beauty and whitewater combine to make this canyon river a thrilling and rewarding experience for all. The South Yuba Trail provides a 13.5-mile link between the trail systems of nearby Malakoff Diggins State Park and the Tahoe National Forest. Within the South Yuba River Recreation Area, camping is restricted to designated sites of the South Fork Campground. The river is rated Class IV to V. From Nevada City, head 12 miles north on State Road 49 and then right on Tyler Foote County Road.

For more information: Contact the BLM Folsom Resource Area, 63 Natoma Street, Folsom, CA 95630; (916) 985-4474.
USGS topographic maps: Washington, North Bloomfield

SQUAW LEAP
camping, hiking, backpacking, horseback riding, mountain biking

Two developed trails enhance the spectacular views of the San Joaquin River Gorge that reward the visitor to this region. Wildflowers abound in the spring. From Fresno, take Highway 168 to Prather. Follow the signs to Auberry. Access is via Power House Road to Smalley Road.

For more information: Contact the BLM Hollister Resource Area, 20 Hamilton Court, Hollister, CA 95023; (408) 637-8183.
USGS topographic maps: Millerton Lake East

TUOLUMNE RIVER
whitewater kayaking/rafting

California's premier whitewater river is a slalom course of boulders of escalating intensity. Staircase rapids, chutes, and pools by the score and the close proximity of Yosemite National Park help to create the ultimate wilderness river adventure—a journey that is both exhilarating and pristine. Take Highway 49 south from Sonora to Highway 120. Head east on Highway 120 past Groveland about 7.5 miles (one-half mile past the turn for County Road J20). Turn left (north) and drive one mile. Turn right onto a dirt road and drive six miles to

Lumsden Campground and the put-in. You must have a permit to run the river or be on a trip with a licensed outfitter. The river is rated Class IV to V.

•See also Best of the State, page 150•
For more information: Contact the BLM Folsom Resource Area, 63 Natoma Street, Folsom, CA 95630; (916) 985-4474.

VOLCANIC TABLELAND / FISH SLOUGH
hiking, horseback riding, mountain biking

This is a lush oasis standing in dramatic contrast to the surrounding stark volcanic tableland. Set between the White Mountains and the Sierra Nevada, the Tableland provides the patient photographer with striking shadow play and dawn/ dusk light shows.

For more information: Contact the BLM Bishop Resource Area, 787 North Main, Suite P, Bishop, CA 93514; (619) 872-4881.
USGS topographic maps: Mount Tom, Bishop, White Mountain Peak, Casa Diablo Mountain

---

TIP: Camp out of sight of the trail.

CALIFORNIA BY REGION

3

SOUTHERN CALIFORNIA

AFTON CANYON
camping, hiking, backpacking, horseback riding, mountain biking

The canyons, nooks and crannies wandered years ago by Native Americans, Spanish missionaries and mountain men practically beg to be explored. Wagon trains once stopped here for rest and water beside the Mojave River, which still flows most of the year.

For more information: Contact the BLM Barstow Resource Area, 150 Coolwater Lane, Barstow, CA 92311; (619) 256-3591.
USGS topographic maps: Dunn, Manix, Hidden Valley West

BIG MORONGO PRESERVE
hiking, wildlife observation, picnicking

This region is nationally recognized for its birdwatching opportunities. The desert springs ecosystem and Mojave riparian woodland are exemplary. Cottonwood Trail follows a creek lined by cottonwood and willow, which creates a haven for raccoons, ringtails, great horned owls, and numerous songbirds. The rare Peninsular bighorn sheep can be spotted here at dawn or dusk during the summer months—the only time you will want to be out because of the oppressive summer heat. To get there from Interstate 10 near Palm Springs, drive Highway 62 north to Morongo Valley. Turn right on East Drive and continue three blocks to the signed entrance. The Preserve is closed on Mondays and Tuesdays.

For more information: Contact the BLM Palm Springs-South Central Coast Resource Area, 63-500 Garnet Avenue, P.O. Box 2000, North Palm Springs, CA 92258; (619) 251-0812.
USGS topographic maps: Morongo Valley

COACHELLA VALLEY PRESERVE
hiking, backpacking, horseback riding, wildlife observation

This 1,000-palm oasis is a joint BLM and Nature Conservancy Preserve established to protect the endangered Coachella Valley fringe-toed lizard. Crystal clear springs shaded by greenery attract a wide variety of wildlife and birds. From Palm Springs, take Interstate 10 east ten miles to the Ramon Road exit. Drive east to Thousand Palms Canyon Drive. Turn north and drive two miles to the signed entrance to the Preserve.

For more information: Contact the BLM Palm Springs-South Central Coast Resource Area, 63-500 Garnet Avenue, P.O. Box 2000, North Palm Springs, CA 92258; (619) 251-0812.
USGS topographic maps: Cathedral City, Myoma

CORN SPRINGS
camping

Set in a deep canyon among the fabled Chuckwalla Mountains, this site produces a wealth of botanical pleasures from groves of native fan palms to lush clumps of cattail.

For more information: Contact the BLM Palm Springs-South Central Coast Resource Area, 63-500 Garnet Avenue, P.O. Box 2000, North Palm Springs, CA 92258; (619) 251-0812.
USGS topographic maps: Corn Spring

DARWIN FALLS
camping, hiking, backpacking

Spring is the best time to visit the falls as this is when the canyon area is teeming with desert wildlife and migrating birds. There is much more to this area than just the falls, however. The Darwin Plateau rises 4,000 feet above the valley floor and is cut by deep chasms through volcanic rock faces. Spring-fed creeks within a number of these canyons create cool and moist oases from the desert which attract wildlife from all around. From Olancha on Highway 395, head 27 miles east on State Road 190. The Darwin Falls area is located south of State Road 190 near the town of Darwin. The falls can be seen from the road.

For more information: Contact the BLM Ridgecrest Resource Area, 300 South Richmond Road, Ridgecrest, CA 93555; (619) 375-7125.
USGS topographic maps: Darwin

DESERT TORTOISE NATURAL AREA
wildlife observation, hiking

Although this is a tortoise preserve, you will have to look hard to spot one—they are a bit shy and reclusive. The best time to view the threatened California State Reptile is between early March and late May. If you spot one, keep your distance. Tortoises traumatize easily and human contact could lead to their death. Wildflowers are spectacular here during the spring with over 150 species in bloom. Check with the visitor's center for guided tours during the spring. Summer is too hot to visit and viewing is poor anyway. From Highway 58 or Highway 14, take the California City exit to California City. Head

---

through town, turning north on Randburg-Mojave Road. Drive 5.5 miles to the signed entrance.

For more information: Contact the BLM Ridgecrest Resource Area, 300 South Richmond Road, Ridgecrest, CA 93555; (619) 375-7125.
USGS topographic maps: California City North

DOS PALMAS PRESERVE
hiking

Yet another BLM and Nature Conservancy Preserve, the Dos Palmas Preserve is an island of biological diversity protecting the endangered pupfish and Yuma clapper rail. From the town of Indio, drive south on Highway 111 approximately 25 miles to Parkside Drive. Turn left here and drive one mile to a right turn onto Desertaire Drive. The paved road will end, but keep driving on a dirt road for three miles to the signed preserve. It's hot here in the summer.

For more information: Contact the BLM Palm Springs-South Central Coast Resource Area, 63-500 Garnet Avenue, P.O. Box 2000, North Palm Springs, CA 92258; (619) 251-0812.
USGS topographic maps: Otocopia Canyon

EAST MOJAVE NATIONAL SCENIC AREA
camping, hiking, backpacking, horseback riding, mountain biking

The sawtooth mountains, salt-encrusted playas, weird yet wonderful Joshua trees, dramatic rock spires, and flat-topped mesas of this region were the inspiration behind many of novelist Zane Grey's western writings.

For more information: Contact the BLM Needles Resource Area, 101 West Spikes Road, Needles, CA 92363; 619) 326-3896.
USGS topographic maps: Granite Spring, Cow Cove, Cima Dome, Cima Hayden, Marl Mountain, Indian Spring, Old Dad Mountain, Kelso

EL PASO MOUNTAINS
camping, hiking, backpacking, wildlife observation, birdwatching

Twenty-two square miles of the El Paso Raptor Management Area are within this site, one of the principal breeding areas for golden eagle, prairie falcon and others. You can be virtually assured of blue-ribbon raptor watching. Last Chance Canyon runs through the region and has been given the BLM thumbs-up as a place of high scenic value. At times, the surrounding slopes of this badland-like area are a wildflower mosaic of color. Located east of State Road 14 and north of Red Rock-Randsburg-Garlock Road (it's just as tough to put on a sign as it is to say).

For more information: Contact the BLM California Desert District Office, 6221 Box Springs Boulevard, Riverside, CA 92507; (714) 697-5217.
USGS topographic maps: El Paso Peaks

EUREKA DUNES
camping, hiking

Climb California's highest sand dune at 700 feet, give or take a few inches. Race downhill to celebrate. Photographers thrill to the interplay of light and shadows among the dunes and playa.

For more information: Contact the BLM Ridgecrest Resource Area, 300 South Richmond Road, Ridgecrest, CA 93555; (619) 375-7125.
USGS topographic maps: Last Chance Range

FORT PIUTE
hiking, horseback riding

Though four-wheel-drive is required for access, a visit here is worth the effort. The mile-long oasis of Piute Creek has enjoyed a checkered history as one of the Mojave's most important watering spots since prehistoric times. Nomadic Native Americans camped here, as did the U.S. military who created a desert outpost. The area is located on the California/Nevada border, west of US 95, east of Lanfair Road and approximately 12 miles north of Needles. Access is via local roads—ask at the BLM office for specific directions.

For more information: Contact the BLM Needles Resource Area, 101 West Spikes Road, Needles, CA 92363; (619) 326-3896.
USGS topographic maps: Needles Northwest, Needles Southwest

FOSSIL FALLS
camping, hiking, backpacking

Black lava, sculpted and polished during the Ice Age, creates a series of dry waterfalls here. Native Americans frequented this exceptional site because of the lavish formations created by volcanic activity—activity that provided materials for toolmaking.

For more information: Contact the BLM Ridgecrest Resource Area, 300 South Richmond Road, Ridgecrest, CA 93555; (619) 375-7125. **USGS topographic maps:** Little Lake

IMPERIAL SAND DUNES
camping, hiking, off-road vehicle use

The dunes of what some call "America's Sahara" rise 300 feet into the sky and stretch for nearly 40 miles along the eastern edge of Imperial Valley and near the ancient shoreline of Lake Cahuilla. Highway 78 bisects the area. South of the highway is known as one of the state's ultimate off-road vehicle playgrounds—a place to stay away from unless you enjoy listening to the incessant growling and whining of engines. North of the highway, however, you can find some peace, as the area is closed to motor vehicle use and open to hiking and other less aggressive forms of recreation.

For more information: Contact the BLM El Centro Resource Area, 1661 South Fourth Street, El Centro, CA 92243; (619) 353-1660. **USGS topographic maps:** Glamis, Glamis Northwest, Glamis Southeast, Glamis Southwest, Ogilby, Hedges, Cactus, Clyde, Acolita, Amos, Mammoth Wash, Tortuga

JAWBONE / DOVE SPRINGS
hiking, backpacking, horseback riding, mountain biking, off-road vehicle use

Located in southern Kern County, this area offers the outdoor enthusiast an opportunity to enjoy just about every non-motorized and motorized recreational activity except watersports. Dramatic views with an equally dramatic blend of mountains, desert shrubs and flatlands provide a superb backdrop and a haven for an impressive inventory of mammals, reptiles and birds. Off-road vehicle activity can be heavy at times.

For more information: Contact the BLM Ridgecrest Resource Area, 300 South Richmond Road, Ridgecrest, CA 93555; (619) 375-7125.
USGS topographic maps: Freeman Junction, Cinco, Cross Mountain, Dove Spring, Pinyon Mountain

JOSHUA TREE NATIONAL MONUMENT AREA
hiking, backpacking, wildlife observation, rock climbing, horseback riding

The BLM has jurisdiction over a wide range of territory surrounding the Joshua Tree National Monument, an area that is sure to convince even the most cynical outdoorsperson that desert terrain is far from boring or monotonous. Wildflower displays in the spring border on the spectacular! To get to the monument, take State Road 26 from Interstate 10 to Twentynine Palms—the entrance to the visitor's center is signed. Be sure to visit the following areas:

Sheephole-Cadiz Recreation Areas: Vast desert valleys bounded by steep granite mountains make up this region of high wilderness that lies to the northeast of the monument. There is a spring in the Sheephole Mountains that provides sufficient water to support a small desert bighorn sheep herd.

Eagle Mountains: Lying to the southeast of the monument, the Eagle Mountains are rugged and highly complex with jumbled boulder piles, numerous small canyons, steep slopes, washes and areas of thick vegetation. There are a number of fan palm oases in the region.

For more information: Contact the BLM Palm Springs-South Central Coast Resource Area, 63-500 Garnet Avenue, P.O. Box 2000, North Palm Springs, CA 92258; (619) 251-0812.
USGS topographic maps: New Dale, Clarks Pass, Cadiz Valley Southeast, Cadiz Valley Southwest, Coxcomb Mountains, East of Victory Pass, Victory Pass Buzzard Spring, Conejo Well, San Bernardino Wash, Placer Canyon, Pinto Wells, Hayfield
Additional maps: *Trails Illustrated Joshua Tree National Monument* park map with backcountry and hiking information, published by Trails Illustrated, P.O. Box 3610, Evergreen, CO 80439; (800) 962-1643.

McCain Valley
camping, hiking, backpacking, horseback riding, off-road vehicle use

The BLM refers to this site as "an ideal family retreat year-round" because it is often uncrowded. Tucked into the In-Ko-Pah Mountains, part of the coastal range, it forms a rocky garden playground for bighorn sheep. A pair of BLM-managed campgrounds shaded by oak trees and cooled by the 3,500-foot elevation offer a generally pleasing alternative to the searing heat of the surrounding desert during the summer months.

For more information: Contact the BLM El Centro Resource Area, 1661 South Fourth Street, El Centro, CA 92243; (619) 353-1660.
USGS topographic maps: Live Oak Springs

Mecca Hills
camping, hiking, backpacking, horseback riding, mountain biking

Picturesque badlands, hidden palm oases, colorful box canyons, and ridgetops with views west to the Salton Sea and Santa Rosa Mountains offer excellent opportunities for adventurous exploration, hiking and photography.

For more information: Contact the BLM Palm Springs-South Central Coast Resource Area, 63-500 Garnet Avenue, P.O. Box 2000, North Palm Springs, CA 92258; (619) 251-0812.
USGS topographic maps: Thermal Canyon, Mortmar, Cottonwood Basin

Providence Mountains State Recreation Area
hiking, backpacking, camping, horseback riding, spelunking

The Providence Mountains extend northeast for about 20 miles from Granite Pass, just south of Kelso. Limestone cliffs and caverns add a unique blend of variety to the rhyolite crags and peaks and the broad bajadas. If you are a Zane Grey fan, you may recognize the large flat-topped Wildhorse Mesa as the setting for his book of the same name—*Wildhorse Mesa*. There are no marked trails for hiking or backpacking, but there are plenty of opportunities for hiking away from it all and discovering a peaceful sense of isolation—check with the BLM office. Located 17 miles northwest of Essex and Interstate 40 on Essex Road. The BLM lands bound the State Park on the west and on the north, off Kelso Road.

For more information: Contact the BLM California Desert District Office, 6221 Box Springs Boulevard, Riverside, CA 92507; (714) 697-5217.

USGS topographic maps: Fountain Peak, Van Winkle Spring

RAINBOW BASIN
camping, hiking, backpacking, horseback riding, mountain biking

The millions of years of geological history are the primary drawing card here. Take a hike down Owl Canyon Wash, or drive, or pedal your mountain bike on the short 1.5-mile loop trail through the basin. To get there, take Camp Irwin Road north from Barstow for five miles and then head west for five more miles on Fossil Beds Road. Harper Dry Lake (no longer completely dry) is a few miles further on.

For more information: Contact the BLM Barstow Resource Area, 150 Coolwater Lane, Barstow, CA 92311; (619) 256-3591.

USGS topographic maps: Mud Hills, Lane Mountain

RAND MOUNTAINS
camping, hiking, backpacking, horseback riding, mountain biking

Hikers, rock hounds, wildlife watchers and mountain bikers will enjoy the wide, open spaces and dramatic ups and downs of existing roads that wind through this historic mining district.

For more information: Contact the BLM Ridgecrest Resource Area, 300 South Richmond Road, Ridgecrest, CA 93555; (619) 375-7125.

USGS topographic maps: Johannesburg, Saltdale Southeast

SANTA ROSA NATIONAL SCENIC AREA
hiking, backpacking, horseback riding, mountain biking

Jolting skyward 7,000 feet in an spectacularly abrupt fashion from the surrounding Coachella Valley, the Santa Rosa

---

Mountains offer the adventurer a playground landscape that varies from desert shrubbery to hidden palm canyons to conifer-capped peaks.

•**See also Best of the State, page 152**•
For more information: Contact the BLM Palm Springs-South Central Coast Resource Area, 63-500 Garnet Avenue, P.O. Box 2000, North Palm Springs, CA 92258; (619) 251-0812.

SPANGLER HILLS
camping, hiking, backpacking, horseback riding, mountain biking, off-road vehicle use

Although a fair number of off-road vehicles frequent this area, there is plenty of room for hikers and mountain bikers to enjoy the recreational pleasures of this high desert site.

For more information: Contact the BLM Ridgecrest Resource Area, 300 South Richmond Road, Ridgecrest, CA 93555; (619) 375-7125.
USGS topographic maps: Spangler Hills East, Spangler Hills West

TRONA PINNACLES
camping, hiking, backpacking, horseback riding, mountain biking

If you are a Star Trek fan, you may recognize the Pinnacles as the setting for the movie, *Star Trek: The Final Frontier*. If not, you will still find ultimate pleasure within this maze of monoliths jutting out of a dry lakebed. Located at Searles Lake, east of State Road 178 near Trona.

For more information: Contact the BLM Ridgecrest Resource Area, 300 South Richmond Road, Ridgecrest, CA 93555; (619) 375-7125.
USGS topographic maps: Searles Lake

TIP: When car camping, set up your camp no more than 300 feet from the nearest road and your vehicle.

STATE INFORMATION OVERVIEW

CALIFORNIA STATE OFFICE
2800 Cottage Way, E-2841, Sacramento, CA 95825; (916) 978-4474

BAKERSFIELD DISTRICT OFFICE
800 Truxtun Avenue, Room 311, Bakersfield, CA 93301; (805) 861-4191

Bishop Resource Area, 787 North Main, Suite P, Bishop, CA 93514; (619) 872-4881

Caliente Resource Area, 4301 Rosedale Highway, Bakersfield, CA 93308; (805) 861-4236

Folsom Resource Area, 63 Natoma Street, Folsom, CA 95630; (916) 985-4474

Hollister Resource Area, 20 Hamilton Court, Hollister, CA 95023; (408) 637-8183

UKIAH DISTRICT OFFICE
555 Leslie Street, Ukiah, CA 95482; (707) 462-3873

Arcata Resource Area, 1125 16th Street, Room 219, Arcata, CA 95521; (707) 822-7648

Clear Lake Resource Area, 555 Leslie Street, Ukiah, CA 95482; (707) 462-3873

Redding Resource Area, 355 Hemsted Drive, Redding, CA 96002; (916) 224-2100

SUSANVILLE DISTRICT OFFICE
705 Hall Street, P.O. Box 1090, Susanville, CA 96130; (916) 257-5381

Alturas Resource Area, 608 West 12th Street, Alturas, CA 96101; (916) 233-4666

Eagle Lake Resource Area, 2545 Riverside Drive, Susanville, CA 96130; (916) 257-5381

Surprise Resource Area, 602 Cressler Street, Cedarville, CA 96104; (916) 279-6101

CALIFORNIA DESERT DISTRICT OFFICE
6221 Box Springs Boulevard, Riverside, CA 92507; (714) 697-5217

Barstow Resource Area, 150 Coolwater Lane, Barstow, CA 92311; (619) 256-3591

El Centro Resource Area, 1661 South Fourth Street, El Centro, CA 92243; (619) 353-1660

Needles Resource Area, 101 West Spikes Road, Needles, CA 92363; (619) 326-3896

Palm Springs-South Central Coast Resource Area, 63-500 Garnet Avenue, P.O. Box 2000, North Palm Springs, CA 92258; (619) 251-0812

Ridgecrest Resource Area, 300 South Richmond Road, Ridgecrest, CA 93555; (619) 375-7125

COLORADO

(SEE MAP A)

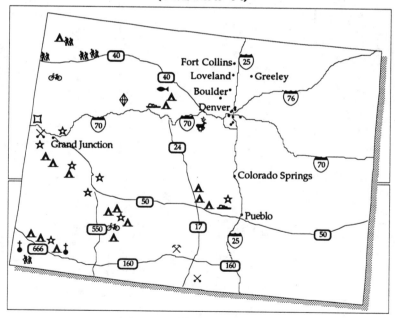

(SEE MAP B)

MAP A—COLORADO

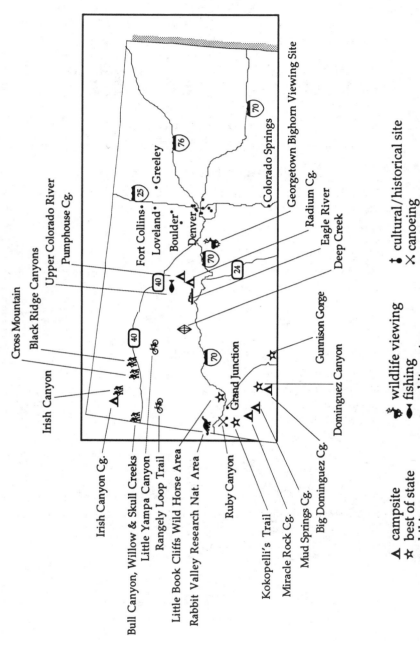

Cross Mountain
Black Ridge Canyons
Upper Colorado River
Pumphouse Cg.

Irish Canyon

Irish Canyon Cg.

Bull Canyon, Willow & Skull Creeks
Little Yampa Canyon
Rangely Loop Trail
Little Book Cliffs Wild Horse Area
Rabbit Valley Research Nat. Area

Ruby Canyon

Kokopelli's Trail
Miracle Rock Cg.
Mud Springs Cg.
Big Dominguez Cg.

Fort Collins
Loveland
Boulder
Denver
Greeley

Georgetown Bighorn Viewing Site

Colorado Springs

Radium Cg.
Eagle River
Deep Creek

Grand Junction

Gunnison Gorge

Dominguez Canyon

△ campsite
☆ best of state
🥾 hiking
🚲 mountain biking

🦌 wildlife viewing
🐟 fishing
〜 whitewater
⚓ general recreation

✝ cultural/historical site
✕ canoeing
✕ rock climbing
🦴 dinosaur relics

MAP REFERENCES

Black Ridge Canyons Wilderness Study Area—p. 209-210
Bull Canyon, Willow Creek & Skull Creek Wilderness Study
    Area—p. 208
Cross Mountain Wilderness Study Area—p. 207-208
Deep Creek—p. 206
Dominguez Canyon—p. 196-198
Eagle River—p. 210
Georgetown Bighorn Viewing Site—p. 205
Gunnison Gorge—p. 198-200
Irish Canyon—p. 206-207
Kokopelli's Trial—p. 203-204
Little Book Cliffs Wild Horse Area—p. 194-195
Little Yampa Canyon—p. 211
Rabbit Valley Research Natural Area—p. 205
Rangely Loop Trail—p. 209
Ruby Canyon—p. 210-211
Upper Colorado River—p. 211-212

CAMPGROUNDS

The following campgrounds are found in this area of Colorado. Please call the BLM office (listed following each campground's name) for reservations and information. Contact information for each BLM office is on pages 221-222 of Colorado.

Big Dominguez Campground, Grand Junction Resource Area
Irish Canyon Campground, Little Snake Resource Area
Miracle Rock Campground, Grand Junction Resource Area
Mud Springs Campground, Grand Junction Resource Area
Pumphouse Campground, Kremmling Resource Area
Radium Campground, Kremmling Resource Area

MAP B—COLORADO

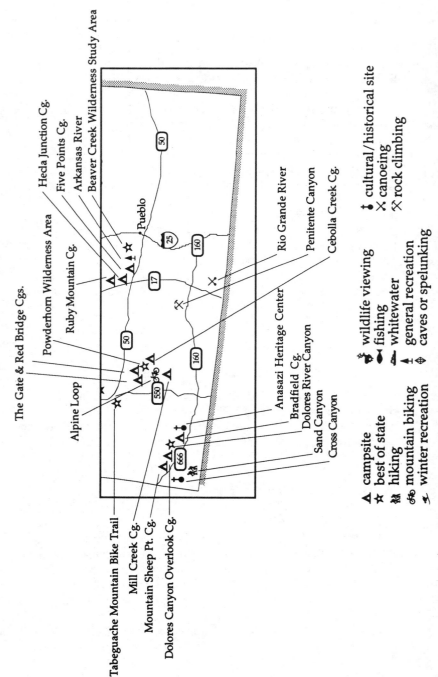

Hecla Junction Cg.
Five Points Cg.
Arkansas River
Beaver Creek Wilderness Study Area

Powderhorn Wilderness Area
Ruby Mountain Cg.

The Gate & Red Bridge Cgs.

Alpine Loop

Tabeguache Mountain Bike Trail
Mill Creek Cg.
Mountain Sheep Pt. Cg.
Dolores Canyon Overlook Cg.

Anasazi Heritage Center
Bradfield Cg.
Dolores River Canyon
Sand Canyon
Cross Canyon

Rio Grande River
Penitente Canyon
Cebolla Creek Cg.

Pueblo

▲ campsite
★ best of state
🛶 hiking
🚴 mountain biking
⚞ winter recreation

🦌 wildlife viewing
🎣 fishing
≈ whitewater
🚶 general recreation
⬙ caves or spelunking

† cultural/historical site
✕ canoeing
⤬ rock climbing

MAP REFERENCES

Alpine Loop—p. 212
Anasazi Heritage Center and Resource Management Area—
        p. 213
Arkansas River/Arkansas Headwaters Recreation Area—p. 219
Beaver Creek Wilderness Study Area—p. 192-193
Cross Canyon—p. 213-214
Dolores River Canyon—p. 189-191
Penitente Canyon—p. 220
Powderhorn Wilderness Study Area—p. 186-188
Rio Grande River—p. 217
Sand Canyon—p. 217-218
Tabeguache Mountain Bike Trail—p. 200-203

CAMPGROUNDS

The following campgrounds are found in this area of Colorado. Please call the BLM office (listed following each campground's name) for reservations and information. Contact information for each BLM office is on pages 221-222 of Colorado.

Bradfield Campground, San Juan Resource Area
Cebolla Creek Campground, Gunnison Resource Area
Dolores Canyon Overlook Campground, San Juan
        Resource Area
Five Points Campground, Royal Gorge Resource Area/
        Arkansas Headwaters Resource Area
Hecla Junction Campground, Arkansas Headwaters
        Resource Area
Mill Creek Campground, Gunnison Resource Area
Mountain Sheep Point Campground, San Resource Area
Red Bridge Campground, Gunnison Resource Area
Ruby Mountain Campground, Arkansas Headwaters
        Resource Area
The Gate Campground, Gunnison Resource Area

1

POWDERHORN WILDERNESS STUDY AREA

You sense the vastness of this area as you trek upon its plateaus. These undulating plains have been recognized as the largest continuous sweep of alpine tundra in the lower 48. Despite the expansive alpine beauty, sculpted escarpments and jewel-like lakes, few travel this backcountry region. This is surprising. You would think that any place offering abundant water, dense forests, open grasslands, and lots of wildlife would be overrun with visitors. Actually, the majority of the thousands who visit this region annually are local Coloradans. Enjoy spectacular views of the San Juan, Elk and Sawatch mountain ranges from on top of the 12,000-foot Calf Creek Plateau. Beaver are numerous, and one can also expect to see elk, mule deer, bighorn sheep, black bear, and marmot. Mountain lion and bobcat also frequent the area but are not often seen.

HIKING

Allow three days to thoroughly enjoy a backpacking trip in this region. Be sure to self-register at the trailhead before entering the trail. By beginning at the Indian Creek Trailhead, a wide variety of options are available to you. Trout fishing can be enjoyed in three lakes, Powderhorn, Devils and Hidden, as well as in the nearly 67 miles of perennial streams. Most of the trails in this area follow streams. From Powderhorn Lakes and Devils Lake, a system of trails interconnect with U.S. Forest Service trails to the south and offer a virtual smorgasbord of possible loops.

Temperatures can range from minus 50°F in the winter to 95°F in the summer. Plan for frost and snow at any time of the year. Thunderstorms are common and are often a daily occurrence in the summer months. Expect strong winds when traveling above timberline—at or above 11,000 feet. If you head up onto Cannibal Plateau, take a moment to contemplate the fate of Alfred Packer's five expedition companions in 1984. Apparently, he dined upon them to stay alive while stranded at the western edge of the Plateau, thereby becoming notorious as a cannibal. To be safe, I suggest packing an extra meal or two along if you are traveling with someone else. The BLM and the U.S. Forest Service share the administration of this area.

MANAGEMENT
BLM Montrose District Office, 2465 South Townsend Avenue, Montrose, CO 81402; (303) 249-6049

LOCATION
Five miles northeast of Lake City and northeast of Durango and Highway 160 in the southwest quadrant of Colorado.

GETTING THERE
Take Highway 149 north from Lake City. Approximately three miles past the Cebolla Creek Road intersection and a settlement named Powderhorn, turn right onto a dirt road that will lead you ten miles up Indian Creek to the Indian Creek Trailhead. All trails that lead into the western half of the Powderhorn Primitive Area begin here.

CAMPING
The BLM maintains a campground at the confluence of Mill Gulch and Lake Fork roads. A camping fee is charged. Water and restrooms are available. Primitive camping is allowed anywhere within the wilderness study area.

PERMITS
Campfire permits are required.

MAPS
USGS topographic maps: Cannibal Plateau, Mineral Mountain, Powderhorn Lakes, Rudolph Hill

ADDITIONAL INFORMATION
Colorado BLM Wildlands, by Mark Pearson and John Fielder, published by Westcliffe Publishers, 2650 South Zuni Street, Englewood, CO 80110.

SEASON

Late spring to early fall is the best time to travel here.

TIP: The most serious damage to a cultural site occurs from innocent visitation. Staying on the trail will minimize the damage.

2

GUNNISON RESOURCE AREA ALPINE GULCH TRAIL

Remnants of historic cabins from turn-of-the-century mining claims and herds of deer and elk add a special flavor to this area.

BACKPACKING

Alpine Gulch Trail begins at 9,000 feet and travels approximately six miles up to Grassy Mountain Saddle, elevation 12,480 feet. The trail is moderately difficult with some steep sections. It follows a narrow canyon with steep cliffs up onto narrow ridges and eventually into a large alpine meadow. This trail is used very lightly even though the views of the San Juan Mountain Range are spectacular. There is also the option of hooking up with the Williams Creek Trail for a one-way shuttle-supported trip beginning at Henson Creek Road and ending up at the Mill Creek Camping Area near Lake San Cristobal.

MANAGEMENT

BLM Gunnison Resource Area, 216 North Colorado, Gunnison, CO 81410; (303) 641-0471

LOCATION

In the Gunnison Resource Area of southwest Colorado.

GETTING THERE

From Lake City, head two miles west on Henson Creek Road to the trailhead of the Alpine Gulch Trail. Parking is available at a wide pull-out on the north side of Henson Creek Road.

CAMPING

Camping is allowed anywhere within the wilderness area. Mill Creek Campground is located at the Williams Creek Trailhead. Restrooms and drinking water are available. A camping fee is charged.

PERMITS

Campfire permits are required.

MAPS

USGS topographic maps: Lake City, Lake San Cristobal
BLM surface maps: Silverton, Montrose

SEASON

The best time to visit this area is from late spring to early fall.

---

*TIP: Keep the development of social trails
in a campsite to a minimum.*

BEST OF THE STATE

DOLORES RIVER CANYON

The 104-mile stretch of the Dolores River takes boaters and adventurers through one of Colorado's most remote river environments. Fishing is excellent due to a superb trout fishery. Wildlife viewing opportunities include the peregrine falcon, bighorn sheep, turkey, hawk, eagle, and river otter. There are numerous opportunities for swimming and picnicking along the Dolores River Canyon Trail. This trail is also great for mountain biking.

MOUNTAIN BIKING

This is a very scenic high desert route that follows the Dolores River. Self-register at the trailhead before heading out on the trail. The trail is rated as intermediate for the first 11 miles and challenging for the remaining 15. It is marked, somewhat sporadically, with bicycle emblem signposts and follows an abandoned jeep trail. Turn around at the 11-mile marker if you are not using the shuttle option. The remaining 15 miles are rather dry and tedious. Most people just enjoy the first 11 miles and then turn around. Five river crossings must be made and these crossings are considered unsafe if the river is running above 200 cubic feet per second. Call the BLM San Juan Resource Area Hotline at (303) 882-7600 for flow information.

RIVER RUNNING

The Upper Dolores River is rated Class II to Class IV. From Bradfield Bridge to Slick Rock, the trip is 45 miles long and takes two to three days. From Slick Rock to Bedrock, the trip is 58 miles and takes two to three days. The Slick Rock River access site is privately owned and a fee is charged. See the owners at the Chuck Wagon Cafe, about one-quarter of a mile west of the Slick Rock Bridge, for permission and to pay the fee. Fire pans and porta-potties are required for all boaters.

The whitewater is fun. Even the names reflect the energy—how does the name "Snaggletooth Rapid" grab you? There is a river hotline during the season; for information phone (303) 882-7600.

MANAGEMENT

BLM San Juan Resource Area, Federal Building, 701 Camino Del Rio, Durango, CO 81301; (303) 247-4082

LOCATION

Located in southwestern Colorado—northwest of Cortez in the San Juan Resource Area

GETTING THERE

To get to the mountain bike trail, drive north on US 666 for 34 miles. Turn right just southeast of Dove Creek at a large brown sign that says "Public Lands Access, Dolores River Canyon and

Overlook." Follow the signs to Dolores Canyon river access and park at the provided area near the pump station. The length of the trail is 26 miles one way, requiring a shuttle if you wish to ride the entire route. For a shuttle, leave a vehicle to the parking area on road 13R. Take US 666 past Dove Creek. Head north on State Highway 141 to the Nicholas Wash sign, four miles past Slick Rock and Dolores River Bridge. Road 13R is a half-mile past the Nicholas Wash sign on the right.

River access is at Bradfield Bridge near the town of Cahone, at Dove Creek pump station, Slick Rock, and at Big Gypsum Valley downriver from Slick Rock and Bedrock Bridge.

CAMPING
Camping is allowed anywhere except on private land. Fires are allowed anywhere, but only if you pack in your own firewood. No campfire permit is necessary. Fire pans are required.

PERMITS
No permits are necessary.

MAPS
USGS topographic maps: Secret Canyon, Joe Davis Hill, Hamm Canyon, Dolores Canyon, The Glade, Horse Range Mesa, Anderson Mesa, Paradox

ADDITIONAL INFORMATION
Western Whitewater, From the Rockies to the Pacific, by Jim Cassady, Bill Cross and Fryar Calhoun, published by North Fork Press, Berkeley, CA; (800) 243-5522.

SEASON
The mountain biking season is from September to mid-October and in early June. In a normal rainfall year, the river crossings preclude safe mountain biking in the canyon. The river running season is from May through June. In wet years, it runs from mid-April through early July.

TIP: Apply a no-trace ethic everyday, everywhere.

4

BEAVER CREEK WILDERNESS STUDY AREA

This is a very wild and pristine area, only lightly impacted by man. The views are superb. Beaver Creek is a cold-water fishery and the fishing is quite good. Vegetation is quite varied, from aspen stands to pinyon pine to Douglas fir. Even the odd cactus or two may be spotted on the valley floor and away from the water. Wildlife includes black bear, bighorn sheep, mountain lion, mule deer, and the endangered peregrine falcon. If you are an amateur geologist, you will recognize the predominant rock formations of granite and migmatitic gneisses and schists.

HIKING

Trail Gulch offers a wonderful 20-mile round-trip excursion into the Beaver Creek Wilderness Study Area. Shortly after leaving the parking area, you come to a fork in the trail. Stay to the right along the ridge paralleling Beaver Creek. Water is generally available along the entire route, with one notable exception—for one mile from Big Saddle down to an excellent camp along the east fork of Beaver Creek. Pack sufficient water reserves just in case. The water is of fairly good quality, although the mineral content of East Beaver Creek continues to taste poor, even after filtering. Turn around at Meadow Camp alongside East Beaver Creek—approximately ten miles from the trailhead. It is possible to continue onward, but you will end your trip along Gold Camp Road between Rosemont and Clyde, which necessitates a car shuttle.

MANAGEMENT
BLM Royal Gorge Resource Area, 3170 East Main Street, P.O. Box 2200, Canon City, CO 81215-2200; (303) 275-0631

LOCATION
Approximately 40 miles southwest of Colorado Springs.

GETTING THERE

From Interstate 25 in Colorado Springs, take State Highway 115 south for approximately 34 miles. Just past Penrose, turn right on State Highway 50 and drive just over four miles. Turn right on County Road 67 (known locally as the Phantom Canyon Road). Continue for just under two miles to another right turn, County Road 123. After approximately one-quarter of a mile, turn left on Beaver Creek Road and drive another 11 miles to its end and the trailhead. Parking is available anywhere next to the fence.

CAMPING

Camping is permitted anywhere within the wilderness area.

PERMITS

No permits are necessary.

MAPS

USGS topographic maps: Phantom Canyon, Big Bull Mountain, Mount Pittsburg, Mount Big Chief

ADDITIONAL INFORMATION

Hikers Guide to Colorado, by Caryn and Peter Boddie, published by Falcon Press, P.O. Box 1718, Helena, MT 59624; (800) 582-2665.

SEASON

This is a prime area to visit all year round.

TIP: Travel or camp in small groups.

5

LITTLE BOOK CLIFFS WILD HORSE AREA

A great area to hike and explore, this area offers views of spectacular canyons, fascinating and intricate rock formations, colorful desert flora, and an opportunity to spot and observe wild horses.

HIKING

Spring Canyon is perhaps the most suitable access route into the area. From the trail, there are an almost infinite number of side canyon exploration opportunities. Although the trail itself is nine miles each way, many more miles may be added with side route and alternate route explorations. Navigation is not too difficult once you are off the route, but adequate map and compass skills are essential.

Canyons can become quickly choked with water, mud, rocks, and logs during a flash flood. Always be ready to head for high ground if there is rain. Clouds filling the upland areas are a sure sign that flash floods are an imminent possibility. There are a number of 1,000-foot-deep canyons that intersect the plateau area. The 1,500-foot escarpment known as the Book Cliffs create a spectacular geological contrast extending up into Utah. Wild horses frequent the area, and if you keep alert, you stand a good chance of spotting one or more before they spot you—and gallop off.

MANAGEMENT

BLM Grand Junction District Office, 2815 H Road, Grand Junction, CO 81506; (303) 244-3050

LOCATION

Ten miles northeast of Grand Junction.

GETTING THERE

From Grand Junction, take Interstate 70 east to the Cameo exit. Drive alongside the highway on the paved road, cross the Colorado River and pass the electrical generating plant. Follow the dirt road that takes you over an irrigation ditch into the canyon ahead. Numerous service roads crisscross the area, but you will remain on the correct one as long as you continue up into the canyon. The road will become progressively narrower and rougher, but should be okay for most vehicles. However, four-wheel-drive vehicles are recommended from this point on if the road is wet and muddy. From the power plant, it is only one-and-a-half miles or so to the trailhead for Spring Canyon.

CAMPING

Camp anywhere within the resource area. Flash floods are always a hazard in this area, so do not camp anywhere near a stream bed or on a narrow canyon floor.

PERMITS

No permits are necessary.

MAPS

USGS topographic maps: Cameo, Round Mountain

ADDITIONAL INFORMATION

Hikers Guide to Colorado, by Caryn and Peter Boddie, published by Falcon Press, P.O. Box 1718, Helena, MT 59624; (800) 582-2665.

SEASON

Spring is the best time to visit this area.

TIP: Never dig holes, trenches, or otherwise alter the campsite for convenience. The perfect campsite is found, not made.

Best of the State

6
Dominguez Canyon

Although there are few formal trails and travel within this area is moderate to strenuously difficult, this area of pristine wilderness canyons is not to be missed. Dominguez Canyon is the largest BLM wilderness study area in Colorado. You must allow at least several days for playful exploration. There is great ecological variety here, from deserts to forests, arid playas to inner canyons filled with verdant pools and water- falls, and canyon rock formations made of sandstone and Precambrian gneiss. Wildlife is also abundant and visible to those who keep a watchful eye out.

Hiking

It is possible to put together a long 20-mile backpacking trip across the length of Big Dominguez Canyon, but that requires a car shuttle between Bridgeport and Dominguez Campground. This is because as yet there is no way of cross- ing the Gunnison River at the campground, other than swim- ming— meaning you either get wet, very wet, or head back the way you came until BLM constructs a foot bridge across the river, which they hope to do soon. Water is available in the canyon bottom, but for traveling out of the canyon area, pack all the water you will need. Insect repellent is a must. In addition, there is at least one old mine shaft and possibly more in the area. Stay away from them as they are very hazardous.

Canoeing

With open canyon scenery and flat water, this section of the Gunnison River is very popular. The quiet, meandering river offers Class I and II boating alongside small ranches and apple orchards—creating a peaceful pastoral scene for relaxing and getting away from it all.

MANAGEMENT
BLM Grand Junction District Office, 2815 H Road, Grand Junction, CO 81506; (303) 244-3050

LOCATION
Approximately 20 miles south of Grand Junction.

GETTING THERE
Perhaps the best access to the canyons is via the Cactus Park Trailhead. Drive approximately nine miles south of Grand Junction on US 50 to Highway 141. Head west 9.5 miles to a sign for Cactus Park. Turn left and keep left at all forks in the road—this will keep you on the east side of Cactus Park. After approximately four miles, turn right at a junction and sign indicating "Dominguez Canyon Trail." After three-tenths of a mile turn left again at what should be another signed road for Dominguez Canyon Trail. Once you come to the wilderness study area boundary, you will need to leave your vehicle unless you have four-wheel-drive. The last two miles to the "official" trailhead can be mighty rough.

CAMPING
There is one organized campground, Dominguez Campground. As of this writing, however, there is no access from the campground across the Gunnison River into the Dominguez Canyon and the Bridgeport Trailhead. The only bridge crossing the river has been condemned, even for foot traffic, necessitating a long drive back around to the Cactus Park Trailhead. Camping is allowed anywhere within the wilderness study area. To get to the Dominguez Campground, take Highway 141 west past Cactus Park Road to Divide Road. Turn left on Divide Road and drive approximately eight miles to another left on Dominguez Conservation Area Road. It's another six miles to the campground.

PERMITS
No permits are necessary.

MAPS
USGS topographic maps: Dominguez, Escalante Forks, Good Point, Jacks Canyon, Keith Creek, Triangle Mesa
BLM surface maps: Delta
USFS maps: Uncompahgre National Forest Map

ADDITIONAL INFORMATION
Hikers Guide to Colorado, by Caryn and Peter Boddie, published by Falcon Press, P.O. Box 1718, Helena, MT 59624; (800) 582-2665.

SEASON
Spring and fall are the best times to visit.

BEST OF THE STATE

7

GUNNISON GORGE

Ute Park and, in particular, the Ute Trail, provide a spectacular introduction to a canyon wilderness area that is world-famous—the Black Canyon of the Gunnison—which lies just above this area. Listed as a gold-medal trout stream, and by all accounts a gold-medal whitewater river for kayaks, this area has been proposed for Wild and Scenic River status. Sandstone and shale are the predominant geological formations. Numerous faults and sequences of sedimentary rock strata are visible and quite stunning.

HIKING

The Ute Trail is known as the traditional route the Ute Indians used to ford the Gunnison River. Only 4.5 miles each way, the trail is an easy and enjoyable introduction to the canyon area. The Ute Trail is open to both horse and foot traffic. Fishing along the river is superb. The trailhead is a great spot for picnicking, with picnic tables that afford beautiful views both to the west, across the Uncompahgre Valley, and to the east, into the Gunnison Gorge. Garçon—table for two please.

There are three other trails within the canyon that are used primarily to access the river for rafting. These are: Bobcat Trail (one mile long), Duncan Trail (one mile long) and, preferred by rafters because it is less steep, Chukar Trail (just over one mile long).

WHITEWATER RAFTING

One of the most remote river experiences in Colorado can by enjoyed by rafting or kayaking the Gunnison Gorge Wilderness Study Area. Access to the river is by horseback or foot only via one of four steep trails in the area. The scenery in the gorge, as well as the abundant wildlife, are major attractions. Rapids range from Class II to Class IV. The trip is 14 miles long and can be made in one or two days.

MANAGEMENT
BLM Uncompahgre Resource Area, 2505 South Townsend Avenue, Montrose, CO 81401; (303) 249-6049

LOCATION
Ten miles north of Montrose.

GETTING THERE
To get to the Ute Trailhead from Delta, take US highway 50 south for eight miles (give or take a one-quarter of a mile or so) to a paved county road, Carnation. Head east to Carnation's end as it forms a T at County Road 62. Turn left and head northeast through the badlands until the road ends at Peach Valley Road. Turn left and drive four-tenths of a mile, keeping a vigilant eye out for a sign indicating the Ute Trail road to the right. From there, the next 2.5 miles are recommended only for four-wheel-drive vehicles. If you have one, drive to the trailhead. If you don't, park your car and walk—otherwise you will be picking up bits and pieces of your car all the way back to the nearest road.

CAMPING
There are three established campsites at Ute Park especially for river runners. Backpackers and fishermen may want to explore less crowded accommodations away from the river's edge or up further into the canyon. Camping is allowed anywhere, but minimum-impact camping rules dictate no camping within 200 feet of the river. Along the canyon itself, there are limited camping opportunities for those who are boating. Porta-potties must be used by all boaters and fire pans are required.

PERMITS
No permits are necessary.

MAPS
USGS topographic maps: Black Ridge, Red Rock Canyon, Lazear
BLM surface maps: Paonia, Gunnison Gorge River

ADDITIONAL INFORMATION
Hikers Guide to Colorado, by Caryn and Peter Boddie, published by Falcon Press, P.O. Box 1718, Helena, MT 59624; (800) 582-2665.
Western Whitewater, From the Rockies to the Pacific, by Jim Cassady, Bill Cross and Fryar Calhoun, published by North Fork Press, Berkeley, CA; (800) 243-5522.

SEASON
Spring through fall is the best time to visit.

---

*TIP: Respect public and private property
including all trail signs and closure signs.
Leave gates open or closed as you find them.*

BEST OF THE STATE

TABEGUACHE MOUNTAIN BIKE TRAIL

The Tabeguache Mountain Bike Trail winds through both public and private land for 142 miles, connecting Montrose and Grand Junction. The trail winds through the Uncompahgre Plateau, where evidence of man's presence dates back over 10,000 years. More recently, the plateau has seen cattle grazing, sheep herding, mining and lumber ventures, and evidence of these past and present uses dot the landscape. It is essential that modern and historic resources are not disturbed, so tread lightly and leave everything as you found it.

This magnificent mountain bike trail, one of the finest in the United States, is a result of a combined effort involving the

---

BLM, the U.S. Forest Service, and dozens of volunteers all coordinated by the Colorado Plateau Mountain Bike Trail Association. Their goal is to create a network of mountain bike trails that will allow mountain bikers to travel off-road from Aspen, Colorado to the Grand Canyon. If you are interested in helping out or want to learn more, contact the COPMOBA at (303) 241-9561.

MOUNTAIN BIKING

The Tabeguache Trail begins in Shavano Valley, eight miles west of Montrose. The trail winds and weaves its way through canyons, mesas and highlands of the Uncompahgre Plateau, ending in "No Thoroughfare Canyon" a few miles west of Grand Junction. The entire route is well marked with brown fiberglass posts every half-mile and at all junctions. If the route is wet, some sections may be impassable. If you plan on having a support vehicle, it is possible (but very difficult) for a high-clearance, four-wheel-drive vehicle to travel all but the single-track sections of the route. Most of the trail is routed through remote and virtually unused BLM and U.S. Forest Service land. A good working knowledge of map and compass reading is a requisite. Water is available, although not abundant, along the route—look for drainages and established campgrounds. All water must be treated before drinking. Campfires are okay with the use of a fire pan. All charcoal must be packed out.

MANAGEMENT
•BLM Grand Junction District Office, 2815 H Road, Grand Junction, CO 81506; (303) 244-3050
•BLM Montrose District Office, 2465 South Townsend Avenue, Montrose, CO 81401; (303) 249-6049

LOCATION
The Tabeguache Trail runs between Grand Junction and Montrose, west of Highway 50 and south of Interstate 70.

GETTING THERE
Montrose Trailhead: Drive six miles west of Montrose on Spring Creek Road. Turn right at 58.75 Road and continue for approximately two miles to Kiowa Road. Turn left on Kiowa Road and cross the valley to the Shavano Valley Road. The

Tabeguache Trail begins as a jeep road near the north end of the Shavano Valley Road.

Grand Junction Trailhead: Drive west on Grand Junction Avenue to Highway 340. Turn left on Monument Road. Continue to the signed trailhead for the Tabeguache Trail.

CAMPING
Camping is allowed anywhere along the trail in designated camping areas or on public land. Stay off private property.

PERMITS
No permits are necessary.

MAPS
USGS topographic maps: Hoovers Corner, Davis Point, Ute, Starvation Point, Windy Point, Keith Creek, Casto Reservoir, Triangle Mesa, Island Mesa, Dry Creek Basin, Antone Spring, Moore Mesa, Kelso Point, Snipe Mountain, Uncompahgre Butte, Jacks Canyon, Whitewater, Grand Junction
BLM surface maps: Grand Junction, Delta, Nulca
USFS maps: Uncompahgre National Forest

ADDITIONAL INFORMATION
•COPMOBA, P.O. Box 4602, Grand Junction, CO 81502; (303) 241-9561
•*The Tabeguache Trail Map and Trail Log* can be obtained from the BLM, U.S. Forest Service or COPMOBA.

SEASON
May through October is the best time to ride the entire trail. Lower elevation sections may be pedaled all year as snow doesn't affect them. Bikers are warned, however, that September and October are prime hunting seasons and if you choose to pedal the route (and I recommend heartily that you don't!), you must wear blazing orange colors. A myopic hunter could mistake you for a deer that has recently taken up bicycling. Of course, good hunters, and there are many, won't shoot at anything unless they are absolutely sure what it is and have a certain and clean kill shot. There are, however, far too many city-bound yo-yos who head out to the mountains for one week every year, armed with a rifle and eager to shoot anything that moves in the hope that it may be what they have a

hunting license for..."What, you mean deer don't wear lycra and ride Specialized bikes? Well I'll be damned!"

KOKOPELLI'S TRAIL

The Kokopelli's Trail meanders its way through desert sandstone canyons and sagebrush prairies that parallel the Colorado River from just west of Grand Junction, Colorado to Moab, Utah. This 128-mile mountain biking trail offers a remote and scenic adventure with an interesting combination of easy and very challenging trail segments. As with the Tabeguache Trail, this trail's existence is a direct result of the hard work and cooperative effort put forth by the BLM, the U.S. Forest Service, the Colorado Plateau Mountain Bike Trail Association and numerous volunteers. It is because of the COPMOBA's effort in developing this trail that I include it within this chapter on Colorado, even though the majority of the ride lies within the state of Utah.

MOUNTAIN BIKING

The trail begins at the Loma Boat Launch near Grand Junction, Colorado and winds for 128 miles through sandstone and shale canyons until it reaches Moab, Utah. The entire route is well marked with brown fiberglass posts every half mile and at all junctions. If the route is wet, some sections may be impassable. If you plan on having a support vehicle, it is possible but very difficult for a high-clearance, four-wheel-drive vehicle to travel all but the single-track sections of the route.

Most of the trail is routed through remote and virtually unused BLM land. A good working knowledge of map and compass reading is a requisite. Water is not readily available along the route. The few water resupply points that exist are spread far apart. Be sure to carry all the water that you will need with you for each day—one gallon per person minimum. Get in the habit of topping off at all available water sources. All water must be treated before drinking. Campfires are okay with the use of a fire pan. All charcoal must be packed out.

MANAGEMENT
•BLM Grand Junction District Office, 2815 H Road, Grand Junction, CO 81506; (303) 244-3050
•BLM Grand Resource Area, P.O. Box M, Sand Flats Road, Moab, UT 84532; (801) 259-8193

LOCATION
The trail begins approximately 15 miles west of Grand Junction and follows the Colorado River all the way to Moab, Utah.

GETTING THERE
To get to the Loma Boat Launch near Grand Junction, Colorado, take the Loma exit 15 on Interstate 70, cross over the Interstate to the south and go left on the gravel road for three-tenths of a mile. The trail begins at the parking lot for the Loma Boat Launch.

CAMPING
Camp anywhere along the trail in designated camping areas or on public land. Stay off of private property.

PERMITS
No permits are necessary.

MAPS
USGS topographic maps: Colorado: Mack, Ruby Canyon
Colorado/Utah: Bitter Creek Well, Westwater
Utah: Agate, Big Triangle, Cisco Northeast, Dewey, Blue Chief Mesa, Fisher Valley, Mount Waas, Warner Lake, Rill Creek, Moab Southeast
BLM surface maps: Grand Junction, Westwater, Moab

ADDITIONAL INFORMATION
•COPMOBA, P.O. Box 4602, Grand Junction, CO 81502; (303) 241-9561.
•*Mountain Bike Adventures in the Four Corners Region,* by Michael McCoy, published by The Mountaineers, Seattle, WA.

SEASON
March through May and September through November are the best times to ride the trail. Summer is possible, but it can get almost too hot to handle in the lower elevations.

1

NORTHWESTERN COLORADO

GEORGETOWN BIGHORN VIEWING SITE
wildlife observation

Jointly managed by the city of Georgetown, the BLM and the Colorado Division of Wildlife, this developed interpretive site overlooks an area that is the habitat for bighorn sheep nearly every month of the year. Best viewing is in the fall, winter and spring. A viewing tower offers excellent opportunities to spot bighorn. Located near the town of Georgetown and Interstate 70.

For more information: Contact the BLM Craig District Office, 455 Emerson Street, Craig, CO 81625-1129; (303) 824-8261.

RABBIT VALLEY RESEARCH NATURAL AREA
hiking, dinosaur fossils

Often referred to as the "trail through time," this interpretive trail is a unique and very special opportunity for a family to enjoy a close-up view of an area that has been excavated for dinosaur fossils since 1982. There are numerous other field sites nearby and are well worth the time if you are interested in prehistoric time and the Jurassic Age. From Grand Junction, drive west on Interstate 70 for approximately 30 miles to the Rabbit Valley exit. Turn right and park on the southwest side of the frontage road. Walk north on the dirt road to the signed trailhead where brochures are available to help guide you along.

For more information: Contact the BLM Grand Junction District Office, 2815 H Road, Grand Junction, CO 81501; (303) 244-3050 or the Museum of Western Colorado at (303) 243-DINO—what else did you expect?

DEEP CREEK
hiking, camping, fishing, spelunking, wildlife observation

Deep Creek is a relatively small area, 2,380 acres, but well regarded for its scenic, deep-walled limestone and sandstone canyon carved over 2,000 feet into the side of White River Plateau. There are a number of limestone caves for spelunking adventures. Fishing is primarily for trout.

For more information: Contact the BLM Glenwood Springs Resource Area, P.O. Box 1009, Glenwood Springs, CO 81602; (303) 945-2341.

IRISH CANYON
hiking, backpacking, camping, mountain biking, wildlife observation, archaeological sites

This scenic area is remote with few people visiting the area. Twelve of the 22 geological formations found in the eastern Uinta Mountains are present here. Although there are no developed or maintained trails, hiking and mountain biking opportunities are excellent. Several miles of primitive dirt roads in the area provide challenges to the mountain biker in this colorful, semi-arid region. Hikers will find cross-country routes up to Limestone Ridge to the west with expansive views of the region. There are also opportunities to explore the colorful badlands of Vermillion Creek to the east. A small campground in the canyon has three campsites, and a picnic site with ancient rock art is located at the south end of Irish Canyon. Water is scarce—snowmelt is often the only available natural source. Pack all the water you will need. The best time to visit is from fall to spring. Summer is often hot and dry. October and November is big game hunting season so wearing blazing orange from head to toe is a must (personally, I would just stay out of the area during that time unless you are hunting). Camping is allowed anywhere, however the area is easily impacted mandating the use of backpacking stoves instead of fires. Wildlife is abundant and includes mule deer, antelope, elk, mountain lion, coyote, fox, golden eagle, bald eagle, vulture and prairie falcon. To get there, take State Route 318 north from US 40 at Maybell. Drive approximately 41 miles to Moffat County Road 10N, turn north and continue for four miles to Irish Canyon.

For more information: Contact the BLM Little Snake Resource Area,

---

1280 Industrial Avenue, Craig, CO 81625; (303) 824-4441.
USGS topographic maps: Irish Canyon, Big Joe Basin

POWDERHORN WILDERNESS STUDY AREA
hiking, backpacking, wildlife observation

The vastness of the Powderhorn region often overcomes those who trek upon the plateaus as these undulating plains have been recognized as the largest continuous sweep of alpine tundra in the lower 48. Despite the expansive alpine beauty with contrasting sculpted escarpments and jewel-like lakes, few travel this backcountry region. This is surprising, as you would think that anywhere offering abundant water, dense forests, open grasslands, and abundant wildlife would be overrun with visitors. But the majority of the thousands who visit this region annually are local Coloradans. Enjoy spectacular views of the San Juan, Elk and Sawatch ranges from the top of the 12,000-foot Calf Creek Plateau. Beaver are numerous and one should expect to see elk, mule deer, bighorn sheep, black bear, and marmot. Mountain lion and bobcat also frequent the area but are not often seen.

•**See also Best of the State, page 186**•
For more information: Contact the BLM Montrose District Office, 2465 South Townsend Avenue, Montrose, CO 81402; (303) 249-6049.

CROSS MOUNTAIN WILDERNESS STUDY AREA
hiking, backpacking, camping, fishing, wildlife observation

Although there are no designated trails within this area, Cross Mountain offers the willing explorer super opportunities to wander through the plateau country of the eastern-most extension of the Uinta Mountains. Views into the 1,000-foot-deep Cross Mountain Canyon are breathtaking. This area has been recommended for wilderness designation. The best times to visit are in late spring and in the fall. Summer can be uncomfortably hot and dry and winter can be bitingly cold. There are a number of archaeological sites within the area and the visitor will enjoy observing bighorn sheep and numerous raptors that at times seem to own the sky. Wildflowers are spectacular in late spring and early summer. Elk, deer, antelope, mountain lion and coyote all frequent this area, though the mountain lion will most likely see you more often than

---

you hope to see it. Water is scarce so carry all that you will need. Rattlesnakes are abundant—not a problem if you stay alert, but a definite problem if you are in the habit of reaching under rock piles or anywhere your eye can't clearly see. Use common sense! The best access is via the National Park service parking area at the mouth of Cross Mountain Canyon. To get there, take US Highway 40 to Deerlodge Park Road, approximately 16 miles west of Maybell. Drive along Deerlodge, skirting the west side of Cross Mountain to the parking area. The best access to the south rim of the canyon is by hiking the first drainage south of the parking area.

For more information: Contact the BLM Little Snake Resource Area, 1280 Industrial Avenue, Craig, CO 81625; (803) 824-4441.
USGS topographic maps: Lone Mountain, Cross Mountain Canyon, Twelve-Mile Mesa, Peck Mesa
BLM surface maps: Canyon of Lodore, Rangely

BULL CANYON, WILLOW CREEK AND SKULL CREEK WILDERNESS STUDY AREA
hiking, backpacking, camping, wildlife observation

Numerous side canyons await exploring, offering the visitor a collage of colorful geological formations. Views from high up are super and wildlife viewing opportunities are good. While spring and fall are the best seasons to visit, they are not without their individual challenges—cedar gnats in the spring (wear plenty of insect repellent) and hunters in the fall (wear plenty of blaze orange and do nothing to imitate a deer). The area is perhaps best suited for hiking. Although backpacking is possible, rough terrain will create some difficulties. There are no maintained trails in this region. Water is scarce, pack in all that you will need. Private property is interspersed throughout the region. Respect signed closures and stay off private land. Cattle is run in parts of this region—leave cattle gates as you find them. To get to Bull Canyon, drive east from Dinosaur on US 40 to the Dinosaur National Monument turnoff, approximately one mile. Drive 3.5 miles up Harper's Corner Road to Plug Hat Rock picnic area and overlook or continue on for three miles to the Escalante overlook and parking area.

For more information: Contact the BLM White River Resource Area, 73455 Highway 64, P.O. Box 928, Meeker, CO 81641; (303) 878-3601.
USGS topographic maps: Plug Hat Rock, Snake John Reef
BLM surface maps: Rangely

Rangely Loop Trail
mountain biking, camping, archaeological sites, wildlife observation

Located in the remote backcountry, south of Rangely, Colorado, this 177-mile-long trail traverses through changing landscapes of harsh desert, stark buttes, high ridges, mountains, and cool forests. There is a variety of climates and country and spectacular vistas from high points to be enjoyed along the entire route. The best times to ride are spring and fall. Gnats can be a problem in the spring. There are springs along the way, however, it is suggested that you pack all the water you will need. Camping is permitted anywhere on BLM lands.

For more information: Contact the BLM White River Resource Area, 73455 Highway 64, P.O. Box 928, Meeker, CO 81641; (303) 878-3601.
USGS topographic maps: Rangely, Water Canyon, Banta Ridge, Texas Creek, Dragon, Davis Canyon, East Evacuation Creek, Baxter Pass, Douglas Pass, Calf Canyon, Brushy Point, Razorback Ridge, Black Cabin Gulch, Sagebrush Hill, Calamity Ridge, Gillam Draw
BLM surface maps: Rangely, Douglas Pass

Black Ridge Canyons Wilderness Study Area
hiking, backpacking, camping, wildlife observation, mountain biking

Located near Colorado National Monument, the Black Ridge Canyons Wilderness Study Area offers an opportunity for the visitor to explore a varied and spectacular desert canyon country. Rattlesnake Canyon in particular is known for its geological faults and numerous arches. Wildlife is abundant and includes desert bighorn sheep, deer, black bear, mountain lion, and many species of raptor including the golden eagle. The best seasons to visit are spring and fall. For an excellent introduction to the area, hike the Pollock Canyon Trail which is not only the most accessible of all the trails in the region, but also the only trail which will guide you through the second largest concentration of natural arches in the world. To reach the trailhead, drive west from Grand Junction on Interstate 70 to the Fruita exit. Bear south on Highway 340 towards the Colorado National Monument. Just after crossing the Colorado River, turn right on King's View Road. At the fork in the road, bear left and follow the signs for Pollock Canyon. After approximately three miles, the road dips into Flume Creek gully, just before reaching the Colorado River. Turn left here on the road and follow it three-tenths of a mile to the trailhead. Mountain biking may be enjoyed on many of the jeep roads that provide access to the area.

Resources: *Western Whitewater, From the Rockies to the Pacific,* by Jim Cassady, Bill Cross, and Fryar Calhoun, published by North Fork Press, Berkeley, CA; (800) 243-5522.

For more information: Contact the BLM Grand Junction District Office, 2815 H Road, Grand Junction, CO 81506; (303) 244-3050.

USGS topographic maps: Mack

EAGLE RIVER
canoeing, rafting, biking, wildlife observation, fishing

With an overall whitewater rating of Class IV and located just of Interstate 70 at the town of Wolcott, the Eagle River flows through colorful canyons of red, yellow and pale brown sandstone dotted with pinyon, juniper and cottonwood. The river trip is approximately eight miles long and takes three to four hours. The BLM point of access is in Wolcott. Much of the river runs through private land and trespassing on the river edge is prohibited. Take-out is on public land once again at Eagle City Park.

Resources: *Western Whitewater, From the Rockies to the Pacific,* by Jim Cassady, Bill Cross, and Fryar Calhoun, published by North Fork Press, Berkeley, CA; (800) 243-5522.

For more information: Contact the BLM Glenwood Springs Resource Area, P.O. Box 1009, Glenwood Springs, CO 81602; (303) 945-2341.

USGS topographic maps: Edwards, Wolcott, Eagle

RUBY CANYON
biking, rafting, kayaking, canoeing, wildlife observation

The beautiful Ruby Canyon of the Lower Colorado River provides excellent flat-water trips for canoeists, rafters and kayakers. In fact, the 25-mile stretch from the Loma Boat Launch, just below Grand Junction, to the Westwater Ranger Station take-out in Utah offers some of the best flat-water canoeing in the state. Along the way, you will gain access to seven spectacular canyons within the Black Ridge Canyons

Wilderness Study Area. This region contains the largest concentration of natural sandstone arches in Colorado. Adventurous and experienced rafters and kayakers can make this the
first leg of a journey into Utah's famed Westwater Canyon—
but you must be an experienced boater and you must have a
permit once past the Westwater Ranger Station! Be prepared
for stiff upstream winds which can slow travel time consider-
ably.

For more information: Contact the BLM Grand Junction District
Office, 2815 H Road, Grand Junction, CO 81506; (303) 244-3050.
USGS topographic maps: Mack, Ruby Canyon, Bitter Creek Well,
Westwater Southwest

LITTLE YAMPA CANYON
*fishing, canoeing, rafting, hiking, backpacking, mountain
biking, wildlife observation*

This 53-mile segment of the Yampa River is a super flat-
water canoeing river. The river offers excellent spring float
trips and an outstanding opportunity for viewing a wide
variety of wildlife. The Yampa Valley Mountain Bike Trail is
being developed at this time and completion is anticipated
sometime in late 1993. Contact the local BLM office for up-to-
date information.

Resources: *Western Whitewater, From the Rockies to the Pacific,* by
Jim Cassady, Bill Cross, and Fryar Calhoun, published by North Fork
Press, Berkeley, CA; (800) 243-5522.
For more information: Contact the BLM Little Snake Resource Area,
1280 Industrial Avenue, Craig, CO 81625; (303) 824-4441.
USGS topographic maps: Craig, Round Bottom, Horse Gulch,
Juniper Hot Springs, Juniper Mountain, Maybell, Sunbeam, Peck
Mesa, Cross Mountain Canyon, 12-mile Mesa
BLM surface maps: Meeker, Canyon of Lodore, Rangely

UPPER COLORADO RIVER
*whitewater rafting, canoeing, kayaking, fishing, horseback
riding, wildlife observation, hiking, mountain biking*

This 50-mile segment of the Colorado River offers Class II
to III whitewater recreation for boaters. It lies within two hours
of the major population concentration of Colorado and consequently receives heavy use. Located near the town of

Kremmling, the Pumphouse recreation site and campground is the major put-in spot, although there are many others along the river.

For more information: Contact the BLM Kremmling Resource Area, 1116 Park Avenue, P.O. Box 68, Kremmling, CO 80459; (303) 724-3437; or the BLM Glenwood Springs Resource Area, P.O. Box 1009, Glenwood Springs, CO 81602; (303) 945-2341.

USGS topographic maps: Kremmling, Radium, McCoy, State Bridge, Blue Hill, Burns North, Burns South, Dotsero

BLM surface maps: Vail

> *TIP: Drive only on established roads and trails
> or in designated open areas where travel
> will not result in lasting impact upon the land.*

COLORADO BY REGION

2

SOUTHWESTERN COLORADO

ALPINE LOOP

Backcountry Byway for off-road vehicle use, mountain biking, wildlife observation

The Alpine Loop is designated as a National Backcountry Byway. A 52-mile circuit of mostly dirt roads, the route is a high-altitude experience, climbing through two 12,000-foot passes, Cinnamon and Engineer. An endurance test for even the most savy rider. Much of the pedal will offer excellent views of the high-alpine tundra and spectacular scenery of the rugged San Juan Mountains. Wildlife viewing is for ptarmigan, marmots, pikas, elk, deer, blue grouse, goshawks, Clark's nutcrackers and more.

For more information: Contact the BLM Gunnison Resource Area, 216 North Colorado, Gunnison, CO 81401; (303) 641-0471.
BLM San Juan Resource Area, Federal Building, 701 Camino Del Rio, Durango, CO 81301; (303) 247-4082.

ANASAZI HERITAGE CENTER AND RESOURCE MANAGEMENT AREA
hiking, camping, archaeological sites, wildlife observation, rock hounding, mountain biking

This 156,000-acre area near the town of Dolores is managed by the BLM in order to "maintain its rich cultural and natural resource diversity for a variety of land uses while allowing visitors to explore the area largely on their own," according to the BLM mandate. Although archaeological artifacts and ruins abound, a greater and more educated insight into the Anasazi culture may be enjoyed by experiencing the outstanding interpretive exhibits, educational programs and outreach efforts of the Anasazi Heritage Center museum and visitor center. This striking facility receives over 40,000 visits annually. Call (303) 882-4811 for more information. The center also serves as a regional research laboratory for continuing archaeological investigations in the Four Corners region—Colorado, New Mexico, Arizona and Utah.

For more information: Contact the BLM San Juan Resource Area, Federal Building, 701 Camino Del Rio, Durango, CO 81301; (303) 247-4082.

CROSS CANYON
hiking, backpacking, archaeological sites

Cross Canyon offers the hiker the very unique experience of walking back through time among the small Anasazi Indian cliff dwellings and ruined pueblos of the 12th and 13th centuries. Much of the hiking follows a scenic route along a cottonwood and willow dominated riparian area at the base of Cross Canyon which cuts through the surrounding plateau country. Water is available from Cross Creek which runs year-round. Wildflowers are spectacular during the late spring and early summer—just the season you want to avoid because of the obnoxious cedar gnats. The best times to visit is in early spring, late summer, or early fall. Winter is accessible depending on the weather conditions.

Trails disappear quickly and good topographic map-reading and orienteering skills are mandatory. The best trailhead for access is reachable only by high-clearance or four-wheel-drive vehicles. From Pleasant View, turn west on

Pleasant Valley Road, near the radio tower. Look for the sign directing you to Lowry Ruin. Drive for 5.5 miles to an intersection and turn left toward Hovenweep. After approximately 24 miles bear right at a sign directing you towards Cross Canyon. It is seven rough miles from here to the trailhead. Park at the Wilderness Study Area boundary.

Camping is allowed within the area, but not at archaeological or historical sites. Fires can be built if the fire rings are dismantled. I would heartily recommend going without a fire and using only a stove. Water is available from Cross Creek, but it must be treated. While the BLM encourages visitation, much of the policing of the area is left up to each of us individually. Report any and all signs of vandalism to the BLM. Look but don't touch is the rule. Take pictures and memories; leave only footprints.

For more information: Contact the BLM San Juan Resource Area, Federal Building, 701 Camino Del Rio, Durango, CO 81301; (303) 247-4082.
USGS topographic maps: Ruin Point, Papoose Canyon, Ruin Canyon, Champagne Spring
BLM surface maps: Bluff, Cortez, Dove Creek

DOLORES RIVER CANYON
mountain biking, rafting, kayaking, canoeing, biking, wildlife observation, camping, backpacking

The 104-mile stretch of the Dolores River guides boaters and adventurers through one of Colorado's most remote river environments. Trout fishing is excellent due to a super trout fishery here. Wildlife viewing opportunities include the peregrine falcon, bighorn sheep, turkey, hawk, eagle and river otter. There are numerous opportunities for mountain biking, swimming and picnicking along the Dolores River Canyon Trail.

•**See also Best of the State, page 189**•
For more information: Contact the BLM San Juan Resource Area, Federal Building, 701 Camino Del Rio, Durango, CO 81301; (303) 247-4082.

DOMINGUEZ CANYON
hiking, backpacking, camping, wildlife observation

Although there are no trails, and travel within this area is of moderate to strenuously difficult, this area of wilderness canyons demands at least several days for playful exploration. The Dominguez Canyon is the largest BLM wilderness study area in Colorado. There is a large variety of ecological lands here, from desert to forest, arid playas to inner canyons filled with verdant pools and waterfalls, and canyon rock formations made of sandstone and Precambrian gneiss. Wildlife is also abundant and visible to those who keep a watchful eye out.

•**See also Best of the State, page 196**•
For more information: Contact the BLM Grand Junction District Office, 2815 H Road, Grand Junction, CO 81506; (303) 244-3050.

GUNNISON GORGE
hiking, backpacking, horseback riding, camping, fishing, rafting, kayaking

Ute Park and, in particular, the Ute Trail, provides a spectacular introduction to a canyon wilderness area that is world famous—the Black Canyon of the Gunnison—which lies just above this area. Listed as a gold-medal trout stream and by all accounts, a gold-medal whitewater river for rafts and kayaks, the area has been proposed for Wild and Scenic River status. Sandstone and shale are the predominant geological formations. Numerous faults and sequences of sedimentary rock strata (love that Geology 101 college class) are visible and quite stunning.

•**See also Best of the State, page 198**•
For more information: Contact the BLM Uncompahgre Resource Area, 2505 South Townsend Avenue, Montrose, CO 81401; (303) 249-6049.

LITTLE BOOK CLIFFS WILD HORSE AREA
hiking, backpacking, camping, wildlife observation

A great area to hike and explore, this area offers views of spectacular canyons, fascinating and intricate rock formations, colorful desert flora, and an opportunity to spot and observe wild horses.

Colorado

•**See also Best of the State, page 194**•
For more information: Contact the BLM Grand Junction District
Office, 2815 H Road, Grand Junction, CO 81506; (303) 244-3050.

TABEGUACHE MOUNTAIN BIKE TRAIL
mountain biking, hiking, backpacking

The Tabeguache Mountain Bike Trail winds through both
public and private land for 142 miles, connecting Montrose
and Grand Junction. The trail winds through the Uncompahgre
Plateau, where evidence of man's presence dates back over
10,000 years. More recently, the plateau has seen cattle grazing, sheep herding, mining and lumber ventures, and evidence
of these past and present uses dot the landscape—it is essential that modern and historical resources are not disturbed, so
tread lightly and leave everything as you found it.

This magnificent mountain bike trail, one of the finest in
the United States, is a result of a combined effort involving the
BLM, the U.S. Forest Service and dozens of volunteers, all
coordinated by the Colorado Plateau Mountain Bike Trail
Association. Their goal is to create a network of mountain bike
trails that will allow mountain bikers to travel off-road from
Aspen, Colorado to the Grand Canyon. If you are interested in
helping out or want to learn more, contact the COPMOBA at
(303) 241-9561.

•**See also Best of the State, page 200**•
For more information: Contact the BLM Grand Junction District
Office, 2815 H Road, Grand Junction, CO 81506; (303) 244-3050.
BLM Montrose District Office, 2465 South Townsend Avenue,
Montrose, CO 81401; (303) 249-6049
COPMOBA, P.O. Box 4602, Grand Junction, CO 81502; (303) 241-
9561

KOKOPELLI'S TRAIL
mountain biking, hiking, backpacking

The Kokopelli's Trail meanders its way through desert
sandstone canyons and sagebrush prairies that parallel the
Colorado River from just west of Grand Junction, Colorado to
Moab, Utah. The 128-mile mountain biking trail offers a remote
and scenic adventure with an interesting combination of easy
to very challenging trail segments. As with the Tabeguache

Trail, this trail's existence is a direct result of the hard work and cooperative effort put forth by the BLM, U.S. Forest Service, the Colorado Plateau Mountain Bike Trail Association and numerous volunteers.

•**See also Best of the State, page 203**•

For more information: Contact the BLM Grand Junction District Office, 2815 H Road, Grand Junction, CO 81506; (303) 244-3050.
BLM Grand Resource Area, P.O. Box M, Sand Flats Road, Moab, UT 84532; (801) 259-8193
COPMOBA, P.O. Box 4602, Grand Junction, CO 81502; (303) 241-9561

RIO GRANDE RIVER

hiking, backpacking, canoeing, rafting, wildlife observation

The Colorado section of the Rio Grande River offers easy floating opportunities for rafters and canoeists. Thirty miles long, the river flows through sagebrush and pinyon pine tucked in among low-lying rock formations. Deer, elk, beaver, muskrat, golden eagle, and a variety of falcons may be seen. The Sangre de Cristo Range provides a spectacular and scenic backdrop to the solitude of the float. A word of caution: Before you become too engrossed in the tranquility, keep in mind that once across the border into New Mexico, the Rio Grande becomes quite turbulent and a little less forgiving. Only experienced rafters and kayakers should venture beyond the Colorado border. The Colorado section usually takes about two days to float. Put-in is at La Sauses Bridge, ten miles east, 8.5 miles north and one-half mile east again from Manassa, off Highway 142. Take-out is at Lobatos Bridge, 15 miles east of Antonito on Country Road G.

For more information: Contact the BLM San Luis Resource Area, 1921 State Street, Alamosa, CO 81101; (719) 589-4975.
USGS topographic maps: Misito Reservoir, Kiowa Hill, Ski Valley Ranch

SAND CANYON

hiking, backpacking, mountain biking, archaeological sites, wildlife observation

Sand Canyon is an excellent area for exploring sandstone canyons and slickrock with numerous hidden Anasazi Indian cliff dwellings. Good views from high up also may be enjoyed and there are excellent opportunities to observe wildlife including cottontail rabbit, coyote and deer. Raptors are abundant in the skies above. Of special note, the Crow Canyon Archaeological Center performs excavation, in conjunction with the BLM, and offers programs that allow for public participation in the excavation process. If you are interested, contact the Crow Canyon Archaeological Center, 23390 County Road K, Cortez, CO 81321; (303) 565-8975.

To get to Sand Canyon, head south from Cortez on US 666 for 2.5 miles to McElmo Canyon Road. Watch for signs indicating the airport and Hovenweep National Monument. Turn right and after 12 miles the road turns to dirt and crosses McElmo Creek. After approximately one-half mile, you will come to a parking area for the Sand and East Rock Canyon. Access to the BLM site is on the right.

For more information: Contact the BLM San Juan Resource Area, Federal Building, 701 Camino Del Rio, Durango, CO 81301; (303) 247-4082.
USGS topographic maps: Battle Rock, Woods Canyon
BLM surface maps: Cortez

TIP: Camping or building fires near cultural sites can cause serious and irreparable damage.

COLORADO BY REGION

3

SOUTHEASTERN COLORADO

ARKANSAS RIVER/ARKANSAS HEADWATERS RECREATION AREA

rafting, kayaking, canoeing, camping, fishing, wildlife observation, rock hounding, picnicking

This national whitewater river, located near Canon City, lies within a two to three-hour drive of over two million Colorado residents—is it any wonder it gets so much use? Still, the 80-mile segment offers challenging whitewater recreation for anyone who loves to kayak, raft or whitewater canoe through rapids rated up to Class V. The river is extremely scenic and trout fishing is quite good. Put-ins and take-outs are spread out all along Highways 24 and 50 near the towns of Leadville, Buena Vista, Salida, Vallie Bridge, Parkdale, Canon City, and Pueblo.

Resources: *Western Whitewater, From the Rockies to the Pacific,* by Jim Cassady, Bill Cross, and Fryar Calhoun, published by North Fork Press, Berkeley, CA; (800) 243-5522.

For more information: Contact the BLM Royal Gorge Resource Area, 3170 East Main Street, P.O. Box 2200, Canon City, CO 81215-2200; (303) 275-0631.

USGS topographic maps: Leadville South, Granite, South Peak, Buena Vista, Poncha Springs, Cameron Mountain, Howard, Cotopaxi, Royal Gorge, Pueblo Reservoir

BEAVER CREEK WILDERNESS STUDY AREA

hiking, backpacking, wildlife observation, fishing

This is a very wild and pristine area, only lightly impacted by man. The views are superb and the fishing is quite good. Beaver Creek is itself a good cold-water fishery. Vegetation is quite varied, from aspen stands to pinyon pine and Douglas fir. Even the odd cactus or two may be spotted on the valley floor and away from the water. Wildlife includes black bear,

---

bighorn sheep, mountain lion, mule deer, and the endangered peregrine falcon.

•See also Best of the State, page 192•
For more information: Contact the BLM Royal Gorge Resource Area, 3170 East Main Street, P.O. Box 2200, Canon City, CO 81215-2200; (303) 275-0631.

PENITENTE CANYON
rock climbing, hiking, mountain biking, fishing, camping

Located approximately 22 miles northwest of the town of Monte Vista in the San Luis Valley, Penitente Canyon offers 2,500 acres of world-class rock climbing on outstanding quality limestone cliffs. Over 300 climbing routes have been identified and bolted. A climbing guide of this area is available at state retail outlets. Trout fishing is also good if you tire of climbing. Cast your line into La Garita Creek. Of additional interest, is the fall chokecherry crop (very tasty) and the historic wagon tracks which have been deeply carved into the limestone bedrock by old logging and mining activity.

For more information: Contact the BLM San Luis Resource Area, 1921 State Street, Alamosa, CO 81101; (719) 589-4975.

TIP: Constantly stay alert for signs of your passing and erase them if possible.

STATE INFORMATION OVERVIEW

COLORADO STATE OFFICE
2850 Youngfield Street, Lakewood, CO 80215; (303) 239-3660

GRAND JUNCTION DISTRICT OFFICE
2815 H Road, Grand Junction, CO 81506; (303) 244-3050

Glenwood Springs Resource Area, P.O. Box 1009, Glenwood Springs, CO 81602; (303) 945-2341

CANON CITY DISTRICT OFFICE
3170 East Main Street, P.O. Box 2200, Canon City, CO 81212; (719) 275-0631

Royal Gorge Resource Area, 3170 East Main Street, P.O. Box 2200, Canon City, CO 81215-2200; (303) 275-0631

San Luis Resource Area, 1921 State Street, Alamosa, CO 81101; (719) 589-4975

MONTROSE DISTRICT OFFICE
2465 South Townsend Avenue, Montrose, CO 81401; (303) 249-6049

Gunnison Resource Area, 216 North Colorado, Gunnison, CO 81230; (303) 641-0471

San Juan Resource Area, Federal Building, 701 Camino Del Rio, Durango, CO 81301; (303) 247-4082

Uconmpahgre Resource Area, 2505 South Townsend Avenue, Montrose, CO 81401; (303) 249-6049

CRAIG DISTRICT OFFICE
455 Emerson Street, Craig, CO 81625-1129; (303) 824-8261

Kremmling Resource Area, 1116 Park Avenue, P.O. Box 68, Kremmling, CO 80459; (303) 724-3437

Little Snake Resource Area, 1280 Industrial Avenue, Craig, CO 81625; (303) 824-4441

White River Resource Area, 73455 Highway 64, P.O. Box 928, Meeker, CO 81641; (303) 878-3601

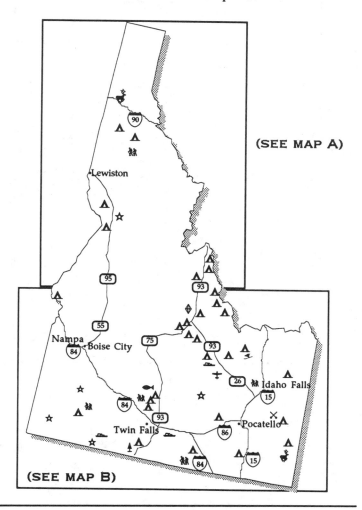

(SEE MAP A)

(SEE MAP B)

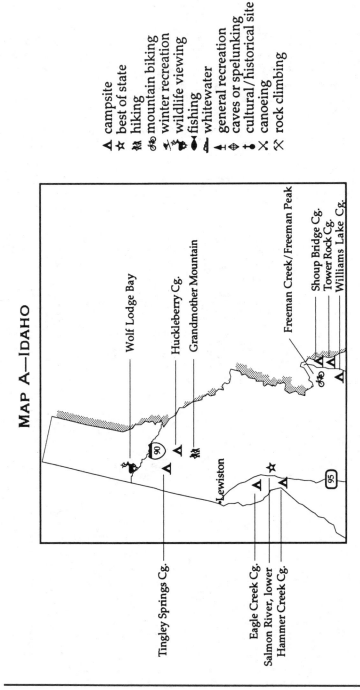

MAP A—IDAHO

campsite
best of state
hiking
mountain biking
winter recreation
wildlife viewing
fishing
whitewater
general recreation
caves or spelunking
cultural/historical site
canoeing
rock climbing

Wolf Lodge Bay

Huckleberry Cg.

Grandmother Mountain

Freeman Creek/Freeman Peak

Shoup Bridge Cg.
Tower Rock Cg.
Williams Lake Cg.

Lewiston

Tingley Springs Cg.

Eagle Creek Cg.
Salmon River, lower
Hammer Creek Cg.

MAP REFERENCES

Freeman Peak/Freeman Creek—p. 250
Grandmother Mountain—p. 244-245
Lower Salmon River—p. 236-238
Wolf Lodge Bay—p. 246

CAMPGROUNDS

The following campgrounds are found in this area of Idaho.
Please call the BLM office (listed following each campground's
name) for reservations and information. Contact information for
each BLM office is on pages 257-258 for Idaho.

Eagle Creek Campground, Coeur d'Alene District Office
Hammer Creek Campground, Coeur d'Alene District Office
Huckleberry Campground, Coeur d'Alene District Office
Shoup Bridge Campground, Salmon District Office
Tingley Springs Campground, Coeur d'Alene District Office
Tower Rock Campground, Salmon District Office
Williams Lake Campground, Salmon District Office

MAP B—IDAHO

East Fork Cg.

Agency Creek Cg.
McFarland Cg.
Smokey Clubs Cg.
Mackay Reservoir
Summit Creek Cg.
John Day Cg.
Birch Creek Valley

Hells Half Acre
Kelly's Island Cg.
Blackfoot River
Blackfoot River Cg.
Dike Lake Cg.
Formation Springs Reserve

Pipeline Cg.

Bayhorse Cg.
Spring Gulch Cg.
Idaho Falls
Pocatello
Hawkins Cg.

The Great Rift & Snake River Plain
McClendon Spring Cg.
Silent City of Rocks National Reserve
Snake River, Murtaugh Section

Herd Lake & Upper Lake Creek Cgs.
Appendicitis Hill
Steck Cg.
Nampa
Boise City

Thorn Creek Reservoir & Campground
Jacks Creek
Cove Campground
Snake River Birds of Prey Area
Owyhee Canyonlands
Jarbridge River
Bruneau River Canyon
Mt. Bennett Hills/Gooding City of Rocks
Lava Creek & Moonstone Cgs.
Salmon Falls Creek & Reservoir
Lud Drexler Park Cg.
Twin Falls

△ campsite
☆ best of state
hiking
mountain biking
winter recreation
wildlife viewing
fishing
whitewater
general recreation
caves or spelunking
✝ cultural/historical site
✕ canoeing
rock climbing

MAP REFERENCES

Appendicitis Hill—p. 247
Birch Creek Valley—p. 248
Blackfoot River—p. 248-249
Bruneau River Canyon—p. 232-234
Formation Springs Reservoir—p. 249-250
Hells Half Acre—p. 251
Jacks Creek—p. 251-252
Jarbridge River—p. 252
Mount Bennett Hills/Gooding City of Rocks—p. 253
Owyhee Canyonlands—p. 229-232
Salmon Falls Creek & Reservoir—p. 254
Silent City of Rocks National Reserve—p. 228-229
Snake River Birds of Prey Area—p. 238-240
Snake River, Murtaugh Section—p. 255
The Great Rift & Snake River Plain—p. 240-243
Thorn Creek Reservoir—p. 256

CAMPGROUNDS

The following campgrounds are found in this area of Idaho. Please call the BLM office (listed following each campground's name) for reservations and information. Contact information for each BLM office is on pages 257-258 for Idaho.

Agency Creek Campground, Salmon District Office
Bayhorse Campground, Salmon District Office
Blackfoot River Campground, Idaho Falls District Office
Cove Campground, Boise District Office
Dike Lake Campground, Idaho Falls District Office
East Fork Campground, Salmon District Office
Hawkins Campground, Burley District Office
Herd Lake Campground, Salmon District Office
John Day Campground, Idaho Falls District Office
Kelly's Island Campground, Idaho Falls District Office
Lava Creek Campground, Shoshone District Office
Lud Drexler Park Campground, Burley District Office
Mackay Reservoir, Salmon District Office
McClendon Spring Campground, Burley District Office
McFarland Campground, Salmon District Office
Moonstone Campground, Shoshone District Office
Pipeline Campground, Burley District Office
Smokey Clubs Campground, Salmon District Office
Spring Gulch Campground, Salmon District Office
Steck Campground, Boise District Office
Summit Creek Campground, Salmon District Office
Thorn Creek Campground, Shoshone District Office
Upper Lake Creek Campground, Salmon District Office

1

SILENT CITY OF ROCKS NATIONAL RESERVE

These fantastic granite monoliths in pillars, knobs, cliffs, pinnacles and hoodoos create a wonderful playground for hikers and rock climbers. Once nearly trashed by irreverent vandals and off-road activity, this area was established as a national reserve in 1988, thanks mainly to the efforts of local residents. It is also noteworthy as the only known area in the state supporting pinyon pine.

ROCK CLIMBING

Rocks with names such as Bath Rock, the Arrow and Turtle Rock are all popular and excellent climbing destinations. A number of outdoor programs use the area for climbing instruction.

MANAGEMENT

City of Rocks National Reserve, P.O. Box 169, Almo, ID 83312; (208) 824-5519

LOCATION

Approximately 45 miles directly southeast of Burley.

GETTING THERE

From Interstate 84, head south to the town of Malta. At Malta, take Highway 77 towards the mountains and then head south at Conner Junction to the hamlet of Almo. At Almo, take a gravel road for approximately one mile south and turn right onto yet another gravel road. Drive approximately four miles, past the ruins of a stone house to another junction and another gravel road. Here, head left to the Twin Sisters. Stay to the right and you will find any number of parking, picnicking and camping areas among the rocks.

CAMPING
Camp at designated sites among the rocks. There are vault toilets and one well for potable water.

PERMITS
No permits are necessary.

MAPS
USGS topographic maps: Almo, Cache Creek

SEASON
April through September is the best time to visit. Spring brings range wildflowers in colorful display soon after the snow melts. Summer can be very hot at times—almost too uncomfortable for climbing. Fall shows aspen trees in golden splendor.

---

*TIP: Pack out all that you bring in—
and a little extra if you find it.*

BEST OF THE STATE

2

OWYHEE CANYONLANDS

Although access to it is challenging, this 450,000-acre region is picturesque, dramatic, wild, isolated and well worth visiting. River runners and hunters are the predominant users, and there are not too many of them. The narrow canyons that cut into the plateau range from several hundred to one thousand feet deep—often with sheer walls from rimrock to river bottom. Mountain lion, bobcat, river otter, pronghorn antelope, and bighorn sheep reside within the Owyhee canyon system.

HIKING
There are no established routes. Hiking consists of either wandering along the canyon edges or along the canyon floors. The North Fork of the Owyhee is perhaps the most accessible

---

area—a gravel road leads to the canyon—and is of particular interest and special beauty during spring wildflower season. Within the canyons themselves, hiking can be tedious and difficult, often requiring frequent rock and talus scrambles and at times river wading or swimming. Only experienced back-packers and those with knowledge and skills in canyoneering should venture into the canyon bottoms. Hiking is much easier on the mile-high desert plateau.

Water is not easily found on the plateau although some springs and hidden swimming holes do exist. Check with the BLM office for specific locations and advice as to potability (all water must be filtered and or treated to guard against Giardia). Always carry adequate reserves just in case—one gallon per person is advised.

BOATING

The Upper Owyhee consists of three forks: the East, South and North Fork. Both the East and South Forks are boatable in rafts, kayaks and canoes. The river is rated Class II through IV with several very arduous portages on the East Fork before its confluence with the South. The BLM lists the North Fork as a river for "world class" expert kayakers only! Enough said.

The Middle Owyhee is a mixture of Class III through Class V+ rapids that are challenging for most boaters. Small 12 to 15-foot rafts and kayaks are recommended. The rapids feature long boulder gardens, some steep drops and several heavy hydraulics. Some portaging is required.

The Lower Owyhee offers Class II through Class IV rapids that any level of boater in all variety of craft—raft, canoe, kayak or drift boat—will find enjoyable. This is the most popular section of the river and is considered ideal for family groups and parties with inexperienced boaters. No party should attempt the river without several members being qualified intermediate boaters capable of navigating Class III and Class IV whitewater safely. The river is somewhat forgiving in that it is of the "pool and drop" variety, meaning that rapids are usually short, followed by calm pool sections to recover.

MANAGEMENT

BLM Boise District Office, 3948 Development Avenue, Boise, ID 83705; (208) 384-3300

LOCATION
In the high-desert region of southwestern Idaho, southwest of Grand View and Highway 78 and southeast of Jordan Valley, Oregon, and US 95.

GETTING THERE
The area is predominantly roadless—hence its attraction. The dirt roads that do exist can become impassable at any time. In fact, one river runner I talked to said that he considers the Owyhee to be a Class II river float with a Class V access. The official *River Runners Guide to Idaho,* published by the BLM and the Idaho Parks and Recreation Department, states that "spring rains are common and the dirt tracks can quickly turn into an impassable quagmire of gumbo." Before visiting, check with the BLM office in Boise to determine which access route would be most appropriate during the time of your visit. Four-wheel-drive is recommended for any route that is not gravel!

The best access is via the Owyhee Uplands National Backcountry Byway, a 103-mile gravel road, suitable for high-clearance vehicles, stretching from Grand View on Idaho State Highway 78 to Jordan Valley in Oregon and US 95. There are numerous pullouts appropriate for overnight camping and embarking on short or extended backpacking explorations.

CAMPING
Camp anywhere within the canyon proper or on the plateau—campsites are evident and frequent. Select sites already established if you have the choice. A primitive campground, the Owyhee North Fork Recreation Site, is maintained by the BLM off the Backcountry Byway—nestled in the bottom of the North Fork of the Owyhee Canyon.

PERMITS
No permits are needed for backpacking. Boaters, however, must register prior to embarking on any of the Owyhee River forks and tributaries.

MAPS
BLM surface maps: Riddle (South Fork, East Fork), Triangle (North Fork)

ADDITIONAL INFORMATION
• *Owyhee River Boating Guide* is available through the Boise District BLM office.
• *Western Whitewater, From the Rockies to the Pacific,* by Jim Cassady, Bill Cross and Fryar Calhoun, published by North Fork Press, Berkeley, CA; (800) 243-5522.

SEASON
For hiking, May and June or September and October are best. July and August are hot and dry. May and early June are best for wildflowers. For boating, the best time is during the spring runoff from March through June. River levels can fluctuate severely with cold or warm spells and periods of heavy rain. Call the River Forecast Center at (503) 249-0666 for current gauge readings.

> *TIP: Always use a river runner's toilet when boating and never bury human waste around river camps. Human waste, including toilet paper, must be packed out.*

BEST OF THE STATE

BRUNEAU RIVER CANYON

Hot springs, a stunning riparian environment and mysterious canyons invite the visitor. Towering hoodoo spires highlight the magnificent geological displays. Expect to see river otter and a variety of waterfowl. The canyon is cut deeply through a high desert plateau, as deep as 800 feet in some places. Its narrowness, closing to only 30 feet wide occasionally and never exceeding 400 to 500 yards, adds to the feeling of drama within the canyon bottom.

HIKING

There is no designated trail—the stream along the canyon floor is the route. Watch out for thick infestations of poison ivy—sometimes so thick that it steers you into the river itself. Rattlesnakes are also prevalent, but shouldn't pose a problem unless you walk with your eyes closed and put your hands and feet into places where you can't see. Anticipate lots of rock scrambling. Some hikers bring along small inner tubes to float their gear in during deep water crossings and sections requiring brief swims.

RAFTING/KAYAKING

Boaters must be able to run sustained sections of Class IV and V whitewater. The BLM recommends that the West Fork of the Bruneau be run only by expert kayakers, due to the demanding nature of the rapids and strenuous portages. Most people run a Jarbidge-Bruneau combination starting near Murphy Hot Springs. Throughout the river, anticipate challenging rapids and numerous portages. At flows of 1,000 cubic feet per second, the route is rocky; at 2,000 cubic feet per second, the river is a foaming, raging torrent of water. At levels much higher than 2,000 cubic feet per second, floating logs and flood debris add to the danger and challenge of running the river. There are several outfitters who run trips on this river—check with the BLM for a current listing of permitted commercial outfits.

MANAGEMENT

BLM Boise District Office, 3948 Development Avenue, Boise, ID 83705; (208) 384-3300

LOCATION

The Bruneau River runs from the Jarbidge Mountains in northeastern Nevada to the Snake River near Boise, Idaho.

GETTING THERE

From Boise, drive 45 miles east on Interstate 84 to Highway 51, then go south to Bruneau (20 miles). Take the Bruneau-Three Creeks Road south to the trailhead. This is a grueling 52-mile gravel road, the last 12 miles requiring dry weather and four-wheel-drive. Not only is this a challenging river to run, but it's a bear of an access. But, it's more than worth the effort to visit. Besides, since you have to earn your pleasure, you can bet the hordes of curiosity seekers will stay away.

CAMPING
Camp anywhere along the river's edge.

PERMITS
No permits are required for backpacking. Registration is required for all boaters.

MAPS
Use the *Bruneau-Jarbidge River Guide* from the BLM Boise District Office.

ADDITIONAL INFORMATION
• *A River Runners Guide to Idaho,* published by the Idaho Department of Parks and Recreation and the BLM.
• *Western Whitewater, From the Rockies to the Pacific,* by Jim Cassady, Bill Cross and Fryar Calhoun, published by North Fork Press, Berkeley, CA; (800) 243-5522.

SEASON
The season for backpacking is from late May or early June to early October, depending on the water flow. The season for boating is April 1 to June 15 with the usual high water peak by May 15.

TIP: Travel or camp in small groups.

BEST OF THE STATE

SAWTOOTH MOUNTAINS/ QUIGLEY CANYON

Wildflowers sprinkle the meadows and mountains during June. The Cove Creek area features a lush mixture of aspen, Douglas fir and sagebrush.

MOUNTAIN BIKING

Traveling the Quigley Canyon Trail, you go along a dirt road for approximately four miles, climbing gradually. Cross Big Witch Creek and, ignoring the road branching right, continue straight for one-half mile. The road soon turns to trail and winds up a ridge, over the summit and past several beaver ponds. Bear right at the intersection with a two-track jeep trail. After approximately three-quarters of a mile, the jeep trail merges with Quigley/Baugh Creek Road. Follow this road over Quigley Summit, downhill to Hailey and take the bike path north to East Fork Road and the return trip to the parking area.

MANAGEMENT
BLM Shoshone District Office, P.O. Box 2B, Shoshone, ID 83352 (208) 886-2206

LOCATION
Quigley Canyon is a 26-mile round-trip ride located in the Sawtooth Mountains, approximately five miles south of Ketchum on Highway 75.

GETTING THERE
Drive south from Ketchum for five miles on State Highway 75. Turn left (east) on East Fork Road. Drive seven miles to Cove Creek Road and park.

CAMPING
Camping is not recommended along the trail. There are nearby primitive campgrounds on East Fork Road and Trail Creek Road. Contact the BLM or the U.S. Forest Service for information.

PERMITS
No permits are necessary.

MAPS
USGS topographic maps: Hailey, Sun Valley, Hyndman Peak, Baugh Creek Southwest
BLM surface maps: Sun Valley Quadrangle

ADDITIONAL INFORMATION

Bike Routes in the Sawtooths, a joint effort of the BLM, the U.S. Forest Service, and local businesses is available for $9.50 from the Ketchum Ranger Station, P.O. Box 2356, Sun Valley Road, Ketchum, ID 83340; (208) 622-5371.

SEASON

The best time to visit this area is in the spring. The trail usually opens about two weeks earlier than rides to the north. Rains tend to make the trail extremely muddy, however, during which time the trail should be avoided.

> *TIP: Use a portable stove whenever possible and minimize fire impacts which can leave unsightly scars.*

BEST OF THE STATE

LOWER SALMON RIVER

This high desert river flows through land and canyon terrain that is both varied and spectacular. The river flows through four major canyons—Green, Cougar, Snowhole and Blue Canyon—which is where most of the Class III to IV whitewater occurs. Between the canyons the river calms to a tranquil float along rolling grassy slopes and smaller rock outcroppings. Since winter in the canyon is relatively mild when compared to the surrounding plains and hills, this is an important wintering ground for mule deer, white-tail deer, elk, bear and mountain lion. River otter, coyote, chukar and golden eagle also frequent the canyon year round. Fishing is considered good for rainbow trout, smallmouth bass and steelhead trout. There are numerous cultural sites throughout the river route, but many are becoming severely impacted and damaged beyond repair. Leave all artifacts where they lie and do not climb on or around old stone wall structures.

RIVER RUNNING

Put-in is at Hammer Creek on the Salmon River and take-out is at Grande Ronde on the Snake River—total mileage 73 river miles. The average trip takes four to five days. Shorter trips are possible by taking out at Pine Bar, 12 river miles from Hammer Creek. The take-out at Grande Ronde is managed by the BLM which charges no fee—what a concept. There is also a privately operated take-out at Beamers Heller Bar. They also charge no fee. Maximum group size on the river is 30 people.

MANAGEMENT
BLM Cottonwood Resource Area, Route 3, P.O. Box 181, Cottonwood, ID 83522; (208) 962-3246

LOCATION
North of Boise and alongside US 95.

GETTING THERE
From Boise, head north on US 95. Exit at the turnoff for Hammer Creek and the put-in. A shuttle will need to be arranged for the full river trip and involves a drive of approximately 125 miles. Shuttle services are available in the towns of White Bird (near Hammer Creek) and Cottonwood. Information regarding shuttles and maps may be obtained from the Cottonwood BLM office.

CAMPING
There are numerous large sandy beaches suitable for camping. The Whitehouse Bar/Snowhole Canyon Area can get congested—avoid it if possible. Smaller groups are asked to leave obviously large camping areas for larger groups and to seek out smaller sites. The BLM no longer maintains campgrounds along the river, allowing them to revert to undeveloped status. Look for several undeveloped sites scattered along the river.

PERMITS
Permits are required on the Salmon River for all overnight trips below Hammer Creek for private outfitters. Permits are available at Hammer Creek and Pine Bar launch sites and the BLM office in Cottonwood. The permits also allow for entry onto the Snake River.

ADDITIONAL INFORMATION
• *A River Runners Guide to Idaho,* published by the Idaho
Department of Parks and Recreation and the BLM.
• *Western Whitewater, From the Rockies to the Pacific,* by Jim
Cassady, Bill Cross and Fryar Calhoun, published by North
Fork Press, Berkeley, CA; (800) 243-5522.

MAPS
Lower Salmon River Guide, published by the BLM, is waterproof and available for $2 from the BLM Cottonwood Office.

SEASON
March and April are perhaps the most colorful months to visit
as spring green-up is in full swing. Wildflowers and fruit trees
are in full bloom. Water is also at its highest, creating increased
river hazards in several of the more significant rapids. The river
can essentially be floated all year, with each season offering
unique perspectives on the area; however, it is considered
unrunnable during the peak of spring runoff for approximately
six weeks around June. July through October is the most
popular time and most crowded. Daily river flow information
may be obtained by calling (208) 962-3245. During fall, in the
hunting and fishing season, power boats are prevalent on the
lower reaches of the Salmon and especially on the Snake.

---

*TIP: Never leave a campfire unattended,
even for a few moments.*

BEST OF THE STATE

6

SNAKE RIVER BIRDS OF
PREY AREA

This area was established in 1980 to protect a unique
environment in southwestern Idaho that supports one of the
world's densest populations of nesting birds of prey. Within

this region, falcons, eagles, hawks, owls and vultures play out the rhythms of life, but not within the usual confines of a zoo. The birds are not on display here. Public facilities are few and very primitive within the area where the nesting birds concentrate. This is nature in all its raw and rough splendor—it's there if you are willing to spend some time to look closely.

With a good spotting scope or binoculars, you can expect to view the following, if your eyes and luck are good: prairie falcon, American kestrel, peregrine falcon, golden eagle, red-tailed hawk, ferruginous hawk, Swainson's hawk, rough-legged hawk, bald eagle, northern harrier, northern goshawk, Cooper's hawk, sharp-shinned hawk, osprey, great horned owl, long-eared owl, short-eared owl, western screech owl, common barn-owl, burrowing owl, turkey vulture, common raven.

RECREATION

Canoeing or rafting are good ways to visit the area. Floating from Grand View to Swan Falls Dam or Walter's Ferry is the most popular trip. It requires one overnight. There are a number of outfitters who guide commercial trips—the BLM can provide a listing of permitted outfitters if you desire their service. Hiking is allowed anywhere within the area; however, you are not allowed to climb on cliff walls or otherwise do anything that might disturb nesting raptors. A 300mm high-speed telephoto lens is a minimum for adequate photography, if that is your interest in this area.

MANAGEMENT

BLM Boise District Office, 3948 Development Avenue, Boise, ID 83705; (208) 334-1582

LOCATION

This area covers 482,000 acres in southwestern Idaho, south of Interstate 84 near Kuna.

GETTING THERE

From Boise and Interstate 84, take Idaho 69 (exit 44) south for eight miles to the town of Kuna. Continue south on Swan Falls Road, following signs for the Snake River Birds of Prey Area. The area officially begins five miles south of Kuna. At mile 15 there is a signed parking area and a short trail for canyon and raptor viewing.

CAMPING

Anywhere within the area except near nesting areas. Pack out everything that you pack in. Please, stoves only, no fires.

PERMITS

No permits are needed for hiking or camping in the area. Boaters must register before heading out on the Snake River.

MAPS

USGS topographic maps: There are many for this area. Once you have determined the exact area you wish to visit, contact the USGS and request maps.
BLM surface maps: Murphy

ADDITIONAL INFORMATION

• *Snake River Birds of Prey,* published by the BLM, Idaho Power Company and Idaho Department of Fish and Game.
• The Idaho Outfitter and Guides Association is an excellent source of information regarding outfitters who run raft trips down the Snake that are geared toward raptor observation. Phone (208) 342-1438.

SEASON

Mid-March through June is the best time to view birds of prey. During this period, the birds are courting, nesting, laying eggs, and raising young. By July, most raptors have left the area with prey becoming very scarce and summer temperatures beginning to reach the scorch and burn level.

BEST OF THE STATE

7

THE GREAT RIFT AND SNAKE RIVER PLAIN

Lying adjacent to the Craters of the Moon National Monument, the Great Rift is every bit equal in its bizarre, twisted, craters convoluted and unusually formed lunar-like landscape. Lava cave tubes abound, creating a unique habitat for nesting birds and other wildlife. June wildflower blooms can be spectacular, depending on the water situation. Cross-country skiing is excellent in the winter. The few visitors who are fascinated by this remarkable area are often drawn to the kipukas—vegetated islands of older lava ranging in size from one acre to several thousand acres, each creating their own unique habitat. Junipers, some as old as 750 years, have found a tenuous hold in the small crevices.

TRAVELING THE GREAT RIFT— WORDS OF WISDOM
reprinted courtesy of the BLM

Roads: Traveling by vehicle along the unimproved dirt roads is slow and difficult. Sharp lava rocks should be traversed with care to avoid puncturing a tire. In many places, wind and water erosion have caused ruts and holes in the road. The desert is remote, but expect to encounter oncoming vehicles. After a rain, roads can be slippery. Some parts of the southern edge of the Wapi Flow require a four-wheel-drive vehicle to negotiate sand. High-clearance vehicles are needed to travel on primitive jeep trails.

Orienteering: The Snake River Plain surrounding the Great Rift is covered by a vast network of roads. Look for landmarks like buttes, wells, survey markers and lava fingers extending into the desert to help locate your position on a map. Big Southern Butte is the most prominent landmark in the area. Orienteering for hikers can be difficult. The high iron content in the volcanic rocks distorts compass readings. The buttes in the area will be your best direction indicators. Park your vehicle on a high knoll so you can find it easily upon return.

Temperature: During the summer season, temperatures often exceed 100°F. The black lava absorbs the sun's rays and intensifies the heat. Shade is not readily available since few trees exist on the flow, but shelter may be found in a lava crack, tube, or behind a ridge. Light-colored clothing, a hat, sunglasses, and sunscreen protect against the sun. Temperatures can be surprisingly cold at night, so carry warm clothing.

Water: Since safe drinking water is a scarce commodity in the desert, it is essential that you bring your own. Hikers should carry at least one gallon per day per person to replace the tremendous amount of body fluid lost through perspiration. On rare occasions, pools or ice may be found within the lava flow, but these are most likely contaminated and must be treated. Although several wells are located on the desert for livestock use, the water may not be safe to drink.

Fire: The desert is susceptible to wild fires. The exhaust system on a car can start a fire while parked or idling in grassy and vegetated areas. Vegetation entwined on the exhaust system can also ignite. Use caution and be fire-conscious. A shovel and fire extinguisher are invaluable equipment.

Terrain: Hiking across the lava is a unique experience. Lava rock is extremely sharp, glassy and fragmented, and can be precariously loose, especially in the jagged "a'a" formation. Open cracks, lava tubes and caves are particularly hazardous. A sturdy pair of hiking boots provides the best foot protection. Before you start your hike, tell someone where you are going and when you will return. Carry a first-aid kit.

Snakes: Rattlesnakes are a natural part of the Snake River Plain. If left alone, they are harmless, but when aggravated or surprised, they may strike. Snakes are found in desert areas and occasionally on the lavas. Yield the right-of-way to snakes.

Ticks: Ticks live on the sagebrush and other vegetation in this area. Periodically check for this insect on your clothing and skin.

Archaeological sites: Since much of the Great Rift is virtually unexplored, you may discover remnants from past cultures. Please leave them undisturbed and report your find to the BLM. Protective measures will be taken so that all may enjoy this resource. Remember, there are substantial penalties for the removal, defacement, or destruction of archaeological sites for artifacts.

MANAGEMENT
•BLM Idaho Falls District Office, 940 Lincoln Road, Idaho Falls, ID 83401; (208) 524-7500
•BLM Shoshone District Office (208) 886-2206
•BLM Burley District Office (208) 678-5514.

LOCATION
South of Craters of the Moon National Monument

GETTING THERE
From Arco, take Interstate 95 southwest for approximately 18 miles past the signs for Craters of the Moon. The Arco-Minidoka Road parallels the area for a section and then cuts into the middle of it. State Road 20 also provides access.

CAMPING
Camping is permitted anywhere within the Great Rift.

PERMITS
No permits are necessary.

MAPS
Obtain *A Guide to the Great Rift and Snake River Plain* from the BLM. It contains a complete and extensive listing of all topographic maps needed to travel throughout the region—a very long list.

SEASON
The peak fair-weather seasons for outdoor activities such as hiking, climbing and camping are from mid-April through mid-June and from September through mid-October. The winter season invites cross-country skiers to tour and explore the Craters of the Moon National Monument.

TIP: Camping or building fires near cultural sites can cause serious and irreparable damage.

NORTHERN IDAHO— THE PANHANDLE

GRANDMOTHER MOUNTAIN

hiking, backpacking, fishing, huckleberry picking, camping, wildlife observation, snowmobiling, cross-country skiing, mountain biking, horseback riding

Grandmother Mountain Roadless Area, managed by both the BLM and the U.S. Forest Service, is an oasis of mountains and trees amid an area that has suffered from extensive clear-cutting and development. Well known to local elk and deer hunters, the high elevation lakes attract numerous visitors during summer months, as do the huckleberries which bears also enjoy. There are a number of notable trails within the 45-mile Marble Creek Trail System. A fun 15-mile loop trip through BLM and the adjacent Panhandle National Forest Service land can be put together by connecting the Delaney Creek Trail, Marble Divide Trail, Gold Center-Marble Creek Trail, and the Marble Creek Trail. Parts of all four trails plus part of the Lookout Mountain Trail (26.7 miles total) have been designated as historic trails.

Located 40 miles northwest of Moscow and 20 miles east of Clarkia, Grandmother Mountain can be really confusing to get to without a detailed map. Before heading out, call the BLM office or the National Forest Service office and get up-to-date details—with your map in front of you. Roughly, the trail systems can be accessed via the BLM campground and the BLM/USFS trailheads on Freezeout Saddle Road / Forest Service Road 301 and also from Forest Service Road 321 at Marble Creek. The best time to visit is from July to mid-October. Most commonly seen wildlife are elk, mule deer, black bear, moose, and forest grouse.

Resources: *The Hikers Guide to Idaho,* by Ralph and Jackie Maughan, published by Falcon Press, P.O. Box 1718, Helena, MT 59624; (800) 582-2665. Also, ask for two brochures from the BLM or Forest Service: *Freezeout Mountain Snowmobile Trail and Hiking; Horse/Pack Saddle Marble Creek Trail System.*

For more information: Contact the BLM Coeur d'Alene District Office, 1808 North Third Street, Coeur d'Alene, ID 83814; (208) 769-5000; or the Avery Ranger District, Panhandle National Forest, Star Route Box 1, Avery, ID 83802; (208) 245-4517 ; or the St. Maries Ranger District, P.O. Box 407, St. Maries, ID, 83861; (208) 245-2531 **USGS topographic maps:** Grandmother Mountain, Widow Mountain

LOWER SALMON RIVER
camping, rafting, canoeing, kayaking, fishing

This high desert river flows through land and canyon terrain that is both varied and spectacular. The river flows through four major canyons—Green, Cougar, Snowhole and Blue Canyon—which is where most of the Class III to IV whitewater occurs. Between the canyons, the river calms to a tranquil float along rolling grassy slopes and smaller rock outcroppings.

•**See also Best of the State, page 236**•
For more information: Contact the BLM Cottonwood Resource Area, Route 3, Box 181, Cottonwood, ID 83522; (208) 962-3246.

UPPER SALMON RIVER / CHALLIS AREA
camping, hiking, backpacking, fishing, rafting, kayaking, canoeing, wildlife observation

The recreation destination in the Challis area is the Upper Salmon River, with 100 or so river miles managed by the BLM. The BLM maintains seven campgrounds and approximately 15 river access points along the Salmon River Scenic Byway, State Highways 9 and 75. Some of the water in the Sawtooth National Recreation Area is challenging, Class IV water for experienced whitewater rafters and kayakers only. There are many sections suitable for open canoes, rated at Class II. Check with the BLM for specific river information, which varies depending on water flow. Hiking or backpacking in the area can be enjoyed along the many primitive roads and jeep tracks. Fishing in the area's creeks and lakes is good—primarily for trout. The BLM Salmon office has a detailed map showing roads, river access points and camping areas.

Resources: A River Runners Guide to Idaho, published by the Idaho Department of Parks and Recreation and the BLM.
For more information: Contact the BLM Challis Resource Area, P.O.

Box 430, Salmon, ID 83467; (208) 756-5400.

USGS topographic maps: Bald Mountain, Bayhorse, Bradbury Flat, Challis, Allison Creek, Goldbug Ridge, Salmon, Bird Creek, North Fork, Hat Creek

WOLF LODGE BAY

hiking, picnicking, wildlife observation, boating

Wolf Lodge is an area that attracts numerous migratory bald eagles when Lake Coeur d'Alene's kokanee salmon spawn and die in November. The Mineral Ridge National Recreation Trail, a wonderful interpretive trail, consists of a 2.7-mile loop as part of its 3.3 total miles and offers excellent opportunities to view bald eagles as well as a wealth of other wildlife. The area is a super birding spot for song birds at other times of the year.

From Coeur d'Alene, take Interstate 90 east for seven miles; exit at Wolf Lodge Bay. Continue driving around the bay by crossing the bridge over Wolf Lodge Creek at the Idaho 97 junction. Established turnouts are excellent wildlife viewing locations. Obtain both the *Bald Eagles of Wolf Lodge Bay* and *Mineral Ridge Trail Guide* brochures from the BLM.

For more information: Contact the BLM Coeur d'Alene District Office, 1808 North Third Street, Coeur d'Alene, ID 83814; (208) 769-5000.

TIP: Always walk single file in the center of a trail. Resist the urge to spread out or walk two abreast.

2

SOUTHERN IDAHO

APPENDICITIS HILL
hiking, backpacking, mountain biking, horseback riding, caves

This area is suitable for weekend backpacking, mountain biking and day hiking. Head into the upper reaches of the region as the lower area is used by cattle quite heavily. Ridges and peaks, up to 8,500 feet in elevation, are cut by picturesque canyons. Aspen, willow and Douglas fir are the primary trees. Hunters use this area heavily in the fall looking for elk, mule deer, chukar partridge, and sage grouse.

From the town of Arco, head northwest eight miles on US 93 to Moore. Drive approximately one mile west on local roads.

For more information: Contact the BLM Idaho Falls District Office, 940 Lincoln Road, Idaho Falls, ID 83401; (208) 524-7500.
USGS topographic maps: There are many for this area. Once you have determined the exact area you wish to visit, contact the U.S. Geological Survey and request maps.

BIG SOUTHERN BUTTE
camping, hiking, hang gliding

Once a landmark for pioneers, this 7,550-foot-high butte is now a National Natural Landmark, towering majestically above the surrounding Snake River plain. With swirling winds, this is a popular launching spot for highly experienced hang gliders and a great spot to picnic and watch the man-made birds soar.

From Atomic City off US 26, head west 15 miles to the butte—shown on most road maps.

For more information: Contact the BLM Idaho Falls District Office, 940 Lincoln Road, Idaho Falls, ID 83401; (208) 524-7500.

BIRCH CREEK VALLEY
hiking, backpacking, camping, fishing, cross-country skiing

The valley itself rests at about a 7,000-foot elevation, nestled between the Beaverhead Mountains to the northeast and the Lemhi Range on the southwest. Incidentally, the Lemhi Range at over 70 miles long is the longest mountain range in Idaho that is uncrossed by any public access road. Birch Creek itself is a blue-ribbon trout stream.

From Interstate 15 north of Idaho Falls, drive west on State Road 33 to Mud Lake and then 20 miles northwest on State Road 28 to the BLM's John Day campground.

For more information: Contact the BLM Idaho Falls District Office, 940 Lincoln Road, Idaho Falls, ID 83401; (208) 524-7500.
USGS topographic: There are many for this area. Once you have determined the exact area you wish to visit, contact the U.S. Geological Survey and request maps.
BLM surface maps: Circular Butte

BLACKFOOT RIVER
hiking, camping, fishing, wildlife observation, canoeing

Little known and consequently lightly visited, the Blackfoot River lies below the Blackfoot Reservoir, a popular watersport and recreation destination. The BLM maintains a campground, Dike Lake, at the south end of the reservoir. Although the river canyon is quite wide below the dam, it narrows the farther down you go.

Approximately 12 miles of the river are suitable for boating, rated Class II from the dam to the BLM Cutthroat Trout campground. From the campground down to a take-out at Trail Creek, the river varies from Class II to Class IV. After Trail Creek, the river begins to boil and becomes unsuitable for boating, with rapids rated conservatively from Class V to Class VI.

The best time to visit is May to November. Wildlife observation opportunities are superb, rather like a miniature version of the Snake River Birds of Prey Area.

From Blackfoot, take US 91 north about seven miles and turn right onto Wolverine Road. Head east for about 10 miles to Wolverine Creek. Turn right and cross the creek onto Cedar Creek Road. Follow this road for the next 10 miles as it parallels the river canyon's rim. This road will turn into Blackfoot

River Road after several miles. Continue to Trail Creek Road, turning right onto it and crossing the river. Within the next six miles you will pass Morgans Bridge and Paradise Road on the left. Trail Creek will turn into Lincoln Creek Road and within the six mile section you will pass Graves Creek, Cutthroat Trout and Sagehen campgrounds. This road will take you all the way to the reservoir.

For more information: Contact the BLM Idaho Falls District Office, 940 Lincoln Road, Idaho Falls, ID 83401; (208) 524-7500.
USGS topographic maps: There are many for this area. Once you have determined the exact area you wish to visit, contact the U.S. Geological Survey and request maps.
BLM surface maps: Soda Springs, Pocatello, Blackfoot

BRUNEAU RIVER CANYON
hiking, backpacking, camping, fishing, rafting, kayaking, canoeing, rock hounding, wildlife observation

Hot Springs, a stunning riparian environment and mysterious canyons invite the visitor. Towering hoodoo spires highlight the magnificent geological displays. Expect to see river otter and a variety of waterfowl.

•**See also Best of the State, page 232**•
For more information: Contact the BLM Boise District Office, 3948 Development Avenue, Boise, ID 83705; (208) 384-3300.

FORMATION SPRINGS PRESERVE
hiking, wildlife observation, caves

A joint partnership between the BLM and The Nature Conservancy preserves this area of crystal clear pools, wetlands, and the Formation Cave—20 feet tall at the entrance and over 1,000 feet long. The spring water which feeds the pools and creek has been determined to be over 13,000 years old—eat your heart out Vichy Springs! The preserve supports a wildlife population that includes elk, mule deer and raptors.

From Soda Springs, take Idaho 34 north for two miles, turn right onto Forest Road 124 and go one mile to the signed preserve on your left.

For more information: Contact The Nature Conservancy at (208)726-3007.
USGS topographic maps: There are many for this area. Once you

---

have determined the exact area you wish to visit, contact the U.S. Geological Survey and request maps.
BLM surface maps: Soda Springs

FREEMAN PEAK / FREEMAN CREEK
hiking, mountain biking, backpacking, climbing, fishing, historic gold and silver mine

Beginning on BLM land and ending in U.S. Forest Service territory, an old mining road leads up from the lower valley to the Continental Divide, offering spectacular views into Montana. The ruins of the Ore Cash mine as well as snowfields, surrounding mountain peaks (often snow-covered) and nearby lakes make this an attractive destination or jumping-off point for longer journeys. Although the mine shafts are open and clearly evident, it is not advised to attempt any spelunking adventures. Entering old mines is highly dangerous!

Drive approximately five miles north from Salmon on US 93 to the town of Carmen. Head right on a paved road leading to Carmen Creek. After approximately six miles, the road turns to gravel and you will turn right onto the signed Freeman Creek Road. Drive 2.5 miles to the junction of Freeman Creek and Kirtley Creek Roads. Head left at the fork towards Freeman Peak. It is advised that you park within the first mile after the junction and begin hiking or biking your way to the top. Although the road is presently legal for all vehicles, travel is highly hazardous. The U.S. Forest Service is contemplating closure of its section near the top and the mine.

For more information: Contact the BLM Salmon District Office, P.O. Box 430, Salmon, ID 83467; (208) 756-5400; or the North Fork Ranger District, Salmon National Forest, P.O. Box 780, North Fork, ID 83466; (208) 867-2382.
USGS topographic maps: Badger Springs Gulch, Homer Youngs Peak

THE GREAT RIFT AND SNAKE RIVER PLAIN
hiking, backpacking, camping, wildlife observation, volcano tubes, archaeological sites

Lying adjacent to the Craters of the Moon National Monument, the Great Rift is every bit equal with its bizarre, twisted, craters convoluted and unusually formed lunar-like landscape. Lava cave tubes abound, creating unique habitat for nesting

birds and other wildlife. June wildflower blooms can be
spectacular, depending on the water situation. Cross-country
skiing is excellent in the winter. The few visitors who are
fascinated by this remarkable area are often drawn to the
kipukas—vegetated islands of older lava ranging in size from
one acre to several thousand acres, each creating its own
unique habitat. Junipers, some as old as 750 years, have
found a tenuous hold in the small crevices.

•**See also Best of the State, page 240**•
For more information: Contact the BLM Idaho Falls District Office,
940 Lincoln Road, Idaho Falls, ID 83401; (208)524-7500.

HELLS HALF ACRE
hiking, volcano tubes

If you haven't gotten enough of the convoluted volcanic
terrain offered in the Great Rift, here's more, and it is every bit
as interesting. It's fascinating to actually view the anatomy of a
volcano flow, even a 4,100-year-old volcano flow. See a source
vent, a shield cone, various volcanic caves, tunnels and
kipukas. Different than the extremely rough and jagged "a'a"
formation of the Great Rift, this volcanic formation is more
twisted, rope-like and billowing—and makes for much easier
wandering.

For more information: Contact the BLM Idaho Falls District Office,
940 Lincoln Road, Idaho Falls, ID 83401; (208) 524-7500.
USGS topographic maps: There are many for this area. Once you
have determined the exact area you wish to visit, contact the U.S.
Geological Survey and request maps.
BLM surface maps: Blackfoot

JACKS CREEK
*hiking, backpacking, fishing, camping, horseback riding,
wildlife observation*

This area consists of absolutely spectacular canyons
offering more than 50 miles of rugged, sheer-walled meandering adventure for the hiker or backpacker. Big Jacks Creek
offers the best hiking, especially in and around Parker Trail.
Fishing is adequate, but primarily limited to the mouth of the
canyon. Mule deer, pronghorn antelope, beaver, sage grouse,
chukar and golden eagles may all be seen.

Take State Road 51, just south of Bruneau to the Wickahoney-Battle Creek Road. This is one point of access, perhaps the best, and places you near the east side of Big Jacks Creek.

For more information: Contact the BLM, Boise District Office, 3948 Development Avenue, Boise, ID 83705; (208) 384-3300.

USGS topographic maps: There are many for this area. Once you have determined the exact area you wish to visit, contact the U.S. Geological Survey and request maps.

BLM surface maps: Sheep Creek

JARBIDGE RIVER
hiking, backpacking, rafting, kayaking, camping, fishing

Before even considering this rugged canyon, head to the Bruneau first, as its access is easier as is the passage. However, once you have the Bruneau under your belt and if you are eager for more, then this is it—a 31-mile-deep canyon trek or float from the Nevada border to the confluence with the Bruneau. If you are hiking the canyon, plan on doing so after June, when the runoff has subsided and the river level is low enough to hike and/or float sections safely with minimum swimming and water hazard. Rock scrambling and creative poison ivy avoidance are the norm.

Floating is good from April to June with water appropriate for small rafts and kayaks. Boaters must register before heading out. Rapids are Class III and IV with numerous log jams and one portage. There are several outfitters who run trips on this river—check with the BLM for a current listing of permitted commercial outfits. Wildlife that may be spotted include bighorn sheep, mule deer, otter, golden eagle and chukar. Fishing is for trout.

Resources: *A River Runners Guide to Idaho,* published by the Idaho Department of Parks and Recreation and the BLM.

Bruneau-Jarbidge River Boating Guide, published by the BLM Boise District.

Western Whitewater, From the Rockies to the Pacific, by Jim Cassady, Bill Cross and Fryar Calhoun, published by North Fork Press, Berkeley, CA; (800) 243-5522.

For more information: Contact the BLM Boise District Office, 3948 Development Avenue, Boise, ID 83705; (208) 384-3300.

MOUNT BENNETT HILLS/
GOODING CITY OF ROCKS
hiking, backpacking, wildlife observation, wildflowers, volcanic rock formations

Hiking this area gives you a unique perspective into what the public rangelands of the West must have been like before cattle roamed the land. The canyon sections, highlighted by weird rock formations, tiny meadows and small creeks, have not been grazed by cattle, allowing for plants not normally seen. Wildlife, too, is more abundant, including elk and black bear. A word of caution: Navigation can be quite tricky in here owing to the myriad of look-alike hoodoos. Your orientation skills and map reading talents must be sharp.

Two recommended hikes in the Gooding City of Rocks are Fourmile Creek and Coyote Creek. Burnt Willow Canyon, several miles south of the City of Rocks and certainly more accessible in wet weather, is ideal for a two-day backpack outing. In early spring (May and June) water is available in several of the canyons in the region from spring runoff. Treat the water before drinking. Camping is allowed anywhere within the area.

Turn off Highway 20 several miles east of Fairfield onto Highway 46 south. Turn right after 14 miles onto a dirt road with BLM signs reading "Fir Grove 7, Coyote Springs 8, City of Rocks 9." After several miles, turn left onto a poor quality dirt road and find a suitable parking spot—this is the trailhead for Burnt Willow Canyon. To reach Gooding City of Rocks, drive several more miles to a signed junction indicating the City of Rocks. Use caution on the dirt roads; if they are wet they quickly become impassable. Four-wheel-drive won't even help you when it's wet—try walking on the stuff if you don't believe me.

For more information: Contact the BLM Shoshone District Office 77, 400 West F Street, P.O. Box 2-B, Shoshone, ID 83352; (208) 886-2206.
USGS topographic maps: Fir Grove Mountain, McKinney Butte, McHan Reservoir, Thorn Creek Southwest

---

Owyhee Canyonlands
hiking, backpacking, rafting, kayaking, canoeing, horseback riding, fishing, camping, mountain biking

Although access is challenging, this 450,000-acre region is picturesque, dramatic, wild, isolated and well worth your time. River runners and hunters are the predominant users, and there are not too many of them. The narrow canyons that cut into the plateau range from several hundred to one thousand feet deep—often with sheer walls from rimrock to river bottom. Mountain lion, bobcat, river otter, pronghorn antelope and bighorn sheep reside within the Owyhee canyon system.

• **See also Best of the State, page 229** •
For more information: Contact the BLM Boise District Office, 3948 Development Avenue, Boise, ID 83705; (208) 384-3300.

Salmon Falls Creek and Reservoir
hiking, camping, fishing, horseback riding, canoeing, swimming

This is a fun area to come and recreate with the entire family, known chiefly to locals. When the reservoir is full (and that's not too often as it gets drained down heavily), it holds 34,000 acre-feet of water. The area upstream of the dam is very scenic and offers opportunities for canoeing, hiking and camping in the spring. The canyons have sheer walls and broad bottoms with willow groves and grassy meadows. Downstream from the dam, the willow-lined canyon area offers opportunities for hiking, backpacking and fishing. Fishing is quite popular in the reservoir, even drawing a contingent of ice anglers in the winter. Fishing is for walleye, perch, salmon and trout. There is a BLM campground, Lud Drexler Park, near the dam.

For more information: Contact the BLM Burley District Office, Route 3, Box 1, Burley, ID 83318; (208) 678-5514.
BLM surface maps: Twin Falls, Rogerson

Silent City of Rocks National Reserve
hiking, picnicking, rock climbing

These fantastic granite monoliths in pillars, knobs, cliffs, pinnacles and hoodoos create a wonderful playground for hikers and rock climbers. Once nearly trashed by irreverent vandals and off-road activity, this area was established as a National Reserve in 1988, thanks mainly to the efforts of local residents.

•**See also Best of the State, page 228**•
For more information: Contact the BLM Burley District Office, Route 3, Box 1, Burley, ID 83318; (208) 678-5514; or the City of Rocks National Reserve, P.O. Box 169, Almo, ID 83312; (208) 824-5519.

SNAKE RIVER BIRDS OF PREY AREA
hiking, canoeing, wildlife observation, camping, wildlife photography, archaeological study

This area was established in 1980 to protect a unique environment in southwestern Idaho which supports one of the world's densest populations of nesting birds of prey. Within this region, falcons, eagles, hawks, owls and vultures play out the rhythms of life, but not within the usual confines of a zoo. The birds are not on display here. Public facilities are few and very primitive within the area where the nesting birds concentrate. This is nature in all its raw and rough splendor—it's there if you are willing to spend some time to look closely enough.

•**See also Best of the State, page 238**•
For more information: Contact the BLM Boise District Office, 3948 Development Avenue, Boise, ID 83705; (208) 334-1582.

SNAKE RIVER, MURTAUGH SECTION
whitewater kayaking for experts

Called "the best one-day whitewater run around" by the BLM, this section of river throws Class III, IV, V and even one section of Class VI water that only a fool wouldn't portage. Put-in is one-half mile north of Murtaugh at the Murtaugh Bridge. If you are feeling your oats and want to wet your kayaking whistle on some tough whitewater, give the BLM a call and they will fill you in on permit and access details.

For more information: Contact the BLM Shoshone District Office 77, 400 West F Street, P.O. Box 2-B, Shoshone, ID 83352; (208) 886-2206.

THORN CREEK RESERVOIR
camping, hiking, fishing

This site has the advantage of close proximity to the Gooding City of Rocks. It also offers excellent trout fishing and is quiet and very scenic owing to the surrounding lava outcrops. Don't expect to see many people here as it is out of the way and primarily enjoyed by locals—they shouldn't mind your out-of-town presence if you are mannerly.

Drive north on State Road 46 from Gooding. At approximately 20 miles and just past the turnoff for Gooding City of Rocks, head right on a dirt road. It's approximately four miles to the reservoir.

For more information: Contact the BLM Shoshone District Office 77, 400 West F Street, P.O. Box 2-B, Shoshone, ID 83352; (208) 886-2206. **BLM surface maps:** Fairfield

---

STATE INFORMATION OVERVIEW

IDAHO STATE OFFICE
3380 Americana Terrace, Boise, ID 83706; (208) 384-3000

BOISE DISTRICT OFFICE
3948 Development Avenue, Boise, ID 83705; (208) 384-3300

Bruneau Resource Area, 3948 Development Avenue, Boise, ID 83705; (208) 384-3300

Cascade Resource Area, 3948 Development Avenue, Boise, ID 83705; (208) 384-3300

Jarbidge Resource Area, 2620 Kimberly Road, Twin Falls, ID 83301; (208) 384-3300

Owyhee Resource Area, 3948 Development Avenue, Boise, ID 83705; (208) 384-3300

BURLEY DISTRICT OFFICE
Route 3, Box 1, Burley, ID 83318; (208) 678-5514

Deep Creek Resource Area, 138 South Main, Malad City, ID 83252; (208) 766-4766

Snake River Resource Area, Route 3, Box 1, Burley, ID 83318; (208) 678-5514

SHOSHONE DISTRICT OFFICE
400 West F Street, P.O. Box 2-B, Shoshone, ID 83352; (208) 886-2206

Bennett Hills Resource Area, 400 West F Street, P.O. Box 2-B, Shoshone, ID 83352; (208) 886-2206

Monument Resource Area, 400 West F Street, P.O. Box 2-B, Shoshone, ID 83352; (208) 886-2206

COEUR D'ALENE DISTRICT OFFICE
1808 North Third Street, Coeur d'Alene, ID 83814; (208) 769-5000

Cottonwood Resource Area, Route 3, Box 181, Cottonwood, ID 83522; (208) 962-3246

Emerald Empire Resource Area, 1808 North Third Street, Coeur d'Alene, ID 83814; (208) 769-5000

IDAHO FALLS DISTRICT OFFICE
940 Lincoln Road, Idaho Falls, ID 83401; (208) 524-7500

Big Butte Resource Area, 940 Lincoln Road, Idaho Falls, ID 83401; (208) 524-7500

Medicine Lodge Resource Area, 940 Lincoln Road, Idaho Falls, ID 83401; (208) 524-7500

Pocatello Resource Area, U.S. Courthouse, 250 South Fourth Avenue, Pocatello, ID 83201; (208) 236-6860

SALMON DISTRICT OFFICE
P.O. Box 430, Salmon, ID 83467; (208) 756-5400

Challis Resource Area, P.O. Box 430, Salmon, ID 83467; (208) 756-5400

Lemhi Resource Area, P.O. Box 430, Salmon, ID 83467; (208) 756-5400

CHAPTER

MONTANA

Maps—p. 260
Best of the State—p. 264
Montana by Region—p. 273
Information Resources—p. 285

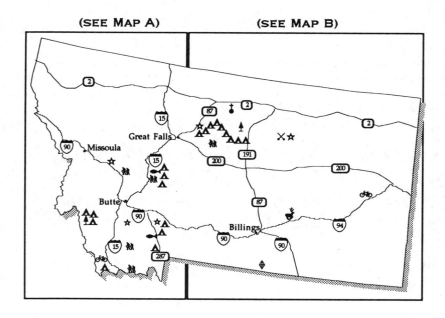

(SEE MAP A)   (SEE MAP B)

MAP A—MONTANA

Legend:

- ▲ campsite
- ☆ best of state
- 🥾 hiking
- 🚲 mountain biking
- ⛷ winter recreation
- 🦌 wildlife viewing
- 🐟 fishing
- whitewater
- general recreation
- ⊕ caves or spelunking
- ● cultural/historical site
- ✕ canoeing
- ✗ rock climbing

Map labels:

Holter Lake Cg.
Log Gulch Cg.
Departure Point Cg.
Bear Trap Canyon
Red Mountain Cg.
West Madison Cg.
Axolotl Lakes
South Madison Cg.
Ruby Mountains
Great Falls
Missoula
Butte
Centennial Mts.
Deadman Gulch Cg.
Garnet
Hoodoo Mts.
Holter Lake State Rec. Area
Sleeping Giant
Divide & Dickie Bridge Cg.
Big Hole River
East Bank Cg.
Humbug Spire Wilderness
Big Sheep Creek

MAP REFERENCES

Axolotl Lakes—p. 280-281
Bear Trap Canyon Wilderness—p. 264-265
Big Hole River—p. 281
Big Sheep Creek—p. 281-282
Centennial Mountains—p. 282-283
Garnet Recreation Trail/Garnet Ghost Town—p. 268-269
Hoodoo Mountains—p. 276
Humbug Spires—p. 266-267
Ruby Mountains—p. 283-284
Sleeping Giant Wilderness Study Area—p. 277

CAMPGROUNDS

The following campgrounds are found in this area of Montana.
Please call the BLM office (listed following each campground's
name) for reservations and information. Contact information
for each BLM office is on pages 285-286 of Montana.

Deadman Gulch Campground, Dillon Resource Area
Departure Point Campground, Headwaters Resource Area
Dickie Bridge Campground, Headwaters Resource Area
Divide Campground, Headwaters Resource Area
East Bank Campground, Headwaters Resource Area
Holter Lake Campground, Headwaters Resource Area
Log Gulch Campground, Headwaters Resource Area
Red Mountain Campground, Butte District Office
South Madison Campground, Dillon Resource Area
West Madison Campground, Dillon Resource Area

MAP B–MONTANA

Legend:

- △ campsite
- ☆ best of state
- 🥾 hiking
- 🚲 mountain biking
- winter recreation
- wildlife viewing
- fishing
- whitewater
- general recreation
- ⊕ caves or spelunking
- † cultural/historical site
- ✕ canoeing
- ⤢ rock climbing

Nez Perce National Historic Trail
Little Rocky Mts. Recreation Area
Upper Missouri National
Wild & Scenic River

Terry Badlands
Howery Island Rec. Area

Pryor Mt. National Wild Horse Range

See next page for complete list
of campsites along the
Upper Missouri River

Upper Missouri National
Wild & Scenic River

Square Butte Natural Area

Billings

MAP REFERENCES

Howery Island Recreation Area—p. 278-279
Little Rocky Mountains Recreation Area—p. 274-275
Nez Perce National Historic Trail—p. 273-274
Pryor Mountain National Wild Horse Range—p. 279
Square Butte Natural Area—p. 277-278
Terry Badlands Wilderness Study Area—p. 279-280
Upper Missouri National Wild & Scenic River—p. 270-272

CAMPGROUNDS

The following campgrounds are found in this area of Montana. Please call the BLM office (listed following each campground's name) for reservations and information. Contact information for each BLM office is on pages 285-286 of Montana.

Upper Missouri National Wild and Scenic River campgrounds:

Coal Banks Landing Campground, Lewiston District Office
Cow Island Landing Campground, Lewiston District Office
Dark Butte Campground, Lewiston District Office
Eagle Creek Campground, Lewiston District Office
Evans Bend Campground, Lewiston District Office
Fort Benton Campground, Lewiston District Office
Hole-In-The-Wall Campground, Lewiston District Office
James Kip Recreation Area, Lewiston District Office
Judith Landing Campground, Lewiston District Office
Little Sandy Campground, Lewiston District Office
Loma Bridge Campground, Lewiston District Office
Slaughter River Campground, Lewiston District Office
Stafford Ferry Campground, Lewiston District Office
Woodhawk Creek Campground, Lewiston District Office

1

BEAR TRAP CANYON WILDERNESS

Bear Trap Canyon was carved by the Madison River as it flowed west from Yellowstone through the Madison Range. Its 1,500-foot walls provide a scenic backdrop for a wide range of recreational activities from backpacking to whitewater rafting to trout fishing. Sections of the east side of the canyon abut with the Gallatin and Beaverhead National Forests. North slopes of the canyon are forested with Douglas fir, juniper and aspen. Sagebrush dots the southerly slopes.

HIKING/BACKPACKING

Bear Trap Canyon National Recreation Trail is nine miles each way. Ticks can be a problem during the spring and summer months. Take the time to perform a tick check daily. Bear-proof camping precautions are necessary, as black bear frequent the canyon and a periodic visit from a grizzly is not unusual.

WHITEWATER RAFTING

The BLM maintains a list of licensed outfitters who run trips through the canyon.

MANAGEMENT

BLM Dillon Resource Area, 1005 Selway Drive, P.O. Box 1048, Dillon, MT 59725; (406) 494-5059

LOCATION

This wilderness is in the southwest corner of Montana, approximately 30 miles west of Bozeman.

GETTING THERE

From Bozeman, travel approximately 30 miles west on State Road 84 to the Bear Trap Canyon Trailhead at the north end of the canyon. Those interested in running the canyon by whitewater kayak or raft will put in at the south end, near the

---

Montana Power Company powerhouse, located 10 miles north of the town of Ennis via local roads.

CAMPING
Red Mountain Campground, managed by the BLM, is located near the Bear Trap Canyon Trailhead. Primitive camping is allowed anywhere within the wilderness area for backpackers. River runners are prohibited from camping within the wilderness area.

PERMITS
No permits are necessary for backpacking.

MAPS
USGS topographic maps: Beartrap Creek, Norris, Ennis Lake. Obtain either the *Bear Trap Canyon Wilderness* folder with map or the *Bear Trap Canyon Floater's Guide* folder with map from the BLM.

ADDITIONAL INFORMATION
• *The Sierra Club Guide to the Natural Areas of Idaho, Montana, and Wyoming* by John and Jane Perry, published by Sierra Club, 730 Polk Street, San Francisco, CA 94109.
• *Western Whitewater, From the Rockies to the Pacific,* by Jim Cassady, Bill Cross and Fryar Calhoun, published by North Fork Press, Berkeley, CA; (800) 243-5522.
• *The Hikers Guide to Montana,* by Bill Schneider, published by Falcon Press, P.O. Box 1718, Helena, MT 59624; (800) 582-2665.

SEASON
The season runs from early May to late September. The canyon is most heavily traveled during July and August. Winter is a super time for exploring the trail via cross-country skis, but expect harsh temperatures and heavy snows.

TIP: Stay on the main trail even if wet or snow-covered.
Leaving the trail to skirt these areas
only creates another trail and point of erosion.

BEST OF THE STATE

2

HUMBUG SPIRES

There are 9,000-plus acres of dense forests, meadows and canyons at the edge of the Big Hole River Valley between the Highland and Pioneer ranges. Moose Creek is the major artery, tumbling through a narrow, boulder-filled canyon. There are numerous pools, beaver ponds and waterfalls. The steepest of the waterfalls create a natural barrier between trout in the lower reaches of the creek and native cutthroat in its upper environs. There are several rare and endangered plants in the canyon including Idaho sedge, Kelsey's milk-vetch, and Rock Mountain douglasia. Weathering and erosion account for the unique spires which name the Humbug area. The size and number of these spires are unequalled in the Northwest. Excellent rock climbing opportunities exist on many of the spires, some that have yet to be climbed.

HIKING/BACKPACKING

The developed trail is a short two-mile route heading northeast from the parking area through old growth Douglas fir and then up over a small ridge to the northeast fork of Moose Creek. From here, the opportunities for the adventurous backpacker are numerous. Utilizing game trails extending in all directions, it is possible to access the many rock spires, some 200 to 600 feet high, that are located throughout the northern section of the area. Terrain is heavily timbered and hikers traveling off the established trail must be adept at using a topographic map and compass. Adequate drinking water should be carried at all times.

MANAGEMENT

BLM Butte District Office, 106 North Parkmont, P.O. Box 3388, Butte, MT 59702; (406)494-5059.

LOCATION

Approximately 25 miles south of Butte along the west slopes of the Highland Mountains.

Getting There
To get to Humbug Spires, turn off Interstate 15 at the Moose Creek interchange and head east for about three miles on an improved gravel road. Parking is available at the trailhead.

Camping
Camping is allowed anywhere in the Humbug Spires.

Permits
No permit is necessary. Campfires may be prohibited due to fire danger in dry season, so call the BLM office for an update.

Maps
USGS topographic maps: Melrose, Tucker Creek, Mount Humbug, Wickiup Creek

Additional Information
For brief descriptive information and pictures of this and other Montana wild areas, get a copy of *Montana Wildlands,* by Bill Cunningham, published by Montana Magazine/American Geographic Publishing.

Season
The season runs from June to late September. You may encounter light snow in late spring and early fall.

TIP: Only gather firewood well away from more popular camping areas. Removing all downed wood from an area severely impacts the ecological balance of the region and removes vital nutrients that the soil and animals need.

GARNET RECREATION TRAIL
GARNET GHOST TOWN

Garnet bustled and prospered as a gold mining town from 1895 to 1911. Although it experienced a slight revival after the Great Depression, it was completely abandoned and left for the ghosts in 1950. Much of the area is filled with old mining shafts. It is also an area that has suffered from logging, and some activity is still ongoing in the vicinity.

Beginning and ending in the historic ghost town of Garnet, this trail system is primarily roads, some well maintained, some not. According to the area recreation specialist, Chuck Hollenbaugh, a mountain biker may see between three to four vehicles during a two-day ride. The trails system is well used in the winter as a signed and well maintained cross-country ski and snowmobile recreation area. Trails wind through open slopes and timber and skirt heavily mined areas. Elevations range up to 7,000 feet. There are excellent vistas of the Blackfoot Valley, Mission Mountains, the Bob Marshall Wilderness, and the Pintlar Range.

MOUNTAIN BIKING/BACKPACKING

The recommended loop begins in Garnet. Parking is good, but let the volunteer on duty know that your car is being left if you are planning an overnight. There are numerous streams and springs in the area, but all water must be treated. From Garnet, head out on the Summit Cabin trail, 4.2 miles to Elk Creek Summit. Continue straight for nine-tenths of a mile on the Keno Creek / Pearl Ridge Loop to the Top O'Deep Trail. Follow Top O'Deep around to rejoin with Keno Creek / Pearl Ridge after 3.5 miles. Go right on Keno Creek / Pearl Ridge 1.7 miles to the intersection with Kennedy Creek Trail. Head straight, now on Kennedy Creek, for 7.1 miles until the road rejoins Keno Creek. Turn right on Keno Creek riding six-tenths of a mile to another junction. Bear left, staying on Keno Creek and pedal one mile to Elk Creek Junction. At Elk Creek, head right on the Range Road Trail and pedal 2.6 miles back to the town of Garnet.

CROSS-COUNTRY SKIING

The Garnet National Winter Recreation Trail system is the hub for winter recreation in the Garnet Range east of Missoula. Cross-country skiing, snowshoeing and snowmobiling lure fun-hogs from all over the U.S. The main trail from Greenough to Garnet is groomed on a regular basis for both cross-country skiing and snowmobiling. Trails immediately around the ghost town are groomed on a regular basis. Outlying trails and lower elevation portions are groomed infrequently if at all.

MANAGEMENT
BLM Garnet Resource Area, 3255 Fort Missoula Road, Missoula, MT 59801; (406) 329-3914.

LOCATION
In the Garnet Range east of Missoula.

GETTING THERE
From Interstate 90, take either the Drummond or Bearmouth exit. Follow old US 10 to the Bear Gulch Road, midway between the two exits. Follow Bear Gulch to the historic ghost town of Garnet.

CAMPING
Camping is allowed anywhere within the resource area. No camping is allowed in the immediate vicinity of Garnet Ghost Town.

PERMITS
Check to see if a campfire permit is necessary. Normally no fire permit is required, however in times of high fire danger, permits must be carried.

MAPS
USGS topographic maps: Greenough, Bata Mountain, Chamberlain Mountain, Union Peak, Elevation Mountain, and Wild Horse Parks. Ask for *Garnet Winter Recreation Trails* map from the BLM Garnet Resource Area.

Season

Heavy snow is typical from mid-September to late May in the higher elevations, and from November to late March in the lower elevations. Hunting season is a time when vehicular use dramatically increases and mountain bikers probably will not want to be on the roads. The general hunting season is from October 21 to December 1.

Best of the State

4

Upper Missouri National Wild and Scenic River

Designated a Wild and Scenic River in 1976, this 149-mile segment is the only portion of the mighty Missouri River to be protected and preserved in its natural and free-flowing state. It is also the premier segment of the Lewis and Clark National Historic Trail. You will enjoy scenic vistas that remain much as they were when first described by Lewis and Clark during their 1805-1806 expedition.

Following the expedition, the river became the major waterway route west toward the Rocky Mountains until the coming of the railroads in the late 1800s. At the riverside trading posts of Forts Lewis, Benton, McKenzie and Piegan, the fur trade flourished for a short time. Steamboats brought gold seekers and supplies as far as Fort Benton. LaBarge Rock, Hole-In-The-Wall, Dark Butte, Citadel Rock—all are landmarks along the scenic White Rock section of the river that recall the period of western expansion. Frame and log dwellings, left behind by homesteaders who found the valley and environment too harsh, remain for visitors to view and get a feeling for the dreams that might have been.

Canoeing / Boating

Most boating trips are launched from either Fort Benton, Coal Banks Landing or Judith Landing. Floaters desiring a one-day outing often float between Fort Benton and Loma. Depending on the speed of travel, the float time between Coal

Banks Landing and Judith Landing, and Judith Landing and Fred Robinson Bridge takes three days. When on shore, you should be aware that rattlesnakes do frequent the area. This is not a hazard if you watch where you place your feet and hands. Beware of the low-hanging cables at each of the ferry crossings.

MANAGEMENT
BLM Judith Resource Area, 80 Airport Road, P.O. Box 1160, Lewiston, MT 59547; (406) 538-7461.

LOCATION
From Fort Benton on US 87 westward to the US 191 bridge crossing at Charles M. Russell National Wildlife Refuge.

GETTING THERE
See the designated put-in and take-out points listed below in tandem with the campgrounds. Access to these areas are via local and county roads. Check with the BLM prior to heading out to determine the best access routes and road conditions.

CAMPING
Camping is allowed anywhere along the river banks, however the BLM recommends that you camp only in designated sites. A great deal of private land bounds the river and if you choose to venture on to it, you are the landowner's guest. Act like one. If you are asked to leave, that is the landowner's right. Camping is formally available at the following sites which also offer toilets and drinking water:
• Fort Benton, put-in or take-out point
• Evans Bend, Loma Bridge, put-in and take-out point
• Coal Banks Landing, put-in and take-out point
• Judith Landing, put-in and take-out point
• Stafford Ferry, put-in and take-out point
• Cow Island Landing, put-in and take out point
• James Kip Recreation Area, put-in and take-out point
• Little Sandy, Eagle Creek, Hole-In-The-Wall, Dark Butte, Slaughter River, Woodhawk Creek

PERMITS
No permits are necessary, but you are required to register for safety and management purposes.

MAPS

The Complete Floaters Guide, including waterproofed maps 1, 2, 3, and 4, is available for $8 from the BLM.

ADDITIONAL INFORMATION

• *Western Whitewater, From the Rockies to the Pacific,* by Jim Cassady, Bill Cross and Fryar Calhoun, published by North Fork Press, Berkeley, CA; (800) 243-5522.
• BLM brochure: *Highlights of the Upper Missouri National Wild and Scenic River and Lewis and Clark National Historic Trail*
• BLM brochure: *Some Hazards on the Upper Missouri National Wild and Scenic River*

SEASON

The season runs from the weekend before Memorial Day (May) to the weekend following Labor Day (September).

TIP: Travel and camp responsibly to protect the environment and preserve opportunities to enjoy recreation in the wilderness.

1

MONTANA (GENERAL)

UPPER MISSOURI NATIONAL WILD AND SCENIC RIVER FROM FORT BENTON
hiking, wildlife observation, canoeing, boating, camping

Designated a Wild and Scenic River in 1976, this 149-mile segment is the only portion of the mighty Missouri River to be protected and preserved in its natural and free-flowing state. It is also the premier segment of the Lewis and Clark National Historic Trail. You will enjoy scenic vistas that remain much as they were when first described by Lewis and Clark during their 1805-1806 expedition.

Following the expedition, the river became the major waterway route west toward the Rocky Mountains until the coming of the railroads in the late 1800s. At the riverside trading posts of Forts Lewis, Benton, McKenzie and Piegan, the fur trade flourished for a short time. Steamboats brought gold seekers and supplies as far as Fort Benton. LaBarge Rock, Hole-In-The-Wall, Dark Butte, Citadel Rock—all are landmarks along the scenic White Rock section of the river that recall the period of western expansion. Frame and log dwellings, left behind by homesteaders who found the valley and environment too harsh, remain for visitors to view and get a feeling for the dreams that might have been.

•**See also Best of the State, page 270**•
For more information: Contact the BLM Judith Resource Area, 80 Airport Road, P.O. Box 1160, Lewiston, MT 59547; (406) 538-7461.

NEZ PERCE NATIONAL HISTORIC TRAIL

Dedicated in 1986 as a National Historic Trail, this is the 1,170-mile trail the Nez Perce Indians followed from Wallowa Lake, Oregon to Bears Paw Battlefield near Chinook, Montana. This trek must go down in history as one of the most remarkable odysseys of a persecuted people in recent times. Long friends of the white man, the Nez Perce found that a treaty guaranteeing them land in 1855 meant nothing in the face of

---

gold fever. During subsequent re-negotiations attempting to force the Nez Perce to cede some of the land to the whites, the tribe became split, with some agreeing to renegotiation and others walking out of the talks. Those that left became known as the "nontreaty" Nez Perce and, after several unfortunate events, they were forced to flee in the face of U.S. Army reprisal. The flight began on June 15, 1877, and ended on October 5, 1877. Many abandoned segments of the trail can be located today, but most are overgrown by vegetation, or altered by floods, powerlines or other manmade structures. The BLM manages an historic site in the Bear Paw Mountains.

For more information: Contact the BLM Miles City District Office, Gary Owen Road, P.O. Box 940, Miles City, MT 59301; (406) 232-4331.
BLM Lewistown District Office, 80 Airport Road, P.O. Box 1160, Lewiston, MT 59457; (406) 538-7461.
BLM Butte District Office, 106 North Parkmont, P.O. Box 3388, Butte, MT 59702; (406) 494-5059.

TIP: Do not pitch your tent directly over vegetation.

MONTANA BY REGION

2

NORTHEASTERN MONTANA

LITTLE ROCKY MOUNTAINS RECREATION AREA
hiking, camping, wildlife observation, horseback riding, fishing

Best known for providing shelter and refuge to assorted outlaws and whiskey traders including the likes of Butch Cassidy, Kid Curry and the Sundance Kid, the Little Rocky Mountains, surrounded by grassy plains and broken by the Missouri River, is now best regarded for its basement cargo of precious metals. Pagasus Gold Company runs an open-pit gold mine within the boundaries of the range. The BLM maintains a recreation area that offers decent hiking, camping and day exploring opportunities.

For more information: Contact the BLM Phillips Resource Area, 501 South Second Street, East, P.O. Box B, Malta, MT 59538; (406) 654-1240.

> *TIP: The most serious damage to a cultural site occurs from innocent visitation. Staying on the trail will minimize the damage.*

MONTANA BY REGION

3

NORTHWESTERN MONTANA

GARNET RECREATION TRAIL SYSTEM / GARNET GHOST TOWN

camping, hiking, backpacking, mountain biking, cross-country skiing, wildlife observation, snowmobiling

Garnet bustled and prospered as a gold mining town from 1895 to 1911. Although it experienced a slight revival after the Great Depression, it was completely abandoned and left for the ghosts in 1950. Much of the area is filled with old mining shafts. It is also an area that has been logged and some impacts are still ongoing in the vicinity.

Beginning and ending in the historic ghost town of Garnet, this trail system is primarily roads, some well maintained, some not. According to the resource area recreation specialist, Chuck Hollenbaugh, a mountain biker may see between three and four vehicles during a two-day ride. The trails system is well used in the winter as a signed and well maintained cross-country ski and snowmobile recreation area. Trails wind through open slopes and timber and skirt heavily mined areas. Elevations range up to 7,000 feet. There are excellent vistas of the Blackfoot Valley, Mission Mountains, the Bob Marshall Wilderness, and the Pintlar Range.

•**See also Best of the State, page 268**•
For more information: Contact the BLM Garnet Resource Area, 3255 Fort Missoula Road, Missoula, MT 59801; (406) 329-3914.

HOODOO MOUNTAINS
camping, backpacking, hiking, cross-country skiing, rock climbing, wildlife observation, fishing

Like the Garnet Recreation Trail System, the Hoodoos lie within the Garnet Range, which stretches from the town of Avon and US 12, just west of Helena, north along State Route 141 to Nevada Lake. The best access to the range is via a primitive road from Nevada Lake. The BLM thought highly enough of this mountain region to designate it as a wilderness study area. Tucked in among dense Douglas fir and lodgepole pine forests are grassy meadows, wet bogs, rocky outcroppings and fishable streams. Wildlife includes black bear, porcupine, elk, whitetail deer, porcupine and blacktail deer. Fishing is chiefly for cutthroat trout, although due to the size of the creeks, expect fish to be small and hardly abundant.

For more information: Contact the BLM Butte District Office, 106 North Parkmont, Butte, MT 59702; (406) 494-5059.
USGS topographic maps: Helmville

HOLTER LAKE STATE RECREATION AREA
camping, hiking, fishing, horseback riding, boating, swimming

From Interstate 15 between the cities of Great Falls and Helena, take the Wolf Creek exit, head east across the bridge and then south to the signed area. Holter Lake is really nothing more than an expansive section of the Missouri River caused by Holter Dam. Numerous agencies and private ownership make up the management of the area. The BLM oversees three campgrounds along Holter Lake near Holter Dam at the southeast end of the "lake" and a much larger region, Sleeping Giant Wilderness Study Area, along the west edge of the lake.

Gates of the Mountains Wilderness, part of the Helena National Forest, lies along the southeast side. The terrain immediately around the lake is hilly to mountainous, semi-arid, and features a number of rocky outcrops and timbered areas. Wildlife around the lake will likely include black bear, porcupine, cottontail, mule deer, whitetail deer, elk, bighorn sheep, and Rocky Mountain goat. Birdwatching is considered very good. Fishing is for trout and salmon.

For more information: Contact the BLM Headwaters Resource Area, 106 North Parkmont, P.O. Box 3388, Butte, MT 59702; (406) 494-5059.

USGS topographic maps: Beartooth Mountain, Sheep Creek Mountain

SLEEPING GIANT WILDERNESS STUDY AREA
hiking, horseback riding, mountain biking, wildlife observation, snowshoeing, cross-country skiing, fishing, camping

Access to this site is available via boat along Holter Lake. To gain access by vehicle, take the Interstate 15 frontage road and then go three miles along the improved gravel Wood Siding Gulch Road, which terminates at a proposed trailhead west of Sheep Creek. From the trailhead, opportunities for mountain biking abound over numerous established roads and trails throughout the 6,000 acres surrounding the Wilderness Study Area. Within the 10,000-acre Wilderness Study Area, hiking opportunities along the scenic ridgelines can be enjoyed eastward to the Missouri River and the Sleeping Giant profile at Beartooth Mountain. No established trails exist, but orientation and route finding is not too difficult. Views from on top of the ridgelines are outstanding. Wildlife includes mountain goats, bighorn sheep, elk, mule deer, red-tailed hawk, osprey, golden eagle and bald eagle. Rock spires in the area attract the more adventurous.

For more information: Contact the BLM Headwaters Resource Area, 106 North Parkmont, P.O. Box 3388, Butte, MT 59702; (406) 494-5059.
USGS topographic maps: Beartooth Mountain, Sheep Creek Mountain

SQUARE BUTTE NATURAL AREA
hiking, wildlife observation, camping

Stretching nearly 2,400 feet above the surrounding prairie, Square Butte is dramatic evidence of the powers of erosion—a spectacular flat-topped mound of igneous rock surrounded by eroded spires. Square Butte was named by the Stevens Intercontinental Railway Search Expedition in 1853. In the centuries before, there is evidence that the Butte was used for ceremonial purposes by early peoples and vision quests by Native Americans. From the summit it is possible to see the Highwood Mountains eight miles away to the west, Bears Paw and Little Rockies Mountains to the northeast and the Bit and Little Snowy Mountains to the southeast.

On the summit, it is interesting to note the vegetation, which has never been grazed by livestock—leaving evidence of the historic vegetation before grazing occurred on the surrounding prairie. Wildlife includes golden eagle, great horned owl, prairie falcon, mule deer and elk. Access to the area is through private property, which the landowner generously grants. Respect the privacy of the owner and his property. This area is accessed via the town of Square Butte on State Route 80, south of Fort Benton and east of Great Falls.

For more information: Contact the BLM Judith Resource Area, 80 Airport Road, P.O. Box 1160, Lewiston, MT 59547; (406) 538-7461. **USGS topographic maps:** Pownal, Jiggs Flat

---

*TIP: Constantly stay alert for signs
of your passing and erase them if possible.*

MONTANA BY REGION

SOUTHEASTERN MONTANA

HOWERY ISLAND RECREATION AREA
wildlife observation, fishing, hiking

Managed jointly with the Montana Department of Fish, Wildlife and Parks, Max Howery, and the BLM, Howery Island is one of only four known active bald eagle nesting sites in southeastern Montana. Occasionally subjected to flooding as evidenced by dry channels, logjams and gravel deposits, the island lies six miles west of Hysham off Highway 311 and is located on the Yellowstone River. To get there, take Interstate 94 to Hysham, then follow Secondary Highway 311 west for 6.9 miles to the Myers Bridge fishing access site turnoff. Continue a short distance past the fishing access site to a dry river channel. Park here and walk to the island—vehicles are restricted on the island itself. There are no established trails on the island, but it is possible to follow old vehicle tracks and wildlife trails. Bring your binoculars, because birdwatching on the island is tremendous with red-tailed hawks, bald eagles, great horned owls, red-headed woodpeckers, great blue herons, warblers, turkeys and wood ducks most common. Wildlife includes deer, red fox and beaver.

For more information: Contact the BLM Big Dry Resource Area, Miles City Plaza, Miles City, MT 59301; (406) 232-7000.
USGS topographic maps: Myers, Eldering Ranch

PRYOR MOUNTAIN NATIONAL WILD HORSE RANGE
hiking, camping, mountain biking, horseback riding, cross-country skiing, wildlife observation, spelunking

Designated in 1968 as a reserve for the protection and management of wild horses, this region sees light use by visitors year-round. Numerous caves attract spelunkers, although the most popular one, Mystery Cave, is gated and may be accessed only with a guide or by permit because of the great harm human impacts will cause. In addition to the 120 or so wild horses that occupy the range, native wildlife includes mule deer, bighorn sheep, elk, black bear and ring-necked pheasant. The terrain is a variety of open and rolling grasslands, steep-walled canyons and grassy mesas. Access is really limited to four-wheel-drive vehicles due to the rugged nature of the access road beginning with Crooked Creek. From Lovell, Wyoming, head north on Bad Pass Highway (37). Just before entering the Bighorn Canyon National Recreation Area, turn left on Crooked Creek Road.

For more information: Contact the BLM Billings Resource Area, 810 East Main Street, Billings, MT 59105; (406) 657-6262.
USGS topographic maps: Dead Indian Hill, East Pryor Mountain, Mystery Cave

TERRY BADLANDS WILDERNESS STUDY AREA
mountain biking, hiking, camping, rock hounding

These badlands are located four miles west of the town of Terry across the Yellowstone River. To get there from Interstate 94, exit at Terry, heading north on County Road 253 for approximately 1.5 miles and then head five miles west on an access road. This will find you at a signed overlook to the region. From here, numerous cattle paths crisscross through the rugged topography of sandstone bridges, spires, mesas and buttes. Visitors will find fossils, petrified wood and interesting rocks. During wet weather, routes within and around Terry Badlands become impassable. The Calypso Trail is a semi-improved trail that runs through the Terry Badlands and lies within the Big Dry Recreation Area. The trail is approximately eight miles in length and is ideally suited for mountain bikes. It can also be travelled by two-wheel-drive vehicles when conditions are ideal, but traffic is considered light.

For more information: Contact the BLM Big Dry Resource Area, Miles City Plaza, Miles City, MT 59301; (406) 232-7000.
USGS topographic maps: Terry, Calypso

TIP: Use a fire pan whenever you must build a campfire.

MONTANA BY REGION

5

SOUTHWESTERN MONTANA

AXOLOTL LAKES
hiking, backpacking, horseback riding, fishing, cross-country skiing, wildlife observation

Southeast of Virginia City and State Route 287, follow a county road approximately four miles to the edge of the site. The BLM refers to this region as an "outstanding natural area" and well it should. Tucked in between the Gravelly Range to the north, with an elevation of 7,000 feet, and the Beaverhead Forest to the south, towering above at 10,500 feet, the Axolotl Lakes is a picturesque land of numerous small lakes (lakettes really), grasslands, meadows, and forests—including aspen. Lightly visited, this area is a must-see opportunity. Wildlife observation will likely include elk, mule deer, moose, golden eagle and red-tailed hawk. Fishing is considered quite good in some of the larger lakes, most notably Axolotl and Blue, for cutthroat and rainbow trout.

For more information: Contact the BLM Butte District Office, 106 North Parkmont, P.O. Box 3388, Butte, MT 59702; (406) 494-5059. **USGS topographic maps:** Varneg, Cirque Lake, Eightmile Creek, Virginia City

BEAR TRAP CANYON WILDERNESS AREA
hiking, backpacking, wildlife observation, cross-country skiing, whitewater rafting, kayaking, canoeing, fishing, camping

Bear Trap Canyon was carved by the Madison River as it flowed west from Yellowstone through the Madison Range. Its 1,500-foot walls provide a scenic backdrop for a wide range of recreational activities from backpacking to whitewater rafting to trout fishing. Sections of the east side of the canyon abut with the Gallatin and Beaverhead National Forests. North slopes of the canyon are forested with Douglas fir, juniper, and aspen. Sagebrush dots the southerly slopes.

•See also Best of the State, page 264•
For more information: Contact the BLM Butte District Office, 106 North Parkmont, Butte, MT 59702; (406) 494-5059.

BIG HOLE RIVER
hiking, horseback riding, canoeing, swimming, camping, fishing

This is primarily a water-based destination recreation area with both primitive and developed camping allowed.

For more information: Contact the BLM Headwaters Resource Area, 106 North Parkmont, P.O. Box 3388, Butte, MT 59702; (406) 494-5059.

BIG SHEEP CREEK
hiking, backpacking, camping, fishing, mountain biking, wildlife observation

This area is under appeal and access may become limited or restricted altogether. Contact the BLM regarding status before heading out.

Running right through the middle of an area separating parts of the Beaverhead National Forest/Bitterroot Mountain Range, the Continental Divide and the Tendoy Mountains, is

---

Big Sheep Creek Backcountry Byway. Now, I know this is a book dealing with non-motorized recreation, but the beauty of this 50-mile route is that it provides super access to a world of adventure that bounds the road. Although the route is traveled by vehicles, it is not heavy enough to deter from the pleasure of pedaling the route. Primitive camping is allowed anywhere along the route on BLM land and a maintained primitive campground is located at Deadman Gulch. Wildlife that frequent the area include elk, mule deer, pronghorn antelope, moose, and a variety of hawks, eagles and owls.

For more information: Contact the BLM Dillon Resource Area, 1005 Selway Drive, P.O. Box 1048, Dillon, MT 59725; (406) 494-5059.
USGS topographic maps: Dell, Dixon Mountain, Deer Canyon, Graphite Mountain, Island Butte

CENTENNIAL MOUNTAINS
camping, hiking, backpacking, fishing, horseback riding, cross-country skiing, wildlife observation, snowmobiling

With the Continental Divide running along its crest, the Centennial Mountain Range is an imposing and often snow-capped wall that straddles the Montana/Idaho border, just east of Monida and Interstate 15. Designated a Wilderness Study Area, elevations range from 6,500 feet to just over 9,000 feet. Much of the region is forested with Douglas fir and lodgepole pine. The Continental Divide Trail runs through the Centennial Mountains, traversing 25 miles of BLM land, a section of the Targhee National Forest and the U.S. Sheep Experiment Station managed by the Agricultural Research Station. June through September is the best time to travel the trail. Bugs can be bothersome—pack plenty of insect repellent.

The trailhead may be best accessed at Red Rock Pass on the gravelled Red Rock Pass Road from Highway 20, south of Henry's Lake in Idaho. The trailhead lies at the western end of the Continental Divide Trail segment at Ching Creek in Idaho—managed by the Dubois Ranger District—and crosses Interstate 15 south of Monida Pass. Fishing in Blair Lake adjacent to the Continental Divide is considered good. A primitive campground exists a few mile east of Lakeview, Montana on the Centennial Road. One final note of caution: although the access points are passable with a two-wheel-drive vehicle in good weather, wet conditions mandate four-wheel-drive.

For more information: Contact the BLM Dillon Resource Area, 1005 Selway Drive, P.O. Box 1048, Dillon, MT 59725; (406) 494-5059.
USGS topographic maps: Winslow Creek, Big Table Mountain, Corral Creek, Monida

HUMBUG SPIRE WILDERNESS STUDY AREA
hiking, backpacking, fishing, camping, cross-country skiing, wildlife observation

There are 9,000-plus acres of dense forests, meadows and canyons at the edge of the Big Hole River Valley between the Highland and Pioneer ranges. Moose Creek is the major artery, tumbling through a narrow, boulder-filled canyon. There are numerous pools, beaver ponds and waterfalls. The steepest of the waterfalls creates a natural barrier between trout in the lower reaches of the creek and native cutthroat in its upper environs. There are several rare and endangered plants in the canyon including Idaho sedge, Kelsey's milk-vetch, and Rock Mountain douglasia. Weathering and erosion account for the unique spires which name the Humbug area. The size and number of these spires are unequalled in the Northwest. Excellent rock climbing opportunities exist on many of these spires, some that have yet to be climbed.
•**See also Best of the State, page 266**•
For more information: Contact the BLM Butte District Office, 106 North Parkmont, P.O. Box 3388, Butte, MT 59702; (406) 494-5059.

RUBY MOUNTAINS
hiking, backpacking, climbing, wildlife observation, camping, cross-country skiing, horseback riding

Getting into the mountains can be a bit of a challenge as access is limited by private land surrounding the range. This necessitates that you check in with the BLM prior to your visit to determine the best route of access. Don't let that deter you, however. This mountainous area is spectacular! Steep and carved with deep canyons, the slopes are carpeted with lodgepole pine, Douglas fir, Englemann spruce and limber pine. Rock walls, small caves, meadows with colorful wildflower displays and small aspen groves add to the charm and splendor of the region. Wildlife includes elk, mule deer, black bear, grouse and porcupine.

For more information: Contact the BLM Dillon Resource Area, 1005 Selway Drive, P.O. Box 1048, Dillon, MT 59725; (406) 494-5059.
USGS topographic maps: Mount Humbug, Tucker Creek

STATE INFORMATION OVERVIEW

MONTANA STATE OFFICE
Granite Tower, 222 North 32nd Street, P.O. Box 36800, Billings, MT 59107; (406) 255-2885

BUTTE DISTRICT OFFICE
106 North Parkmont, P. O. Box 3388, Butte, MT 59702; (406) 494-5059

Dillon Resource Area, 1005 Selway Drive, P.O. Box 1048, Dillon, MT 59725; (406) 683-2337

Garnet Resource Area, 3255 Fort Missoula Road, Missoula, MT 59801; (406) 329-3914

Headwaters Resource Area, 106 North Parkmont, P.O. Box 3388, Butte, MT 59702; (406) 494-5059

DICKINSON DISTRICT OFFICE
2933 Third Avenue West, Dickinson, North Dakota 58601; (701) 225-9148

LEWISTOWN DISTRICT OFFICE
80 Airport Road, P. O. Box 1160, Lewiston, MT 59457; (406) 538-7461

Great Falls Resource Area, 812 14th Street North, Great Falls, MT 59401; (406)727-0503

Havre Resource Area, West Second Street, P.O. Drawer 911, Havre, MT 59501; (406) 265-5891

Judith Resource Area, 80 Airport Road, P.O. Box 1160, Lewiston, MT 59547;(406) 538-7461

Phillips Resource Area, 501 South Second Street, East, P.O. Box B, Malta, MT 59538; (406) 654-1240

Valley Resource Area, RR 1-4775, Glasgow, MT 59230; (406) 228-4316

MILES CITY DISTRICT OFFICE
Gary Owen Road, P.O. Box 940, Miles City, MT 59301; (406) 232-4331

Big Dry Resource Area and Powder River Resource Area, Miles City Plaza, Miles City, MT 59301; (406) 232-7000

Billings Resource Area, 810 East Main Street, Billings, MT 59105; (406) 657-6262

Area Manager, BLM, 310 Round Up, Belle Fourche, South Dakota 57717; (605) 892-2526

NEVADA

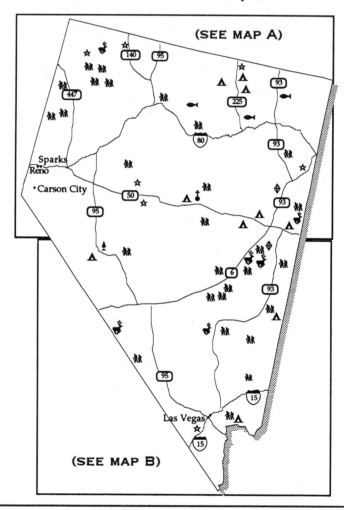

MAP A—NEVADA

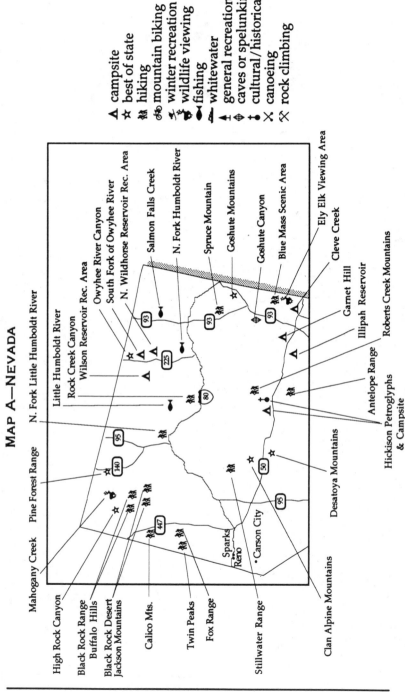

- △ campsite
- ☆ best of state
- 舲 hiking
- ⥁ mountain biking
- ⛷ winter recreation
- 🦌 wildlife viewing
- 🐟 fishing
- ◀ whitewater
- ⊕ general recreation
- ⌖ caves or spelunking
- ⸉ cultural/historical site
- ✕ canoeing
- ⚔ rock climbing

MAP REFERENCES

Antelope Range—p. 315-316
Black Rock Desert—p. 307-308
Black Rock Range—p. 308
Blue Mass Scenic Area—p. 316
Buffalo Hills—p. 308
Calico Mountains—p. 309
Clan Alpine Mountains—p. 296-297
Desatoya Mountains—p. 298-299
Ely Elk Viewing Area—p. 310-311
Fox Range—p. 311
Goshute Canyon and Goshute Canyon Natural Area—
    p. 316-317
Goshute Mountains—p. 303-304
Hickison Petroglyphs—p. 318
High Rock Canyon—p. 294-296
Jackson Mountains—p. 312
Little Humboldt River—p. 318
Mahogany Creek and Lahontan—p. 313-314
North Fork Humboldt River—p. 319
North Fork Little Humboldt River—p. 312-313
Owyhee River Canyon—p. 300-303
Pine Forest Range—p. 292-294
Roberts Creek Mountains—p. 320
Rock Creek Canyon—p. 320-321
Salmon Falls Creek—p. 321
Spruce Mountain—p. 321-322
Stillwater Range—p. 314
Twin Peaks—p. 314-315

CAMPGROUNDS

The following campgrounds are found in this area of Nevada. Please call the BLM office (listed following each campground's name) for reservations and information. Contact information for each BLM office is on page 330 of Nevada.

Cleve Creek, Ely District Office
Garnet Hill, Ely District Office
Hickison Petroglyphs Campsite, Ely District Office
Illipah Reservoir, Ely District Office
North Wildhorse Reservoir Recreation Area, Elko District Office
South Fork of the Owyhee River, Elko District Office
Wilson Reservoir Recreation Area, Elko District Office

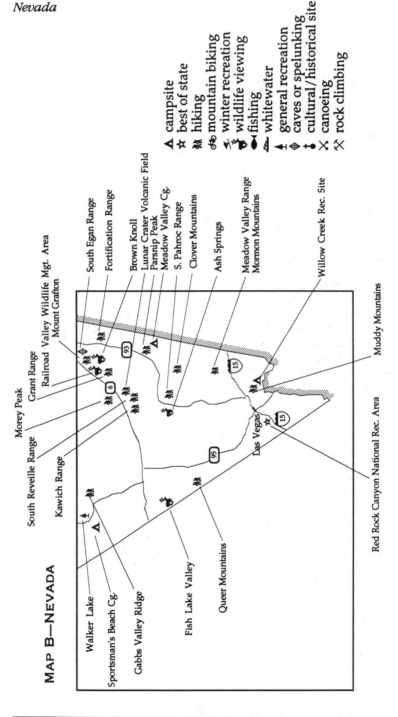

MAP B—NEVADA

campsite
best of state
hiking
mountain biking
winter recreation
wildlife viewing
fishing
whitewater
general recreation
caves or spelunking
cultural/historical site
canoeing
rock climbing

South Egan Range
Fortification Range
Brown Knoll
Lunar Crater Volcanic Field
Parsnip Peak
Meadow Valley Cg.
S. Pahroc Range
Clover Mountains
Ash Springs
Meadow Valley Range
Mormon Mountains
Willow Creek Rec. Site
Muddy Mountains
Railroad Valley Wildlife Mgt. Area
Mount Grafton
Morey Peak
Grant Range
South Reveille Range
Kawich Range
Walker Lake
Sportsman's Beach Cg.
Gabbs Valley Ridge
Fish Lake Valley
Queer Mountains
Red Rock Canyon National Rec. Area
Las Vegas

MAP REFERENCES

Ash Springs—p. 322
Brown Knoll—p. 322-333
Clover Mountains—p. 323
Fish Lake Valley—p. 323
Fortification Range—p. 324
Gabbs Valley Ridge—p. 324
Grant Range—p. 324
Kawich Range—p. 325
Lunar Crater Volcanic Field—p. 325
Meadow Valley Range and Mormon Mountains—p. 325-326
Morey Peak—p. 326
Mount Grafton—p. 318-319
Muddy Mountains—p. 326
Parsnip Peak—p. 327
Queer Mountains—p. 327
Railroad Valley Wildlife Management Area—p. 320
Red Rock Canyon National Conservation Area—p. 304-306
South Egan Range—p. 328
South Pahroc Range—p. 329
South Reveille Range—p. 329
Walker Lake—p. 329

CAMPGROUNDS

The following campgrounds are found in this area of Nevada. Please call the BLM office (listed following each campground's name) for reservations and information. Contact information for each BLM office is on page 330 of Nevada.

Meadow Valley Campground, Ely District Office
Sportsman's Beach Campground, Carson District Office
Willow Creek Recreation Site, Las Vegas District Office

PINE FOREST RANGE

The outstanding scenic quality of this region is worth the effort required to get there—cathedral-like peaks, high mountain meadows, clear, subalpine lakes, steep topography, colorful aspen groves, and abundant water. Spectacular views from many of the high points in the area yield panoramic vistas that extend into nearby California and Oregon.

Always inquire locally for current road conditions before heading out on unimproved roads. Nevada secondary and dirt roads can become impassable and even hazardous when wet. For this reason, many area locations given in this chapter are not specific, requiring you to ask for additional directions.

HIKING

Because access is moderately difficult—15 miles of rough road—day-use is very light. Most visitors are overnight campers seeking fishing, backpacking, hunting, wildlife watching, or other recreational pursuits. There is an obvious trail that leads from Onion Reservoir to Blue Lakes, a popular overnight destination for trout fishing. But many more opportunities for backpacking explorations exist for the experienced and moderately adventurous backpacker. Duffer Peak at 9,400 feet is the highest mountain in the Pine Range. It lies several cross-country miles south of Blue Lakes. Water is moderately plentiful, but hikers are cautioned to carry adequate reserves.

MOUNTAIN BIKING

Mountain biking opportunities exist on the four-wheel-drive roads that are open outside of the vehicle-closure boundary. An approximately 15-mile loop may be put together by including Alder Creek Road, Sand Basin Road, Cove Camp Road, and Alta Creek Road. A connecting trail from Rodeo Flat over to Cove Camp Road makes the loop possible. No mountain bikes are allowed within the Wilderness Study Area which encompasses Duffer Peak, Blue Lakes and part of Little Onion Valley Reservoir.

MANAGEMENT
BLM Winnemucca District Office, 705 East Fourth Street, Winnemucca, NV 89445; (702) 623-3676

LOCATION
Approximately 70 miles north of Winnemucca and Interstate 80 in the northwestern corner of the state.

GETTING THERE
From Winnemucca, drive 30 miles north on US 95 and then 40 miles west on State Highway 140. Turn left onto Alder Creek Road, just south of the highway maintenance station. It is a dirt road and only suitable for high-clearance vehicles. Four-wheel-drive vehicles are recommended. The trailhead for Blue Lakes and Duffer Peak is at the Onion Valley Reservoir, approximately 15 miles from Highway 140. Mountain bikers must camp outside of the vehicle closure area at Onion Valley or at another appropriate site.

CAMPING
Onion Valley Reservoir has designated primitive camping sites and porta-potties. Primitive camping is allowed anywhere else in the region. One word of caution: Nevada state law prohibits camping within 300 feet of watering holes that are used by livestock.

PERMITS
No permits are necessary.

MAPS
USGS topographic series: Railroad Point, Denio, Idaho Canyon, Duffer Peak

ADDITIONAL INFORMATION
The Hikers Guide to Nevada, by Bruce Grubbs, published by Falcon Press, P.O. Box 1718, Helena, MT 59624.

SEASON
While summer temperatures may climb into the 90s during the day, the nights are usually quite chilly. The best season to visit this area is from May to September. Snow in the winter closes the roads, but the more adventurous may find enjoyment in

---

exploring the area via cross-country skis—check at the BLM office for the snow report.

> *TIP: Look at and photograph, never pick up or collect.*
> *Leave any artifacts you find where they lie.*

2

HIGH ROCK CANYON

The area from High Rock Canyon to Cottonwood Canyon is considered one of the most historic desert canyon routes in the West. First documented by John C. Fremont during his 1843-1844 expedition to Oregon and California, and then subsequently used by settlers and wagon parties as an alternate route to the established Oregon Trail, the canyon became known as the Applegate Trail. During 1849, it is estimated that nearly half of the '49ers (no, not the football team) used this route to get to the gold fields of California, thinking it was the shortest way there. Troubles with Native Americans and the realization that this route was in fact longer than alternate routes, reduced the use somewhat. However, from 1851, when gold was discovered in the Siskiyou Mountains of northern California, up until modern railroads and roads provided alternative routes in the late 1800s, the Applegate Trail through High Rock Canyon remained the primary path into and out of southern Oregon.

HIKING

The High Rock Canyon Trail has been recognized by the BLM as an area of historical importance and is now designated as an Area of Critical Environmental Concern. A Cooperative Management Agreement has been signed by the BLM, the Friends of High Rock Canyon and the Desert Trail Association for the "express purpose of protecting the cultural and natural values of the canyon." Beginning at High Rock Lake, the trail meanders in a northwest direction along sandy washes and

through sagebrush, rice grass, juniper, willow, and greasewood. The geological formations are spectacular, as centuries
of wind and rain have carved basaltic rock and volcanic ash
into awesome canyons. Deer, antelope, rabbits, sage grouse,
and an unusually large population of raptors frequent the area.
The High Rock Canyon Trail section ends at Cottonwood
Canyon in the Sheldon National Wildlife Refuge.

MANAGEMENT
BLM Susanville District Office, 705 Hall Street, Susanville, CA
96130; (916) 257-5381

LOCATION
160 miles due north of Reno and approximately 100 miles
south of Oregon; just east of the California/Oregon borders.

GETTING THERE
Take Interstate 80 east to Wadsworth. Go north on State
Highway 447 to Gerlach. Bear right on the county road just
past Gerlach, north to Leadville and Vya. After approximately
60 miles, bear right on the road to High Rock Lake (the BLM
sign designates this turnoff). It's approximately 15 miles to
High Rock Lake. Park near the signed gate for the High Rock
Canyon Area of Critical Environmental Concern.

CAMPING
There is designated camping in this area. The first good water
stop is an area called Steven's Camp—17 miles from the
parking area. Carry plenty of water.

PERMITS
No permits are necessary.

MAPS
USGS topographic maps: High Rock Lake, Mahogany Moun-
tain, Yellow Hills West, Yellow Hills East, Badger Mountain
Southeast

ADDITIONAL INFORMATION
High Rock Canyon Hiking Guide is published by the Desert
Trail Association, P.O. Box 589, Burns, OR 97720.

SEASON

The best time to travel through the High Rock Canyon area is during the spring and fall. Fires, pets and radios are prohibited on the trail. Water is unreliable and hikers are advised to carry all that they will need. Water, if found, should be treated before drinking. The canyon is closed from mid-February to April 1, for raptor nesting season. It is open the rest of the year. The best times to backpack are in May and from September to November. Summer is uncomfortably warm. Temperatures can be extreme at any time so prepare accordingly.

TIP: Stay on the main trail even if it is wet or snow-covered. Leaving the trail to skirt these areas only creates another trail and point of erosion.

BEST OF THE STATE

3

CLAN ALPINE MOUNTAINS

With a high point of 9,960 feet at Mount Augusta, this canyon-dissected range towers nearly 6,500 feet above the Dixie Valley to the west. The Clan Alpine Mountains are highly scenic, with a number of canyons sporting perennial streams and springs. Rock formations are colorful and abundant. Views from the ridgetops extend to the Sierra crest—100 miles westward. Aspen line the canyons, and mountain mahogany (rare in this part of Nevada) and pinon/juniper forests dot the slopes. The wildlife here includes the sage grouse, golden eagle, prairie falcon, mule deer, wild horses, and mountain lion. Rainbow and brown trout have been introduced here, but don't hold your breath waiting for them to bite—the fish are scarce.

BACKPACKING / CROSS-COUNTRY SKIING

This is a wild area that is quite easily accessible and suitable for all types of wilderness exploration. Although water is available in many of the canyons, there is no guarantee of its presence so carry all that you will need (one gallon per person per day). Game trails and old unmaintained roads make good foot and horse routes.

MANAGEMENT

BLM Carson City District, 1535 Hot Springs Road, Suite 300, Carson City, NV 89706; (702) 885-6000

LOCATION

Due east of Reno and North of US 50 along Highway 121.

GETTING THERE

From Reno, head east on Interstate 80, bearing right at Fernley on US 50. Follow US 50 past Frenchman then turn left and north on Highway 121. Follow 121 north to the Dixie Valley turnoff, right, and then on to Dixie Valley, just south of Humboldt Salt Marsh. There are a number of roads that branch off Highway 121 along the way and lead into the Clan Alpine Range. Dixie Valley is a good place to ask directions. Services are few and far between—gas up at every opportunity.

CAMPING

Camping is allowed anywhere. Several unimproved roads in Deep Canyon, Horse Creek, Cow Canyon (all on the west side) and Bench Creek, Cherry Creek, and War Canyon (all on the east side) provide vehicle access into the range and are suitable areas to set up a base-camp for day-hiking enjoyment.

PERMITS

No permits are necessary.

MAPS

USGS topographic maps: Wonder Mountain, Mount Augusta, Byers Creek, Shoshone Meadows, Cow Canyon, Clan Alpine Ranch, Tungsten Mountain

SEASON

This area is available for year-round use. Access to winter recreation sites is difficult at best, and requires a four-wheel-drive vehicle. Inquire at the BLM office for updated access information. Summer months can be uncomfortably hot in the lower elevations, but should be tolerable once above 7,000 feet.

TIP: *Travel or camp in small groups.*

DESATOYA MOUNTAINS

This is an extremely scenic range with outstanding wind-swept views to the east of the Toiyabe Range, to the northwest of the Clan Alpine Range, and to the far west on clear days of the Sierra Nevada. Standing tall above the surrounding desert with a high point of 9,973 feet at Desatoya Peak, the range is sharply dissected by canyons—many of them narrow, rocky and featuring perennial streams. Big Den Canyon is the most noteworthy and well known for its 30-foot waterfall and colorful rock spires. Aspen, willow and wild rose line many of the canyon bottoms. Pinyon pine and juniper dot the slopes at the lower elevations. The wildflowers are super during the spring. According to the BLM, this is one of the best mountain ranges in northwestern Nevada for adventuring because of the scenery, accessibility and availability of water.

HIKING/BACKPACKING

There are no formal hiking trails here. Follow the ridgeline or seek out game trails along the canyons that drop down from the ridge. Desatoya Peak, 9,973 feet, lies north of the Carroll Summit Pass access point. Follow the ridgeline to get there.

CROSS-COUNTRY SKI TOURING

Ski touring is quite good along the ridgeline above 7,500 feet, from December to March. Access can be challenging in the winter. Be prepared for very strong winds. Avalanche safety and rescue skills are a must for venturing into the backcountry.

MANAGEMENT
BLM Carson City District, 1535 Hot Springs Road, Suite 300, Carson City, NV 89706; (702) 885-6000

LOCATION
Roughly 112 miles east of Reno at Eastgate on Highway 722.

GETTING THERE
From Reno, head east on Interstate 80. Turn right, south, on US Highway 50 at Fernley towards Fallon. Follow US Highway 50 to its intersection with State Highway 722 to Eastgate. Eastgate is a good place to stop and get specific directions to a good place you wish to visit in the range. Access to the Desatoya Mountains is possible from various points off Highway 722, which cuts the range into roughly equal parts, north and south. The best access to this area is at the Carroll Summit pass—elevation 7,452 feet.

CAMPING
Camping is permitted anywhere within this area.

PERMITS
No permits are necessary.

MAPS
USGS topographic maps: Buffalo Summit, Desatoya Peak, Carroll Summit, Cold Springs, Basque Summit

SEASON
This area is available for year-round use. Access to winter recreation sites is difficult at best and requires a four-wheel drive vehicle. Inquire at the BLM office for updated access information. Summer months can be uncomfortably hot in the lower elevations, but should be tolerable once above 7,000 feet.

TIP: Never dig holes, trenches, or otherwise alter a campsite for convenience. The perfect campsite is found, not made.

5

OWYHEE RIVER CANYON

Although access is challenging, this 450,000-acre region (much of it lying to the north in Idaho and known as the Owyhee Canyonlands) is picturesque, dramatic, wild, isolated and well worth your time. River runners and hunters are the predominant users, and there are not too many of those. The narrow canyons that cut into the plateau range anywhere from several hundred to one thousand feet deep—often with sheer walls from rimrock to river bottom. Mountain lion, bobcat, river otter, pronghorn antelope, and bighorn sheep reside within the Owyhee canyon system.

HIKING

There are no established hiking routes here. Hiking trips are either wandering along the canyon edges or along the canyon floors—following the game trails when available. Within the canyons themselves, hiking can be tedious at best, often requiring frequent rock and talus scrambles, and at times, river wading or swimming. Only experienced backpackers and those with knowledge and skills in canyoneering should venture into the canyon bottoms. Hiking is much easier on the mile-high desert plateau. Although some springs and hidden swimming holes do exist, water is not easily found on the plateau. Check with the BLM office for specific locations and potability information (all water must be filtered and/or treated to guard against Giardia). Always carry adequate reserves just in case—one gallon per person is advised.

BOATING

Upper Owyhee
This river consists of three forks, the east (Idaho), south (Nevada into Idaho) and north fork (Idaho). Both the east and south forks are floatable in rafts, kayaks and canoes. The river is rated Class II through IV, with several very arduous portages on the east fork before its confluence with the south. The

south fork is quite scenic with Class I to II water. The BLM lists the north fork as a river for "world class" expert kayakers only! Enough said. If you continue on after the Nevada/Idaho section this is what to expect in Idaho:

Middle Owyhee
The Middle Owyhee is a mixture of Class III through Class V+ rapids that are challenging for most boaters. Small 12 to 15-foot rafts and kayaks are recommended. The rapids feature long boulder gardens, some steep drops and several heavy hydraulics. Some portaging is required.

Lower Owyhee
The Lower Owyhee offers Class II through Class IV rapids that any level of boater in all variety of crafts—raft, canoe, kayak or drift boat—will find enjoyable. This is the most popular section of the river and is considered ideal for family groups and parties with inexperienced boaters. No party should attempt the river without several members being qualified intermediate boaters capable of navigating Class III and Class IV whitewater safely. The river is somewhat forgiving because it is of the "pool and drop" variety, meaning that rapids are usually short followed by calm, pool sections giving you time to recover.

MANAGEMENT
BLM Elko District Office, P.O. Box 831, 3900 East Idaho Street, Elko, NV 89801; (702) 753-0200

LOCATION
The northeastern high-desert region is north of Interstate 80 and west of Highway 225 and the town of Owyhee. Also, the vast region includes the high-desert region of southwestern Idaho—southwest of Grand View and Highway 78 and south-east of Jordan Valley, Oregon and US 95.

GETTING THERE
This area is predominantly roadless—hence its attraction. The dirt roads that do exist can become impassable at any time. In fact, one river runner I talked to said that he considered much of the Owyhee a Class II river float with a Class V access. The official *River Runners Guide to Idaho*, published by the BLM and the Idaho Parks and Recreation states that "spring rains are

common and the dirt tracks can quickly turn into an impassable quagmire of gumbo." The same is true for the Nevada portion of the Owyhee. Before visiting, check with the BLM office in Elko to determine which access route would be most appropriate during the time of your visit. Four-wheel-drive vehicles are recommended for any route not graveled! The best access in Nevada takes you 28 miles west of the town of Owyhee on local and unimproved roads—river put-in is at Petan Ranch. The best access in Idaho is via the Owyhee Uplands National Backcountry Byway, a 101-mile gravel road, suitable for high-clearance vehicles. This road stretches from Grand View, on Idaho State Highway 78, and Jordan Valley in Oregon and US 95. There are numerous take-outs appropriate for overnight camping and embarking on short or extended backpacking explorations.

CAMPING
Camping is permitted anywhere within the canyon proper or on the plateau. Campsites are evident and frequent—select sites already established if you have the choice.

PERMITS
No permits are necessary for backpacking. Boaters, however, must register prior to embarking on any of the Owyhee River forks and tributaries.

MAPS
BLM surface maps: Riddle (south fork and east fork), Triangle (north fork)

ADDITIONAL INFORMATION
• *Owyhee River Boating Guide* is available through the Boise District BLM office.
• *Western Whitewater, From the Rockies to the Pacific,* by Jim Cassady, Bill Cross, and Fryar Calhoun, published by North Fork Press, Berkeley, CA; (800) 243-5522.

SEASON
The best hiking is in May and June or in September and October. July and August are hot and dry. May and early June are best times for wildflowers. The best boating is during the spring runoff from March through June. River levels can fluctuate severely with cold or warm spells and periods of

heavy rain. Call the River Forecast Center in Idaho at (503) 249-0666 for current gage readings.

BEST OF THE STATE

5

GOSHUTE MOUNTAINS

Located within the Goshute Mountains is the Goshute Raptor Migration Area. A lookout site in a small limestone outcrop, at approximately 9,000 feet, may be reached providing you have a high-clearance vehicle. Raptors fly along the Goshute Range, taking advantage of the uplift created by the mountains and avoiding the Bonneville Salt Flats to the east in Utah. This area is considered the best migration lookout in the western United States. It is possible to observe over 200 raptors in a single day—days with over 1,000 sightings are not uncommon either. Primary sightings include the sharp-shinned hawk, Cooper's hawk, northern goshawk, red-tailed hawk, American kestrel, golden eagle, turkey vulture, and northern harrier. It is possible, if you are interested, to participate in counting or banding studies as well.

MANAGEMENT
BLM Elko District Office, P.O. Box 831, 3900 East Idaho Street, Elko, NV 89801; (702) 753-0200

GETTING THERE
From Wendover, drive south on US Highway Alternate 93 for approximately 24 miles to the old Ferguson Highway Maintenance Station. Turn right and drive by the station on a dirt road for about two miles to a T junction. Turn right and go about one mile on the main road. Bear left at the top of the hill, proceeding up the rocky jeep road into Christmas Tree Canyon. The trail to the top of the ridge is about a two-mile hike, considered moderately strenuous with 1,600 feet of elevation gain.

PERMITS
No permits are necessary.

MAPS
USGS topographic maps: Goshute Peak, Lion Spring, Morgan Pass

ADDITIONAL INFORMATION
Hawk Watch International, P.O. Box 35706, Albuquerque, NM 87176; (505) 255-7622

SEASON
Raptor migration begins in mid-August and continues into November.

TIP: Take the time to animal proof your campsite for the protection of your gear, yourself, and the animal.

BEST OF THE STATE

6

RED ROCK CANYON NATIONAL CONSERVATION AREA

The predominant geological feature in Red Rock Canyon, and a feature that attracts rock climbers from all over, is a spectacular 3,000-foot sandstone escarpment extending for much of the region's length. Named for the bright red colors of the stone, this canyon region contains over 40 springs as well as many natural catch basins known as tanks. It is this presence of water, more prevalent than anywhere in the surrounding desert region, that supports a rich and concentrated plant and animal population. Joshua trees are predominant on the canyon floor. As the elevation rises, pinyon pine and juniper trees take over.

HIKING

There are many trails suitable for day hiking and a number of longer routes that are good choices for overnight backpacking. The BLM publishes a brochure *Red Rock Canyon National Conservation Area Hiking* which lists and briefly describes 15 routes.

MOUNTAIN BIKING

There are a number of suitable mountain bike routes that provide good views of the surrounding terrain. The most notable trail is the Scenic Loop Ride, suggested by the BLM. You will share these roads with other vehicles, so watch your speed and control.

WILDLIFE OBSERVATION

Wild horses and burros are popular attractions in the canyon—these were brought to the Great Basin area by early explorers. Over 100 species of birds have been identified in the area. The cooler canyons of Pine Creek and First Creek echo with the calls of canyon wrens. Keep an eye out for the occasional roadrunner streaking across the trails and roads. The desert tortoise, native to this area and listed as a threatened species, is most commonly seen after a summer rain or during cool spring days. The tortoise hibernates from October to March. Desert bighorn can be enjoyed in the White Rock Spring area and the Willow Spring picnic area. Mating season occurs in late summer, with the reverberations of vigorous head butting echoing up the canyon walls.

MANAGEMENT

BLM Las Vegas District Office, 4765 West Vegas Drive, Las Vegas, NV 89108; (702) 385-6403

LOCATION

Approximately 15 miles west of Las Vegas

GETTING THERE

From Las Vegas, head west on State Route 159 (West Charleston Boulevard) to the visitor's center. From Interstate 15, head west on State Route 160, and then west again on State Route 159.

CAMPING

Primitive camping is allowed, but only in certain areas. You must register for overnight camping. Check with the BLM.

PERMITS

No permits are necessary for day use. Registration is required for overnight use.

MAPS

USGS topographic maps: La Madre Mountain, La Madre Spring, Blue Diamond
BLM surface maps: Las Vegas

ADDITIONAL INFORMATION

The Hikers Guide to Nevada, by Bruce Grubbs, published by Falcon Press, P.O. Box 1718, Helena, MT 59624; (800) 582-2665.

SEASON

The best season for this area is the spring. Summers can be uncomfortably hot.

TIP: Mountain biking should be only on open roads and trails. Riding cross-country is destructive and leaves an obvious path that tempts others to follow.

1

NORTHWESTERN NEVADA

Always inquire locally for current road conditions before heading out on unimproved roads. Nevada secondary and dirt roads can become impassable and even hazardous when wet. For this reason, many area locations given in this chapter are not specific, requiring you to ask for additional directions.

BLACK ROCK DESERT
hiking, rock hounding, camping (along the edges only!), mountain biking

The Black Rock Desert is located roughly north of State Roads 48 and 49, between the towns of Gerlach and Winnemucca. If you look as far as you can in every direction, all you will see is bare, white playa surrounded by distant mountain ranges. If you gaze at the Black Rock Desert from above, you will see that it is shaped roughly like a giant Y. The western arm extends up to Soldier Meadows, has low shrub vegetation and is bordered on the west by the Calico Range. The eastern arm is bounded by the Jackson Mountains and follows the water course of the Quinn River. The main body of the Y is all playa. This area is the remains of the ancient Lake Lahontan, a Pleistocene-age lake that formed other valley bottoms in northwestern Nevada. Would you believe that in some places, the silt underfoot is nearly a mile deep?

This barren area is appropriate for hiking, rock hounding, mountain biking, and four-wheel-drive explorations—but only in the cooler months. Locals and those familiar with this vast desert, drive the playa during dry months. They either follow an historic route that links Gerlach and Winnemucca or venture freely into the interior. If you don't know the playa, don't wander into its vastness alone—strangers to the area have died from exposure once their vehicles became inextricably stuck. When the playa is wet, it becomes a quagmire of monumental proportions, impassable even on foot in many places.

For more information: Contact the BLM Winnemucca District Office, 705 East Fourth Street, Winnemucca, NV 89445; (702) 623-1500.
BLM surface maps: Highrock Canyon, Gerlache, Jackson Mountains, Eugene Mountain

BLACK ROCK RANGE
camping, hiking, backpacking, horseback riding

The Black Rock Range divides the two arms of the Black Rock Desert and is accessed by Soldier Meadows Ranch Road (County Road HU 217.) Backpacking, hiking and camping are good here, but be prepared for a difficult access and a very rugged trip. The southern sections of the range feature deep drainages and rugged, rocky outcroppings. Several springs, some of them hot, may be found here. The northern sections include the Lahontan Cutthroat Trout Natural Area, Mahogany Creek and areas of higher elevations cut with aspen and at times deep drainages. I suggest backpacking in the Big Mountain area. Camping is considered best here. Camping is also good at Colman Creek and Soldiers Creek.

For more information: Contact the BLM Winnemucca District Office, 705 East Fourth Street, Winnemucca, NV 89445; (702) 623-1500.
USGS topographic maps: Pidgeon Spring, Clapper Creek, Big Mountain, Paiute Meadows, Burnt Springs, Red Mountain, Summit Lake, Idaho Canyon Spring, New York Peak

BUFFALO HILLS
camping, backpacking, hiking, horseback riding

The Buffalo Hills are bounded on the east by State Road 447 and lies approximately 15 miles northwest of Gerlach. Since the area is so easily accessible, it is well suited for recreational uses. Water is readily available from many of the more than 50 springs (some on private land) and three major streams (Buffalo, Jones and Frog). From the air, it is easy to see that the area is one giant plateau with deep canyons radiating out to the surrounding desert like spokes from a wheel. The canyons provide the best access from the desert floor up to the top of the plateau. Wildlife includes pronghorn antelope, deer, mountain lion, sage grouse and chukar.

For more information: Contact the BLM Winnemucca District Office, 705 East Fourth Street, Winnemucca, NV 89445; (702) 623-1500.

USGS topographic maps: Squaw Valley, Poodle Mountain, Hillside Spring, Cruther Canyon, Wall Spring, Horse Canyon

CALICO MOUNTAINS
camping, hiking, rock hounding, horseback riding

The western border of the western arm of the Black Rock Desert is an outstanding location for rock hounding with jasper, fire opal, agate, and petrified wood. However, access is limited to this area. High Rock Lake offers poor access and Soldier Meadows Ranch Road offers fair to good access. Your best bet is to inquire at the BLM Winnemucca office or locally in the town of Gerlach. Wildlife observation is limited, as is the water. Pronghorn, mule deer, chukar, sage grouse, and quail can be seen in this area. Donnelly Creek provides the best opportunity for wildlife viewing and water. Water is scarce everywhere else so pack all that you will need. The camping is best along Donnelly Creek and near the few springs that may be found around the Donnelly Peak area. The best hiking is around High Rock Lake, Fly Canyon, Donnelly Creek, and Box Canyon.

For more information: Contact the BLM Winnemucca District Office, 705 East Fourth Street, Winnemucca, NV 89445; (702) 623-1500. **USGS topographic maps:** High Rock Lake, Mud Meadows, McConnel Canyon, Wagner Spring, Donnelly Peak, Division Peak

CLAN ALPINE MOUNTAINS
camping, hiking, backpacking, wildlife observation, horseback riding, cross-country skiing

With a high point of 9,960 feet at Mount Augusta, this canyon-dissected range towers nearly 6,500 feet above the Dixie Valley to the west. The Clan Alpine Mountains are highly scenic with a number of canyons sporting perennial streams and springs. Rock formations here are colorful and abundant. The views from the ridgetops extend to the Sierra crest—100 miles westward. Aspens line the canyons, and mountain mahogany (rare in this part of Nevada) and pinyon/juniper forests dot the slopes. The wildlife includes sage grouse, golden eagle, prairie falcon, mule deer, wild horse and mountain lion. Rainbow and brown trout have been introduced here, but don't hold your breath waiting for them to bite—the fish are scarce.

•**See also Best of the State, page 296**•
For more information: Contact the BLM Carson City District, 1535
Hot Springs Road, Suite 300, Carson City, NV 89706; (702) 885-6000.

DESATOYA MOUNTAINS
*camping, hiking, backpacking, horseback riding, wildlife
observation, cross-country skiing*

An extremely scenic range, the Desatoya Mountains offer
outstanding windswept views: to the east the Toiyabe Range,
to the northwest the Clan Alpine Range, and to the far west,
on clear days, the Sierra Nevada. Desatoya Peak stands tall
above the surrounding desert at 9,973 feet. The range is
sharply dissected by canyons—many of them narrow and
rocky and featuring perennial streams. Big Den Canyon is the
most noteworthy and is well known for its 30-foot waterfall
and colorful rock spires. Aspen, willow and wild rose line
many of the canyon bottoms. Pinyon pine and juniper dot the
slopes at the lower elevations. The wildflowers are superb
during the spring. This is one of the best mountain ranges in
northwestern Nevada for adventuring because of its scenery,
accessibility and availability of water.

•**See also Best of the State, page 298**•
For more information: Contact the BLM Carson City District, 1535
Hot Springs Road, Suite 300, Carson City, NV 89706; (702) 885-6000.

ELY ELK VIEWING AREA
wildlife observation

Located in the Egan Resource Area, south of Ely along
Highway 93, the Ely Elk Viewing Area provides visitors an
excellent opportunity to observe up to several hundred elk.
The elk in this area are very tolerant of visitors providing you
stay in your vehicle and drive slowly along the area dirt roads.
The elk are generally found on the east side of the highway.
Peak viewing times are in early November, before elk hunting
season begins in mid-November, and in early spring during
March and April. Bald eagles winter in the area as do golden
eagles. Pronghorn antelope and mule deer may also be seen
here.

For more information: Contact the BLM Ely District Office, Egan Resource Area, 702 North Industrial Way, HC Box 33500, Ely, NV 89301; (702) 289-4865.

USGS topographic maps: Comins Lake, Ward Charcoal Ovens

FOX RANGE

camping, hiking, backpacking, horseback riding, wildlife observation

The Fox Range is located southwest of Gerlach and north of the Pyramid Lake Indian Reservation. Access to this area is via a maintenance road, several local roads leading from Gerlach or a power line road along the northeastern boundary. Water is very scarce; perennial streams run in Rodeo Creek on the east side of the range and in Wild Horse Canyon in the southwest of the range (please respect the private land in the canyon area). The southern part of the range is the best area for backpacking, especially along the ridge to Pah-Rum Peak and in the narrow and colorful canyons that carve through this area.

For more information: Contact the BLM Winnemucca District Office, 705 East Fourth Street, Winnemucca, NV 89445; (702) 623-1500.

USGS topographic maps: Pah-Rum Peak, Fox Canyon, Smith Canyon

HIGH ROCK CANYON

camping, hiking, backpacking, wildlife observation

High Rock Canyon to Cottonwood Canyon is considered one of the most historic desert canyon routes in the West. First documented by John C. Fremont during his 1843 to 1844 expedition to Oregon and California, and then subsequently used by settlers and wagon parties as an alternate route to the established Oregon Trail, the canyon became known as the Applegate Trail. During the year 1849, it is estimated that nearly half of the '49ers (no, not the football team) used this route to get to the gold fields of California thinking that it was the shortest route there. Indian troubles and the realization that this route was in fact longer, reduced its use somewhat. However, from 1851, when gold was discovered in the Siskiyou Mountains of Northern California, up until modern railroads and roads provided alternative routes in the late

---

1800s, the Applegate Trail through High Rock Canyon remained the primary path into and out of southern Oregon.

•See also Best of the State, page 294•
For more information: Contact the BLM Susanville District Office,
P.O. Box 1090, Susanville, CA 96130; (916) 257-5385.

JACKSON MOUNTAINS
camping, hiking, backpacking, horseback riding

The Jackson Mountains are located just east of the Black
Rock Desert. Access to this area is via county roads south of
Highway 140 or northeast of Gerlach and Highway 447. East
Jackson Creek Road, north from Sulphur, runs along the
western boundary of the region. Unlike many other desert
ranges in Nevada, water is relatively easy to find and this
proves attractive to a wide variety of wildlife. King Lear Peak,
at 8,910 feet is the highest peak in the range. Much of the
range lies above 5,000 feet. Towards the north, the deep
canyons of Deer Creek, Mary Sloan, Happy Creek, and Jackson
Creek feature perennial streams and lush vegetation. The
ridges and slopes are covered with juniper, snowberry, gooseberry, and dogwood. Due to the rugged nature of the northern
area, it is better to base-camp and day-hike in this area. In the
south, you will find King Lear, McGill Canyon and other
spectacular peaks lining the hike-able ridgeline. The backpacking is good, but be prepared for rugged hiking.

For more information: Contact the BLM Winnemucca District Office,
705 East Fourth Street, Winnemucca, NV 89445; (702) 623-1500.
USGS topographic maps: Hobo Canyon, King Lear Peak, Parrot
Peak, Deer Creek Peak

NORTH FORK LITTLE HUMBOLDT RIVER
camping, backpacking, hiking, horseback riding, wildlife
observation

Originating in the Humboldt National Forest, the North
Fork of the Little Humboldt River flows southeast and then
southwest, merging with the South Fork approximately 20
miles east of the town of Paradise Valley. Access to this river is
via BLM road 2003, also called Little Owyhee Road. The river
gorge is the major feature within this region, and is also the

best place for hiking, camping and wandering. Within the 14-mile long canyon, you will find steep colorful walls interrupted with numerous spires, cliffs, small caves, and narrow side canyons. The wildlife is abundant and includes pronghorn antelope, mule deer, beaver, muskrat, mink, coyote, raccoon, bobcat, and bats. Birds are also abundant—so bring your binoculars for sure! Great blue heron, turkey vulture, red-tailed hawk, sage grouse, great horned owl, belted kingfisher, a variety of swallows, northern oriole, and a variety of wrens can be viewed here. Hiking and backpacking is best in the gorge. Camping is good in the gorge and at Button Lake.

For more information: Contact the BLM Winnemucca District Office, 705 East Fourth Street, Winnemucca, NV 89445; (702) 623-1500.
USGS topographic maps: Little Poverty, Willow Point, Gumboot Lake

PINE FOREST RANGE
camping, hiking, backpacking, fishing, horseback riding, wildlife observation, mountain biking

The outstanding scenic quality of this region is worth the effort required to get there. Cathedral-like peaks, high mountain meadows, clear sub-alpine lakes, steep topography, colorful aspen groves, and abundant water are all found in this area. Spectacular views from many of the high points in the area yield panoramic vistas that extend into nearby California and Oregon.

•**See also Best of the State, page 292•**
For more information: Contact the BLM Winnemucca District Office, 705 East Fourth Street, Winnemucca, NV 89445; (702) 623-1500.

MAHOGANY CREEK AND LAHONTAN
Cutthroat Trout Natural Area, wildlife observation, hiking

Mahogany Creek is a habitat for the endangered Lahontan cutthroat trout and a spawning habitat for Lahontan cutthroat trout from Summit Lake—some of whom have reached 30 inches in length. Fishing of any kind is not allowed! Spawning occurs from April through May. Bird watching is superb in the area as it is both a migration corridor and a habitat for a variety of songbirds.

Two points of access are possible with a high-clearance vehicle. From Winnemucca, head to Denio Junction on State Route 140/291. Turn west at Denio Junction and travel 12 miles. Turn left on Gridley Lake Road and drive approximately 19 miles to the Little Idaho Canyon Road. Turn right and drive approximately another 14 miles to the Summit Lake Indian Reservation. Bear left and drive approximately two miles to the Lahontan Cutthroat Natural Area.

From Fernley in the south, head to Gerlach on State Road 34. Continue past Gerlach for 15 miles to the Soldier Meadows Ranch Road. Turn right and travel about 56 miles to the ranch and then another 13 miles to the Summit Lake Indian Reservation. Turn right past the north end of the lake and drive about three miles to the Lahontan Cutthroat Trout Natural Area.

For more information: Contact the BLM Winnemucca District Office, 705 East Fourth Street, Winnemucca, NV 89445; (702) 623-1500.
USGS topographic maps: Idaho Canyon Spring, New York Peak

STILLWATER RANGE
camping, hiking, backpacking, horseback riding

This area is accessed via Highway 121 north of US 50, just east of Dixie Valley via Dixie Hot Springs Road to the canyons of Hare, Mississippi and White Rock. Water is not readily available; there are few springs and streams. Backpacking is best along the ridgeline, but remember to pack all the water you will need for your journey. Since there is periodic mine and oil/gas exploration (some of the range lies within gas and oil leases), check with the BLM for current and suggested best routes to avoid areas of development.

For more information: Contact the BLM Carson City District, 1535 Hot Springs Road, Suite 300, Carson City, NV 89706; (702) 885-6000.
USGS topographic maps: Table Mountain, Job Peak, Cox Canyon, IXL Canyon, Fondaway Canyon, Dixie Hot Spring, Dixie Hot Spring Northwest, Logan Peak

TWIN PEAKS
camping, hiking

This area lies immediately west of Buffalo Hills and is bounded by the Home Springs-Painter Flat Road to the north, and Sand Pass-Gerlach Road or Buffalo Meadow Road to the southeast. Access is from the town of Gerlach and west of State Road 447. Twin Peaks, the area's namesake, sits at 6,605 feet, watching over the surrounding range with elevations roughly around 4,000 feet. Shinn Creek and Smoke Creek provide perennial water to the region. The best hiking and exploring is found within Willow Creek Canyon, Buffalo Creek Canyon and Chimney Rock Creek Canyon. Willow and aspen may be found in some of the drainages.

For more information: Contact the BLM Susanville District Office, P.O. Box 1090, Susanville, CA 96130; (916) 257-5385.

USGS topographic maps: Buffalo Creek, Mixie Flat, Smoke Creek Ranch, Salt Marsh

---

TIP: Desert soils are particularly susceptible to impacts and erosion. Stay on established trails and minimize social wandering around campsites.

NEVADA BY REGION

2

NORTHEASTERN NEVADA

Always inquire locally for current road conditions before heading out on unimproved roads. Nevada secondary and dirt roads can become impassable and even hazardous when wet. For this reason, many area locations given in this chapter are not specific, requiring you to ask for additional directions.

ANTELOPE RANGE
camping, hiking, backpacking, horseback riding

If you are looking for wilderness with unvisited and pristine meadows, dense aspen groves, perennial streams, and abundant wildlife, this is it. You can hike for miles without seeing any sign of human intrusion. Ninemile Peak sits as ruler of the range at 10,014 feet. You can expect snow in the higher elevations during the winter months. It is appropriate that the BLM has recommended this region for Wilderness Designation. From the town of Eureka, head west on US 50 for approximately 16 miles. Turn south on secondary State Route 82 and drive for approximately 23 miles. Then head east for about five miles on a local road to the northern boundary of the area and an intersection with another local road forming the western boundary.

For more information: Contact the BLM Battle Mountain District, P.O. Box 1420, Battle Mountain, NV 89820; (702) 635-5181.
USGS topographic maps: Segura Ranch, Fish Springs Northeast, Snowball Ranch, Ninemile Peak, Cockalorum Spring
BLM surface maps: Summit Mountain

BLUE MASS SCENIC AREA
camping, hiking

The mountains here are not spectacular, but they are scenic. Blue Mass Creek flows through a winding canyon and can be easily accessed by an unimproved road running through the canyon. Hoodoo rocks weathered into all sorts of interesting shapes are the most memorable feature of this area, and they provide an interesting foreground to the backdrop of pinyon pine and aspen that dot the slopes. From Interstate 80 and Wells, head south on US 93 to approximately 20 miles past the town of Lages. Once past Lages, pick up the local road and drive approximately 33 miles east to Tippett and then 15 miles southeast to Blue Mass Canyon.

For more information: Contact the BLM Ely District Office, 702 North Industrial Way, HC Box 33500, Ely, NV 89301; (702) 289-4865.
USGS topographic maps: Tippet, Tippet Canyon, Blue Mass Canyon, Grass Valley Wash

GOSHUTE CANYON AND GOSHUTE CANYON NATURAL AREA
camping, hiking, backpacking, horseback riding, rock climbing, spelunking, wildlife observation, cross-country skiing, fishing

This is an outstanding area for hikers, backpackers, spelunkers, and other recreational users who revel in scenery. Be prepared, however, for rugged terrain. Don't miss the Goshute Canyon Natural Area; it is narrow near the road leading from Cherry Creek and widens as it heads west, opening into the Goshute Basin. The Goshute Basin is a large amphitheater rimmed by tall mountains and it serves as the headwaters for Goshute Creek. The entire canyon is wonderful to hike and camp in; it has limestone crags, cool springs (always treat water before drinking), aspen groves and pristine meadows.

Spelunkers head to the area to enjoy the 1,500 feet of limestone passages of Goshute Cave. Rare limestone formations may be viewed from within the cave. However, you must be experienced before venturing into any cave and know how to minimize the impacts of your explorations. Human damage to a cave is virtually irreparable! It ruins future experiences for everyone. The wildlife here includes the great horned owl, golden eagle, Cooper's hawk, mule deer, mountain lion, yellow-bellied marmot, and bobcat.

From Ely, head north on US 93 for approximately 45 miles to State Route 489. Drive west on 489 for another nine miles. From here, a local road will take you in a northeasterly direction for eleven miles to Goshute Creek. There are a number of spur roads that lead you off the local route as they head into the surrounding canyons.

For more information: Contact the BLM Ely District Office, 702 North Industrial Way, HC Box 33500, Ely, NV 89301; (702) 289-4865.
USGS topographic maps: Cherry Creek Station, Goshute Creek

GOSHUTE MOUNTAINS
camping, hiking, backpacking, horseback riding, wildlife observation

Located within the Goshute Mountains is the Goshute Raptor Migration Area. A lookout site, in a small limestone outcrop at approximately 9,000 feet, may be reached providing you have a high-clearance vehicle. Considered the best migration lookout in the western United States, it is possible to observe over 200 raptors in a single day—days with over 1,000 sightings are not uncommon either.

•**See also Best of the State, page 303**•
For more information: Contact the BLM Elko District Office, P.O. Box 831, 3900 East Idaho Street, Elko, NV 89801; (702) 753-0200.

HICKISON PETROGLYPHS
camping, hiking, archaeological site

The BLM maintains a campground here which serves as a good base from which to take day hikes into the surrounding open country as well as enjoy historic examples of Native American petroglyphs. This area is located 20 miles east of the town of Austin on US 50, and just west of Hickison Summit. Look for the signed entrance road on the north side. The campground is dry so you will need to bring in all the water for your stay. The nearest town for supplies is Austin.

For more information: Contact the BLM Battle Mountain District, P.O. Box 1420, Battle Mountain, NV 89820; (702) 635-5181.
USGS topographic maps: Hickison Summit, Cape Horn

LITTLE HUMBOLDT RIVER
camping, backpacking, hiking, fishing, wildlife observation

The Little Humboldt River is located approximately 60 miles northwest of Elko, near the ghost town of Midas and west of Willow Creek Reservoir. The canyon that the Little Humboldt River flows through is super for hiking and back-packing. The wildlife includes wild horses and the endangered Lahontan cutthroat trout. Water is readily available. Game trails and old cattle trails make the best hiking routes; no formal hiking trail exists. You will need a four-wheel-drive vehicle for access to this area.

For more information: Contact the BLM Elko District Office, P.O. Box 831, 3900 East Idaho Street, Elko, NV 89801; (702) 753-0200.
USGS topographic maps: Rodear Flat, Haystack Peak, Oregon Canyon, Snowstorm Mountain

MOUNT GRAFTON
camping, hiking, backpacking, fishing, horseback riding, wildlife observation

This is an outstanding scenic area with the centerpiece being Mount Grafton at 10,993 feet. Much of the ridge in the immediate vicinity of Mount Grafton lies above 10,000 feet, creating wonderful opportunities for enjoying spectacular views. In addition to the sub-alpine vegetation at the peak, the surrounding rocky crags sport stands of white fir and bristle-

cone pine. Just north of the mountain, in the North Creek
Scenic Area, is a steep canyon with crystal water flowing down
its course. The perennial creek provides water (purify before
drinking) and decent trout fishing. Mount Patterson Pass, south
of Ely and just east of US 93 on a local road, provides the best
access to the mountain area. The pass lies approximately
seven miles south (as the crow flies) of Mount Grafton.

For more information: Contact the BLM Ely District Office, 702 North
Industrial Way, HC Box 33500, Ely, NV 89301; (702) 289-4865.
USGS topographic maps: Mount Grafton, Parker Station, Bullwhack
Summit, Cattle Camp Spring

NORTH FORK HUMBOLDT RIVER
hiking, fishing

This is a relatively small area located approximately 35
miles north of Elko and east of State Road 225. Much of the
river runs through private land after it leaves the Humboldt
National Forest, but a short section of approximately 12 miles
is on BLM land. The BLM area runs through Devil's Gap and
past Cottonwood Creek. The terrain is rolling and is well
suited to day-hiking, but forget about backpacking.

For more information: Contact the BLM Elko District Office, P.O.
Box 831, 3900 East Idaho Street, Elko, NV 89801; (702) 753-0200.
USGS topographic maps: Mahala Creek East, Tule Valley

OWYHEE RIVER CANYON
*camping, backpacking, hiking, fishing, rafting, canoeing,
kayaking*

The South Fork of the Owyhee flows northwest into Idaho
through a rugged and serpentine canyon system. Although the
access to this area is challenging, this 450,000-acre region (the
majority lies in Idaho) is picturesque, dramatic, wild, isolated
and well worth your time. River runners and hunters are the
predominant users, and there are not too many of those. The
narrow canyons that cut into the plateau range anywhere from
several hundred to one thousand feet deep—often with sheer
walls from rimrock to river bottom. Mountain lion, bobcat,
river otter, pronghorn antelope, and bighorn sheep reside
within the Owyhee canyon system.

• **See also Best of the State, page 300** •
For more information: Contact the BLM Elko District Office, P.O.
Box 831, 3900 East Idaho Street, Elko, NV 89801; (702) 753-0200.

RAILROAD VALLEY
WILDLIFE MANAGEMENT AREA
wildlife observation, fishing

This area can be accessed via US 6 northeast of Tonopah,
about halfway to Ely. There are four separate areas that
provide suitable habitats for migratory and nesting waterfowl,
non-game birds, mammals and fish. You cannot see the site
from the highway, so it is somewhat of a surprise to head off
on the dirt road and suddenly come upon a wetland full of tall
reeds. March to June and early fall are the best times to visit.

For more information: Contact the BLM Battle Mountain District,
P.O. Box 1420, Battle Mountain, NV 89820; (702) 635-5181.
USGS topographic maps: Blue Eagle Springs Southwest, Blue Eagle
Springs, Blue Eagle Springs Northeast, Meteorite Crater

ROBERTS CREEK MOUNTAINS
camping, hiking, horseback riding

These mountains are located eleven miles west of Eureka
on US 50, and 20 miles north via local roads past Roberts
Creek Ranch and up Roberts Creek. The peaks of this range
are very rugged and broken. Roberts Creek Mountain sits at
10,133 feet, the highest point in the range. Hanson Creek
features a nice waterfall and there are a number of small
ponds and intermittent streams that water the rest of the area.
It is quite scenic.

Resources: *Hiking the Great Basin,* by John Hart, published by Sierra
Club Books, San Francisco, CA.
For more information: Contact the BLM Battle Mountain District,
P.O. Box 1420, Battle Mountain, NV 89820; (702) 635-5181.
USGS topographic maps: Cooper Peak, Roberts Creek Mountain

ROCK CREEK CANYON
hiking

From the town of Battle Mountain, drive 23 miles north on
Izzenhood Road and then eight miles east on local roads—ask

at the BLM for specific directions. It's a small area, but the riparian environment of the eight-mile long canyon is interesting and quite attractive.

For more information: Contact the BLM Elko District Office, P.O. Box 831, 3900 East Idaho Street, Elko, NV 89801; (702) 753-0200. **USGS topographic maps:** Sheep Creek Range Northwest, Rock Creek Canyon

SALMON FALLS CREEK
camping, hiking, backpacking, fishing, canoeing, kayaking, raft floating

Salmon Falls Creek is located approximately 50 miles north of the town of Wells and just west of US 93. Boating is possible along a very quiet Class I section of the creek near the Nevada/Idaho border. Just past the border boundary, the stream dumps into the Salmon Creek Reservoir. The creek's winding route has cut a narrow, steep, relatively shallow canyon through a badlands topography. There isn't much vegetation in the area, other than within the canyon. The fishing here is for rainbow and brown trout. There is a rest area near the town of Jackpot along US 93 which is suitable as a put-in for the river float to the reservoir. You will need to portage around the fish barrier downstream. Camping spots along the canyon are available, though limited and at times, creative.

For more information: Contact the BLM Elko District Office, P.O. Box 831, 3900 East Idaho Street, Elko, NV 89801; (702) 753-0200. **USGS topographic maps:** Jackpot

SPRUCE MOUNTAIN
hiking

Spruce Mountain is adjacent to US 93, on the east side, and lies about 45 miles south of Wells. Access is easy from the highway. There is a wintering bald eagle roost in the range. On Spruce Mountain itself, there is a small grove of bristlecone pine. The area really isn't that noteworthy, other than the bald eagle roost and the superb views of the spectacular Ruby Mountains to the west.

For more information: Contact the BLM Elko District Office, P.O. Box 831, 3900 East Idaho Street, Elko, NV 89801; (702) 753-0200.
USGS topographic maps: Spruce Mountain

TIP: Camp out of sight of the trail.

NEVADA BY REGION

3

SOUTHERN NEVADA

Always inquire locally for current road conditions before heading out on unimproved roads. Nevada secondary and dirt roads can become impassable and even hazardous when wet. For this reason, many area locations given in this chapter are not specific, requiring you to ask for additional directions.

ASH SPRINGS
wildlife observation

Ash Springs, a significant, crystal-clear, spring-fed pool is located just east of State Route 93 in the town of Ash Springs. The part of the pool nearest the highway is privately owned. The source and the back side of the pool are public. Besides being a good area for observing songbirds, the water is a protected habitat for the endangered White River spring fish.

For more information: Contact the BLM Las Vegas District Office, Caliente Resource Area, P.O. Box 237, Caliente, NV 89008; (702) 726-8100.
USGS topographic maps: Ash Springs

BROWN KNOLL
wildlife observation

Brown Knoll is located one mile south of Lund on State Highway 318; there are several access roads leading east of the highway that lead to the Knoll. A large population of up to 3,000 mule deer can be observed in this area. Rocky Mountain elk, from the Ward Mountain herd, sometimes stray into the

---

area. The best season for wildlife observation is from late November through April.

For more information: Contact the BLM Ely District Office, Egan Resource Area, 702 North Industrial Way, HC Box 33500, Ely, NV 89301; (702) 289-4865.

USGS topographic maps: Preston

CLOVER MOUNTAINS
camping, hiking, backpacking, horseback riding, wildlife observation

This is a rugged land of deep, serpentine canyons, jagged peaks, steep cliffs, colorful rocks, and abundant water. Cattle roam the area, so you will have to be careful selecting drinking water and subsequently treating it. Located roughly 100 miles northeast of Las Vegas, this area can be accessed by State Route 317 south of Caliente and US 93. The road between Elgin and Carp is dirt and is frequently washed out. Four-wheel-drive vehicles are highly recommended for any travel in this region. Check with BLM before heading out to ascertain road conditions.

For more information: Contact the BLM Las Vegas District Office, 4765 West Vegas Drive, Las Vegas, NV 89108; (702) 385-6403.

USGS topographic maps: Ella Mountain, Fife Mountain, Bunker Peak, Jacks Mountain, Garden Springs, Leith

FISH LAKE VALLEY
wildlife observation

For bird watching enthusiasts, Fish Lake Valley is a very exciting area to visit during the spring migration (May to early June) and fall migration (mid-September through late October). This is one area where "off-course" migratory birds may be seen—if you are lucky or persistent. Most strays are warblers, especially eastern wood warblers. Other recorded sightings include the Philadelphia vireo, brown thrasher, rose-breasted grosbeak, little blue heron, and upland sandpiper. The usual western migrants can be observed here in large numbers.

For more information: Contact the BLM Battle Mountain District Office, Tonopah Resource Area, P.O. Box 911, Tonopah, NV 89049; (702) 885-6000.

USGS topographic maps: Dyer, Chiatovica Ranch

FORTIFICATION RANGE
camping, hiking, wildlife observation

Although the range itself is not all that remarkable, one canyon, Cottonwood Canyon, is worth the visit alone. The canyon is remarkable, stunning and exceptional. I leave it to you to agree or disagree. The head of the Cottonwood Canyon forms a natural amphitheater of towering and jagged rock formations, colored white, pink and mauve.

For more information: Contact the BLM Ely District Office, 702 North Industrial Way, HC Box 33500, Ely, NV 89301; (702) 289-4865.
USGS topographic maps: The Gouge Eye, Indian Spring Knolls

GABBS VALLEY RIDGE
camping, hiking, backpacking, horseback riding

US 361 bisects this range, from just south of the town of Gabbs to just north of the town of Luning. The BLM has created a wilderness study area that includes the range to the west of the highway. The range is quite scenic with two notable canyons, Lost Canyon and Red Rock Canyon. Both canyons offer water and pleasant camping. Access to this area is via unmaintained roads that run east and west from US 361. Wildlife, though not abundant, includes mule deer, wild horse, bobcat, and golden eagle.

For more information: Contact the BLM Carson City District, 1535 Hot Springs Road, Suite 300, Carson City, NV 89706; (702) 885-6000.
USGS topographic maps: Mount Ferguson, Gabbs Mountain, Luning, WinWan Flat

GRANT RANGE
camping, backpacking, hiking, horseback riding

Located south of the town of Currant on US 6, the Grant Range sits just east of the unpaved road connecting Current and Nyala. It also features high mountains cut with deep and narrow canyons that wind through the region. You will find white fir and bristlecone pine on Blue Eagle Mountain.

For more information: Contact the BLM Battle Mountain District, P.O. Box 1420, Battle Mountain, NV 89820; (702) 635-5181.
USGS topographic maps: Blue Eagle Mountain, Heath Canyon, Currant

KAWICH RANGE
camping, hiking, backpacking

Although this area is near the Bombing and Gunnery Range, it is a nice respite for those seeking solitude among mountains. The Kawich Range offers high-basin lakes and canyon streams. Longstreet's Canyon is noteworthy for its diverse vegetation. Trails do exist but they are indistinct and unmarked. Kawich Peak is the high point, sitting at 9,404 feet. Located south of the town of Warm Springs and US 6, Kawich Range is accessed by local and unimproved roads.

For more information: Contact the BLM Battle Mountain District, P.O. Box 1420, Battle Mountain, NV 89820; (702) 635-5181.
USGS topographic maps: Kawich Peak, Bellehelen, Stinking Spring, Kawich Peak Northeast

LUNAR CRATER VOLCANIC FIELD
camping, hiking, wildlife observation

This is a very large colorful region, especially in years of good water which helps to create a virtual carpet of wildflowers in some areas. NASA considered this area to be so lunar-like that early astronauts trained here. Lunar Crater, a National Natural Landmark, at 430 feet deep and 3,800 feet in diameter, is located approximately seven miles south of US 6. The region can be accessed from US 6, and lies approximately 30 miles northeast of Warm Springs, just past Sandy Summit.

For more information: Contact the BLM Battle Mountain District, P.O. Box 1420, Battle Mountain, NV 89820; (702) 635-5181.
USGS topographic maps: Lunar Crater

MEADOW VALLEY RANGE
AND MORMON MOUNTAINS
camping, hiking, backpacking, horseback riding, spelunking

Driving south, from Caliente and US 93, on State Route 317 will take you right into the middle of the Meadow Valley Range. To the south and east lies the Mormon Mountains, which protect several limestone caverns that are of interest to spelunkers. The area is rugged and predominantly dry, but strangely attractive because of its vastness. It is interesting to note that the Mormon Mountains derive their name from the old Spanish Trail/Mormon Road that passed through here.

For more information: Contact the BLM Las Vegas District Office, 4765 West Vegas Drive, Las Vegas, NV 89108; (702) 385-6403.
USGS topographic maps: Vigo Northwest, Vigo Northeast, Sunflower Mountain, Vigo, Carp, Toquop Gap, Wildcat Wash Northeast, Rox, Rox Northeast, Moapa Peak Northwest, Davidson Peak

MOREY PEAK
camping, hiking

Morey Peak, 10,246 feet, sits as the monarch of this tiny range. Sixmile Canyon extends to the south and features a number of springs and nice meadow vegetation. The region is quite scenic and untrammeled by man. The best access is via local roads that extend north from US 6 approximately 20 miles northeast of the town of Warm Springs and just south of Sandy Summit. For a detailed description, refer to John Hart's book, listed below.

Resources: *Hiking the Great Basin,* by John Hart, published by Sierra Club Books, San Francisco, CA.
For more information: Contact the BLM Battle Mountain District, P.O. Box 1420, Battle Mountain, NV 89820; (702) 635-5181.
USGS topographic maps: Morey Peak, Hobble Canyon, Moores Station, Moores Station Southwest

MUDDY MOUNTAINS
camping, hiking, backpacking, wildlife observation, rock hounding

Lying along the edge of Lake Mead National Recreation Area and just south of Valley of Fire State Park, the Muddy Mountains offer super hiking opportunities among colorful and at times, jagged sandstone formations. Opportunities to observe bighorn sheep are excellent here. The best time to visit is between September and May. Summer is too darn hot! The following are ideal destinations for hiking in the area: Hidden Valley, Color Rock Quarry, Wild Sheep Valley, Muddy Peak, and Anniversary Narrows. Rock hounders will enjoy hunting for jasper, agate, amethyst and opal.

For more information: Contact the BLM Las Vegas District Office, 4765 West Vegas Drive, Las Vegas, NV 89108; (702) 385-6403.
USGS topographic maps: Dry Lake Southeast, Muddy Peak, Bitter Spring, Government Wash, Caliente Bay

PARSNIP PEAK
camping, hiking, backpacking, horseback riding, wildlife observation

The area's chief attraction is its remoteness, which virtually guarantees solitude and isolation. There are a number of ridges in the area, all cut by deep canyons. Ponderosa pine and aspen dot the slopes, and springs may be found within this region. Parsnip Peak, the area's namesake, sits at a moderate 8,942-foot elevation, but the unique and colorful granite rock formations that surround the peak more than make up for its lack of altitude. It is located south of Great Basin National Park and northeast of the town Pioche and US 93. Eagle Valley Road provides distant access, but to get into the range you have to hoof it. It will take you two to three hours of hard hiking just to get to the area.

For more information: Contact the BLM Ely District Office, 702 North Industrial Way, HC Box 33500, Ely, NV 89301; (702) 289-4865.
USGS topographic maps: Parsnip Peak, Buckwash Well, Eagle Valley Reservoir, Pierson Summit

QUEER MOUNTAINS
camping, hiking, backpacking, horseback riding

This area has no outstanding redeeming features, but it makes a good stopping-off point and place to unroll your sleeping bag if you are headed somewhere else. The mountains in this range are rugged and will be of interest to geologists (amateur and otherwise) for the many geological features. Since it is also adjacent to Death Valley National Monument, it is a good area to romp around if you need some time to stretch your legs. There is no water to be found; bring all that you will need. State Route 267 bisects this range.

For more information: Contact the BLM Las Vegas District Office, 4765 West Vegas Drive, Las Vegas, NV 89108; (702) 385-6403.
USGS topographic maps: Bonnie Claire Lake, Bonnie Claire, Bonnie Claire Southwest, Bonnie Claire Southeast, Gold Mountain

RED ROCK CANYON
NATIONAL RECREATION AREA
*camping, hiking, backpacking, climbing, horseback riding,
mountain biking*

The predominant geological feature in Red Rock Canyon,
and a feature that attracts rock climbers from all over, is a
spectacular 3,000-foot sandstone escarpment extending for
much of the region's length. Named for the bright red colors of
the stone, the canyon region contains over 40 springs as well
as many natural catch basins known as tanks. It is this presence of water, more prevalent than anywhere in the surrounding desert region, that supports a rich and concentrated plant
and animal population. Joshua trees are predominant on the
canyon floor. As the elevation rises, pinyon pine and juniper
trees take over.

•**See also Best of the State, page 304**•
For more information: Contact the BLM Las Vegas District Office,
4765 West Vegas Drive, Las Vegas, NV 89108; (702) 385-6403.

SOUTH EGAN RANGE
*camping, hiking, backpacking, horseback riding, spelunking,
rock climbing*

The South Egan Range is located south of Ely and east of
State Route 318, extending from the town of Lund south for
approximately 35 miles. Although there is an abundance of
streams and springs, there is also an abundance of cattle—so
you must treat all the water thoroughly before drinking. This
limestone mountain range is rugged and beautiful with dense
groves of aspen, white fir, ponderosa pine, and even bristlecone pine. Angel Cave and other caves in the area attract
many spelunkers. The cliffs are quite climbable and attract a
number of climbers every year.

For more information: Contact the BLM Ely District Office, 702 North
Industrial Way, HC Box 33500, Ely, NV 89301; (702) 289-4865.
USGS topographic maps: Sawmill Canyon, Brown Knoll, Haggerty
Spring, Parker Station, Shingle Pass, Shingle Pass Southeast, Cave
Valley Well

SOUTH PAHROC RANGE
camping, hiking, backpacking, horseback riding

Canyons, washes, cliffs and interesting boulder fields are the main fare here. Though not exceedingly spectacular, the area is scenic enough to warrant a visit. Access is quite easy via local roads. US 93, west of Caliente, passes right over Pahroc Summit and through the middle of the range.

For more information: Contact the BLM Las Vegas District Office, 4765 West Vegas Drive, Las Vegas, NV 89108; (702) 385-6403.
USGS topographic maps: Hiko Southeast, Alamo Northeast

SOUTH REVEILLE RANGE
camping, hiking, backpacking, horseback riding, wildlife observation

The South Reveille Range lies west of State Highway 375 and south of Warm Springs. The proximity to the Bombing and Gunnery Range does not significantly detract from the scenery which includes steep-sided mountains and narrow canyons. The wildlife is abundant.

For more information: Contact the BLM Battle Mountain District, P.O. Box 1420, Battle Mountain, NV 89820; (702) 635-5181.
USGS topographic maps: Reveille Peak, Reveille Peak Southeast, Reveille Peak Northwest, Freds Well, Reveille Southeast

WALKER LAKE
camping, hiking, fishing, swimming, canoeing, boating

Walker Lake is located southeast of Reno and just north of Hawthorne alongside US 95. A very scenic destination for the entire family at any time of the year; but summer redefines the word hot. Regal Mount Grant towers above the lake to the southwest at 11,239 feet. Hiking in the wooded canyons all around the area is very pleasant. The BLM maintains one campground, Sportsman's Beach. This does not preclude you from setting up an informal camp elsewhere around the lake, however. Miles of sandy beaches make the lake a great recreational destination.

For more information: Contact the BLM Carson City District, 1535 Hot Springs Road, Suite 300, Carson City, NV 89706; (702) 885-6000.
USGS topographic maps: Reese River Canyon, Gillis Canyon, Copper Canyon, Walker Lake, Mount Grant, Hawthorne West

---

STATE INFORMATION OVERVIEW

NEVADA STATE OFFICE
850 Harvard Way, P.O. Box 12000, Reno, NV 89520-0006;
(702) 785-6586

BATTLE MOUNTAIN DISTRICT OFFICE
P.O. Box 1420, Battle Mountain, NV 89820; (702) 635-4000

CARSON CITY DISTRICT OFFICE
1535 Hot Springs Road, Suite 300, Carson City, NV 89706;
(702) 885-6000

ELKO DISTRICT OFFICE
BLM, P.O. Box 831, 3900 East Idaho Street, Elko, NV 89801;
(702) 753-0200

ELY DISTRICT OFFICE
702 North Industrial Way, HC Box 33500, Box 150, Ely, NV
89301-9408; (702) 289-4865

LAS VEGAS DISTRICT OFFICE
P.O. Box 26569, 4765 West Vegas Drive, Las Vegas, NV 89126;
(702) 647-5000

WINNEMUCCA DISTRICT OFFICE
705 East Fourth Street, Winnemucca, NV 89445; (702) 623-1500

NEW MEXICO

(SEE MAP A)

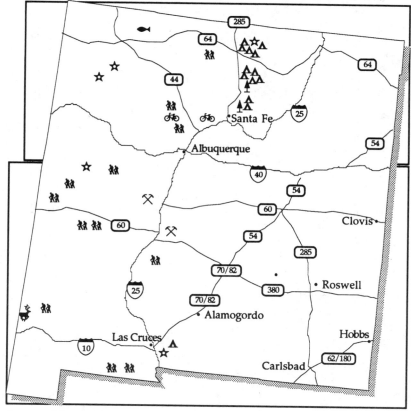

(SEE MAP B)

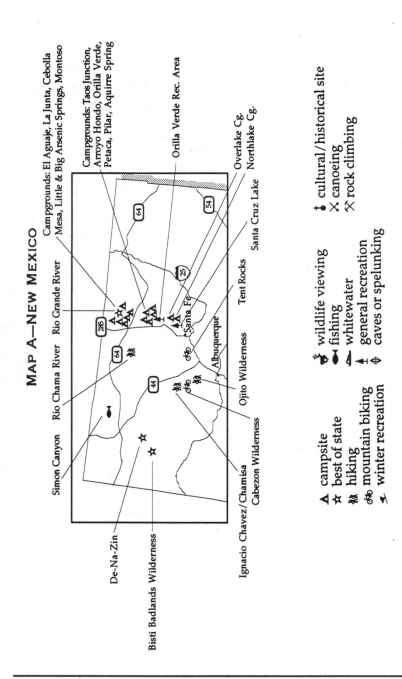

MAP A—NEW MEXICO

Campgrounds: El Aguaje, La Junta, Cebolla
Mesa, Little & Big Arsenic Springs, Montoso

Campgrounds: Taos Junction,
Arroyo Hondo, Orilla Verde,
Petaca, Pilar, Aquirre Spring

Orilla Verde Rec. Area

Overlake Cg.
Northlake Cg.

Santa Cruz Lake

Simon Canyon   Rio Chama River   Rio Grande River

De-Na-Zin

Bisti Badlands Wilderness

Ignacio Chavez/Chamisa
Cabezon Wilderness

Ojito Wilderness

Tent Rocks

Albuquerque

Santa Fe

▲ campsite
★ best of state
⅍ hiking
⑯ mountain biking
≼ winter recreation

♈ wildlife viewing
⬤ fishing
⬣ whitewater
⊕ general recreation
⬦ caves or spelunking

† cultural/historical site
✕ canoeing
✕ rock climbing

MAP REFERENCES

Bisti Badlands Wilderness—p. 339-340
Cabezon Wilderness Study Area—p. 349-350
De-Na-Zin Wilderness—p. 341-342
Ignacio Chavez/Chamisa Wilderness Study Area—p. 350-351
Ojito Wilderness Study Area—p. 351
Orilla Verde Recreation Area—p. 352
Rio Chama Wild and Scenic River—p. 353-354
Rio Grande/Wild Rivers Recreation Area—p. 344-346
Santa Cruz Lake—p. 354-355
Simon Canyon—p. 355
Tent Rocks Area of Critical Environmental Concern—
    p. 355-356

CAMPGROUNDS

The following campgrounds are found in this area of New
Mexico. Please call the BLM office (listed following each
campground's name) for reservations and information. Contact
information for each BLM office is on pages 365-366 for New
Mexico.

Aquirre Spring Campground, Mimbres Resource Area
Arroyo Hondo Campground, Taos Resource Area
Big Arsenic Springs Campground, Taos Resource Area
Cebolla Mesa Campground, Taos Resource Area
El Aguaje Campground, Taos Resource Area
La Junta Campground, Taos Resource Area
Little Arsenic Spring Campground, Taos Resource Area
Montoso Campground, Taos Resource Area
Northlake Campground, Taos Resource Area
Orilla Verde Campground, Taos Resource Area
Overlake Campground, Taos Resource Area
Petaca Campground, Taos Resource Area
Pilar Campground, Taos Resource Area
Taos Junction Campground, Taos Resource Area

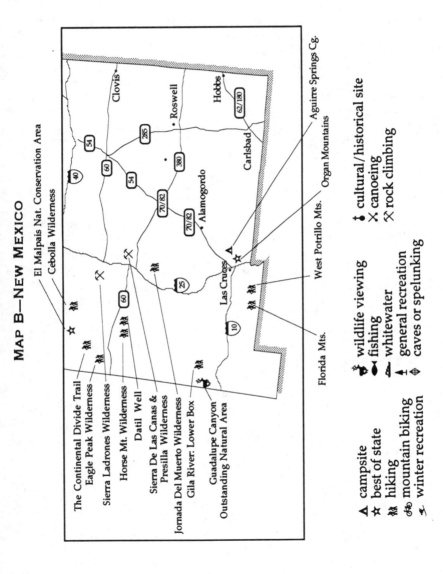

MAP B—NEW MEXICO

El Malpais Nat. Conservation Area
Cebolla Wilderness

The Continental Divide Trail
Eagle Peak Wilderness
Sierra Ladrones Wilderness
Horse Mt. Wilderness
Datil Well
Sierra De Las Canas & Presilla Wilderness
Jornada Del Muerto Wilderness
Gila River: Lower Box
Guadalupe Canyon Outstanding Natural Area

Clovis
Roswell
Hobbs
Carlsbad
Alamogordo
Las Cruces

West Potrillo Mts.
Organ Mountains
Aguirre Springs Cg.
Florida Mts.

△ campsite
☆ best of state
朲 hiking
ᴔ mountain biking
➘ winter recreation

🦌 wildlife viewing
🐟 fishing
⬆ whitewater
⬆ general recreation
⊕ caves or spelunking

† cultural/historical site
✕ canoeing
⤬ rock climbing

MAP REFERENCES

Cebolla Wilderness—p. 352-353
Continental Divide Trail—p. 347
Datil Well—p. 357
Eagle Peak Wilderness Study Area—p. 357
El Malpais National Conservation Area—p. 336-338
Florida Mountains—p. 358
Gila River: Lower Box—p. 358-359
Guadalupe Canyon Outstanding Natural Area—p. 359
Horse Mountain Wilderness Study Area—p. 359-360
Jornado Del Muerto Wilderness Study Area—p. 360
Organ Mountains—p. 342-344
Sierra De Las Canas Wilderness Study Area; Presilla Wilderness
    Study Area—p. 361
Sierra Ladrones Wilderness Study Area—p. 361-362
West Potrillo Mountains—p. 362

CAMPGROUNDS

The following campgrounds are found in this area of New Mexico. Please call the BLM office (listed following each campground's name) for reservations and information. Contact information for each BLM office is on pages 365-366 for New Mexico.

Aguirre Springs Campground, Mimbres Resource Area

1

EL MALPAIS NATIONAL CONSERVATION AREA

Travelers speak of a ghostly silence within the El Malpais National Conservation Area, a silence occasionally broken by a rush of wind or the growl of a passing vehicle. While Native Americans made use of the area, early Spanish and American explorers disdained the rugged terrain, referring to it as El Malpais—the badlands. Indeed, the area is forbidding with a dramatic landscape created from numerous cinder and spatter cones, ice caves, pressure ridges, and some of the longest lava tubes on the continent. High sandstone bluffs add a remarkable contrast to the lava flows, with winds leaving balancing stones and creative sculptures that rival anything seen in the world's best art galleries.

The lava crevices harbor an amazing amount of vegetation including grasses, cacti, aspen and more. Naturalists at the visitor's center say that lava fields create a kind of microclimate which is more moist than the surrounding terrain. In some of the island-like depressions (Hole-In-The-Wall, described below, is the biggest), wind-blown debris has collected, allowing trees such as the pinyon pine, juniper, ponderosa pine, and Douglas fir to take root. This area demands a light touch, however, as archaeological sites continue to be vandalized, trees cut for firewood and signed vehicle closures ignored. Every impact eventually leads to the destruction of an irreplaceable resource valuable to us all.

HIKING

Numerous backpacking and exploring opportunities present themselves within the 40,000-acre wilderness of the West Malpais Wilderness. Hiking is very rugged—hiking for one mile on lava is equivalent to several miles on regular terrain. For those who are not experienced in desert-type backpacking, setting up a base-camp near your vehicle and spending the time day-hiking is recommended. Hiking is generally easiest on the jeep roads (closed to all vehicle traffic in the wilderness, making them ideal for foot traffic). There is no water to be had within the National Conservation Area or National Monument, so you must carry all you need—one gallon per person per day is the minimum recommended amount. The north plains of the area are primarily grasslands interspersed with juniper trees. Six thousand acres of this wilderness, named Hole-In-The-Wall, forms a peninsula that juts out northeast into the National Monument (many more exploration possibilities exist there). Hole-In-The-Wall is an island of older lava flow blanketed with ponderosa pine. Gloves, long sleeves and long pants are recommended as are sturdy leather boots. Lava can be very unforgiving on the skin as it is sharp and brittle. Lava tubes may be explored at your own risk as long as you have three sources of light, a helmet and protective clothing.

MOUNTAIN BIKING

Brazo Canyon features several remote and forested canyons that demand exploration. Although four-wheel-drive vehicles are allowed, the route is traveled lightly enough that mountain biking becomes an attractive alternative. Carry a copious amount of water—two quarts just won't cut it. Be sure to pack extra parts and plenty of patching material. Mountain bikes are not allowed in the nearby wilderness areas; respect the closures.

MANAGEMENT
•BLM Grants Field Station, 620 East Santa Fe, Grants, NM 87020; (505) 285-5041.
•El Malpais Information Center, 620 East Santa Fe Avenue, Grants, NM 87020; (505) 285-5406.

LOCATION
Approximately ten miles south of Grants, New Mexico and south of Interstate 40 in the northwestern quadrant of the state.

GETTING THERE
From Grants, drive south on Highway 117 to the east boundary of this area. Highway 117 cuts through the eastern edge of the region and is very scenic. High-clearance vehicles are required on all the dirt county roads for access into the wilder-

ness areas—anything less and you are liable to leave body
parts behind (the car's, not yours). Without a high-clearance
vehicle, stick to Highway 53 or Highway 117. Limited pull-outs
for overnight parking are available along the highways. Do not
leave your vehicle in the two signed places prohibiting overnight stays.

CAMPING
Several commercial camping sites do exist. Primitive camping
is allowed throughout the BLM conservation and wilderness
areas. Water is not available anywhere within the wilderness
areas—pack plenty.

PERMITS
A permit is required. Campfires are prohibited at times—check
with the ranger. The gathering of firewood is prohibited, so
you must bring your own.

MAPS
El Malpais Recreation Guide Map, published by BLM and
distributed through the visitor's center. Topographic maps
needed for your particular venture may be purchased at the El
Malpais Ranger Station.

ADDITIONAL INFORMATION
New Mexico Mountain Bike Guide, published by Big Ring
Press, P.O. Box 8266, Albuquerque, NM 87198.

SEASON
Spring and fall are the best seasons to visit this area. Summer
can be exceedingly hot. Winter brings periodic snowfalls and
freezing temperatures.

---

*TIP: Respect public and private property
including all trail signs and closure signs.
Leave gates open or closed as you find them.*

2

BISTI WILDERNESS

The 3,946-acre Bisti Wilderness is very remote and stark. The weathered sandstone of the region forms spectacular formations known as hoodoos. Once heavily populated by diverse primitive forms of animal life living in swamps and forests, the area is now desolate badlands. This world of bizarre rock formations and prehistoric remains, sometimes referred to as an eerie moonscape, is a wilderness monument to a primeval wonderland. Very little wildlife inhabits this region. An occasional lizard, snake, tarantula, or scorpion may be seen scuttling along among petrified wood remains. Even ferruginous hawks or golden eagles may be observed riding the thermals overhead. Mostly, silence and solitude reign supreme.

HIKING/BACKPACKING

There is no set hiking trail. Travel is by map and compass, leaving the visitor free to wander and explore the twisted and magical topography. You must be proficient with a map and compass to safely and easily navigate your way through the region.

MANAGEMENT

BLM Farmington District Office, 1235 La Plata Highway, Farmington, NM 87401; (505) 327-5344

LOCATION

Located 170 miles northwest of Albuquerque near the "four corners" region where New Mexico meets Utah, Arizona and Colorado.

GETTING THERE

From Albuquerque, take Interstate 40 to State Highway 371. Take 371 north to Crown Point. From Crown Point, continue north another 46 miles until you arrive at an unmarked gravel

---

road known locally as Old State Highway 371. BLM is planning to place signs in the near future, but at press time this road is unmarked. Follow this gravel road for six miles past the old Bisti Trading Post to an undeveloped parking area and the trailhead—actually just an opening in the barbed wire fence.

CAMPING
Camping is allowed anywhere within the wilderness area at the present time. BLM is anticipating prohibiting camping in the commonly visited day-use areas. Minimum impact camping techniques will encourage you to stay away from these areas, regardless. Bring all the water you will need as there is none available at the site.

PERMITS
No permits are necessary. Campfires are not permitted anywhere. Parts of this region are closed seasonally by the BLM to protect nesting raptors. Check with the office for closure information.

MAPS
USGS topographic: Bisti Trading Post, Alamo Mesa West, Tanner Lake

ADDITIONAL INFORMATION
The Hikers Guide to New Mexico, by Laurence Parent, published by Falcon Press, P.O. Box 1718, Helena, MT 59624; (800) 582-2665.

SEASON
The best time to visit this area is in late winter, spring and fall. Summer is brutally hot.

TIP: Apply a no-trace ethic everyday, everywhere.

DE-NA-ZIN WILDERNESS

Designated as wilderness, the De-Na-Zin has no formal trails or any designated entrance to speak of. It's just there, spread out for wandering among the wind-carved bluffs, badlands, mesas, and striking color variations which are accented at sunset. Although there isn't much plant life save the small areas of rolling grassland and pockets of pinyon pine and juniper, there is an interesting animal population which includes desert cottontails, prairie dogs, coyotes, and badgers. Expect to find petrified wood and numerous fossils within the boundaries, although collecting is strictly prohibited by federal law. You can pick up and look, just don't pocket and carry.

HIKING/BACKPACKING

There is no set hiking trail. Travel is by map and compass, leaving the visitor free to wander and explore the twisted and magical topography. You must be proficient with a map and compass to safely and easily navigate your way through the region.

MANAGEMENT

BLM Farmington District Office, 1235 La Plata Highway, Farmington, NM 87401; (505) 327-5344

LOCATION

The De-Na-Zin Wilderness is 170 miles northwest of Albuquerque near the "four corners" region where New Mexico meets Utah, Arizona and Colorado.

GETTING THERE

From Bloomfield, drive approximately 30 miles south on State Route 44 to El Huerfano Trading Post and then continue 11 miles southwest on County Road 7500 to the parking area. The road is generally good, although it can become slippery when wet. This usually occurs in the spring and late summer.

CAMPING

Camping is allowed anywhere within the wilderness area. BLM is anticipating prohibiting camping in the commonly visited day-use areas. Minimum impact camping techniques will encourage you to stay away from these areas, regardless. Bring all the water you will need as there is none available at the sites.

PERMITS

No permits are necessary. Campfires are not permitted anywhere. Parts of this region are closed seasonally by the BLM to protect nesting raptors. Check with the office for closure information.

MAPS

USGS topographic maps: Alamo West, Alamo Mesa East, Huerfano Trading Post Southwest
BLM surface maps: Chaco Canyon, Toadlena

SEASON

The best times to visit are in late winter, spring and fall. Summer will cook your brains for sure.

TIP: Pack out all that you bring in—
and a little extra is you find it.

BEST OF THE STATE

4

ORGAN MOUNTAINS

There is a tremendous diversity of life within the arid environment of the Organ Mountains. In the lower elevations you will find creosote bush and mesquite giving way to juniper and oak as the elevation increases. In the highest reaches of the mountains, enclaves of ponderosa pine, juniper and mountain mahogany may be found. There are also many species of birds, mammals and reptiles to be seen. Most common are quail, rabbits, deer, tree lizards, and rattlesnakes. The geology is severe, looking rather like a dried up Swiss Alps.

Mountain Biking

The Baylor Pass National Recreation Trail is one of the few trails in these BLM holdings limited to hiking, horseback riding and mountain biking. No vehicles are allowed. Total riding distance is six miles each way. Beginning at Aguirre Spring Campground, with elevation of approximately 5,540 feet, the trail winds and climbs to 6,340 feet, the highest point of the trail. From there, the trail descends rapidly to an elevation of 4,865 feet and intersects with Baylor Canyon Road. The Baylor Pass National Recreation Trail is an out-and-back proposition.

Rock Climbing

The needles and a rock formation known as Sugarloaf attract climbers from all over.

Hiking

There are a number of trails that wind through the region including the Baylor Pass Trail described above. The Pine Tree Trail is for hiking only and is a loop trail requiring approximately three hours to walk and covering four-and-a-half miles. It begins and ends in the Aguirre Spring Campground.

Management
BLM Mimbres Resource Area, 1800 Marquess Street, Las Cruces, NM 88005; (505) 525-4300

Location
In the Organ Mountains, 3.5 miles east of Organ and just south of US Highway 70.

Getting There
Drive 25 miles northeast from Las Cruces on US 70. Follow the signs to the Organ Mountains.

Camping
Camping is available at the Aguirre Spring Campground—it's crowded but it's the only game in town. There is a seven-day camping limit. The only drinking water available in the recre-

ation area is located at the A. B. Cox Visitor Center just off
Baylor Canyon Road.

PERMITS
No permits are necessary.

MAPS
USGS topographic maps: Organ Peak, Organ New Mexico
BLM surface maps: Las Cruces
Additional maps: Recreation maps for the Organ and Franklin
Mountains are available from the BLM Mimbres office.

SEASON
The best time to visit this area is from fall to spring. Summers
can be uncomfortably hot.

TIP: Travel or camp in small groups.

BEST OF THE STATE

5

RIO GRANDE / WILD RIVERS RECREATION AREA

The Rio Grande was one of the first rivers in the lower 48
to achieve protected status under the Wild and Scenic Rivers
Act. The protected area includes 48 river miles south of the
Colorado border and also the lower four miles of the Red River
tributary. The Rio Grande cuts an ever-deepening swath
through the Taos Plateau, beginning at the Colorado border at
a 200-foot depth and then slicing even deeper, ending up
flowing nearly 880 feet below the Plateau, down at the
confluence with the Red River. The gorge is a picture in stark
contrast—dry and forbidding on top with sparse vegetation,
yet lush and inviting along the river's edge with a riparian
environment of cottonwood, ponderosa pine, willow, horsetail,

and the ever-present poison ivy. Transitional vegetation on the slopes and benches include oak, cactus, pinyon pine, juniper and various wildflowers. Expect to see numerous birds attracted by the water and all the available food, and expect also to view wildlife that includes mule deer, elk, coyote, beaver, muskrat, raccoon, porcupine, black bear, bobcat, and mountain lion. The fishing for rainbow and German brown trout and northern pike is excellent.

HIKING/BACKPACKING

Guided hikes and campfire talks are offered each weekend from Memorial Day through Labor Day. There are 12 miles of developed and maintained trails with trailheads located near each of the campgrounds—the system is made up of five separate trails, ranging from three-quarters to one and one-quarter miles in length connecting with a trail along the river. The trails system has received designation as part of the National Recreation Trails System. A new five-mile loop trail winds through the pinyon along the canyon rims.

MOUNTAIN BIKING

There are ten miles of mountain biking trails.

WHITEWATER RAFTING

Upper Box run begins at Lobatos Bridge in Colorado. Upper Box is closed to boating from March 1 to June 1 each year to protect wildlife. Since some downstream sections are unrunnable, boaters must obtain detailed portage and river information prior to putting in. Taos Box is the most popular run and begins at the John Dunn Bridge Recreation Site. The river is rated Class I to Class IV within this section. The length of the Lower Box run is approximately 16 river miles. Take-out is at Taos Junction Bridge. Write to the BLM for a current listing of commercial river companies offering half-day to overnight trips on the Rio Grande or Rio Chama.

MANAGEMENT

BLM Taos Resource Area, 224 Cruz Alta Road, Taos, NM 87571; (505) 758-8851

LOCATION
Beginning one hour north of Taos, near the Colorado/New Mexico border and ending 20 miles south of Taos near Pine, New Mexico.

GETTING THERE
Three miles north of the town of Questa on State Route 522, turn left on State Route 378. Follow the signs which mark the access points and the Visitor's Center.

CAMPING
Camping is allowed only in designated sites on the rim and along the river. There are five campgrounds along the rim with 47 sites available and one group site. Rim campground fees are $7 per site.

PERMITS
No permits are necessary for hiking or backpacking. All whitewater use requires a permit and is issued only if you can demonstrate adequate experience and proper equipment. Permits are available at the Art Zimmerman Visitor's Center or at the John Dunn Bridge.

ADDITIONAL INFORMATION
• *Western Whitewater, From the Rockies to the Pacific,* by Jim Cassady, Bill Cross, and Fryar Calhoun, published by North Fork Press, Berkeley, CA; (800) 243-5522.
• BLM brochure and map, *Rio Grande Wild and Scenic River*

MAPS
USGS topographic maps: Guadalupe Mountain
BLM surface maps: Wheeler Peak

SEASON
The boating season runs from May to July, depending on the water levels.

1

NEW MEXICO (GENERAL)

THE CONTINENTAL DIVIDE TRAIL
backpacking

The Continental Divide Trail runs roughly along the lower ridge that stretches northeast to southwest through the western half of the state. Expect blistering temperatures in the south during the months of May to September and snow on the higher reaches in the north from November through February. The route is not marked at all on BLM land except within Socorro Resource Area (posts with emblem only—no developed treadway). No permits are needed. There are no designated campsites. Permission to cross Native American land is required. Contact the Jicarilla Apache Tribe, Tourism Director, P.O. Box 507, Dulce, NM 87528, and the Ramah Navajo Tribe, Ramah, NM 87321. Other landowners may require permission to cross their land as well, so it is critical that you obtain information and maps from the BLM detailing the approximate trail route and land ownership information.

Maps: The following BLM surface maps will provide initial planning assistance by showing land ownership, major topographical features, major roads and trails, cities and towns: Chama, Chaco Canyon, Abiquiu, Chaco Mesa, Zuni, Fence Lake, Quemado, Tularosa Mountains, San Mateo Mountain, Truth or Consequences, Silver City, Lordsburg, and Animas. There is a fee for each map and maps may be ordered by calling or writing the BLM at New Mexico State Office, 1474 Rodeo Road, P.O. Box 27115, Santa Fe, NM 87505; (505) 438-7400.

> *TIP: Look up and photograph—
> never pick up and collect.*

2

NORTHWESTERN
NEW MEXICO

BISTI WILDERNESS
backpacking, hiking, horseback riding

The 3,946-acre Bisti Wilderness is very remote and stark. The weathered sandstone of the region forms spectacular formations known as hoodoos. Once heavily populated by diverse primitive forms of animal life living in swamps and forests, the area is now desolate badlands. This world of bizarre rock formations and prehistoric remains, sometimes referred to as an eerie moonscape, is a wilderness monument to a primeval wonderland. Very little wildlife inhabits this region. An occasional lizard, snake, tarantula, or scorpion may scuttle among petrified wood remains. Even ferruginous hawks or golden eagles may be observed riding the thermals overhead. Mostly, silence and solitude reign supreme.

•**See also Best of the State, page 339**•
For more information: Contact the BLM Farmington District Office, 1235 La Plata Highway, Farmington, NM 87401; (505) 327-5344.

DE-NA-ZIN WILDERNESS
backpacking, hiking, horseback riding

Designated as wilderness, the De-Na-Zin has no formal trails. It's just there, spread out for wandering with wind-carved bluffs, badlands, mesas, and striking color variations which are accented at sunset. Although there isn't much plant life save the small areas of rolling grassland and pockets of pinyon pine and juniper, there is an interesting animal population which includes desert cottontail, prairie dog, coyote, and badger. Expect to find petrified wood and numerous fossils within the boundaries, although collecting is strictly prohibited by federal law. You can pick up and look, just don't pocket and carry.

• See also Best of the State, page 341 •
For more information: Contact the BLM Farmington District Office, 1235 La Plata Highway, Farmington, NM 87401; (505) 327-5344.

EL MALPAIS NATIONAL CONSERVATION AREA
camping, backpacking, hiking, mountain biking, historical sites

Travelers speak of a ghostly silence within the El Malpais National Conservation Area, a silence occasionally broken by a rush of wind or the growl of a passing vehicle. While Native Americans made use of the area, early Spanish and American explorers disdained the rugged terrain, referring to it as El Malpais—the badlands. Indeed, it is forbidding with a dramatic landscape created from numerous cinder and spatter cones, ice caves, pressure ridges and some of the longest lava tubes on the continent. High sandstone bluffs add a remarkable contrast to the lava flows, with winds leaving balancing stones and creative sculptures that rival anything seen in the world's best art galleries. The lava crevices harbor an amazing amount of vegetation including grasses, cacti, aspen, and more. Naturalists at the visitor's center say that lava fields create a kind of microclimate which is more moist than the surrounding terrain. In some of the island-like depressions, wind-blown debris has collected allowing trees such as the pinyon pine, juniper, ponderosa pine, and Douglas fir to take root. This area demands a light touch, however, as archaeological sites continue to be vandalized, trees cut for firewood, and signed vehicle closures ignored. Every impact eventually leads to the destruction of an irreplaceable resource valuable to us all.

• See also Best of the State, page 336 •
For more information: Contact the BLM Rio Puerco Resource Area, 435 Montano Road, Northeast, Albuquerque, NM 87107; (505) 761-8700.
El Malpais Information Center, 620 East Santa Fe Avenue, Grants, NM 87020; (505) 285-5406.

CABEZON WILDERNESS STUDY AREA
camping, backpacking, hiking, horseback riding, wildlife observation, mountain biking

Views from the mesas and rolling hills are superb and the entire region is richly dotted with historical, archaeological and geological features. You will need to carry all your water as there are no guaranteed water sources within the region. Camping is allowed anywhere, but minimum impact camping techniques are essential. Gravel and dirt roads network a large portion of this region and are suitable (outside the Wilderness Study Area) for four-wheel-drive access, mountain biking and car camping base camps. Once again, even if base-camping, practice minimum impact camping techniques.

Cabezon Peak is a 7,775-foot-high volcanic plug. There is a primitive trail along the south side of the peak which takes two and a half to four hours to climb. A visitor's register at that summit indicates that hikers from as far away as Europe come to experience a climb that is appropriate for both beginning and intermediate hikers.

Wildlife is abundant and includes badgers, bobcats, coyotes, porcupine, chipmunks, prairie dogs, and numerous and varied rodents. Birds are also abundant here, as are raptors, which feed upon the population of rodents. State Route 279, located approximately 20 miles north of San Ysidro, off State Route 44, travels through the village of San Luis and to the northwestern boundary of Cabezon Wilderness Study Area near the privately-owned ghost town of Cabezon. Be sure to top off your gas tanks at San Ysidro before heading out.

Resources: BLM publishes an informal booklet entitled *Rio Puerco Mountain Bike Routes* and a brochure entitled *Cabezon.*
For more information: Contact the BLM Rio Puerco Resource Area, 435 Montano Road, Northeast, Albuquerque, NM 87107; (505) 761-8700.
USGS topographic maps: Cabezon Peak

IGNACIO CHAVEZ/CHAMISA WILDERNESS STUDY AREA
camping, backpacking, hiking, horseback riding, wildlife observation, mountain biking, rock climbing

This is a lightly visited area with a variety of terrain and scenic canyons. It is through the Ignacio Chavez/Chamisa Area across the level terrain of the mesas that the proposed Continental Divide National Scenic Trail will cross. Views from the mesas and rolling hills are superb and the entire region is richly dotted with historical, archaeological and geological features. You will need to carry all your water as there are no guaranteed water sources within the region. Camping is allowed anywhere. BLM Road 1103 is opened on a seasonal basis for vehicle access. All other roads, even though evident, are closed to vehicle traffic within the wilderness study areas. Wildlife is abundant and includes badger, bobcat, coyote, porcupine, chipmunks, prairie dogs, and numerous and varied rodents. Birds are also abundant as are raptors, which feed upon the populations of rodents. State Route 279, located approximately 20 miles north of San Ysidro off State Route 44, travels through the village of San Luis and turns into County Road 25, following the northern border of Ignacio Chavez/ Chamisa Area. Be sure to top off your gas tanks at San Ysidro before heading out. BLM 1103 is a seasonal road that travels to the top of the mesa and over Forest Service Road 239A.

For more information: Contact the BLM Rio Puerco Resource Area, 435 Montano Road, Northeast, Albuquerque, NM 87107; (505) 761-8700.

USGS topographic maps: Mesa Cortada, Cerro Parido, Guadalupe

OJITO WILDERNESS STUDY AREA
biking, backpacking, camping, rock climbing, wildlife observation

To get to Ojito, drive State Route 44 south from San Ysidro for two miles. A maintained dirt road heads west to Ojito, seven miles away. The Ojito area is made up of steep, rocky terrain interspersed with steep canyons and pockets of badlands topography. Roads outside of the Wilderness Study Area are suitable for mountain biking, four-wheel-drive base-camping from your car. This site lies just south of the Cabezon boundary and offers super views of the imposing volcanic plug known as Cabezon Peak.

Resources: BLM publishes a brochure entitled *Ojito.*
For more information: Contact the BLM Rio Puerco Resource Area, 435 Montano Road, Northeast, Albuquerque, NM 87107; (505) 761-8700.
USGS topographic maps: Ojito Spring, San Ysidro, Sky Village Northeast, Sky Village Northwest

ORILLA VERDE RECREATION AREA

fishing, camping, canoeing, flat-water rafting, picnicking, hiking

Formerly Rio Grande State Park, the Orilla Verde Recreation Site is a good family destination for water recreation and side hiking activities. Fishing is for rainbow and brown trout and northern pike. There are petroglyphs and artifacts remaining in the area—help to protect the resources by looking but not touching. There are a number of trails within the area that are suitable for exploring the side canyons. Camp in the designated campgrounds or primitive sites along the river. There are organized and guided nature hikes and interpretive programs scheduled from Memorial Day through Labor Day.

For more information: Contact the BLM Taos Resource Area, 224 Cruz Alta Road, Taos, NM 87571; (505) 758-8851.
USGS topographic maps: Carson, Taos Southwest
BLM surface maps: Taos

CEBOLLA WILDERNESS

camping, backpacking, hiking, horseback riding, wildlife observation

Lying adjacent to El Malpais (although officially it is still part of the El Malpais National Conservation Area), just east of State Route 117, is an area of scenic sandstone bluffs, canyons, mesas, and draws that provide easier access than the challenging and forbidding volcanic terrain of El Malpais. There are primitive roads in Cebolla Canyon, Sand Canyon, and Armijo Canyon that are suitable for foot or horse. Pack all the water you will need because there is none naturally available within this region. A notable feature within Cebolla is La Ventana, one of the largest natural arches in New Mexico. There is a signed parking area just off State Route 117, approximately 17 to 18 miles south of Interstate 40. Be careful that you do not travel within the adjacent Acoma Indian Reservation or disturb archaeological sites that they consider very sacred.

For more information: Contact the BLM Rio Puerco Resource Area, 435 Montano Road, Northeast, Albuquerque, NM 87107; (505) 761-8700; or the El Malpais Information Center, 620 East Santa Fe Avenue, Grants, NM 87020; (505) 285-5406.

USGS topographic maps: Arrosa Ranch, Bonine Canyon, Cebollita Peak, Laguna Honda, Los Pilares, North Pasture, Sand Canyon

RIO CHAMA WILD AND SCENIC RIVER
camping, backpacking, hiking, wildlife observation, fishing, canoeing, rafting

Although the upland area is rather unspectacular (unless you are particularly attracted to open grazing range), the meandering canyon through which the Rio Chama Wild and Scenic River flows is stunning with its colors and unique rock formations. The "gorge" begins at El Vado Reservoir, flowing for the first ten miles through BLM-managed lands, including a wilderness study area. The next 20 miles wind through Chama River Canyon Wilderness of the Santa Fe National Forest. The final seven miles, which include the majority of rapids, flow past Christ in the Desert Monastery before dumping into Abiquiu Reservoir.

To access the canyon from Tierra Amarilla, head approximately two miles south on US 112 and then west on BLM 1023. There are a number of branch roads, suitable for four-wheel-drive, high-clearance vehicles, which access the canyon from the east side. Do not head out before checking with the BLM office in Taos to determine road conditions. The river is usually floatable from April to early June and mid July to late August with Class I to Class III water. Permits are required for the upper sections of the river, although no permits are as yet required for the lower seven miles.

Fishing is considered good for rainbow and brown trout. Hiking and backpacking are good throughout the canyon. Wildlife of the region includes mule deer, elk, mountain lion, bobcat, beaver, raccoon. Coopers Ranch, the official put-in, provides the launching facilities as well as camping. There is a per-person charge for launching and a per-vehicle charge for parking overnight. They also offer a vehicle shuttle service to the take-out at Big Eddy. Contact Coopers Ranch at (505) 588-7354.

Resources: *Western Whitewater, From the Rockies to the Pacific,* by Jim Cassady, Bill Cross, and Fryar Calhoun, published by North Fork Press, Berkeley, CA; (800) 243-5522.
For more information: Contact the BLM Taos Resource Area, 224 Cruz Alta Road, Taos, NM 87571; (505) 758-8851.

Maps: BLM/Carson and Santa Fe National Forests/US Army Corps of
Engineers publish a map and brochure entitled *Rio Chama: A Wild
and Scenic River.*

RIO GRANDE WILD AND SCENIC RIVER / WILD RIVERS RECREATION AREA
*camping, backpacking, hiking, wildlife observation, fishing,
canoeing, rafting, kayaking*

The Rio Grande was one of the first rivers in the lower 48
to achieve protected status under the Wild and Scenic Rivers
Act. The protected area includes 48 river miles south from the
Colorado border and also the lower four miles of the tributary
Red River. The Rio Grande cuts an ever-deepening swath
through the Taos Plateau, beginning at the Colorado border at
a 200-foot depth and slicing even deeper, ending up nearly
880-feet-deep down at the confluence with the Red River. The
gorge is a picture in stark contrast—dry and forbidding on top
with sparse vegetation, yet lush and inviting along the river's
edge with a riparian environment of cottonwood, ponderosa
pine, willow, horsetail, and the ever-present poison ivy.
Transitional vegetation on the slopes and benches includes
oak, cactus, pinyon pine, juniper, and various wildflowers.
Expect to see numerous birds attracted by the water and all
the available food, and expect to view wildlife that includes
mule deer, elk, coyote, beaver, muskrat, raccoon, porcupine,
black bear, bobcat, and mountain lion.
•**See also Best of the State, page 344**•
For more information: Contact the BLM Taos Resource Area, 224
Cruz Alta Road, Taos, NM 87571; (505) 758-8851.

SANTA CRUZ LAKE
camping, hiking, fishing, canoeing, boating

This is a good family destination for water recreation.
Santa Cruz Lake is an irrigation lake with decent access via a
paved road leading to the boat launch ramp maintained by
BLM. From US 84/285, approximately 20 miles north of Santa
Fe, bear right on State Route 503. Travel nine miles to reach
the Overlook Campground turnoff and an additional four miles
to State Route 596. Make a left turn to reach Northlake Campground. Several trails provide access on foot to most of the
lakeshore and the banks of the creek that feeds the lake. There

is also an easy trail from the Overlook Campground leading to the south shore. Scenery in this badlands area is spectacular. For a campground-style getaway with a boat and fishing pole, this is a good escape. Couple that with the fact that BLM officials say this is one of their most beautiful recreation areas and you have all the elements necessary for a fun, family escape. Fishing is for rainbow and brown trout. Summer temperatures range from 54°F to 82°F and winter temperatures from 15°F to 45°F. Historical sites and artifacts are located within the region—please help to protect the resources.

For more information: Contact the BLM Taos Resource Area, 224 Cruz Alta Road, Taos, NM 87571; (505) 758-8851.
BLM surface maps: The BLM publishes a map/brochure entitled *Santa Cruz Lake*

SIMON CANYON
camping, backpacking, hiking, fishing

From just below the Navajo Dam to the San Juan River lies the Simon Canyon, which is easily accessible. This area is recovering nicely from illegal off-road vehicle activity in the past. This is a super site when no one is around. Side canyons are pretty and worth exploring. If you visit during the week or off-season, you will likely have the canyon area to yourself. The predominant use of the area is by fishermen working the quality waters of the San Juan. Archaeological sites are within the region, although most have been thoroughly vandalized.

To get there, from US 550 at the town of Aztec, head approximately 23 miles east on State Route 173. A signed exit and three-mile unpaved access road leads to the site and the Cottonwood Campground, run by the state parks. Tent camping only at Simon. RVs are required to stay at Cottonwood.

For more information: Contact the BLM Farmington District Office, 1235 La Plata Highway, Farmington, NM 87401; (505) 327-5344.
USGS topographic maps: Archuleta, Anastacio Spring

TENT ROCKS AREA OF CRITICAL ENVIRONMENTAL CONCERN
camping, hiking, mountain biking

The BLM told me "the brochure doesn't even begin to describe the remarkable beauty of this place." Upon further checking, I was frankly amazed that even though Tent Rocks is so close to both Santa Fe and Albuquerque, it receives only light visitation—not that I'm complaining. It is sometimes used as a movie location because of its unique rock formations and badlands topography. Most unique are the tent-shaped rocks (looking like huge tepees at 40- to 90-feet high) for which the area is named. Climbing is not allowed on any of the tent formations due to their fragile nature—they were formed by erosion. They are in a constant state of erosion—one day this site will no longer be here. Best access is by driving approximately three miles via USFS Road 266, just off State Route 22 near Cochiti Pueblo. U.S. Forest Service Road 266 turnoff from 22 is marked by a colorful water tower.

Resources: BLM publishes an informal booklet entitled *Mountain Bike Excursions in Tent Rocks* and a map/brochure entitled *Tent Rocks*.

For more information: Contact the BLM Rio Puerco Resource Area, 435 Montano Road, Northeast, Albuquerque, NM 87107; (505) 761-8700.

USGS topographic maps: Canada

USFS maps: Santa Fe National Forest

TIP: When car-camping set up your camp no more than 300 feet from the nearest road and your vehicle.

3

SOUTHWESTERN
NEW MEXICO

DATIL WELL
camping, hiking

The site of a well along the historic Magdalena Stock Driveway livestock trail is now a BLM maintained campground. A three-mile nature and hiking trail winds through pinyon pine and juniper woodlands to viewpoints that overlook the Plains of San Agustine. BLM publishes a leaflet about the site and the campground. Located just off US 60 approximately one mile northwest of the town of Datil. A $5 overnight fee is charged.

For more information: Contact the BLM Socorro Resource Area, 198 Neel Avenue, Northwest, Socorro, NM 87801; (505) 835-0412.
USGS topographic maps: Datil

EAGLE PEAK WILDERNESS STUDY AREA
camping, hiking, wildlife observation

A generally arid and barren area that offers pleasant enough desert hiking through various volcanic landforms, sandstone mesas and canyons, and rolling hills. There are even a few small cinder cones. The largest, Cerro Pomo, shelters Zuni Salt Lake—an historic source of salt for Native American tribes and a neutral ground of spiritual importance. Flashflooding is possible in this area during the rainy season of July through September—watch out for serious thunderstorms. From Quemado on US 60, drive northwest on unpaved State Route 32 to the town of Salt Lake. Head south on County A007 to Eagle Peak.

For more information: Contact the BLM Socorro Resource Area, 198 Neel Avenue, Northwest, Socorro, NM 87801; (505) 835-0412.
USGS topographic maps: Zuni Salt Lake, Blaines Lake, Tejana Mesa, Lake Armijo, Tejana Mesa Southwest, Armstrong Canyon

FLORIDA MOUNTAINS
camping, hiking, backpacking, wildlife observation, rock hounding

Rising up out of the surrounding desert for nearly 3,000 feet, the Florida Mountains are the most noteworthy geological feature for miles. The topography is jagged and rugged, carved open with steep canyons—many with near vertical walls. Four-wheel-drive roads skirt the entire range making access quite easy when the roads are dry. Numerous springs and small seeps dot the region creating mini-oases of riparian vegetation. The wildlife here includes mule deer, coyote, kit fox, ringtail, badger, and Persian ibex—yep, you read it right. The Persian ibex were released here in the early '70s and have flourished. Rock hounding is a big draw to the area, chiefly because of the close proximity to Rockhound State Park which actually encourages rock hounding and tills the soil to help rock hounders unearth geodes, jasper, agate, rhyolite, and more. The state park has a campground with approximately 30 sites that is open all year.

For more information: Contact the BLM Las Cruces District Office, 1800 Marquess Street, Las Cruces, NM 88005; (505) 525-4300.
USGS topographic maps: Capitol Dome, South Peak, Florida Gap, Gym Peak

GILA RIVER: LOWER BOX
camping, hiking, backpacking, wildlife observation, canoeing, kayaking

This tranquil and relatively shallow section of the Gila River flows through a highly scenic and lightly visited area just south of the Gila National Forest. Large rock outcroppings and a periodically steep-walled canyon with numerous side canyons provide ample opportunity for exploring on foot. Hoodoos and columns add an almost magical nature to the area. Camping is allowed anywhere within the area. Water levels are low and the river is best floated in March or immediately following a rainy period. The water flow is rated Class I throughout the river. Access to the canyon and the river is best from the Red Rock Bridge on State Route 464 north of Lordsburg. There are a number of local roads offering access to other points along the canyon, but it is best to ask locals regarding these put-in spots.

Resources: *Western Whitewater, From the Rockies to the Pacific,* by
Jim Cassady, Bill Cross, and Fryar Calhoun, published by North Fork
Press, Berkeley, CA; (800) 243-5522.
For more information: Contact the BLM Las Cruces District Office,
BLM, 1800 Marquess Street, Las Cruces, NM 88005; (505) 525-4300.
USGS topographic maps: Canador Peak, Nichols Canyon

GUADALUPE CANYON OUTSTANDING NATURAL AREA
hiking, backpacking, wildlife observation

Well known to avid birders for the excellent birdwatching
opportunities to be found here, the Guadalupe Canyon is a
remote and special destination for anyone who enjoys solitude
and shallow canyonland geography. Since the area borders on
the wilderness study area of the Coronado National Forest,
extended backpacking trips are possible. There is a stream that
flows periodically through the canyon, most commonly during
the late summer and early fall when the thunderstorms of New
Mexico are frequent. Over 159 species of birds have been
sighted and recorded within the canyon—many at their most
northerly point of migration. Camping is allowed anywhere,
but for safety's sake, camp only on high ground because flash
flooding is a real, not imagined, hazard. There is a trail that
leads to Bunk Robinson Peak within the Peloncillo Mountains
of the Coronado National Forest.

For more information: Contact the BLM Las Cruces District Office,
1800 Marquess Street, Las Cruces, NM 88005; (505) 525-4300.
USGS topographic maps: Guadalupe Spring, Guadalupe Canyon
USFS maps: Coronado National Forest

HORSE MOUNTAIN WILDERNESS STUDY AREA
camping, hiking, horseback riding, wildlife observation

This is a nice destination for a view or peak-bagging hike
as the mountain's 9,490-foot elevation practically towers above
the Plains of San Agustine below. When the weather is clear,
you can see for up to 100 miles in all directions. The routes up
are steep, but for the sure-footed, the going is relatively easy.
There are a number of undeveloped trails that date back to
logging days that have since grown over and offer sure foot-
ing. This is a perfect place to set up a weekend base-camp

from which to explore the peak and surrounding area. From the town of Datil off US 60, head southwest for 26 miles on State Route 12 to Horse Springs. At Horse Springs, head north for approximately four miles on an unpaved county road. Then turn east on a very primitive access road nearly one mile to the boundary of the site. Summer temperatures are warm to hot in the day and cooling at night. Winter temperatures hover around the freezing mark.

For more information: Contact the BLM Socorro Resource Area, 198 Neel Avenue, Northwest, Socorro, NM 87801; (505) 835-0412.

USGS topographic maps: Wallace Mesa, Log Canyon, Horse Mountain West, Horse Mountain East

JORNADA DEL MUERTO WILDERNESS STUDY AREA
hiking, geological sightseeing

Where else can you hike within a missile range, I ask you? Imagine moseying along and then being evacuated for a test firing—don't laugh. It could happen since this site is entirely within the safety net imposed by the White Sands Missile Range. But that's not why this place is called the Journey of Death. Rather, it is because of the harsh and forbidding volcanic terrain of tubes and ridges—many silted in by blowing sand and clay. El Camino Real Trail is in the same geographic area dating back to the Spanish explorers who journeyed through this area. Located south of San Antonio and US 380 off County Roads 2268 and 2322.

For more information: Contact the BLM Socorro Resource Area, 198 Neel Avenue, Northwest, Socorro, NM 87801; (505) 835-0412.

USGS topographic maps: Harriet Ranch, Fuller Ranch

ORGAN MOUNTAINS
camping, backpacking, hiking, horseback riding, mountain biking, rock climbing, wildlife observation

There is a tremendous diversity of life within the arid environment of the Organ Mountains. In the lower elevations you will find creosote bush and mesquite giving way to juniper and oak, as the elevation increases. In the highest reaches of the mountains, enclaves of Ponderosa pine, juniper, and mountain mahogany may be found. There are also many species of bird, mammal and reptile to be seen. Most common are quail, rabbit, deer, tree lizards, and rattlesnake. The geology is severe, looking rather like a dried-up Swiss Alps.

•**See also Best of the State, page 342•**
For more information: Contact the BLM Las Cruces District Office, 1800 Marquess Street, Las Cruces, NM 88005; (505) 525-4300.

SIERRA DE LAS CANAS WILDERNESS STUDY AREA; PRESILLA WILDERNESS STUDY AREA
camping, hiking, wildlife observation, horseback riding, rock climbing

Both units are located east of the Rio Grande at the town of Socorro. Cross the bridge from US 85 at Escondido and continue driving east on BLM maintained Quebradas Road—rough but okay in a high-clearance vehicle. Popular with locals from Socorro, the area is used primarily for hiking, rock climbing, camping, horseback riding, and rock hounding. Within Presilla lies the Tinajas Natural Area of Critical Environmental Concern, which protects numerous Native American pictographs. Sierra De Las Canas is further away from Socorro and sees only light visitation. Rugged and multicolored rock escarpments, narrow canyons, sharp ridges, and broad mesas make up the topography of this region. There are also many good opportunities for sightseeing and outdoor photography during rainstorms which create rainbows.

For more information: Contact the BLM Socorro Resource Area, 198 Neel Avenue, Northwest, Socorro, NM 87801; (505) 835-0412.
USGS topographic maps: Sierra De Las Canas: Loma De Las Canas, Bustos Well, Canon Agua Bueno, San Antonio. Presilla: Loma De Las Canas

SIERRA LADRONES WILDERNESS STUDY AREA
camping, backpacking, hiking, horseback riding, wildlife observation, rock climbing, rock hounding, fossil seeking

Sitting in the car at Interstate 25 near Bernardo and looking west, it is not hard to imagine the ruggedness that the Sierra Ladrones embody—the jagged escarpments of the range virtually dominate the horizon. Ladron Peak, at 9,176 feet, is forbidding in its size, with the peak towering nearly 4,000 feet above the base. Rock climbers come here to enjoy the technical rock. Fall through spring are the best times to visit—summer is too damn hot! The Sevilleta National Wildlife Refuge lies on the east side of the range and is closed to the public. Pinyon pine and juniper dominate the slopes with some aspen and Douglas fir sneaking into the mix among the canyons. Wildlife is abundant and includes coyote, bobcat, badger, cottontail, jackrabbit, gray fox, and a number of bats. Bighorn sheep were recently released into the area and may be seen with a sharp eye. To get there, head west on County Road 67 from Interstate 25 at Bernardo.

For more information: Contact the BLM Socorro Resource Area, 198 Neel Avenue, Northwest, Socorro, NM 87801; (505) 835-0412.
USGS topographic maps: Ladron Peak, Riley, Carbon Springs, Silver Creek

WEST POTRILLO MOUNTAINS
camping, hiking, rock hounding, wildlife observation

This area is volcanic and then some. Over 48 volcanic cones cluster in the area and range from 1,000 to 3,000 feet in diameter. Indian Basin, a large depression in the southwestern part of the mountains, is rimmed with sand dunes and sometimes filled with water, giving ducks a temporary home. Aden Crater is a nearly circular crater with a one-quarter mile diameter and lies within the Aden Lava Flow. There is a four-wheel-drive vehicle trail wandering through the area that locals use. Kilbourne Hole is approximately two miles south of Aden Lava Flow and has been designated a National Natural Landmark. Kilbourne is defined as a "maar," a crater caused by a volcanic explosion of gas, not lava and more rare than cinder cones. Kilbourne is up to two miles across and 450 feet deep in places. Wildlife watchers will enjoy knowing that golden eagles, great horned owls and bats nest among the formations. The abundance of rodents has made for a very healthy raptor population.

For more information: Contact the BLM Las Cruces District Office, 1800 Marquess Street, Las Cruces, NM 88005; (505) 525-4300.
USGS topographic maps: POL Ranch, Potrillo Peak, Guzman's Lookout Mountain, Mount Riley, Mount Riley Southeast, Mount Aden Southwest, Aden Crater

3

SOUTHEASTERN NEW MEXICO

CHOSA DRAW
spelunking

BLM manages more than 150 caves from the Carlsbad Resource Area office. The caves are formed in three different rock types: limestone, gypsum and lava. Seventeen of the caves are gated and require permits for access. The rest are open for general public use and enjoyment. The Chosa Draw has been designated an Area of Critical Environmental Concern because of the outstanding and complex system of gypsum caves—many tied together hydrologically by underwater passages. In fact, the second longest gypsum cave in the U.S. is located in this region. More than 160 sinkholes and cave entrances provide for point sources of groundwater recharge. Some of the underwater river systems in the area support species of cave-adapted fish and fresh-water shrimp.

Caving is a risky activity, as well as a potentially damaging activity to the environment if not done with care. For that reason, I have chosen not to print specific locations of caves within this region. If you are serious about wanting to explore the caves in the area and can prove your competence, the BLM will be more than happy to provide you with all the assistance possible.

For more information: Contact the BLM Carlsbad Resource Area, 101 East Mermod Street, P.O. Box 1778, Carlsbad, NM 88220; (505) 887-6544.

FORT STANTON CAVE
spelunking

Once again, I am not giving specific directions to a site, only because caving requires skill, knowledge and care. If you have the proper equipment and expertise, then the BLM will be happy to issue you a permit to enter this cave, which is second only to Carlsbad Caverns in size. If you would like a permit, you must request it at least ten days in advance by mail or in person. The cave entrance is gated and locked. At this time, the total length of mapped passages is eight miles. Many of the passages are twisting and very narrow. The cave is well regarded for its rare formations of velvet as well as helictites, selenite needles and forms of gypsum. Townsend big-eared bats hibernate here in the winter.

Resources: BLM provides a leaflet with a cave map included.
For more information: Contact the BLM Roswell District Office, 1717 West Second Street, P.O. Box 1397, Roswell, NM 88202; (505) 622-9042.

TIP: Educate yourself by obtaining travel maps and regulations from public agencies, complying with signs and barriers, and asking an owner's permission before crossing private property.

STATE INFORMATION OVERVIEW

NEW MEXICO STATE OFFICE
1474 Rodeo Road, P.O. Box 27115, Santa Fe, NM 87505; (505) 438-7400

TULSA DISTRICT OFFICE
9522-H East 47th Place, Tulsa, OK 74145; (918) 581-6480

Oklahoma Resource Area, 221 North Service Road, Moore, OK 73160; (404) 794-9624

ROSWELL DISTRICT OFFICE
1717 West Second Street, P.O. Box 1397, Roswell, NM 88202; (505) 622-9042

Roswell Resource Area, Federal Building, Room 216, Fifth and Richardson, P.O. Drawer 1857, Roswell, NM 88202; (505) 624-1790

Carlsbad Resource Area, 101 East Mermod Street, P.O. Box 1778, Carlsbad, NM 88220; (505) 887-6544

ALBUQUERQUE DISTRICT OFFICE / RIO PUERCO RESOURCE AREA
435 Montano Road, Northeast, Albuquerque, NM 87107; (505) 761-8700

Rio Puerco Resource Area, 435 Montano Road, Northeast, Albuquerque, NM 87107; (505) 761-8700

Grants Field Station, 620 East Santa Fe Avenue, Grants, NM 87020; (505) 758-8851

Taos Resource Area, 224 Cruz Alta Road, Taos, NM 87571; (505) 758-8851

FARMINGTON DISTRICT OFFICE
1235 La Plata Highway, Farmington, NM 87401; (505) 327-5344

LAS CRUCES DISTRICT OFFICE
1800 Marquess Street, Las Cruces, NM 88005; (505) 525-4300

Mimbres Resource Area, 1800 Marquess Street, Las Cruces, NM 88005; (505) 525-4300

Caballo Resource Area, 1800 Marquess Street, Las Cruces, NM 88005; (505) 525-4300

Socorro Resource Area, 198 Neel Avenue Northwest, Socorro, NM 87801; (505) 835-0412

OREGON

(SEE MAP A)

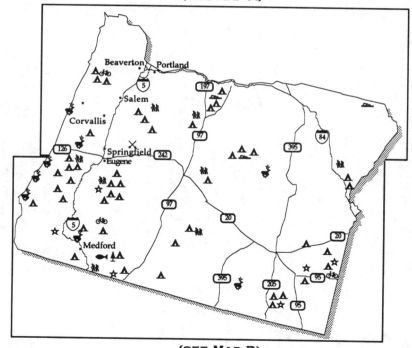

(SEE MAP B)

MAP A—OREGON

Grande Ronde River

Campgrounds: Beavertail, Macks Canyon, Blue Hole

Campgrounds: Muleshoe, Lone Pine, Big Bend

Table Rocks

Deschutes River/Sherar's Falls

John Day River

Middle Deschutes River

Trout Creek Cg.

Nestucca River

Portland

Beaverton

Salem

Campgrounds: Elkhorn Valley,
Fisherman's Bend, Yellowbottom

McKenzie River

Corvallis

Springfield

Lake Creek Falls   Alsea Falls Cg.

Campgrounds: Alder Glen,
Dovre, Fan Creek, Elk Bend

Yaquina Head Oustanding Area

△ campsite
✫ best of state
⚔ hiking
🚲 mountain biking
🎿 winter recreation

🦌 wildlife viewing
🎣 fishing
⚓ whitewater
♠ general recreation
⊕ caves or spelunking

† cultural/historical site
✗ canoeing
⚔ rock climbing

MAP REFERENCES

Deschutes Wild and Scenic River/Sherar's Falls—p. 397
Grand Ronde Wild and Scenic River—p. 401
John Day River—p. 398
Lake Creek Falls—p. 387
McKenzie River—p. 390
Middle Deschutes River—p. 399-400
Nestucca River—p. 391
Table Rocks—p. 393
Yaquina Head Outstanding Natural Area—p. 394-395

CAMPGROUNDS

The following campgrounds are found in this area of Oregon.
Please call the BLM office listed following each campground's
name for reservations and information. Contact information for
each BLM office is on page 404 for Oregon.

Alder Glen Campground; Salem District Office
Alsea Falls Campground; Salem District Office
Beavertail Campground; Prineville District Office
Big Bend Campground; Prineville District Office
Blue Hole Campground; Prineville District Office
Elk Bend Campground; Salem District Office
Elkhorn Valley Campground; Salem District Office
Dovre Campground; Salem District Office
Fan Creek Campground; Salem District Office
Fisherman's Bend Campground; Salem District Office
Lone Pine Campground; Prineville District Office
Macks Canyon Campground; Prineville District Office
Muleshoe Campground; Prineville District Office
Trout Creek Campground; Prineville District Office
Yellowbottom Campground; Salem District Office

Map B—Oregon

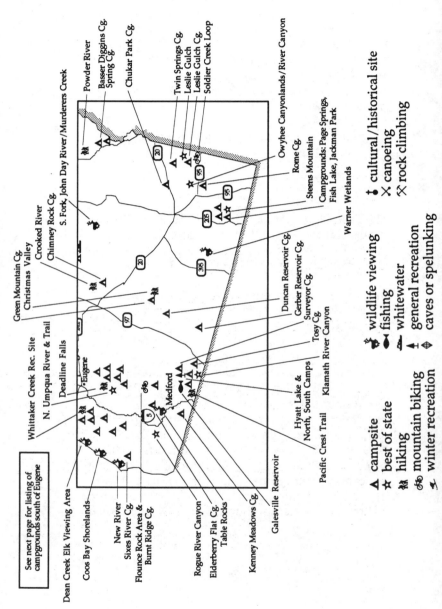

Powder River
Basser Diggins Cg.
Spring Cg.
Chukar Park Cg.
Twin Springs Cg.
Leslie Gulch
Leslie Gulch Cg.
Soldier Creek Loop
S. Fork, John Day River/Murderers Creek
Owyhee Canyonlands/River Canyon
Rome Cg.
Steens Mountain
Campgrounds: Page Springs,
Fish Lake, Jackman Park
Warner Wetlands

Green Mountain Cg.
Christmas Valley
Crooked River
Chimney Rock Cg.
Duncan Reservoir Cg.
Gerber Reservoir Cg.
Surveyor Cg.
Tosy Cg.
Klamath River Canyon
Hyatt Lake &
North, South Camps
Pacific Crest Trail
Galesville Reservoir
Kenney Meadows Cg.
Elderberry Flat Cg.
Table Rocks
Rogue River Canyon
Burnt Ridge Cg.
Flounce Rock Area &
Sixes River Cg.
New River
Coos Bay Shorelands
Dean Creek Elk Viewing Area
Whittaker Creek Rec. Site
N. Umpqua River & Trail
Deadline Falls

Eugene
Medford

See next page for listing of
campgrounds south of Eugene

Δ campsite
☆ best of state
🚶 hiking
🚴 mountain biking
⟋ winter recreation

🦌 wildlife viewing
🐟 fishing
— whitewater
⧊ general recreation
⊕ caves or spelunking

† cultural/historical site
✕ canoeing
✕ rock climbing

MAP REFERENCES

CAMPGROUNDS

The following campgrounds are found in this area of Oregon. Please call the BLM office listed following each campground's name for reservations and information. Contact information for each BLM office is on page 404 for Oregon.

Campgrounds south of Eugene and north of Medford:
Tucker Flat Campground; Medford District Office / Wildcat Campground; Medford District Office / Smith River Falls Campground; Coos Bay District Office / Loon Lake Campground; Coos Bay District Office / East Shore Campground; Coos Bay District Office / Park Creek Campground; Coos Bay District Office / Bear Creek Campground; Coos Bay District Office / Burnt Ridge Campground; Coos Bay District Office / Sixes River Campground; Coos Bay District Office / Tyee Campground; Roseburg District Office / Mill Pond Campground; Roseburg District Office / Rock Creek Campground; Roseburg District Office / Scared Man Campground; Roseburg District Office / Susan Creek Campground; Roseburg District Office / Cavitt Creek Campground; Roseburg District Office / Whittaker Creek Campground; Eugene District Office / Clay Creek Campground; Eugene District Office / Sharps Creek Campground; Eugene District Office

Other campgrounds: Basser Diggins Campground; Vale District Office / Burnt Ridge Campground; Coos Bay District Office / Chimney Rock Campground; Prineville District Office / Chukar Park Campground; Vale District Office / Duncan Reservoir Campground; Lakeview District Office / Elderberry Flat Campground; Medford District Office / Fish Lake Campground; Burns District Office / Gerber Reservoir Campground; Lakeview District Office / Green Mountain Campground; Lakeview District Office / Hyatt Lake Campground; Medford District Office / Hyatt Lake North Campground; Medford District Office / Hyatt Lake South Campground; Medford District Office / Jackman Park Campground; Burns District Office / Kenney Meadows Campground; Medford District Office / Leslie Gulch Campground; Vale District Office / Page Springs Campground; Burns District Office / Rome Campground; Vale District Office / Sixes River Campground; Coos Bay District Office / Spring Campground; Vale District Office / Surveyor Campground; Lakeview District Office / Tosy Campground; Lakeview District Office / Twin Springs Campground; Vale District Office

1

STEENS MOUNTAIN

Steens Mountain stands as a 9,773-foot-high reminder of the earth's power—a 30-mile-long fault-block mountain rising abruptly one mile above the Alvord Desert to the east. Glacial action has added to the visual drama by carving half-mile deep trenches that have formed four immense U-shaped gorges and a number of hanging valleys. The Donner Und Blitzen National Scenic River cuts through the region and numerous streams, springs and lakes dot the landscape. Wildlife abounds, including the local speed demon, the pronghorn antelope. Elk, bighorn sheep and mule deer are also frequently spotted.

HIKING/BACKPACKING

The best route on foot is via the Desert Trail, part of the Oregon State Recreational Trails System and a designated National Recreation Trail. Beginning at the Page Springs Campground, the first section of trail is approximately 25 miles in length, terminating at Fish Lake Campground. From Fish Campground to the Alvord Desert and the completion of the Steens Mountain section of the trail, the distance is approximately 15 miles. Hiking time for the entire trail is an estimated seven to eight days. Water is plentiful throughout the Steens Mountain area, but hikers are advised to carry adequate reserves at all times. Water sources must be purified. Lightning and thunderstorms are common in July and August. Take appropriate precautions to prevent being caught exposed on the high ridges.

FISHING

Mann Lake is said to be one of the best kept fishing secrets in Oregon. Well, the word's out now for sure. Lahontan cutthroat trout, up to 20 inches, are taken regularly from the lake, which also provides for excellent ice fishing in the winter.

MANAGEMENT
BLM Burns District, 12533 Highway 20 West, Hines, OR 97738; (503) 573-5241.

LOCATION
Approximately 60 miles south of Burns, Oregon and Interstate 395.

GETTING THERE
If you are going to be based out of Page Springs Campground, a passenger car is suitable. Further travel along the Steens Mountain Loop Road requires a four-wheel-drive vehicle, and at times the road may be impassable due to muddy conditions and/or snow. Check at the BLM Burns office for current road conditions before heading out. Hiking from Page Springs to the Alvord Desert requires a shuttle. Inquire at the BLM office about appropriate parking areas near Frog Spring—the termination point of the Steens Mountain section. To get to Page Springs from Burns, drive south for 62 miles on State Highway 205. At Frenchglen, take the Steens Mountain Loop Road for approximately three miles to Page Springs Campground.

CAMPING
There are several formal BLM campgrounds with pit toilets and drinking water along the Steens Mountain Loop Road Backcountry Byway—Page Springs, Fish Lake and Jackman Park. A camping fee is charged. Another private campground, Camper Corral, has RV facilities, a phone and a store for last-minute munchies. Primitive camping is allowed anywhere along the Desert Trail. Campfires are discouraged—use a stove. Campsites should be set up at least 200 feet from the nearest spring or waterhole so wildlife can drink without fear. A new campground is currently being planned with construction expected to begin sometime in 1993 at the south limb of the Steens Loop Road near the entrance to Big Indian Gorge.

PERMITS
No permits are necessary.

MAPS
The best maps for this area are published by the Desert Trail Association, P.O. Box 589, Burns, OR 97720. Ask for both the

Steens Mountain to the Alvord Desert and *Steens Mountain to Page Springs* maps.

SEASON

The season runs from mid-June to mid-September. Fall colors are superb in late September, with Fish Lake being particularly beautiful. Spring wildflowers are often at their best in the high country from late June to early July.

TIP: Always use a river runner's toilet when boating and never bury human waste around river camps. Human waste, including toilet paper, must be packed out.

BEST OF THE STATE

ROGUE RIVER CANYON

The backpacker is likely to see black-tailed deer, black bear, raccoon, mink, California ground squirrel, and perhaps the ring-tailed cat in this canyon. Rattlesnakes may also be encountered and caution is advised. The Rogue River has a rich and diverse pioneer past and vestiges of these days may still be viewed on the river. Cabin ruins, artifacts (look, don't touch), abandoned mine shafts, and bits and pieces of old mining equipment are evidence of the Rogue's historic heritage. The cabin at Whiskey Creek is a Registered National Historic Landmark maintained by the BLM. A museum at Rogue River Ranch is on the National Register of Historic Places and is open to the public from May through October.

WHITEWATER RAFTING

Rafts and kayaks are ideal, and although the BLM doesn't recommend it, whitewater canoe enthusiasts do run the river every year. Rapids are rated Class III+. This is considered an ideal river trip for families. Quite a number of river outfitters offer trips on this river. Contact the Rand Visitor's Center at (503) 479-3735, for more information.

Hiking / Backpacking

The Rogue River National Recreation Trail, between Grave Creek and Illahe, falls completely within the portion of the river protected by the Wild and Scenic Rivers Act of 1986. The first 24 miles of this trail, from Grave Creek to Marial, are administered by the BLM. The remaining 16 miles are administered by the Siskiyou National Forest Service. The BLM maintains a series of small campsites located at convenient points along the trail. Many of these sites have pit toilets. Once on Forest Service land, there is only one maintained site, but there are numerous areas suitable for camping. Fire pans are required within 400 feet of the Rogue River. Since the surrounding terrain is steep, the best campsites fall within this 400 feet. Backpackers should plan on carrying several sheets of heavy gauge aluminum foil with them to fashion into a fire pan. All ashes and remaining garbage must be packed out, not buried—use a triple layer of garbage bags for this purpose. The alternative is to use a backpacking stove.

If hiking this trail in the summer, be aware that the heat can be sweltering. It is recommended that you hike in reverse, from Illahe to Grave Creek, during this time so the afternoon sun is at your back. The 15-mile section of trail from Kelsey Creek to Grave Creek is the hilliest and least sheltered section of the trail. Keep in mind that in some of the canyons, the white rock reflects the heat turning the area into a veritable oven—Mule Creek Canyon temperatures have been recorded in excess of 120°F. I recommend bear-bagging your food, as bears are becoming increasingly bold along the river.

Management

This land is jointly managed by the BLM and the U.S. Forest Service. BLM Medford District Office, USDI, 3040 Biddle Road, Medford, OR 97504; (503) 770-2200

Location

Southwestern Oregon just west of Interstate 5 between Grants Pass and Gold Beach.

Getting There

From Interstate 5 north of Medford, take the Merlin exit and follow the Merlin-Galice Road approximately 27 miles northwest to the Grave Creek boat landing. There is a car shuttle

---

service at the store/restaurant that will arrange to have your car at the Foster Creek landing at a prearranged time. A fee is charged. Or you can call Rand Visitor's Center from June 1 to September 15 at (503) 479-3735 to inquire about other shuttle options and to obtain river and trail information. If hiking, the trail is 40 miles long. Plan on five days hiking time.

CAMPING
Camping is allowed anywhere within the Rogue River Wild and Scenic area. The BLM maintains camps in the area and in order to minimize impact in the land, they request that you use them.

PERMITS
No permits are necessary for hiking. Permits are required for floating the section from Grave Creek to Foster Bar between May 15 and September 15. Commercial permits are required for floating any section of the river.

MAPS
USGS topographic maps: Glendale, Galice, Marial, Agness
Additional maps: *Rogue River Recreation Guide* from BLM Medford District

ADDITIONAL INFORMATION
• *Where the Trails Are,* by Bill Williams; published by Independent Publishing Company, Ashland, OR.
• *Western Whitewater, From the Rockies to the Pacific,* by Jim Cassady, Bill Cross, and Fryar Calhoun, published by North Fork Press, Berkeley, CA; (800) 243-5522.

SEASON
The hiking season is all year. The best seasons are spring and fall. The best boating times are from June 1 to September 15.

TIP: Always walk single file in the center of a trail. Resist the urge to spread out or walk two abreast.

3

WILD ROGUE
WILDERNESS AREA

HIKING

Two maintained trails exist within the BLM section of the
Wild Rogue Wilderness. The West Fork of Mule Creek Trail
starts at Tucker Flat Campground, a semi-primitive drive-in
campground outside the wilderness. The trail crosses the
wilderness through three historic miles and provides access to
Hanging Rock, another popular hike in the Forest Service
section of the wilderness. The second developed trail climbs
Mount Bolivar, the highest point in this section of the wilderness, and provides an outstanding view of the surrounding
area. The remainder of the public lands within the Wild Rogue
Wilderness are open to hiking and other non-motorized or
mechanized forms of travel.

MANAGEMENT
BLM Medford District Office, Glendale Resource Area, 3040
Biddle Road, Medford, OR 97504; (503) 770-2399

LOCATION
The Wild Rogue Wilderness is in the heart of the Siskiyou
Mountains along the wild section of the Rogue River, northwest of Grants Pass. Both trails are accessed by narrow, one-
lane, mostly gravel roads, a section of which has been designated as the Grave Creek to Marial National Backcountry
Byway. The West Fork of Mule Creek Trail lies about 2.5 hours
from Grants Pass. The Mount Bolivar Trail is approximately
two hours from Grants Pass.

GETTING THERE
From the small town of Merlin, follow the Backcountry Byway
signs, staying on the main road past Rand Visitor's Center to
BLM road #34-8-1, the Mount Reuben Road. Stay on this road
for about 14 miles until it turns into BLM #32-7-19.3, the Dutch

Henry Road. Another mile farther and you turn left onto #32-8-31, the Kelsey-Mule Road. Four miles more is Ninemile Saddle. If you remain on this road, no longer following the Backcountry Byway signs, you will reach the Mount Bolivar trailhead in approximately nine miles. Or, continue to follow the Backcountry Byway signs to get to the West Fork of Mule Creek Trail by turning onto BLM road #32-9-14.2, the Marial Road. Follow it approximately 12 miles farther to Marial and the trailhead.

CAMPING
A semi-primitive campground is located just outside the wilderness at the Mule Creek entrance. Pit toilets and non-treated water are available. Camping within the wilderness is allowed, however no sites are maintained.

PERMITS
No permits are necessary except for floating the river. Contact the Rand Visitor's Center for permit information at (503) 479-3735.

MAPS
USGS topographic maps: Marial Northwest, Marial, Bone Mountain Southwest, Eden Valley, Bone Mountain Southeast, Mount Bolivar
Additional maps: BLM Medford District Transportation, Wild Rogue Wilderness Topographic—available from the Siskiyou National Forest at (503) 479-5301.

SEASON
Spring is an especially good time to visit this area as the wildflowers will be out and the weather will still be cool. Two creek crossings become impassable with rain—check with the BLM office for access information. Summer temperatures can range as high as 105°F, though the canyon remains quite beautiful—just think cool thoughts.

TIP: The most serious damage to a cultural site occurs from innocent visitation. Staying on the trail will minimize the damage.

4

HISTORIC KELSEY PACKTRAIL

HIKING

One of the original trails in the Rogue Canyon, the Historic Kelsey Packtrail was reopened in 1990 for hiking use. The trail provides another opportunity for hikers who enjoy history as much as scenery.

MANAGEMENT

BLM Medford District Office, Glendale Resource Area, 3040 Biddle Road, Medford, OR 97504; (503) 770-2303

LOCATION

The Historic Kelsey Packtrail is accessed from approximately 14 miles down the Rogue River National Recreation Trail adjacent to the wild section of the Rogue River. Another access point for the trail is from Marial, about a two-hour drive from the trailhead. The walk from this access point is about four miles back along the river.

GETTING THERE

From the small town of Merlin, follow the Backcountry Byway signs staying on the main road past the Rand Visitor's Center to BLM Road #34-8-1, the Mount Reuben Road. Turn onto Mount Reuben Road and follow it to the Grave Creek Bridge, the second crossing of the Rogue River. At the bridge, a road on the left drops down to the river. This is the trailhead for the Rogue River National Recreation Trail. The Kelsey Historic Packtrail is approximately 14 miles down this hiking-only trail.

An alternate route to the trail can be taken by continuing past the Grave Creek Bridge turn-off up the Mount Reuben Road, #34-8-1, the Grave Creek to Marial Backcountry Byway. Stay on this road for about 14 miles, at which point it turns into BLM #32-7-19.3, the Dutch Henry Road. Continue another mile, now on the Dutch Henry Road, to a left turn onto #32-8-

31, the Kelsey-Mule Road. Four miles farther is Ninemile Saddle. Continue to follow the Backcountry Byway signs and turn onto BLM road #32-9-14.2, the Marial Road. Stay on Marial Road for 12 miles to Marial and another access point to the Rogue River Trail. The Kelsey Historic Packtrail is located about four miles east.

CAMPING
No designated or maintained campsites are along the trail. Campsites are available at either end of the Rogue River National Recreation Trail.

PERMITS
No permits are necessary.

ADDITIONAL INFORMATION
Historic Kelsey Packtrail Brochure and *Rogue River Trail Guide*, are available from the BLM office.

MAPS
USGS topographic maps: Marial Northeast, Kelsey Peak
Additional maps: BLM Medford District Transportation, Wild Rogue Wilderness Topographic—available from the Siskiyou National Forest at (503) 479-5301.

SEASON
Spring is an especially good time as the wildflowers will be out and the weather will be cool. Summers can be quite hot—sometimes the mercury creeps as high as 105°F.

TIP: Wash 200 feet away from the nearest water source.

BEST OF THE STATE

NORTH UMPQUA RIVER AND TRAIL

Umpqua was the Native American name of the locality of the Umpqua River. The name was adopted by European settlers as both the name of the river and the Native Americans who fished and hunted in the area until the 1850s when white settlers began to push them out. The area is perhaps best known for winter and summer steelhead fishing, which brought novelist Zane Grey to the river for many years.

MOUNTAIN BIKING

The entire trail consists of an 11-mile segment on BLM lands with 66 additional miles on U.S. Forest Service land. Mountain bikes are allowed on all but a three-mile segment of Boulder Creek Wilderness and an approximately ten-mile segment of the Mount Thielsen Wilderness. Riders report that the best mountain biking with minimum equestrian use is on the BLM section. The trail is close to the river, with excellent overlook opportunities. The trail width is a minimum 36 inches wide, making it ideal for mountain biking, horseback riding and hiking. The trail condition is good, but riders should be alert for slides and loose rocks that may contribute pedaling hazards at any time. Bob Butte within the BLM section is a steep grade approximately one-half mile long.

WHITEWATER RAFTING

The river is rated Class III to IV and is considered good for families and first-timers as long as experienced boaters are along on the trip. A number of outfitters run commercial trips on the river. Check with the BLM for a list of licensed outfitters. This is the river many whitewater guides head to on their days off since the rapids are lively, the water clear and the canyon thickly forested.

MANAGEMENT
Jointly managed by the BLM and the U.S. Forest Service. BLM Roseburg District, 777 Northwest Garden Valley Boulevard, Roseburg, OR 97470; (503) 440-4930

LOCATION
Located near Roseburg, Oregon.

GETTING THERE
Take State Highway 138 to Swiftwater Bridge just one mile east of Idleyld Park. Parking is available on both sides of the river. Restroom and an information kiosk are at the trailhead.

CAMPING
Campgrounds are available, but typically they are on the opposite side of the river and inaccessible to trail-users. Camping is allowed along the trail, but always set up camp away from meadows, shorelines and the trail.

PERMITS
No permits are necessary for the trail. Permits are required for commercial boating.

MAPS
USGS topographic maps: Southerlin and Roseburg
Additional maps: Umpqua National Forest Visitors Map

ADDITIONAL INFORMATION
Western Whitewater, From the Rockies to the Pacific, by Jim Cassady, Bill Cross, and Fryar Calhoun, published by North Fork Press, Berkeley, CA; (800) 243-5522.

SEASON
The ideal season for mountain biking is May through October. Be sure to check on weather conditions—the trail can sometimes be very muddy in the rainy season. Large numbers of trees often fall across the trail, which could make it very frustrating for a mountain biker to ride the trail prior to its annual maintenance—maintenance is usually in May. The boating season is from June to July.

6

KLAMATH RIVER CANYON

This steep-walled canyon stretches for 15 miles from the John C. Boyle Dam south to the California/Oregon border. The dramatic cliffs, rimrock and large pines offer a haven for raptors who nest and hunt in the canyon. Wildlife visible along the river banks include black-tailed deer, Roosevelt elk, black bear, rabbits, beaver, and waterfowl. Access into the canyon is possible in a high-clearance vehicle from the Oregon side via the J.C. Boyle Dam Road or from the California side via the community of Copco. Camping and picnicking facilities are available at Tosy Recreation Site beside the John C. Boyle Reservoir.

WHITEWATER RAFTING

Whitewater rafting here is for experts only as it is rated at Class IV+. The rapids come one after another, in an almost out-of-control rush to get to the sea. Wetsuits are recommended, not because the water is cold, but because if you get tossed and go for a swim, the wetsuit will protect you from the sharp volcanic rock which lines the river bottom and canyon walls.

MANAGEMENT

BLM Lakeview District Office, 1000 Ninth Street South, P.O. Box 151, Lakeview, OR 97630; (503) 947-2177

LOCATION

Near Ashland and Interstate 5 in southern Oregon.

GETTING THERE

Access into the canyon is possible in a high-clearance vehicle from the Oregon side via the John C. Boyle Dam Road or from the California side via the community of Copco.

CAMPING
Camping and picnicking facilities are available at Tosy Recreation Site beside the John C. Boyle Reservoir. Otherwise, primitive camping is allowed anywhere along the river.

PERMITS
Permits are required for all boating on the river.

MAPS
USGS topographic maps: Mule Hill, Chicken Hills

ADDITIONAL INFORMATION
Western Whitewater, From the Rockies to the Pacific, by Jim Cassady, Bill Cross and Fryar Calhoun, published by North Fork Press, Berkeley, CA; (800) 243-5522.

SEASON
The best time to visit the canyon is between April and June, although the roads are usually passable until August. Whitewater seekers will want to run the river April through June—later depending on water levels.

> *TIP: Travel responsibly to protect the environment and preserve opportunities to enjoy recreation on wild lands.*

BEST OF THE STATE

7

LESLIE GULCH

Leslie Gulch is, by most accounts, a highly scenic and even spectacular area. The well-graded road makes it accessible by a car during the summer months. Not only are the rock formations, pinnacles and monoliths in the eight miles of Leslie Gulch spectacular, but each side canyon, Slocum Canyon, Timber Gulch, Juniper Gulch and several lesser side canyons, offer some of the most extraordinary and awe-inspiring formations to be seen anywhere in the U.S. Leslie Gulch is within the north rim of the ancient Mahogany Mountain Caldera with formations composed chiefly of deeply eroded volcanic ash and tufaceous material. Bighorn sheep, deer and chuckar are readily seen as are a variety of raptors. Warm water fishing in Lake Owyhee is good.

HIKING

Hiking is primarily along the dry washes of canyon floors which make for quite easy walking.

MANAGEMENT

BLM Vale District Office, 100 Oregon Street, Vale, OR 97918; (503) 473-3144.

LOCATION

Good access is off US Highway 95, approximately 25 miles on a well-graded gravel road. The signed exit is located approximately 18 miles north of Jordan Valley or 35 miles south of Ontario, Oregon.

GETTING THERE

Eight miles south of Adrian, Oregon (or seven miles west of Homedale, Idaho), take the Oregon State Highway 201 and follow the Leslie Gulch/Succor Creek National Backcountry Byway signs on the graded Succor Creek Road. Or take the graded McBride Creek Road from US Highway 95, south of Homedale, Idaho. You are advised that roads may become hazardous or impassable in wet or winter conditions. Towing large trailers is discouraged due to the steep, narrow and winding road that leads into the upper reaches of the Gulch. The best road conditions exist from mid-April to October, although the canyon is subject to flash-flooding at any time.

CAMPING

There is an established primitive campground near the lower end with tables and vault toilets. Water is obtainable at a developed spring on a small parcel of private land at Dago Canyon. A boat ramp provides water access to the southern portion of Owyhee Reservoir.

PERMITS
No permits are necessary.

MAPS
USGS topographic maps: Rooster Comb
BLM surface maps: Mahogany Mountains

SEASON
The best time to visit this area is during the spring and fall. The summer can be brutally hot.

TIP: Camp only in established
or previously used sites if available.

OREGON BY REGION

1

WESTERN OREGON

LAKE CREEK FALLS
hiking, wildlife observation

This is an excellent spot to view chinook and coho salmon between November and December and steelhead trout from February to March. The site features several waterfalls, two fish ladders, five concrete weirs, and interpretive signs. From Eugene take Highway 36 east to Triangle Lake and park at the Blachly-Lane Campground. Follow the path along the highway to the fish ladder access point.

For more information: Contact the BLM Eugene District Office, 2890 Chad Drive, P.O. Box 10266, Eugene, OR 97440; (503) 683-6600.
USGS topographic maps: Triangle Lake
BLM surface maps: Eugene

COOS BAY SHORELANDS
hiking, wildlife observation

The Coos Bay Shorelands are composed of the North Spit, a sand spit five miles long and up to one mile in width, and Coos Head, a rugged coastal headland with rocky cliffs more than 100 feet high. More than 270 bird species reside in or migrate through Coos Bay, Oregon's largest estuary. Unique birds here include the brown pelican, tufted puffins and peregrine falcons. Seals and California sea lions are also common in this area. The North Spit has the largest great blue heron rookery on Oregon's south coast. In early September, the annual Shorebird Festival is held by the Cape Arago Audubon Society, which offers guided trips.

The North Spit may be reached from Highway 101. Take the turnoff to Horsefall Beach and Dune Access and then turn left on the Trans-Pacific Highway. Access beyond the highway, to the interior of the spit, is limited to foot traffic and all-terrain or four-wheel-drive vehicles because of the sand. A BLM boat ramp is available.

For more information: Contact the BLM Coos Bay District Office, 1300 Airport Lane, North Bend, OR 97459; (503) 756-0100.
USGS topographic maps: Empire, North Bend, Charleston

DEADLINE FALLS
hiking, backpacking, mountain biking, horseback riding, fishing, wildlife observation

Located along the North Umpqua Trail on the Tioga segment, Deadline Falls offers a unique opportunity to view chinook and coho salmon and steelhead trout attempting to migrate up the falls. The best time to view this phenomenon is between May and September. To get there, from Roseburg head 23 miles east on Highway 138 to the Swiftwater Bridge. Immediately after crossing the bridge, park in the lot on the left. Follow the North Umpqua Trail approximately one-quarter mile to the spur trail leading to an observation point.

•**See also North Umpqua Trail in Best of the State, page 381**•
For more information: Contact the BLM Roseburg District, 777 Northwest Garden Valley Boulevard, Roseburg, OR 97470; (503) 440-4930.

DEAN CREEK ELK VIEWING AREA
hiking, wildlife observation

Roosevelt elk commonly graze the pastures and bottomlands near Dean Creek, adjacent to Highway 38, three miles east of Reedsport. Most of the year, the elk can be viewed at any time of the day, except in early spring when cows seek cover to give birth and raise calves. Large numbers of waterfowl will also be visible including mallards, wood ducks, great blue heron, Canada geese, snow geese, as well as osprey and bald eagle.

For more information: Contact the BLM Coos Bay District Office, 1300 Airport Lane, North Bend, OR 97459; (503) 756-0100.

FLOUNCE ROCK AREA OF CRITICAL ENVIRONMENTAL CONCERN
mountain biking, wildlife observation

From Stewart State Park at Lost Creek Reservoir, take Crater Lake Highway 62 drive northeast for 3.7 miles and turn left on Ulrich Road. Ulrich Road is an 8.6-mile tour along a volcanic ridgetop offering nice views and good wildlife viewing possibilities. The wildlife here includes golden eagle, red-tailed hawk, black-backed woodpecker (you'll hear them well before you see them), deer, Roosevelt elk, and mountain chickadees.

For more information: Contact the BLM Medford District Office, 3040 Biddle Road, Medford, OR 97504; (503) 770-2200.
USGS topographic Map: Battle Falls Northeast

GALESVILLE RESERVOIR
biking, picnicking, wildlife observation, boating, fishing

The Galesville Reservoir is located 30 miles north of Grants Pass and 36 miles south of Roseburg on Interstate 5. Take the Azalea exit and drive east on Upper Cow Creek Road for approximately seven miles to the Galesville dam and reservoir. Wildlife observation possibilities include osprey, bald eagles, numerous waterfowl, raptors and black-tail deer.

For more information: Contact the BLM Medford District Office, 3040 Biddle Road, Medford, OR 97504; (503) 770-2200.
USGS topographic map: Dayscreek Southwest

HYATT LAKE SPECIAL RECREATION MANAGEMENT AREA
biking, mountain biking, fishing, camping, wheelchair access, boating, wildlife observation

This is an excellent recreation spot with good opportunities for wildlife viewing. Bald eagles, osprey, Canada geese, cormorants, caspian terns and numerous ducks, black-tailed deer, gray and Douglas squirrels, porcupines, coyotes, and chipmunks are all common. Osprey and eagles are the most active between April and June when they are fishing and feeding their young. September is an excellent time for observing the many species of waterfowl who utilize Hyatt during their annual migrations. Take Interstate 5 to the Ashland exit and then proceed east on Highway 66 for 17.5 miles to the East Hyatt Lake access road. Turn north here and continue for approximately three miles and then turn left on Howard Prairie Road. Follow this road for one mile to Hyatt Lake.

For more information: Contact the BLM Medford District Office, 3040 Biddle Road, Medford, OR 97504; (503) 770-2200.

HYATT LAKE-HOWARD PRAIRIE LAKE SPECIAL RECREATION MANAGEMENT AREA
cross-country skiing, snowmobiling, snowshoeing, camping, mountain biking, inner-tubing

Winter sports opportunities for general snow play on Table Mountain, cross-country skiing on three groomed loop trails and snowmobile access on seasonally closed roads in the area is provided by the Medford District. From Interstate 5 and the Highway 66 exit, head east and travel to the Dead Indian County Road. Turn left and travel 17 miles to the Buck Prairie parking lot for cross-country skiing enthusiasts. Access is also available from Interstate 5 at the Highway 66 exit, by turning east and traveling 20 miles to the Hyatt/Prairie Road. Turn left and travel three-tenths of a mile to the snowmobile parking area, one-and-a-half miles to the Camper's Cove cross-country skiing parking lot, or four miles to the winter play hill.

Warmer months bring a different, yet equally enthusiastic recreational user to this area. Camping, mountain biking and inner-tubing are but a few of the activities possible.

For more information: Contact the BLM Medford District Office, 3040 Biddle Road, Medford, OR 97504; (503) 770-2200.
USGS topographic maps: Hyatt Reservoir Northwest

MCKENZIE RIVER
hiking, float boating, canoeing, wildlife observation, camping

Wildlife is common year-round along this river area and may be viewed best from the river. Expect to see a variety of raptors, waterfowl, songbirds, beavers, and deer. From Springfield, take Highway 126 east to the BLM-managed section of river between Vida and Blue River. Perhaps the most popular boating trip is from a put-in at Finn Rock Bridge to a take-out at the Dorris State Park.

For more information: Contact the BLM Eugene District Office, 2890 Chad Drive, P.O. Box 10266, Eugene, OR 97440; (503) 683-6600.
USGS topographic maps: Vida
BLM surface maps: McKenzie River

NESTUCCA RIVER
wildlife observation, mountain biking, hiking, inner-tubing, camping

The Nestucca River is a lush riparian system that supports nearly 200 species of wildlife and anadromous fish—chinook and coho salmon and steelhead trout. Bear Creek and Alder Creek are the best sites for wildlife viewing. The Nestucca River Road provides access to numerous recreation sites along the river and is designated as a National Backcountry Byway, but be cautious of logging traffic on the road. Deer, elk, songbirds, and bald eagles may be seen here. From Interstate 5, exit at Wilsonville and proceed west to Newberg. Follow State Highway 240 west to State Highway 47 at Yamhill and then continue south to Carlton. From Carlton, take Meadow Lake Country Road west for approximately 12 miles where it becomes the BLM's Nestucca River Road.

For more information: Contact the BLM Salem District Office, 1717 Fabry Road Southeast, Salem, OR 97306; (503) 375-5646.
BLM surface maps: Yamkill

NEW RIVER
hiking, wildlife observation

New River is like none other because it is less than 100 years old. Beginning at the point where Floras Creek intersects the foredune of the Pacific Ocean, New River flows north about nine miles, separated from the ocean by only the single foredune, dumping eventually and abruptly into the ocean. The landscape of shore pine, grasses and bare sand supports a rich population of wildlife including migrating birds. Several are endangered including the snowy plover, peregrine falcon, bald eagle, and Aleutian Canada goose. The best waterfowl viewing season is from April to May and from August to September. To get there from Bandon, drive 10.5 miles south on Highway 101, then turn west onto Croft Road. Look for the directional signs indicating public access at the Storm Ranch.

For more information: Contact the BLM Coos Bay District Office, 1300 Airport Lane, North Bend, OR 97459; (503) 756-0100.

NORTH UMPQUA RIVER AND TRAIL
hiking, backpacking, mountain biking, wildlife observation, camping, horseback riding, fishing, whitewater rafting, kayaking

Umpqua was the Native American name of the locality of the Umpqua River. The name was adopted by European settlers as both the name of the river and the Native Americans who fished and hunted in the area until the 1850s when white settlers began to push them out. The area is perhaps best known for winter and summer steelhead fishing, which brought novelist Zane Grey to the river for many years.

•**See also Best of the State, page 381**•
For more information: Contact the BLM Roseburg District, 777 Northwest Garden Valley Boulevard, Roseburg, OR 97470; (503) 440-4930. This area is jointly managed by the BLM and the U.S. Forest Service.

PACIFIC CREST NATIONAL SCENIC TRAIL
fishing, cross-country skiing, hiking, backpacking

The Pacific Crest National Scenic Trail extends from Mexico to Canada, a distance of approximately 2,500 miles. Predominantly managed by the U.S. Forest Service in Oregon, there is a significant 40-mile section in southern Oregon that is managed by the BLM. The trail begins in the south along the transition zone and runs between the Klamath River Basin and the Rogue River Basin. This portion of the trail could be divided into two excellent weekend hikes. Hyatt Lake, approximately the half-way point, has campgrounds and hot showers if you are so inclined. Attractions along this segment of trail include Pilot Rock, Bean Cabin, Soda Mountain Wilderness Study Area, Little Hyatt Lake, Hyatt Lake, and several segments of the National Historic Applegate Trail.

Access to the trail is available at a number of public road crossings. The most common are:
•Interstate 5 at the Mount Ashland exit and east to the Callahans Restaurant parking lot;
•Highway 66 at Greensprings Summit, 19 miles east of the Highway 66 exit off Interstate 5;
•Little Hyatt Lake, three miles from Greensprings Summit on Little Hyatt Lake County Road;
•Keno Road, from Interstate 5 at the Highway 66 exit, turning

east to the Dead Indian County Road and then left 20 miles to the Keno Road and right five miles to the Keno Road Trailcrossing.

For more information: Contact the BLM Medford District Office, 3040 Biddle Road, Medford, OR 97504; (503) 770-2200.
USGS topographic maps: Hyatt, Ashland, Mount McLoughlin
BLM surface maps: Medford District

ROGUE RIVER CANYON
hiking, backpacking, camping, wildlife observation, whitewater rafting, canoeing, kayaking

The visitor is likely to see black-tailed deer, black bear, Roosevelt elk, raccoon, mink, Douglas squirrel, and perhaps the ring-tailed cat in this canyon. Rattlesnakes may also be encountered and caution is advised. The Rogue River has a rich and diverse pioneer past and vestiges of these days are still seen on the river. Cabin ruins, artifacts (look, don't touch), abandoned mine shafts, and bits and pieces of old mining equipment are evidence of the Rogue's historic heritage. The cabin at Whiskey Creek is a Registered National Historic Landmark maintained by the BLM.

•**See also Rogue River Canyon, Wild Rogue Wilderness Area and the Historic Kelsey Packtrail in Best of the State, pages 374, 377 and 379**•
For more information: Contact the BLM Medford District Office, USDI, 3040 Biddle Road, Medford, OR 97504; (503) 770-2200.

TABLE ROCKS
hiking, wildflowers observation, wildlife observation

Not only is this a great place to hike and observe wildlife, but the wildflowers are spectacular between March and June. Stay on the trails though, because poison oak is everywhere. From Medford, take Interstate 5 north to Central Point. Exit and continue north on Table Rock Road. Turn west on Wheeler Road to Lower Table Rock or turn east on Modoc Road to reach Upper Table Rock. The wildlife here includes red-tailed hawk, osprey, great blue heron, blue-grey gnatcatcher, and the California kangaroo rat.

For more information: Contact the BLM Medford District Office, 3040 Biddle Road, Medford, OR 97504; (503) 770-2200.
USGS topographic maps: Medford Northwest

TABLE ROCK WILDERNESS AREA
hiking, backpacking, horseback riding, wildlife observation, camping

Table Rock Wilderness Area is located in Clackamas County along the western foothills of the Cascade Range. Molalla, with a population of approximately 3,100, is the largest town near the wilderness; the town lies 19 miles by road to the northwest. The terrain is steep and rugged and is the largest block of undeveloped forest land in an otherwise heavily logged or developed area. The wilderness area is also the habitat for the northern spotted owl. Deer and elk use the area as a wintering range. There are 17 miles of developed trails within the wilderness area and from on top of the ridges you can see Mount Rainier, Mount St. Helens, Mount Adams, Mount Hood, Mount Jefferson, and the North, Middle and South Sisters.

Four trailheads provide access into the region: Old Bridge, Table Rock, Rooster Rock Road, and Peachuck Lookout. From Molalla, just off Highway 211, drive to the eastern end of town and head right at the fork in the road. This places you on South Mathias Road. After three-tenths of a mile, the road curves and turn into South Freyer Park Road. Drive 1.9 miles to a junction and turn right on South Dickey Prairie Road. Continue for 5.2 miles and cross the Molalla River, at which point the road changes names again—this time it's South Molalla Road. Drive 12.7 miles to the junction of Middle Fork and Copper Creek Roads and make a left on Middle Fork Road. Then drive 2.6 miles to the Table Rock Access Road. Turn right and head 6.6 more miles to the signed trailhead.

For more information: Contact the BLM Salem District Office, 1717 Fabry Road Southeast, Salem, OR 97306; (503) 375-5646.
USGS topographic maps: Rooster Rock
BLM surface maps: North Santiam River
Additional maps: Table Rock Wilderness Map, available from the BLM office.

YAQUINA HEAD OUTSTANDING NATURAL AREA
hiking, tidepooling, wildlife observation

This coastal headland and off-shore rocky area provides vital habitat for a variety of marine wildlife. Tidepool invertebrates such as hermit crabs, sea anemones, sea stars, and sea urchins may be enjoyed year-round as can harbor seals. Gray whales may be seen migrating at Christmas-time and from March to May every year. There is an historic lighthouse, built in 1872, that is maintained by the BLM and overlooks the Pacific. The site is located just north of Newport along US Highway 101.

For more information: Contact the BLM Salem District Office, 1717 Fabry Road Southeast, Salem, OR 97306; (503) 375-5646.
BLM surface maps: Corvallis

WHITTAKER CREEK RECREATION SITE
hiking, camping, fishing, wildlife observation

Drive Highway 126 west from Eugene to Austa. Turn south on Siuslaw River Road #18-8-34. Drive 1.5 miles to BLM Road #18-8-21. Turn right and proceed to Whittaker Creek Recreation Site. Follow the trails to the creek for wildlife viewing opportunities of migrating coho and chinook salmon in November and December as well as deer, elk, and songbirds the rest of the year.

For more information: Contact the BLM Eugene District Office, 2890 Chad Drive, P.O. Box 10266, Eugene, OR 97440; (503) 683-6600.
USGS topographic maps: Roman Nose Mountain
BLM surface maps: Eugene

OREGON BY REGION

2

CENTRAL OREGON

CHRISTMAS VALLEY
spelunking, hiking, backpacking, camping, wildlife observation, rock hounding, mountain biking

The Fort Rock Basin and Christmas Valley is an amazingly diverse region set right in the middle of central Oregon's dramatic volcanic features. There is a National Backcountry Byway that winds through the region—in some places requiring a high-clearance vehicle for access. The route is suitable for mountain bikes, although you will want to watch for drivers who are more intent on the scenery than the road in front of them. The byway takes you through sagebrush, lava flows, cinder cones, sand dunes, alfalfa fields, and a beautiful forested area. Primitive camping is allowed anywhere along the backcountry route, but please use only previously established sites. The region is located about 70 miles southeast of Bend with the backcountry byway loop beginning at the Fort Rock turnoff on Oregon Highway 31—18 miles north of Silver Lake.

The following are some of the more significant natural features in the area:

Derrik Cave is an unique lava tube cave over 440 yards long and, in places, over 30 feet high. The cave was used as a civil defense fallout shelter site in the early 1950s and was stocked with provisions during that time.

The Devil's Garden, Squaw Ridge and Four Craters Lava Beds are classified as Wilderness Study Areas with unique geological and botanical features to enjoy. Rugged boots and protective clothing are a must for hiking in this region.

Crack-In-The-Ground is a large fracture in basalt which is 40 feet deep and nearly two miles long.

For more information: Contact the BLM Lakeview District Office, 1000 Ninth Street South, P.O. Box 151, Lakeview, OR 97630; (503) 947-2177.
BLM surface maps: Christmas Valley

CROOKED RIVER
hiking, camping, fishing, wildlife observation

Crooked River is a designated Wild and Scenic River, and for good reason—it's beautiful. Many call this spectacular river canyon one of the best areas the BLM has to offer in Oregon. There is a BLM campground at Chimney Rock, 17 miles south of Prineville. There are also nine primitive campgrounds along the canyon and river. Oregon State Highway 27 south from Prineville is designated a National Backcountry Byway and provides access to much of the river canyon and camping areas.

On the other side of Prineville Reservoir, to the east and still on the Crooked River, is an excellent spot to view bald eagles and other birds of prey. The best viewing of bald eagles is between February and March. From Prineville, drive one mile east on Highway 26 and then turn south onto the Paulina Highway. Drive for 25 miles to Post and then continue on the Paulina Highway along the Crooked River.

For more information: Contact the BLM Prineville District Office, 185 East Fourth Street, P.O. Box 550, Prineville, OR 97754; (503) 447-4115.

Maps: Central Oregon Public Lands Map

DESCHUTES WILD AND SCENIC RIVER / SHERAR'S FALLS
whitewater kayaking, rafting, hiking, camping, wildlife observation, fishing

At the Sherar's Falls site, one can view Native Americans using traditional dip-netting methods for catching steelhead trout and chinook salmon. The heaviest fishing takes place from April to June for spring chinook and from August to October for fall chinook and steelhead. From Maupin, 30 miles south of Ralles on Highway 197, follow the Deschutes River Access Road (a National Backcountry Byway) downstream along the river for eight miles to the falls. Continue down the road to find Beavertail and Macks Canyon campgrounds as well as river access to the Deschutes. You will enjoy the scenery of this river area as it follows a serpentine route carved deeply into the ancient lava flows of the Columbia River Plateau. Four small BLM campgrounds exist upriver from Maupin and eight more below Maupin—this is in addition to the larger sites at Beavertail and Macks Canyon.

Resources: *Western Whitewater, From the Rockies to the Pacific,* by Jim Cassady, Bill Cross, and Fryar Calhoun, published by North Fork Press, Berkeley, CA; (800) 243-5522.

For more information: Contact the BLM Prineville District Office, 185 East Fourth Street, P.O. Box 550, Prineville, OR 97754; (503) 447-4115.

BLM surface maps: Lower Deschutes River Map. Order this map from the BLM for $4.

JOHN DAY RIVER
hiking, backpacking, whitewater rafting, kayaking, canoeing, camping

A trip on the lower John Day River will usually involve two to five days with weather ranging from the extremely hot to the extremely cold—talk about having to pack layers. The best time to run the John Day is March through June. Much of the river, downstream from Service Creek, located 15 miles southeast of the town of Fossil on Highway 19, is a leisurely waterway with several Class III and one Class IV rapids to be negotiated. The river runs through semi-arid, high-desert country and is ideally suited to the novice as long as there are boaters with experience along in the group. You will enjoy floating by sheer cliffs and bluffs that are home to a variety of wildlife as well as the area for historical and archaeological sites.

Resources: *Western Whitewater, From the Rockies to the Pacific,* by Jim Cassady, Bill Cross, and Fryar Calhoun, published by North Fork Press, Berkeley, CA; (800) 243-5522.
For more information: Contact the BLM Prineville District Office, 185 East Fourth Street, P.O. Box 550, Prineville, OR 97754; (503) 447-4115.
Maps: Lower John Day River Public Lands Map

KLAMATH RIVER CANYON
hiking, backpacking, rafting, kayaking, whitewater canoeing, wildlife observation, camping

The steep-walled canyon stretches for 15 miles from the John C. Boyle Dam south to the California/Oregon border. The dramatic cliffs, rimrock and large pines offer a haven for raptors who nest and hunt in the canyon. The wildlife visible along the river banks include black-tailed deer, Roosevelt elk, black bear, rabbits, beavers, and waterfowl. Access into the canyon is possible in a high-clearance vehicle from the Oregon side, via the John C. Boyle Dam Road or from the California side, via the community of Copco. Camping and picnicking facilities are available at Tosy Recreation Site beside the John C. Boyle Reservoir.

•**See also Best of the State, page 383**•
For more information: Contact the BLM Lakeview District Office,

1000 Ninth Street South, P.O. Box 151, Lakeview, OR 97630; (503) 947-2177.

SOUTH FORK OF THE JOHN DAY RIVER / MURDERERS CREEK
hiking, fishing, camping, wildlife observation, mountain biking

Along the South Fork of the John Day River is the site known as Murderers Creek; an excellent area to view mule deer, Rocky Mountain elk, bighorn sheep, and a variety of waterfowl and raptors. Four-wheel-drive or high-clearance vehicles are recommended as the road can be rough and rutted—even impassable in the winter. Mountain bikes are suitable on the route, just watch out for motorized vehicles. From Prineville, drive east on Highway 26 to Dayville and then south along the South Fork of the John Day River—this road is a National Backcountry Byway. Camping is allowed anywhere along the river on public lands—do not camp on private land. Please use only sites that have already been established to minimize impact. This scenic canyon offers much in the way of views, solitude and quiet hiking opportunities.

For more information: Contact the BLM Prineville District Office, 185 East Fourth Street, P.O. Box 550, Prineville, OR 97754; (503) 447-4115.

Maps: Upper John Day River Public Lands Map

MIDDLE DESCHUTES RIVER
hiking, backpacking, fishing, camping, wildlife observation

The Middle Deschutes River is located upriver from Lake Billy Chinook and northwest of Redmond, Oregon. A 19-mile river segment from Odin Falls to the upper end of Lake Billy Chinook has been designated a component of the National Wild and Scenic River system. Outstanding scenic, recreational, cultural, geological, wildlife and historical values exist within the rugged, steep-walled basalt canyon. The canyon increases in depth as it proceeds northward. Three waterfalls and a wide variety of riparian vegetation enhance the qualities of this region. Fishing is excellent for rainbow and German brown trout, dolly varden, and Kokanee. The region also harbors prehistoric sites, rock art, rock shelters, and an historic river crossing.

For more information: Contact the BLM Prineville District Office, 185 East Fourth Street, P.O. Box 550, Prineville, OR 97754; (503) 447-4115.

Map: Central Oregon Public Lands Map

WARNER WETLANDS
canoeing, hiking, wildlife observation

The Warner Wetlands have been designated an Area of Critical Environmental Concern. This special habitat of inter-connected lakes, marshes, wet meadows and sand dunes supports thousands of birds. There are over 400 miles of shoreline to walk and/or canoe. The best wildlife viewing times are during the nesting season of April through July and the migration season from September through October. The area is a natural one which goes through periodic wet and dry cycles that are important to its health. It is best to call the BLM prior to heading out to determine the conditions. To get there, travel north from the store (that's right, the store) in the town of Plush, nine-tenths of a mile on Lake County Road 3-10. Turn east on County Road 3-12. Follow this paved road for five miles to the Warner Wetlands sign and interpretive area.

For more information: Contact the BLM Lakeview District Office, 1000 Ninth Street South, P.O. Box 151, Lakeview, OR 97630; (503) 947-2177.

BLM surface maps: Adel, Bluejoint Lake

> *TIP: Use a fire pan whenever you must build a campfire.*

3

EASTERN OREGON

GRANDE RONDE WILD AND SCENIC RIVER
hiking, backpacking, rafting, canoeing, kayaking, camping, wildlife observation, fishing

The Grande Ronde river system, which includes part of the Wallowa River, is considered to be one of Oregon and Washington's most scenic rivers. A segment of the river, the Goosenecks, has been established as a National Natural Landmark. The river corridor is about 90 miles in length with an overall rating of Class III and is suitable for rafts, kayaks or canoes. Located in northeastern Oregon and southeastern Washington, principle river access points are located in small communities such as Minam and Troy in Oregon and Boggan's Oasis and Hellers Bar in Washington.

For more information: Contact the BLM Vale District Office, 100 Oregon Street, Vale, OR 97918; (503) 473-3144.
USGS topographic maps: Minam, Tros (Oregon); Mountain View, Lime Kiln Rapids (Washington)
BLM surface maps: Wallowa (Washington/Oregon); Clarkston (Washington)

LESLIE GULCH
hiking, backpacking, fishing, wildlife observation, camping

Leslie Gulch is a very scenic and even spectacular area. The well-graded road makes it accessible by passenger car during the summer months. Not only are the rock formations, pinnacles and monoliths in the six miles of Leslie Gulch spectacular, but each side canyon, Slocum Canyon, Timber Gulch, Juniper Gulch, and several lesser side canyons, offer some of the most extraordinary and awe-inspiring formations to be seen anywhere in the U.S. Leslie Gulch is within the north rim of the ancient Mahogany Mountain Caldera with formations composed chiefly of deeply-eroded volcanic ash and tufaceous material. Bighorn sheep, deer and chuckar are

Oregon

readily seen here, as are a variety of raptors. Warm-water
fishing in Lake Owyhee is good.

•**See also Best of the State, page 384**•
For more information: Contact the BLM Vale District Office, 100
Oregon Street, Vale, OR 97918; (503) 473-3144.

OWYHEE CANYONLANDS / OWYHEE RIVER CANYON
*hiking, backpacking, rafting, kayaking, canoeing, fishing,
camping*

Although access is challenging, this 450,000-acre region
(much of it lying within Idaho along the Oregon/Idaho border)
is picturesque, dramatic, wild, isolated, and well worth your
time. River runners and hunters are the predominant users,
and there are not too many of those. The narrow canyons that
cut into the plateau range anywhere from several hundred to
one thousand feet deep—often with sheer walls from rimrock
to river bottom. Mountain lion, bobcat, river otter, mule deer,
and bighorn sheep reside within the Owyhee Canyon system.
Within the Oregon region, there is a 13-mile access road to
Owyhee Dam and the Lower Owyhee River Canyon that
provides an excellent introduction to the canyon habitats
typical of eastern Oregon. Songbirds, raptors, waterfowl, and
upland birds are all readily visible from the road, especially
where cottonwood and willows are well established along the
river bottom. The access road is located west of Highway 201,
7.5 miles south of Nyssa, Oregon.

•**See also the Owyhee River Canyon in Best of the State in
Nevada, page 300**•
For more information: Contact the BLM Vale District Office, 100
Oregon Street, Vale, OR 97918; (503) 473-3144.
BLM Boise District Office, 3948 Development Avenue, Boise, ID
83705; (208) 384-3300

POWDER WILD AND SCENIC RIVER
hiking, camping, fishing, wildlife observation

Located 13 miles northeast of Baker and extending from
the Thief Valley Reservoir to the Keating Valley (Highway
203), this river segment is 11.7 miles long and provides excellent raptor nesting and foraging habitat as well as bald eagle

habitat and recreational possibilities. The spring and summer seasons are the best times to visit.

For more information: Contact the BLM Vale District Office, 100 Oregon Street, Vale, OR 97918; (503) 473-3144.

SOLDIER CREEK LOOP
hiking, backpacking, mountain biking, wildlife observation

This route is primarily a graded and gravel access road that passes through some of the best pronghorn antelope and sage grouse areas in Oregon. The best viewing is from April to September. Driving is limited to high-clearance vehicles and in dry weather. From Jordan Valley, follow the North Fork Owyhee Backcountry Byway east into Idaho, then south to the 3-Forks turnoff. The loop is completed by returning to Highway 95 on Soldier Creek Road.

For more information: Contact the BLM Vale District Office, 100 Oregon Street, Vale, OR 97918; (503) 473-3144.

STEENS MOUNTAIN
hiking, backpacking, fishing, wildlife observation, camping, mountain biking

Steens Mountain stands as a 9,773-foot-high reminder of the earth's power—a 30-mile-long fault-block mountain rising abruptly one mile above the Alvord Desert to the east. Glacial action has added to the visual drama by carving half-mile deep trenches that have formed four immense U-shaped gorges and a number of hanging valleys. The Donner Und Blitzen National Scenic River cuts through this region and numerous streams, springs and lakes dot the landscape. Wildlife abounds here, including the local speed demon, the pronghorn antelope. Elk, bighorn sheep and mule deer are also frequently spotted.

•**See also Best of the State, page 372**•
For more information: Contact the BLM Burns District, 12533 Highway 20 West, Hines, OR 97738; (503) 573-5241.

TIP: When mountain biking, leave behind your "need for speed" mentality when in wilderness areas.

STATE INFORMATION OVERVIEW

OREGON STATE OFFICE
1300 Northeast 44th Avenue, P.O. Box 2965, Portland, OR 97208; (503) 280-7001

BURNS DISTRICT OFFICE
HC 74-12533, Highway 20 West, Hines, OR 97738; (503) 573-5241

ROSEBURG DISTRICT OFFICE
777 Northwest Garden Valley Boulevard, Roseburg, OR 97470; (503) 440-4930

COOS BAY DISTRICT OFFICE
1300 Airport Lane, North Bend, OR 97459; (503) 756-0100

EUGENE DISTRICT OFFICE
2890 Chad Drive, P.O. Box 10266, Eugene, OR 97440; (503) 683-6600

PRINEVILLE DISTRICT OFFICE
185 East Fourth Street, P.O. Box 550, Prineville, OR 97754; (503) 447-4115

LAKEVIEW DISTRICT OFFICE
1000 Ninth Street South, P.O. Box 151, Lakeview, OR 97630; (503) 947-2177

SALEM DISTRICT OFFICE
1717 Fabry Road Southeast, Salem, OR 97306; (503) 375-5646

MEDFORD DISTRICT OFFICE
3040 Biddle Road, Medford, OR 97504; (503) 770-2200

Klamath Falls Resource Area, 2795 Anderson Suite 25, Klamath Falls, OR 97601; (503) 883-6916

VALE DISTRICT OFFICE
100 Oregon Street, Vale, OR 97918; (503) 473-3144

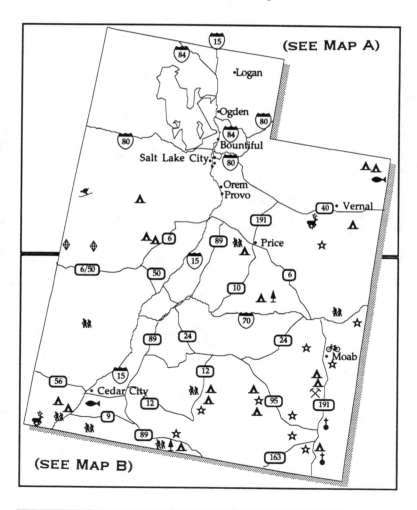

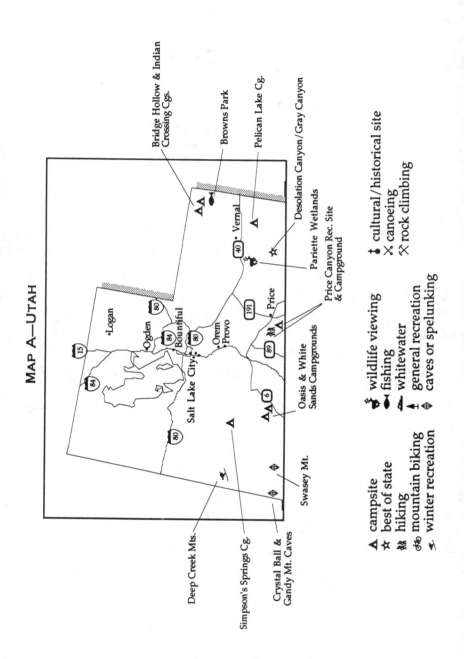

MAP A—UTAH

Bridge Hollow & Indian
Crossing Cgs.

Browns Park

Pelican Lake Cg.

Desolation Canyon/Gray Canyon

Pariette Wetlands

Price Canyon Rec. Site
& Campground

Vernal

40

Logan

80

Ogden

Bountiful

84

80

Orem
Provo

191

Price

89

15

84

Salt Lake City

Oasis & White
Sands Campgrounds

80

6

Swasey Mt.

Deep Creek Mts.

Simpson's Springs Cg.

Crystal Ball &
Candy Mt. Caves

▲ campsite
☆ best of state
🐾 hiking
🚴 mountain biking
⛷ winter recreation

🦌 wildlife viewing
🎣 fishing
🛶 whitewater
⚓ general recreation
⬦ caves or spelunking

† cultural/historical site
✕ canoeing
𝍖 rock climbing

MAP REFERENCES

Browns Park—p. 428
Crystal Ball and Gandy Mountain Caves—p. 429
Deep Creek Mountains—p. 429-430
Desolation Canyon/Gray Canyon—p. 421-423
Pariette Wetlands—p. 430
Price Canyon Recreation Site—p. 436-437
Swasey Mountain—p. 430

CAMPGROUNDS

The following campgrounds are found in this area of Utah. Please call the BLM office listed following each campground's name for reservations and information. Contact information for each BLM office is on pages 445-446 for Utah.

Bridge Hollow Campground; Vernal District Office
Indian Crossing Campground; Vernal District Office
Oasis Campground; Warm Springs Resource Area
Pelican Lake Campground; Vernal District Office
Price Canyon Camground; San Rafael Resource Area
Simpson's Springs Campground; Salt Lake District Office
White Sands Campground; Warm Springs Resource Area

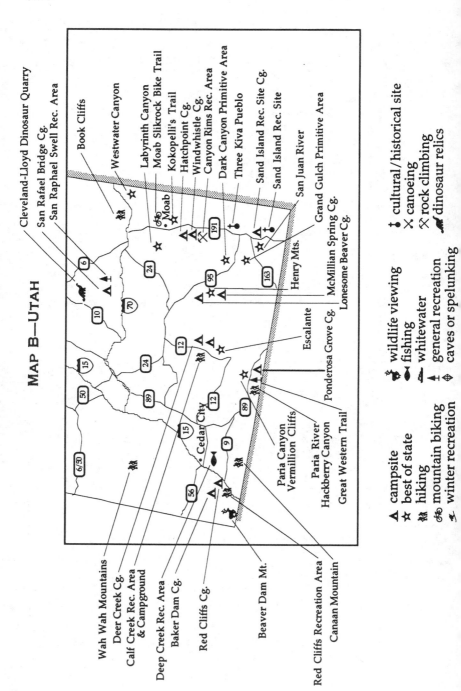

MAP B—UTAH

Cleveland-Lloyd Dinosaur Quarry
San Rafael Bridge Cg.
San Raphael Swell Rec. Area

Book Cliffs

Westwater Canyon

Labyrinth Canyon
Moab Slickrock Bike Trail
Kokopelli's Trail
Hatchpoint Cg.
Windwhistle Cg.
Canyon Rims Rec. Area
Dark Canyon Primitive Area
Three Kiva Pueblo
Sand Island Rec. Site Cg.
Sand Island Rec. Site

San Juan River

Grand Gulch Primitive Area

McMillian Spring Cg.
Lonesome Beaver Cg.

Henry Mts.

Escalante

Ponderosa Grove Cg.

Paria Canyon
Vermillion Cliffs

Paria River
Hackberry Canyon

Great Western Trail

Moab

Cedar City

Wah Wah Mountains
Deer Creek Cg.
Calf Creek Rec. Area
& Campground
Deep Creek Rec. Area
Baker Dam Cg.

Red Cliffs Cg.

Beaver Dam Mt.

Red Cliffs Recreation Area
Canaan Mountain

△ campsite
☆ best of state
🥾 hiking
🚲 mountain biking
⛷ winter recreation

🦌 wildlife viewing
🐟 fishing
🚣 whitewater
⚲ general recreation
⬦ caves or spelunking

♦ cultural/historical site
✕ canoeing
✗ rock climbing
🦴 dinosaur relics

MAP REFERENCES

Beaver Dam Mountain—p. 439
Book Cliffs—p. 428
Calf Creek Recreation Area—p. 439-440
Canaan Mountain—p. 440
Canyon Rims Recreation Area—p. 431-432
Cleveland-Lloyd Dinosaur Quarry—p. 432
Dark Canyon Primitive Area—p. 412-414
Deep Creek Recreation Area—p. 441
Escalante Resource Area—p. 414-417
Grand Gulch Primitive Area—p. 410-412
Great Western Trail—p. 427
Henry Mountains—p. 417-419
Kokopelli's Trail—p. 435
Labyrinth Canyon—p. 423-425
Moab Slickrock Bike Trail—p. 436
Paria Canyon-Vermillion Cliffs—p. 441-442
Paria River-Hackberry Canyon—p. 442
Red Cliffs Recreation Area—p. 443
San Juan River—p. 425-426
San Rafael Swell Recreation Area—p. 437
Sand Island Recreation Site—p. 438
Three Kiva Pueblo—p. 438
Wah Wah Mountains—p. 443-444
Westwater Canyon—p. 419-421

CAMPGROUNDS

The following campgrounds are found in this area of Utah. Please call the BLM office listed following each campground's name for reservations and information. Contact information for each BLM office is on pages 445-446 for Utah.

Baker Dam Campground; Dixie Resource Area
Calf Creek Campground; Escalante Resource Area
Deer Creek Campground; Escalante Resource Area
Hatchpoint Campground; Moab District Office
Lonesome Beaver Campround; Henry Mtns. Resource Area
McMillian Spring Campground; Henry Mtns. Resource Area
Ponderosa Grove Campground; Kanab District Office
Red Cliffs Campground; Dixie Resource Area
San Rafael Bridge Campground; San Rafael Resource Area
Sand Island Recreation Site; San Juan Resource Area
Windwhistle Campground; Moab District Office

1

GRAND GULCH
PRIMITIVE AREA

It is within this twisting canyon maze that some of the most bewitching scenery and the largest concentrations of Anasazi ruins in all of southeastern Utah reside. Beginning at an elevation of 6,400 feet, Grand Gulch cuts a serpentine swath through Cedar Mesa, running southwest to the San Juan River, dropping a tortuous 2,700 feet in just 53 miles. Sheer cliffs, sharp pinnacles, Anasazi cliff dwellings, rock art sites, natural bridges, and sandstone amphitheaters make up Grand Gulch and its many surrounding tributaries. Keep your eyes peeled for signs of mountain lion, black bear, bobcat, fox, mule deer, coyote, ringtail cat, and skunk. Raptors frequently carve and slice their way through the blue sky above. Pinyon pine, juniper, cottonwood, willow, sagebrush, and prickly pear cactus are the predominant species of vegetation.

The Anasazi have left a legacy that includes hundreds of cliff dwellings and thousands of pictographs and petroglyphs, and historical evidence has shown that their influence on the canyon dates back as far as 200 A.D. Take special care not to touch or climb on the ruins, as this kind of wear and tear can cause what the BLM refers to as "innocent vandalism." Souvenir hunting is also a major problem within the entire region. Please leave what you find in its place and report any suspicious activity to the BLM. Vandalism ruins the experience for everyone.

HIKING

If you want to hike from Collins Spring to Kane Gulch Ranger Station, plan on five days to navigate the route. You will cover approximately 38 very arduous miles through the best this area has to offer. This particular section of the Grand Gulch Primitive Area offers the hiker a chance to cover not only more ground, but view more ruins and experience more solitude than anywhere else in the region. Careful navigation is required in some parts to prevent becoming confused and heading off-route down a side canyon. Expect tedious bush-whacking between mile 16 and 20 of the hike. Take a break at Step Canyon, around mile 18.5, as Anasazi sites abound. Spend enough time to locate Two Story Ruin, concealed by thick overgrowth to the right of the canyon. Springs provide the primary water source throughout the canyon, but they aren't always reliable. Check at the ranger station for current water conditions and always carry at least one gallon per person with you.

MANAGEMENT
BLM San Juan Resource Area, 435 North Main, P.O. Box 7, Monticello, UT 84535; (801) 587-2141.

LOCATION
Located approximately ten miles north of Mexican Hat and 25 miles east of Blanding in southeastern Utah.

GETTING THERE
Travel south of Blanding on Highway 191. Turn west onto Highway 95. At the intersection with Highway 261, turn south on Highway 261. Drive approximately four miles to the Kane Gulch Ranger Station. A car shuttle must be taken between the Collins Spring trailhead and the Kane Gulch Ranger Station—it's 29 miles, including nine on dirt. Shuttle services are some-times available. Inquire at the Monticello Interagency Information Center.

CAMPING
Primitive camping is allowed anywhere along the trail.

PERMITS
Permits are required for all travel within the Grand Gulch Primitive Area. Permits are $5; the money goes to enhance on-the-ground management of the region. Groups over 15 people are prohibited.

MAPS
USGS topographic maps: Bears Ears, Cedar Mesa, Grand Gulch.
Additional maps: The Canyonlands Natural History Associa-

tion publishes a catalog and sells topographic maps and other information useful to visitors in this region. Call (801)259-6003.
•*Grand Gulch Plateau, Utah Map Series,* published by Trails Illustrated, P.O. Box 3610, Evergreen, CO 80439; (800) 962-1643.

ADDITIONAL INFORMATION
•*Hiking the Southwest's Canyon Country,* by Sandra Hinchman, published by The Mountaineers, 1011 Southwest Klickitat Way, Suite 107, Seattle, WA 98134; (800) 553-4453.
•*Utah Handbook,* by Bill Weir, published by Moon Publications, 722 Wall Street, Chico, CA 95928; (916) 345-5473.
•*The Hikers Guide to Utah,* by Dave Hall, published by Falcon Press, P.O. Box 1718, Helena, MT 59624; (800) 582-2665.

SEASON
The spring and autumn seasons are the ideal times to travel in this region. Summer months are possible, but you will want to avoid the mid-day heat. Winter brings snow and ice, which can make travel on slickrock sections extremely hazardous.

TIP: Travel or camp in small groups.

BEST OF THE STATE
2
DARK CANYON PRIMITIVE AREA

Dark Canyon runs from the Manti-La Sal National Forest down to the desert environment along Lake Powell. This remote canyon system features outstanding backpacking opportunities. Mountain biking is good along four-wheel-drive roads outside of the designated wilderness area managed by the U.S. Forest Service and the Dark Canyon Primitive Area administered by the BLM. Deep canyons, open valleys and sloping plateaus fill the menu here. Dark Canyon dazzles visitors with its 1,400-foot-high stair-stepped walls. Many canyons within this region feature this unique sandstone/limestone combination which creates numerous benches from which rainwater runs off in spectacular waterfalls, forming picturesque "water curtains" and refreshing pools. From upper plateaus, excellent views of the nearby Henry Mountains and the Colorado River may be enjoyed. Wildlife includes black bear, bobcat, mountain lion, coyote, beaver, fox, mule deer, and bighorn sheep.

HIKING/BACKPACKING

Water is scarce in some areas, most notably Dark Canyon itself. You must be prepared to carry at least one gallon of water per person per day at all times. Many of the routes you will follow have no trail—just stay along the canyon floors. You must also be wary of flash floods at all times.

MANAGEMENT

BLM San Juan Resource Area, 435 North Main, P.O. Box 7, Monticello, UT 84535; (801) 587-2141.

LOCATION

Twenty-five miles west of Blanding and south of Canyonlands National Park.

GETTING THERE

North of State Highway 95, travel toward Natural Bridges National Monument. After about a mile on Natural Bridges Road, turn right and follow the graded road up Little Maverick Point and then over Bears Ears Pass. Approximately two miles north of Bears Ears, you will turn left at a junction. Two miles from the junction is a corral at the turnoff to Twin Springs and the head of Peavine Canyon. Park here.

CAMPING

Camping is allowed anywhere within the canyon area. Always camp above the high-water mark as flash flooding is a constant possibility.

PERMITS

No permits are necessary.

MAPS

USGS topographic maps: Poison Canyon, Warren Canyon, Black Steer Canyon, Bowdie Canyon, Fable Valley
Additional maps: *National Forests in Utah Map Series: Trails Manti-Lasal National Forest featuring Dark Canyon,* published by Trails Illustrated, P.O. Box 3610, Evergreen, CO 80439; (800) 962-1643.

ADDITIONAL INFORMATION

The Hikers Guide to Utah, by Dave Hall, published by Falcon Press, P.O. Box 1718, Helena, MT 59624; (800) 582-2665.

SEASON

The best time to visit this area is in late spring to early summer and in the fall.

> *TIP: Never dig holes, trenches, or otherwise alter the campsite for convenience. The perfect campsite is found, not made.*

BEST OF THE STATE

3

ESCALANTE RESOURCE AREA

The Escalante, an outstanding example of Utah's slickrock and riparian canyon environments, consists of a mind-boggling intricate network of canyons, plateaus, cliffs, sandstone arches, natural bridges, domes, water pockets, meandering streams, and more. The area is so difficult to navigate that it has proved a formidable barrier to vehicle traffic since the days of the horse and buggy. In fact, the Escalante River was not even bridged until 1935, crediting Boulder City as one of the last communities to gain automobile access. Over 60 mammals, 150 birds and 20 reptiles call the Escalante home. Some of the more common animals are mountain lion, mule deer, gray fox, coyote, deer mice, Ord's kangaroo rat, scrub jay, canyon wren, and numerous hawks.

HIKING

The Escalante Canyons continue to retain their reputation as one of the premier backpacking regions in the Southwest. Expect this area to be crowded throughout the spring, summer and fall. Many different routes and trip lengths are possible to help avoid the crowds. The westside tributary canyons are accessible from trailheads on the Hole-In-The-Rock Scenic Byway. The eastern canyons are accessible from trailheads on the Burr Trail Road and Circle Cliffs. The main stem of the Escalante River Canyon is entered at the Highway 12 bridge or in Escalante. Death Hollow is accessible from the Hells Backbone Road.

Rain and water runoff can occur anytime during the spring. It is vital that you contact the Escalante Resource Area office for current trail and road conditions. Fall is an excellent time to backpack in the Escalante River backcountry. Evenings are cool, water levels are low and insects are less bothersome.

Calf Creek to Harris Wash is one of many hiking/backpacking trails available in this area. It is a moderately strenuous 26.4-mile one-way trip, offering an excellent three to four-day backpacking opportunity. There is a ruin of a homestead settled in 1890 along the way, adding an historical flavor. The season runs from late March through June and from early September through October. The route description is quite detailed and can be tricky in places. *Hiking the Escalante*, by Rudi Lambrechtse, provides a detailed six-page explanation of the route. (See Additional Information.)

Parking for this trail is approximately fifteen miles east of Escalante on Highway 12, where the highway crosses the river. Park next to the BLM sign. The trail begins on the south side at the trail register. There is a designated location to cross the river to the north side—cross only at this point as both sides of the river are private property. After two river crossings, you will enter BLM property on the south side, designated by a fence. The maps needed for this trail include the BLM *Escalante Resource Area Recreation Map and Visitor Information,* as well as the USGS topographic maps for Calf Creek, King Bench and Red Breaks.

MOUNTAIN BIKING

Wolverine Loop Route is one of many possible mountain biking routes, and is approximately 34.2 miles. A two-day trip is recommended for easy cycling. The mountain biking season runs from late fall to early spring. Mountain bikes are not allowed in any of the natural areas—please respect signed closures. Abuse and misuse of closed trails has been a problem, and if it continues, more trails may be closed to mountain bike access. There is no guaranteed water along the route and mountain bikers are reminded to carry adequate supplies.

From the parking area, pedal 10.4 miles to Wolverine Petrified Wood Natural Area. Approximately 2.8 miles past this area, the route forks. Bear left. After eight miles, the trail runs into Burr Road. Head left and pedal eight miles through White Canyon Flat. Remain on Burr Road through all intersections, keeping to the left. Once you are through White Canyon Flat, head east on Burr Trail Road five more miles back to the parking area. To get to the parking area from Boulder, take Burr Trail Road 19 miles to the Wolverine turnoff. Park at the designated area.

Helpful maps for this route include the BLM *Escalante Resource Area Recreation Map and Visitor Information,* as well as the USGS topographic maps for King Bench, Steep Creek Bench, Wagon Box Mesa, and Moody Creek.

MANAGEMENT
BLM Escalante Resource Area, P.O. Box 225, Escalante, UT 84726; (801) 826-4291.

LOCATION
North of the Arizona border, east of Bryce Canyon and west of Glen Canyon National Recreation Area.

GETTING THERE
From Cedar City on Interstate 15, take Highway 14/148 east to Highway 89. Drive north on Highway 89 to Highway 12 and Bryce Canyon National Park. Stay on Highway 12 to Escalante.

CAMPING
Camping is allowed anywhere within the Escalante Resource Area. Fires are allowed, but using a fire leaves questionable impacts.

PERMITS

Hiking in the Escalante Natural Area requires a permit. Permits can be obtained for free from the BLM office. Hiking in areas outside of the Escalante Natural Area does not require a permit, but registration at the trailhead is requested for safety reasons.

ADDITIONAL INFORMATION

Hiking the Escalante, by Rudi Lambrechtse, published by Wasatch Publishers, Salt Lake City, UT.
Hiking the Southwest's Canyon Country, by Sandra Hinchman, published by The Mountaineers, Seattle, WA.

MAPS

Canyons of the Escalante, Utah Map Series, published by Trails Illustrated, P.O. Box 3610, Evergreen, CO 80439; (800) 962-1643.

> *TIP: Apply a no-trace ethic everyday, everywhere.*

BEST OF THE STATE

HENRY MOUNTAINS

The Henry Mountains, called the Unknown Mountains by the Powell Expedition, were the last range to be explored and named in the lower 48 states. They have remained largely undeveloped and remote. In addition to historic gold mining sites and artifacts scattered throughout the region, bison are often seen. The bison were transplanted into the Burr Desert below the mountains in 1941. Since then they have established themselves on the Henry Mountains and have become a popular attraction for both viewing and hunting.

This resource area contains spectacular geological structures and associated erosional features in the heart of the Colorado Plateau. Colorful canyons abound. Until the damming of Glen Canyon, the region was only accessible by a dirt

---

road. Even today, there are few paved roads and services are very limited. Small towns provide the basic tourist facilities.

HIKING

There are very few trails within the mountain range. Much of your travel will be cross-country. Good map and compass skills are requisite. Water is available, but it is suggested that you always carry ample supplies with you just in case.

MANAGEMENT

BLM Henry Mountains Resource Area, P.O. Box 99, Hanksville, UT 84734; (801) 542-3461

LOCATION

Just north of Glen Canyon National Recreation Area.

GETTING THERE

Access to the Henry Mountains is off State Routes 276 and 24. The best starting point is in the town of Hanksville, where you can check in at the BLM office and inquire about current road conditions and the best access points for the area you wish to roam.

CAMPING

Three campgrounds are maintained in and around the Henry Mountains. McMillan Spring Campground, located on the west side of the Henry Mountains, is 8,400 feet and set in a Ponderosa pine forest. Excellent views of the Waterpocket Fold and high plateaus can be enjoyed from here. No camping fee is charged and this campground is open from May to November. The Starr Spring Campground is located on Mount Hillers, at 6,300 feet, and set in an oak grove. Views of the area surrounding Mount Hillers are spectacular. This campground is open from April through October. There is a camping fee charged. The third campground is Lonesome Beaver Campground, located in the Sawmill Basin at 8,000 feet. Open from May through October, this site is tucked in among spruce, fir and aspen. A hiking trail leads from the camp to nearby Mount Ellen, 11,506 feet. No camping fee is charged. Primitive camping is allowed anywhere within the Henry Mountains region.

PERMITS
No permits are necessary.

MAPS
The Henry Mountains and Surrounding Deserts General Recreation Map, available from the BLM in Hanksville.

ADDITIONAL INFORMATION
Back Country Byways, by Stewart M. Green, published by Falcon Press, P.O. Box 1718, Helena, MT 59624; (800) 582-2665.

SEASON
In the upper elevations, the season runs from April through October. The season is year-round in the lower reaches.

TIP: Always use a river runner's toilet when boating and never bury human waste around river camps. Human waste, including toilet paper, must be packed out.

BEST OF THE STATE

5

WESTWATER CANYON

Westwater Canyon, located within the Westwater Canyon Wilderness Study Area, is considered by many to be one of the nation's best overnight whitewater river trips. The combination of major rapids and a spectacular 17-mile-long canyon setting draws boaters from all over, but you must be experienced or go with a skilled outfitter. The river is nothing to be trifled with as it has killed seven people since 1982. A small seasonal waterfall is located on the Little Dolores River about 200 yards upstream from its confluence with the Colorado River. Several small arches are located near the Little Dolores River and one large arch is located just below Star Canyon along the skyline. You will see an old miner's cabin, the "outlaw cave" and some Native American sites within the canyon. These are protected by law, but more importantly, they should be respected as

---

remnants of our cultural heritage—leave all you find for others to appreciate.

WHITEWATER RAFTING

The float time for this river is one or two days. This is a serious whitewater trip with 11 rapids rated up to Class IV depending on the water level. The Western River Guides Association publishes a list of licensed operators running river trips. Call (303) 377-4811 for this information. For a list of authorized (permitted) operators running the Westwater, call the BLM at (801) 259-8193.

MOUNTAIN BIKING

A section of the Kokopelli's Trail (refer to the Best of the State in the Arizona chapter) runs just north of the Westwater Canyon area.

MANAGEMENT

BLM Grand Resource Area, 885 South Sand Flats Road, Moab, UT 84532; (801) 259-8193

LOCATION

Northeast of Moab, the first canyon along the Colorado River within Utah.

GETTING THERE

From Interstate 70 north of Moab and east of Green River, take the Westwater Exit, number 225.

CAMPING

Campsites are assigned at the ranger station at launch time. There are only ten sites. Minimum impact camping techniques are suggested and all solid waste must be packed out. River runner's toilets are mandatory.

PERMITS

Permits and fees are required for river use. No permits are necessary for hiking or primitive camping.

MAPS

USGS topographic maps: Agate, Westwater, Cisco, Big Triangle, Marble Canyon
BLM surface maps: Westwater

ADDITIONAL INFORMATION

Western Whitewater, From the Rockies to the Pacific, by Jim Cassady, Bill Cross, and Fryar Calhoun, published by North Fork Press, Berkeley, CA; (800) 243-5522.

SEASON

The season runs from May through September.

TIP: Look at and photograph, never pick up or collect.

BEST OF THE STATE

6

DESOLATION CANYON / GRAY CANYON

Besides being the deepest canyon in Utah and rich in Fremont and Ute Indian cultural sites, the Desolation Canyon and the Gray Canyon are on the National Register of Historic Places. They earned this distinction because of explorer John Wesley Powell who traveled the canyons in the late 1800s and named them. Other famous and infamous characters were also drawn here during the early 1800s. Trapper Denis Julian left his mark in the form of canyon graffiti in 1830, and Butch Cassidy and the Sundance Kid escaped the law within the mazes of canyons here.

Cutting through the Tavaputs Plateau above the Desolation and the Gray is the Green River. Side canyons beg to be hiked and reveal archaeological sites, abandoned homesteads and excellent camping among verdant cottonwoods and sandy beaches.

WHITEWATER RAFTING

The float time on this river is four to seven days. It is 75 miles from the put-in at Sand Wash Ranger Station to the first take-out point at Nefertiti Rapid or 84 miles to the second take-out point at Swaseys Rapid at the end of Green River Daily. Of the 67 rapids you will encounter, most are Class II, but several are rated up to Class IV, depending on the water level. The Western River Guides Association publishes a list of licensed operators running river trips. Call (303) 377-4811 for this information. For a list of authorized (permitted) operators running the Desolation, call the BLM at (801) 637-4584.

MANAGEMENT
BLM Price River Resource Area, 900 North Seventh East, Price, UT 84501; (801) 637-4584

LOCATION
Located along the Green River, just north of the town of Green River.

GETTING THERE
From Myton, drive 42 miles south of US 40 to the Sand Wash Ranger Station.

CAMPING
Camping is allowed anywhere along the river. Minimum impact camping techniques are suggested and all solid waste must be packed out. River runner's toilets are mandatory.

PERMITS
Advanced reservations, permits and fees are necessary for all private and commercial river trips.

MAPS
USGS topographic maps: Nutters Hole Southwest, Firewater Canyon Northwest, Flat Canyon Northeast, Butter Canyon, Gunnison Butte Southeast
BLM surface maps: Vernal, Seep Ridge, Price, Huntington, Westwater

ADDITIONAL INFORMATION

Western Whitewater, From the Rockies to the Pacific,
by Jim Cassady, Bill Cross, and Fryar Calhoun, published by
North Fork Press, Berkeley, CA; (800) 243-5522.

SEASON

The season runs from May through August 30th.

BEST OF THE STATE

7

LABYRINTH CANYON

Located along the Green River between the town of Green
River and Canyonlands National Park, the Labyrinth Canyon
Recreation Management Area encompasses 49,000 acres in and
around 70 river miles. Labyrinth Canyon is best suited to lazy
floating through deep, multi-colored canyons and enjoying
side hikes to visit Native American ruins and petroglyphs as
well as refreshing waterfalls.

WHITEWATER RAFTING

It is 68 river miles from the launch point at Green River
State Park in Green River City to the take-out at Mineral
Bottom, or 123 miles to Spanish Bottom just below the
confluence of the Green and Colorado Rivers. There are no
rapids along this section of the Green River, making it excellent for multi-day canoe trips. Visitors using rafts should plan
on plenty of time to float as the river flows at a leisurely pace.
Sandbars can, at times, present problems for rafts. Ruby Ranch,
located 20 miles below Green River State Park is an alternate
access point. A fee is charged for parking and launching.
Mineral Bottom is the last take-out point accessible by road
before the rapids of Cataract Canyon. If you choose to continue your float and take-out at the confluence of the Green
and Colorado Rivers or just below at Spanish Bottom, you will
need to make arrangements to have you and your boats taken
back up river by a jet boat. There is no road access to Spanish
Bottom. Jet boat service is offered by two companies at this
time: Tag-A-Long Expeditions (801) 259-8946, or Tex's

Riverways (801) 259-5101. Both companies are based in Moab. The Western River Guides Association publishes a list of licensed operators running river trips. Call (303) 377-4811 for this information.

HIKING

The hike to the top of the neck at Bowknot Bend offers expansive views of the river and its canyon setting.

MANAGEMENT
BLM San Rafael Resource Area, 900 North Seventh East, Price, UT 84501; (801) 637-4584

LOCATION
Just south of the city of Green River.

GETTING THERE
Boaters can launch from either Green River State Park or from a private launching area downstream at Ruby Ranch. Mineral Bottom is the take-out point for some, and also a put-in point for trips running Cataract Canyon. There are two outfitters that rent canoes and provide a jet boat pick-up service back to Moab from just below the confluence of the Colorado and Green Rivers. These outfitters are Tag-A-Long Expeditions, (801) 259-8946 and Tex's Riverways, (801) 259-5101.

CAMPING
Camping is allowed anywhere in the canyon. Practice minimum impact river camping.

PERMITS
Presently no permits are necessary for Labyrinth Canyon. But you must obtain one from the National Park Service to enter Stillwater Canyon. The BLM anticipates initiating a permit system for river use within Labyrinth Canyon—call for current river status.

MAPS
USGS topographic maps: Green River, Daly East, Horsebench, Green River Southeast, 10 Mile Point, Bowknot Bend, Mineral Canyon
BLM surface maps: San Raphael Desert, Moab

ADDITIONAL INFORMATION

Western Whitewater, From the Rockies to the Pacific,
by Jim Cassady, Bill Cross, and Fryar Calhoun, published by
North Fork Press, Berkeley, CA; (800) 243-5522.

SEASON

The season runs from May through September 30.

TIP: Use a fire pan whenever you must build a campfire.

BEST OF THE STATE

8

SAN JUAN RIVER

The BLM manages the river from Montezuma Creek for 104
miles downstream to Clay Hills Crossing. The lower 39 miles
flow through Glen Canyon National Recreation Area and are
jointly managed with the National Park Service. The upper San
Juan is well known for the superb Indian rock art left by the
Anasazi culture. Visitors may also want to hike around to view
the ruins of Anasazi dwellings and the remains of an historic
trading post. The lower San Juan cuts through Cedar Mesa and
has carved the deepest set of entrenched "goosenecks" in
North America. There is also an excellent opportunity to hike
into the lower reaches of Grand Gulch to view rarely seen
Anasazi ruins. You must preregister your hike before heading
out on the river if you intend to wander more than three miles
from the river. The Western River Guides Association publishes
a list of licensed operators running river trips. Call (303) 377-
4811 for this information. For a list of BLM authorized (permitted) operators running the San Juan, call the BLM office at
(801) 587-2141.

WHITEWATER RAFTING

Upper San Juan from Sand Island to Mexican Hat offers
one to three-day float opportunities on rapids up to Class III.
The Lower San Juan from the BLM boat ramp at Mexican Hat

---

to the take-out at Clay Hills Crossing offers three to five-day float opportunities on rapids up to Class III.

MANAGEMENT
BLM San Juan Resource Area, 435 North Main, P.O. Box 7, Monticello, UT 84535; (801) 587-2141

LOCATION
Upper San Juan is located approximately three miles west of Bluff; Lower San Juan is located to the west of Mexican Hat.

GETTING THERE
Sand Island is near Bluff on US 163.

CAMPING
Camping is allowed anywhere along the river. Practice minimum impact river camping. There is a campground at Sand Island.

PERMITS
Permits and fees are necessary for river trips.

MAPS
USGS topographic maps: Horse Bench West, Horse Bench East, Spring Canyon, Moonshine Wash, Green River Southeast
BLM surface maps: Bluff, Navajo Mountain

ADDITIONAL INFORMATION
Western Whitewater, From the Rockies to the Pacific, by Jim Cassady, Bill Cross, and Fryar Calhoun, published by North Fork Press, Berkeley, CA; (800) 243-5522.

SEASON
The season runs from May 15 to early July.

1

UTAH (GENERAL)

GREAT WESTERN TRAIL

hiking, backpacking, mountain biking, horseback riding, cross-country skiing, snowmobiling, camping

The Great Western Trail is a partnership effort involving several public land management agencies, thousands of volunteers, community leaders, and business partners, all with the goal of linking a trail that runs all the way from Canada to Mexico. Much of the route, when complete, will become a corridor of existing trails and passageways designed to serve the interests of many recreational users. Approximately 90% of the Utah portion of the Great Western Trail utilizes existing roads and trails. It enters the state in the north, near Beaver Mountain in the Wasatch-Cache National Forest, and continues south through the Uinta, Manti-La Sal, Fishlake, and Dixie National Forests. The trail crosses BLM administered land before exiting into Arizona. The entire trail will be signed with the Great Western Trail symbol.

For information about how you can participate as a volunteer to help build or maintain the trail, contact: Great Western Trail Association, P.O. Box 1428, Provo, UT 84602.

For more information: Contact the BLM Cedar City District Office, 176 East D.L. Sargent Drive, Cedar City, UT 84720; (801) 586-2401.

TIP: If you must use a campfire, collect only dead and downed wood. Standing dead wood is an important part of the ecological balance of the area and may, in fact, already be in use as a home for a wild animal.

2

NORTHERN UTAH

BOOK CLIFFS AND SURROUNDING REGION
hiking, backpacking, camping, rock climbing, mountain biking

Bordered by the Green River to the north and bisected by the White River, the Book Cliffs area sees relatively light usage, although canoeing on the White River is increasing in popularity. Nearby Fantasy Canyon, a region of weird and fascinating rock formations, is a great destination. This is rugged, high-elevation canyon country. Head east of the town of Green River on Interstate 70. Turn left into the little town of Thompson Springs after 25 miles. Drive through town and into Thompson Canyon on a graded road. You can choose to head up either Sego Canyon, to the left, or Thompson Canyon, to the right. You will be on private property in some areas so be respectful. Water is scarce in this area, and even if available, it may be too alkaline to drink—pack all the water you will need. Map reading and navigation skills are requisite if you wish to venture deep into the interior. Wildlife includes elk, deer and mountain lion.

For more information: Contact the BLM Vernal District Office, 170 South 500 East, Vernal, UT 84078; (801) 789-1362.

BROWNS PARK
hiking, rafting, canoeing, camping, fishing

Browns Park is an alluvial valley surrounded by high mountain plateaus and located in the northeastern corner of Utah. The focus of recreation in this region is fishing the Green River, a blue-ribbon fishery that attracts visitors from all over the world.

For more information: Contact the BLM Vernal District Office, 170 South 500 East, Vernal, UT 84078; (801) 789-1362.

CRYSTAL BALL AND GANDY MOUNTAIN CAVES
spelunking

Located approximately 60 miles north of the Great Basin National Park along the Utah/Nevada border, the Gandy Mountains rise above the valley floor dramatically. This mountain range contains two caves, Crystal Ball and Gandy Mountain, both of which are attractive to spelunkers interested in exploring limestone solution caverns. Crystal Ball is noteworthy as it is one of the few caves in the world with unique deposits of dogtooth spar, Icelandic spar, helictites, and other speleothems. Pleistocene mammal bones have been excavated from within. Gandy Cave is smaller, but was once suggested as a national monument site. Unfortunately, the caves exist under a mining claim. The owner has been protecting the site, but could exercise claim rights and mine the area at any time, irreparably destroying the cave environment. BLM is working to ensure that doesn't happen. If you wish to visit the caves, you must first check with the BLM office in Richfield to obtain safety information and access directions.

For more information: Contact the BLM Richfield District Office, 150 East 900 North, Richfield, UT 84701; (801) 896-8221.

DEEP CREEK MOUNTAINS
hiking, backpacking, cross-country skiing, camping, wildlife observation, fishing

The Deep Creek Mountains are located approximately 140 miles southwest of Salt Lake City and 72 miles northwest of Delta. It is the only mountain range with an abundance of water in the interior of Utah's Great Basin. Six perennial streams on the eastern slopes of the range support populations of rainbow and cutthroat trout. Mule deer, bighorn sheep, mountain lion, antelope, grouse, and chukar can all be seen. With 12,000-foot peaks, streams, lush vegetation, and a rich wildlife population, the mountain could be a pristine wilderness escape. Unfortunately, mining, range work and hunting have led to extensive off-road vehicle use—scarring the land in many places. The BLM is looking to limit further damage from off-road use and to manage a significant portion of the area for wilderness enjoyment. Despite the past damage, the region is well worth a peek. The BLM suggests that backcountry skiers have a working knowledge of avalanche safety before venturing out.

For more information: Contact the BLM Richfield District Office, 150 East 900 North, Richfield, UT 84701; (801) 896-8221.
USGS topographic maps: Indian Farm Creek, Partoun, Trout Creek, Trout Creek Southwest
BLM surface maps: Fish Springs

PARIETTE WETLANDS
hiking, wildlife observation

A relatively unique marsh in the middle of miles and miles of desert. Wet meadows, freshwater ponds and alkali bulrush shelter a wide variety of waterfowl, shorebirds and raptors. From US 40 to Fort Duchesne, head south approximately five miles to the Myton Y, turn south off the road to Myton onto a dirt road and drive another 16 miles across Leland Bench to Pariette Wash. Follow the signs to the overlook.

For more information: Contact the BLM Vernal District Office, 170 South 500 East, Vernal, UT 84078; (801) 789-1362.

SWASEY MOUNTAIN
hiking, horseback riding, camping, fossil collection, spelunking

Swasey Mountain is a part of the House Range which consists of high distinct peaks, narrow twisting canyons and palisade cliffs to the north, descending into low washes and indistinct flat desert terrain to the south. There are wild horses, small caves and trilobite rock hounding areas within the range. A three-mile gravel road winds across a plateau to the Sinbad Overlook where, unfortunately, tree cutting detracts from the potential scenic qualities of the area. Access to this area is via local and county roads leading northwest from Highway 50/6, just south of Hinckley.

For more information: Contact the BLM House Range Resource Area, P.O. Box 778, Fillmore, UT 84631; (801) 743-6811.
USGS topographic maps: Sand Pass, Swasey Peak Southest, Swasey Peak Northwest, Swasey Peak Southwest, Swasey Peak, Whirlwind Valley Northwest, Whirlwind Valley Southwest, Marjum Pass
BLM surface maps: Tule Valley, Fish Springs

> *TIP: Camp only in established or*
> *previously used sites, if available.*

3

SOUTHEASTERN UTAH

Visitors to Monticello can now get information about southeastern Utah's parks, forests and recreation areas from the relatively new Monticello Interagency Information Center. The information center is the result of a partnership arrangement that includes San Juan County, the San Juan County Economic Development Board, the BLM, the U.S. Forest Service, the National Park Service, and the Canyonlands Natural History Association. The facility is located in the San Juan County Courthouse. Winter hours from October to April 15 are 9 a.m. to 5 p.m., Monday through Friday. From April 15 to September, the center is open seven days a week from 9 a.m. to 6 p.m. Call (801) 587-3235 for information.

CANYON RIMS RECREATION AREA
hiking, backpacking, mountain biking, horseback riding, rock climbing, camping, wildlife observation

The Canyon Rims region sprawls out along the eastern and southern boundaries of Canyonlands National Park and is located in both the Grand and San Juan BLM Resource Areas. Two developed viewpoints are accessible by vehicles. The Needles and Anticline overlooks offer excellent examples of the spectacular vistas that have made canyon country famous. The many canyons, mesas and pinnacles within the area offer outstanding settings for hiking, outdoor photography and rock climbing. Windwhistle and Hatch Point are two developed campsites within this region. A camping fee is charged for both. Water is available from mid-April through October. To get there from Monticello, drive north on Highway 191 for 17 miles to the Canyon Rims Recreation Area entrance road (Hatch Point area). Then, drive west on the paved BLM road. The southern region of this area is accessible from Utah Scenic Byway 211.

For more information: Contact the BLM Grand Resource Area, 885
South Sand Flats Road, Moab, UT 84532; (801) 259-8193.
BLM San Juan Resource Area, 435 North Main, P.O. Box 7,
Monticello, UT 84535; (801) 587-2141.
USGS topographic maps: Shafer Basin, Trough Springs Canyon,
Kane Springs, Lockhart Basin, Eightmile Rock, LaSal Junction, North
Six Shooter Peak, Harts Point North, Hatch Rock.
BLM surface maps: LaSal

CLEVELAND-LLOYD DINOSAUR QUARRY
nature walk, dinosaur bones

Cleveland-Lloyd is a National Natural Landmark and one of
the most productive dinosaur bone quarries in the world. Since
1931, scientists have removed more than 14,000 fossil bones,
representing over 70 dinosaurs of 14 different species. The
BLM operates a visitor's center, near the quarry, which features
an assembled allosaurus skeleton and on-site interpretation by
a naturalist. Other facilities at the quarry include the Rock
Walk Nature Trail, a picnic area and drinking water. The
quarry is usually open on weekends from Easter through
Memorial Day, and seven days a week from Memorial Day
through Labor Day. It is closed the remainder of the year. To
get there from Price, drive south on Highway 10 and follow
the dinosaur signs to the quarry.

For more information: Contact the BLM Price River Resource Area,
900 North Seventh East, Price, UT 84501; (801) 637-4584.

DARK CANYON PRIMITIVE AREA
*hiking, backpacking, wildlife observation, camping, mountain
biking (outside of the Primitive Area)*

Dark Canyon runs from the Manti-La Sal National Forest
down to the desert environment along Lake Powell. This
remote canyon system features outstanding backpacking
opportunities. The mountain biking is good along four-wheel-
drive roads outside of the designated wilderness area, managed by the National Forest Service, and the Dark Canyon
Primitive Area, administered by the BLM. Deep canyons, open
valleys and sloping plateaus fill the menu here. Dark Canyon
dazzles visitors with its 1,400-foot-high stair-stepped walls.
Many canyons within the region feature this unique sandstone/

limestone combination creating numerous benches from which rain-water run-off pours in spectacular waterfalls forming picturesque "water curtains" and refreshing pools. From upper plateaus, excellent views of the nearby Henry Mountains and the Colorado River may be enjoyed.

•**See also Best of the State, page 412**•
For more information: Contact the BLM San Juan Resource Area, 435 North Main, P.O. Box 7, Monticello, UT 84535; (801) 587-2141.

DESOLATION CANYON / GRAY CANYON
whitewater rafting, kayaking, canoeing, wildlife observation, camping, hiking, backpacking

Besides being the deepest canyons in Utah and rich in Fremont and Ute Indian cultural sites, the Desolation Canyon and the Gray Canyon are on the National Register of Historic Places because of explorer John Wesley Powell. Powell and his expedition traveled the canyons in the late 1800s and named them. Other famous and infamous characters were also drawn here during the early 1800s. Trapper Denis Julian left his mark in the form of canyon graffiti in 1830 and Butch Cassidy and the Sundance Kid escaped the law within the mazes of canyons here.

Cutting through the Tavaputs Plateau above the Desolation and the Gray is the Green River. Side canyons beg to be hiked and reveal archaeological sites, abandoned homesteads and excellent camping among verdant cottonwoods and sandy beaches.

•**See also Best of the State, page 421**•
For more information: Contact the BLM Price River Resource Area, 900 North Seventh East, Price, UT 84501; (801) 637-4584.

GRAND GULCH PRIMITIVE AREA
hiking, backpacking, wildlife observation, camping, Anasazi ruins

It is within this twisting canyon maze that some of the most bewitching scenery and the largest concentrations of Anasazi ruins in all of southeastern Utah reside. Beginning at an elevation of 6,400 feet, Grand Gulch cuts a serpentine swath through Cedar Mesa, southwest to the San Juan River, dropping a tortuous 2,700 feet in just 53 miles. Sheer cliffs, sharp pinnacles, Anasazi cliff dwellings, rock art sites, natural bridges, and sandstone amphitheaters make up Grand Gulch and its many surrounding tributaries. Keep your eyes peeled for signs of mountain lion, black bear, bobcat, fox, mule deer, coyote, ringtail cat, and skunk. Raptors frequently carve and slice their way through the blue sky above. Pinyon pine, juniper, cottonwood, willow, sagebrush and prickly pear cactus make up the predominant species of vegetation. The Anasazi have left a legacy that includes hundreds of cliff dwellings and thousands of pictographs and petroglyphs, and historical evidence has shown their influence on the canyon to date back as far as 200 A.D. Take special care not to touch or climb on the ruins as this kind of wear and tear can cause what the BLM refers to as "innocent vandalism." Pot hunting is also a major problem within the entire region. Please, leave all that you find in its place and report any suspicious activity to the BLM. Vandalism ruins the experience for everyone.

•**See also Best of the State, page 410**•
For more information: Contact the BLM San Juan Resource Area, 435 North Main, P.O. Box 7, Monticello, UT 84535; (801) 587-2141.

HENRY MOUNTAINS
backpacking, hiking, camping, wildlife observation, rock hounding, horseback riding, mountain biking, rock climbing

The Henry Mountains, called the Unknown Mountains by the Powell Expedition, were the last range to be explored and named in the lower 48 states. They have remained largely undeveloped and remote. In addition to historic gold mining sites and artifacts scattered throughout the region, bison are often seen here. The bison were transplanted into the Burr Desert below the mountains in 1941. They have established themselves on the Henry Mountains and have become a popular attraction for both viewing and hunting. The resource area contains spectacular geological structures and associated erosional features in the heart of the Colorado Plateau. Colorful canyons abound. Until the damming of Glen Canyon, this region was only accessible by dirt roads. Even today, there are few paved roads, and services are very limited with small towns providing the basic tourist facilities.

•**See also Best of the State, page 417**•
For more information: Contact the BLM Henry Mountains Resource Area, P.O. Box 99, Hanksville, UT 84734; (801) 542-3461.

KOKOPELLI'S TRAIL
mountain biking, hiking, backpacking, wildlife observation, camping

Kokopelli's Trail connects Moab with Loma, Colorado. This rugged 140-mile mountain bike trail follows seldom-visited back roads and some newer single-track trail. The route traverses spectacular forest, canyon and desert country. The trail may be ridden in day-long segments or as a multi-day adventure. Most of the trail can be accessed or ridden by high-clearance, four-wheel-drive support vehicles. There are a series of mini-camps along the route, constructed in 1990. The trailheads are located at the Moab Slickrock Bike Trail and the Loma Boat Ramp, just west of Fruita, Colorado. The higher elevations of this trail are impassable during the winter.

•**See also Best of the State in Colorado, page 203**•
For more information: Contact the BLM Grand Resource Area, 885 South Sand Flats Road, Moab, UT 84532; (801) 259-8193.

LABYRINTH CANYON
canoeing, hiking, camping

Located along the Green River between the town of Green River and Canyonlands National Park, the Labyrinth Canyon Recreation Management Area encompasses 49,000 acres in and around 70 river miles. Boaters launch from either Green River State Park or from a private launching area downstream at Ruby Ranch. Mineral Bottom is the take-out point for some trips and a put-in point for trips running Cataract Canyon. There are two outfitters that rent canoes and provide a jet boat pick-up service back to Moab from just below the confluence of the Colorado and Green Rivers. These outfitters are Tag-A-Long Expeditions (801) 259-8946, and Tex's Riverways (801) 259-5101. Both companies are based in Moab. The Western River Guides Association publishes a list of licensed operators running river trips. Call (303) 377-4811 for this information. Labyrinth Canyon is best suited to lazy floating through deep, multi-colored canyons and enjoying side hikes to visit Native American ruins and petroglyphs.

•**See also Best of the State, page 423**•
For more information: Contact the BLM San Rafael Resource Area, 900 North Seventh East, Price, UT 84501; (801) 637-4584.

MOAB SLICKROCK BIKE TRAIL
NATIONAL RECREATION TRAIL
mountain biking, biking

This 10-mile-long mountain bike and motorcycle loop trail follows a roller coaster route through a maze of sandstone domes and fins to overlooks of the Colorado River and Arches National Park. Additional connecting and spur trails are available for more skilled riders—test your metal on this loop before branching out on the connecting alternatives. Trailhead facilities include a parking area, restrooms and an information board. The fall is one of the best times to ride due to cooler temperatures and the absence of gnats. Expect the trail to be covered with snow during January and February. To reach the trailhead, drive 2.3 miles east on Sand Flats Road from the BLM Grand Resource Area office. It is important to note that desert soils are delicate—stick to the route; do not create your own path. You will encounter pockets of sand, little gardens of cactus, juniper, grass, and cryptogamic soil, that will be destroyed if you ride through them. Ride around! At Shrimp Rock, you may find a pool of water full of little creatures. Do not ride through or bathe in the pool or other potholes along the trail as you will destroy a delicate balance of life. This is one of the most popular destinations in the West for mountain bikers. You can expect mammoth crowds during the spring and fall. The BLM recommends utilizing the Moab Bike Trail Brochure for finding alternative, equally appealing and less traveled routes.

For more information: Contact the BLM Grand Resource Area, 885 South Sand Flats Road, Moab, UT 84532; (801) 259-8193.
USGS topographic maps: Moab
BLM surface maps: Moab

PRICE CANYON RECREATION SITE
hiking, camping, nature walks, wildlife observation

The Price Canyon Campground is a high-elevation site that offers cool summer temperatures and the shade of large ponderosa pine trees. Reservations are required for group sites. A camping fee is charged for all sites. Drinking water is available here. A Price Canyon Recreation Site brochure is available. To get there, drive 15 miles north of Price on Highway 6/50, and then three miles west on the paved BLM road. This area is not accessible during winter months.

For more information: Contact the BLM Price River Resource Area, 900 North Seventh East, Price, UT 84501; (801) 637-4584.

SAN RAPHAEL SWELL RECREATION AREA
hiking, backpacking, mountain biking, camping, wildlife observation, rafting, canoeing

The San Rafael Swell rises above the desert, west of the Green River, as a complex area of canyons, colorful rock formations and mesas. The recreation area includes approximately 876,000 acres of public land. The San Rafael Campground is a primitive site in the northern region—no water is available nor is a fee charged. The campground is located alongside the San Rafael River. The fall months are the best for visiting, as temperatures are cool and the gnats (voracious little buggers) have all but departed. There is a BLM brochure, *Recreation Guide to the San Rafael Swell,* available. The region is located south of the town of Price and west of the Green River. The San Rafael River is floatable during select times of the year depending on the water levels from runoff—check with the BLM. The Wedge Overlook is worth visiting and is alongside the river.

For more information: Contact the BLM Price River Resource Area, 900 North Seventh East, Price, UT 84501; (801) 637-4584.
USGS topographic maps: Hadden Holes, Horn Silver Gulch, Sids Mountain, Bottleneck Peak, Devils Hole, Drowned Hole Draw, Mexican Mountain, Spotted Wolf Canyon, Jessie's Twist
BLM surface maps: Huntington, San Rafael Desert

SAN JUAN RIVER
whitewater rafting, kayaking, canoeing, camping, wildlife observation

The BLM manages the river from Montezuma Creek to 104 miles downstream to Clay Hills Crossing. The lower 39 miles flow through Glen Canyon National Recreation Area and are jointly managed by the National Park Service. The upper San Juan is well known for superb Indian rock art, left by the Anasazi. Visitors may also want to hike around to view the ruins of Anasazi dwellings and the remains of an historic trading post. The lower San Juan cuts through Cedar Mesa and has carved the deepest set of entrenched "goosenecks" in North America. There is also an excellent opportunity to hike into the lower reaches of Grand Gulch to view rarely seen Anasazi ruins. You must preregister your hike before heading out on the river if you intend to wander for more than three miles from the river.

•**See also Best of the State, page 425**•

For more information: Contact the BLM San Juan Resource Area, 435 North Main, P.O. Box 7, Monticello, UT 84535; (801) 587-2141.

SAND ISLAND RECREATION SITE
camping, San Juan River put-in site

Sand Island is a small tree-shaded campground nestled below a sandstone bluff adjacent to the San Juan River. Of special interest to visitors is the large Indian rock art panel just a short stroll from the campground. The site is popular as a launch area for raft trips. No fee is charged for camping. No drinking water is available at this site. To get there from Bluff, drive three miles west on Highway 191 and turn left at the entrance sign.

For more information: Contact the BLM San Juan Resource Area, 435 North Main, P.O. Box 7, Monticello, UT 84535; (801) 587-2141.

THREE KIVA PUEBLO
archaeological site

This ancient Indian ruin was once the scene of a small Anasazi Indian settlement. The ruins have been stabilized by the BLM and are open for visits. The ruins are located in Montezuma Creek Canyon, east of Blanding, Utah. To get specific directions and a tour map, contact the BLM office.

For more information: Contact the BLM San Juan Resource Area, 435 North Main, P.O. Box 7, Monticello, UT 84535; (801) 587-2141.

WESTWATER CANYON WILDERNESS STUDY AREA
whitewater rafting, hiking, mountain biking (on the plateau overlooking the Westwater Canyon), camping, wildlife observation, fishing

Westwater Canyon is considered by many to be one of the nation's best overnight whitewater river trips. The combination of major rapids and a spectacular 17 mile-long canyon setting draws boaters from all over, but you must be experienced or go with a skilled outfitter. The river is nothing to be trifled with, as it has killed seven people since 1982.

•**See also Best of the State, page 419**•
For more information: Contact the BLM Grand Resource Area, 885 South Sand Flats Road, Moab, UT 84532; (801) 259-8193.

TIP: Camping or building fires near cultural sites can cause serious and irreparable damage.

UTAH BY REGION

4

SOUTHWESTERN UTAH

BEAVER DAM MOUNTAIN
wildlife observation, hiking, whitewater rafting

Managed as a habitat for bighorn sheep and desert tortoise, the Beaver Dam region is located in the southwestern corner of Utah along Interstate 15 as it winds through the spectacular Virgin River Gorge. Extreme faulting, folding, and natural erosion from the river has resulted in a complex mix of steep craggy cliffs and sandstone buttes made up of colorful layers of sandstone and fossil-laden limestone.

For more information: Contact the BLM Cedar City District Office, 176 East D.L. Sargent Drive, Cedar City, UT 84720; (801) 586-2401. **BLM surface maps:** St. George

CALF CREEK RECREATION AREA
hiking, backpacking, wildlife observation, camping

This recreation area is located 15 miles east of Escalante on Scenic Byway 12. There are 14 camping units with water and they are available on a first-come first-served self-registration

---

basis. A fee is charged. A free trail guide to the Lower Calf Creek Falls Nature Trail is available at the campground. If the BLM campground is full, seek out the Boulder Mountain Forest Service campground on Scenic Byway 12 or the Escalante State Park Campground located two miles south of Escalante.

For more information: Contact the BLM Escalante Resource Area, P.O. Box 769, Escalante, UT 84726; (801) 826-4291.
BLM surface maps: Smokey Mountain, Escalante

CANAAN MOUNTAIN
hiking, backpacking, camping, wildlife observation, horseback riding

Along US Highway 50, the spectacular Canaan Mountain plateau is made up of three closely-connected sandstone terraces. The 54,000-acre plateau is considered part of the Grand Staircase unit of the Colorado Plateau. The escarpment towers majestically 2,000 feet above the highway. The top of the plateau is a panorama of rippling slickrock, sandstone pinnacles, cones, balanced boulders, fractures, and scours interspersed with lush pockets of aspen and ponderosa pine— some say the terrain compares favorably with that found in nearby Zion. Within the Canaan Mountain Wilderness Study Area, points of high beauty and outstanding geological scenery are Water Canyon, Eagle Crags, Squirrel Canyon, Canaan Mountain, and Broad Hollow Trails. Access for the trails is from Eagle Crags Trail (Rockville) or Water and Squirrel Canyons (Hildale-Colorado City). To reach the Squirrel Canyon Trailhead, from the town of Hurricane, drive southeast on Highway 59 for approximately 24 miles to the town of Hildale. At the northeastern end of town, drive along a dirt road north for 1.5 miles to a small parking lot and the trailhead. If you wish to leave a vehicle on the other side of the mountains take Highway 9 to Rockville and at the eastern end of town, head south on the paved road and cross the Virgin River at the Rockville Bridge. After a short distance, the road will swing right, but you continue straight, on a dirt road one-and-a-half miles to the trailhead parking.

For more information: Contact the BLM Dixie Resource Area, 225 North Bluff, St. George, UT 84770; (801) 673-4654.
USGS topographic maps: Springdale West, Springdale East, Smithsonian Butte, Hildale
BLM surface maps: Dixie S

DEEP CREEK RECREATION AREA
fishing, hiking, wildlife observation, camping, snowmobiling, cross-country skiing

This area is only 9,000 acres, but it's packed! Deep Creek, Crystal Creek, Box Canyon, Volcano Knoll, Indian Trail, Kolob Creek, and Giant Oak Tree sites offer ample opportunity for stream-based and primitive recreation activities.

For more information: Contact the BLM Dixie Resource Area, 225 North Bluff, St. George, UT 84770; (801) 673-4654.
USGS topographic maps: Kolob Reservoir, Cogswell Point, The Guardian Angels, Temple of Sinawava
BLM surface maps: Dixie S, Dixie T

ESCALANTE RESOURCE AREA
hiking, backpacking, camping, rock climbing, mountain biking, camping

The Escalante, an outstanding example of Utah's slickrock and riparian canyon environments, is made up of a mind-boggling intricate network of canyons, plateaus, cliffs, sandstone arches, natural bridges, domes, water pockets, meandering streams, and more. The area is so difficult to navigate that they have proved a formidable barrier to vehicle traffic since the days of the horse and buggy. In fact, the Escalante River was not even bridged until 1935, making Boulder City one of the last communities to gain automobile access. Over 60 mammals, 150 birds, and 20 reptiles call the Escalante home. Some of the more common animals here are the mountain lion, mule deer, gray fox, coyote, deer mice, Ord's kangaroo rat, scrub jay, canyon wren, and numerous hawks.

•**See also Best of the State, page 414**•
For more information: Contact the BLM Escalante Resource Area, P.O. Box 225, Escalante, UT 84726; (801) 826-4291.

PARIA CANYON-VERMILLION CLIFFS WILDERNESS
hiking, backpacking, camping, wildlife observation

The 120,000-acre Paria Canyon-Vermilion Cliffs Wilderness was officially designated by Congress in 1984. Since then, the four-day backpacking trip in the Paria River Canyon and

Buckskin Gulch to Lees Ferry, Arizona, has become one of the most popular backpacking excursions in the Southwest. Trailhead access is through the Paria Ranger Station (Highway 89) at White House Trailhead. Buckskin Gulch access is from the Wire Pass or Buckskin Trailheads. Water conditions in the Paria River are ankle-deep with several waist-deep crossings to be expected. Commercial car shuttles are available. You can obtain free hiking permits at the Paria Ranger Station or by calling (801) 644-2672, no more than 24 hours in advance. Flash flood information is available at the Kanab Resource Office or the National Weather Service at (801) 524-5133. The length of the hike in Paria Canyon is 34 miles. The Buckskin Gulch section is 11 miles.

You can obtain the *Hikers Guide to Paria* by mail or at the BLM Kanab office for $1. Group size is limited to 15—but I would recommend far less to ensure minimizing impacts on the canyon (even eight is too many.) Another major attraction is the ghost town and old movie set contained within the wilderness area.

•**See also Paria Canyon in the Best of the State in the Arizona chapter, page 98**•

For more information: Contact the BLM Kanab Resource Area, 320 North 100 East, P.O. Box 459, Kanab, UT 84741; (801) 644-2672.

PARIA RIVER-HACKBERRY CANYON
hiking, backpacking, camping

This backpacking area is upstream from the Paria Canyon Wilderness. It is a very colorful and scenic canyon area with many different route and trip length options. Although use is on the increase, visitation remains far below that of the Paria Canyon region. It is recommended that you consult with the Paria Ranger Station or the BLM Kanab office to help you plan an appropriate route. A good book, *Hiking and Exploring the Paria River* by Michael Kelsey is available through the Kanab Resource Area office.

For more information: Contact the BLM Kanab Resource Area, 320 North 100 East, P.O. Box 459, Kanab, UT 84741; (801) 644-2672.

RED CLIFFS RECREATION AREA
hiking, camping, wildlife observation, horseback riding

The Red Cliffs Campground, north of St. George on Interstate 15 (4.5 miles southwest of Leeds) offers overnight camping on a self-registered, first-come first-served basis. The campground is ideal because it is centrally located between the Kolob Canyons and Zion Canyon areas of Zion National Park, Snow Canyon State Park and the Pine Valley Mountain. A day-use or campsite fee is charged. Red Cliffs Recreation Area, Quail Lake Recreation Area, the Sand Mountain dune riding area, Cottonwood Canyon Wilderness Study Area, the Dinosaur tracks paleontological site, and the Fort Pearce historic site can all be enjoyed from the Red Cliffs campground base.

For more information: Contact the BLM Dixie Resource Area, 225 North Bluff, St. George, UT 84770; (801) 673-4654.
USGS topographic maps: Harrisburg Junction
BLM surface map: Dixie S

WAH WAH MOUNTAINS
hiking, backpacking, cross-country skiing, horseback riding, wildlife observation

Located 20 miles from the Utah/Nevada border, approximately 35 miles west of Beaver, Utah, the Wah Wah mountain range is one of the most remote and untouched areas in Utah's western desert region. The sense of vastness within the range is amplified by the broad valleys and often snow-capped peaks. Crystal Peak, visible from distances of 50 miles or more, is the most prominent of the range and draws picnickers from local areas. There is a stand of bristlecone pine within the range that is of particular interest. Of additional note is the fact that this range is a critical year-round habitat for the golden eagle.

To get there from Interstate 15 at Beaver, drive 24 miles west on State Route 21. Where the route passes through the San Francisco Mountains, at milepost 54, turn left on a gravel road. Drive approximately 2.5 miles and bear right, continuing southwest for approximately 13 miles to the interior of the Wah Wahs. Leave your car at the high point. There are no trails. Hiking is cross-country, so you must have strong navigational skills.

Resources: *The Hikers Guide to Utah,* by Dave Hall; published by Falcon Press, P.O. Box 1718, Helena, MT 59624; (800) 582-2665.
For more information: Contact the BLM Richfield District Office, 150 East 900 North, Richfield, UT 84701; (801) 896-8221.
USGS topographic maps: Crystal Peak, Middle Mountain, Pine Valley Hardpan, Pine Valley Hardpan North, Grassy Cove, Wah Wah Cove, Wah Wah Summit
BLM surface maps: Wah Wah Mountains North

TIP: If you must use a campfire, collect only dead and downed wood. Standing dead wood is an important part of the ecological balance of the area and may already be in use as a home for a wild animal.

STATE INFORMATION OVERVIEW

UTAH STATE OFFICE
P.O. Box 45155, Salt Lake City, UT 84145; (801) 539-4010

SALT LAKE DISTRICT OFFICE
2370 South 2300 West, Salt Lake City, UT 84119; (801) 977-4300

Pony Express Resource Area, 2370 West, Salt Lake City, UT 84119; (801) 977-4300

Bear River Resource Area, 2370 South 2300 West, Salt Lake City, UT 84119; (801) 977-4300

CEDAR CITY DISTRICT OFFICE
176 East D.L. Sargent Drive, Cedar City, UT 84720; (801) 865-3053

Dixie Resource Area, 225 North Bluff, St. George, UT 84770; (801) 673-4654

Kanab Resource Area, 320 North 100 East, P.O. Box 459, Kanab, UT 84741; (801) 644-2672

Escalante Resource Area, P.O. Box 769, Escalante, UT 84726; (801) 826-4291

Beaver River Resource Area, 444 South Main, Suite C, Cedar City, UT 84720; (801) 586-2458

MOAB DISTRICT OFFICE
82 East Dogwood, P.O. Box 970, Moab, UT 84532; (801) 259-6111

Price River Resource Area, 900 North Seventh East, Price, UT 84501; (801) 637-4584

San Rafael Resource Area, 900 North Seventh East, Price, UT 84501; (801) 637-4584

Grand Resource Area, 885 South Sand Flats Road, Moab, UT 84532; (801) 259-8193

San Juan Resource Area, 435 North Main, P.O. Box 7, Monticello, UT 84535; (801) 587-2141

VERNAL DISTRICT OFFICE
170 South 500 East, Vernal, UT 84078; (801) 789-1362

RICHFIELD DISTRICT OFFICE
150 East 900 North, Richfield, UT 84701; (801) 896-8221

Sevier River Resource Area, 180 North 100 East, Suite F, Richfield, UT 84701; (801) 896-8221

Henry Mountains Resource Area, P.O. Box 99, Hanksville, UT 84734; (801) 542-3461

House Range Resource Area, P.O. Box 778, Fillmore, UT 84631; (801) 743-6811

Warm Springs Resource Area, P.O. Box 778, Fillmore, UT 84631; (801) 743-6811

WASHINGTON

(SEE MAP A)

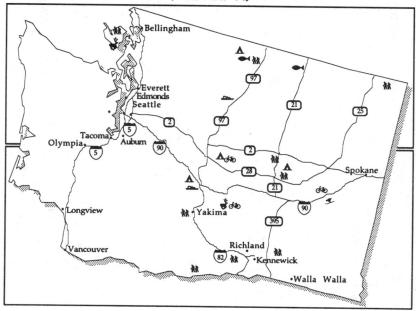

(SEE MAP B)

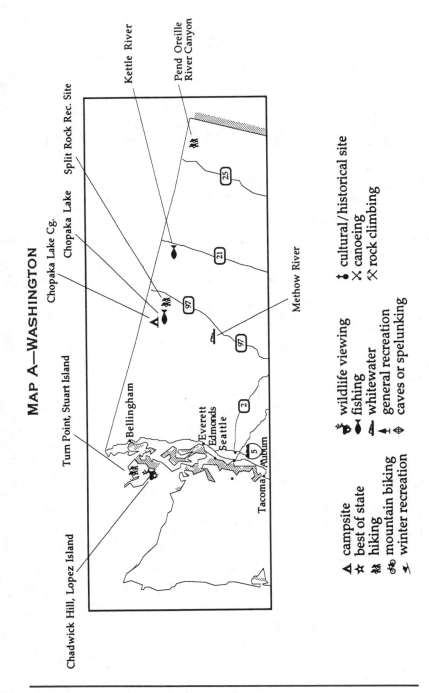

MAP A—WASHINGTON

Kettle River

Pend Oreille
River Canyon

Split Rock Rec. Site

Chopaka Lake Cg.

Chopaka Lake

Turn Point, Stuart Island

Chadwick Hill, Lopez Island

Bellingham

Everett
Edmonds
Seattle

Tacoma
Auburn

Methow River

△ campsite
☆ best of state
🏃 hiking
🚵 mountain biking
⛷ winter recreation

🦌 wildlife viewing
🎣 fishing
🌊 whitewater
🏕 general recreation
⬦ caves or spelunking

✝ cultural/historical site
✕ canoeing
✕ rock climbing

MAP REFERENCES

Chadwick Hill, Lopez Island—p. 456-457
Chopaka Lake—p. 457-458
Kettle River—p. 461
Methow River—p. 462
Pend Oreille River Canyon—p. 453-454
Split Rock Recreation Site—p. 464
Turn Point, Stuart Island—p. 456

CAMPGROUNDS

Chopaka Lake Campground—Call the Spokane District Office at (509) 353-3144 for reservations and information.

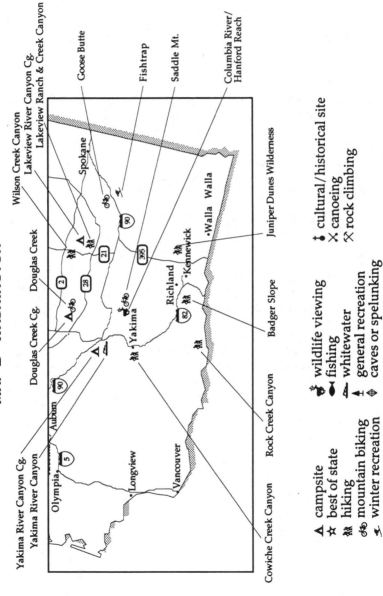

MAP B—WASHINGTON

Yakima River Canyon Cg.
Yakima River Canyon

Wilson Creek Canyon
Lakeview River Canyon Cg.
Lakeview Ranch & Creek Canyon

Goose Butte

Fishtrap

Saddle Mt.

Columbia River/
Hanford Reach

Douglas Creek Cg.
Douglas Creek

Spokane

Walla Walla

Kennewick

Richland

Juniper Dunes Wilderness

Badger Slope

Yakima

Olympia

Auburn

Longview

Vancouver

Rock Creek Canyon

Cowiche Creek Canyon

△ campsite
☆ best of state
🏃 hiking
🚴 mountain biking
🎿 winter recreation

🦌 wildlife viewing
🐟 fishing
🚣 whitewater
⊕ general recreation
◈ caves or spelunking

✝ cultural/historical site
✕ canoeing
⋈ rock climbing

MAP REFERENCES

Badger Slope—p. 457
Columbia River/Hanford Reach—p. 458
Cowiche Creek Canyon—p. 459
Douglas Creek—p. 459
Fishtrap—p. 460
Goose Butte—p. 460
Juniper Dunes Wilderness—p. 460-461
Lakeview Ranch & Creek Canyon—p. 461-462
Rock Creek Canyon—p. 452-453
Saddle Mountain—p. 463-464
Wilson Creek Canyon—p. 464
Yakima River Canyon—p. 454-455

CAMPGROUNDS

The following campgrounds are found in this area of Washington. Call the Spokane District Office at (509) 353-3144 for reservations and information.

Douglas Creek Campground
Lakeview River Canyon Campground
Yakima River Canyon Campground

1

ROCK CREEK CANYON

This is a remote, narrow canyon running through a very wild and scenic area. Ponderosa pine and oak woodlands grow on the slopes with the creek creating a well-defined riparian zone. Fishing is for resident rainbow trout, although Coho salmon and steelhead do spawn in the lower stream.

BACKPACKING

The lower canyon walls rise 1,000 feet above the creek and hiking into and out of the canyon may be strenuous. There are no established trails. Once down in the inner canyon, the explorer will find that the area is quite remote, scenic and peaceful. You must carry or treat all drinking water.

MANAGEMENT

BLM Spokane District Office, East 4217 Main Avenue, Spokane, WA 99202; (502) 353-3144

LOCATION

Near Goldendale in Klickitat County.

GETTING THERE

Few access points to this area exist. The best one is off Highway 97, eight miles north of Goldendale and two miles south of Brooks Memorial Park. Here, a forest access road leads east 3.5 miles to the creek crossing. Park at the bridge and hike down the canyon. Other access points lead off the forest road further south, but parking is limited and you must cross private lands (although most of the canyon itself is either state or BLM lands, some private ownership does occur). Please respect private lands that may or may not be marked.

CAMPING

There are good backpacking campsites along the creek.

PERMITS
No permits are necessary.

MAPS
USGS topographic maps: Status Pass, Goodnoe Hills
BLM surface maps: Goldendale

SEASON
The season runs from May to October

TIP: Camp out of sight of the trail.

BEST OF THE STATE

2

PEND OREILLE RIVER CANYON

This remote stretch of river meanders through a steep-walled limestone canyon, bordered by U.S. Forest Service and BLM land. The wildlife here includes osprey, bald eagle, deer, elk, bighorn sheep, as well as a variety of other birdlife. Fishing is for both cold and warm-water species. The sheer canyon walls rise straight up from the river in many locations, and the effect is striking.

HIKING

Recreational hiking is possible from both shores where roads and trails come down to the river. Shorelines are steep and forested for the most part. The lake behind Boundary Dam is popular for boating, but is never crowded. Streams and waterfalls dot the canyon walls in a few locations. There is a boat launch site at Boundary Dam and near Metaline Falls. The Falls are visible at lower water levels, and must be floated with care due to currents, eddies and upwellings caused by underwater turbulence. The balance of the float is in flat, though moderate, currents.

MANAGEMENT
BLM Spokane District Office, East 4217 Main Avenue, Spokane, WA 99202; (502) 353-3144

LOCATION
The Pend Oreille River Canyon runs north from the town of Metaline Falls to Boundary Dam on the Canadian border.

GETTING THERE
Metaline Falls is located on Highway 31, 100 miles northeast of Spokane near the Canadian border. This highway parallels the Pend Oreille River for many miles.

CAMPING
Camping is allowed along the river on BLM lands only.

PERMITS
No permits are necessary.

MAPS
USGS topographic maps: Metaline Falls, Boundary Dam
BLM surface maps: Colville

SEASON
The season runs from May to October.

TIP: Travel responsibly to protect the environment and preserve opportunities to enjoy recreation on wild lands.

BEST OF THE STATE

YAKIMA RIVER CANYON

Along the canyon, it is possible to see bighorn sheep, songbirds of many varieties and numerous raptors. The best place for viewing bighorn is during the spring and winter, 1.5 to 2.5 miles north of Umtanum and across the river.

RECREATIONAL ACTIVITIES

Power boating, waterskiing, canoeing, picnicking, hiking, horseback riding, fishing, and hunting are all popular activities in this area. The river is regarded as a blue ribbon trout stream. Hiking trails for fishermen and hikers run along the west bank.

MANAGEMENT

BLM Spokane District Office, East 4217 Main Avenue, Spokane, WA 99202; (502) 353-3144

LOCATION

East of the Cascade Mountain Range between the cities of Ellensburg and Yakima.

GETTING THERE

West of Interstate 82, access to the canyon area is along Highway 821 between Ellensburg and Selah. The Yakima River Canyon Recreation Area extends for nearly 24 of the more than 30 river miles that separate the cities of Ellensburg and Yakima.

CAMPING

Three recreation sites with primitive campgrounds are along the route: Umtanum Creek, Squaw Creek and Roza. Each has restrooms and boat launching facilities.

PERMITS

No permits are necessary for boating or hiking.

MAPS

BLM surface maps: Yakima

SEASON

This area is available for access year-round for wildlife viewing and hiking. Boating is best during the warm spring and summer months—but also the most crowded!

1

WESTERN WASHINGTON

TURN POINT, STUART ISLAND
(SAN JUAN ISLANDS)
hiking, wildlife observation, photography, sea kayaking, boating

With a view towards Canada across the Boundary Pass, this old lighthouse station and surrounding area offers expansive scenery of forest and seas as well as an opportunity to view bald eagles, seabirds, deer, marine mammals, and to explore tidepools and coves along the coast. The old lighthouse, though not open to the public, is an historic landmark. Accessible by charter or rental boat from Friday harbor, a 1.5-mile hike from the boat dock at Prevost, or from Reid Harbor State Park on Stuart Island.

For more information: Contact the BLM Spokane District Office, East 4217 Main Avenue, Spokane, WA 99202; (509) 353-3144.
USGS topographic maps: Stuart Island

CHADWICK HILL, LOPEZ ISLAND
(SAN JUAN ISLANDS)
mountain biking, hiking, wildlife observation

This forested headland on Lopez Island offers spectacular views of the Cascades to the east, Rosario Strait, and the San Juan Islands. The "hill" has many diverse plant communities, and offers good wildflower viewing in the spring. Bald eagle and peregrine falcon frequent the cliffs and a marsh lies adjacent to the property on the south. Seabirds, sea lions and whales may often be viewed. From the ferry terminal on Lopez Island, go southeast on the Mud Bay Road to Watmaugh Bay Road, then south 1.5 miles to the property boundary. Private property in the area is posted. Please stay off private land and respect the owners' rights. The cliffs on the south and east drop sharply to the ocean—exercise extreme caution!

For more information: Contact the BLM Spokane District Office, East 4217 Main Avenue, Spokane, WA 99202; (509) 353-3144.
USGS topographic maps: Lopez Pass

> *TIP: Respect public and private property including all trail signs and closure signs. Leave gates open or closed as you find them.*

WASHINGTON BY REGION

2

EASTERN WASHINGTON

BADGER SLOPE
hiking, wildlife observation, hang gliding

A north-facing escarpment overlooking the lower Yakima River Valley, Badger Slope offers expansive vistas, showy spring wildflowers and soaring raptors. Golden eagles, ferruginous and red-tailed hawks, prairie falcons and other birds may be enjoyed during the spring and summer—bring binoculars! The slope is covered with wildflowers in April and early May. The ridge line can be hiked from east to west using the McBee Grade Road from Kiona Junction, off Interstate 12, eleven miles west of Richland. Drive to the top of the grade and hike west along the top of the slope. Keep a sharp eye out for rattlesnakes. Note that the wheat fields to the south are private lands and must be avoided.

For more information: Contact the BLM Spokane District Office, East 4217 Main Avenue, Spokane, WA 99202; (509) 353-3144.
USGS topographic maps: Webber Canyon, Whitstran Northeast
BLM surface maps: Richland

CHOPAKA LAKE
boating, canoeing, mountain biking, fishing, hiking, camping, wildlife observation

Located ten miles north of Loomis, Washington in northeast Okanogan County, Chopaka Lake offers spectacular views of the east Cascade slope and is the gateway to hiking in the Chopaka Mountain Wilderness Study Area. The two-mile ridge trail around Bowers Lake to the north is considered an excellent introduction to the region. Chopaka is rimmed by forest and meadow, and some limited camping is available at BLM and state sites. No vehicles are permitted past the Wilderness Study Area boundary. The boat launch on state land is not developed—canoes and small boats only. There is good fishing for rainbow trout. The mile-long waterway offers a chance for solitude and boat access to some remote hiking opportunities. Wildlife includes deer, waterfowl, bear, and mountain goat in the Wilderness Study Area. To get to Chopaka, drive three miles north of Loomis and watch for a gravel road to the left, leading up the mountain. The lake is located in a basin above the main valley. The road junction may not be signed; inquire at the Loomis store.

For more information: Contact the BLM Spokane District Office, East 4217 Main Avenue, Spokane, WA 99202; (509) 353-3144.
USGS topographic maps: Loomis, Nighthawk
BLM surface maps: Oroville

COLUMBIA RIVER-HANFORD REACH
boating, canoeing, fishing, wildlife observation

This last free-flowing stretch of the Columbia River is located between Wanapum Dam and the city of Richland, Washington. There are a number of access points and boat launch sites along the river. For canoeing or floating, the undeveloped launch at the Vernita Bridge is popular. Fishing is for steelhead and king salmon. Bald eagles concentrate along the river in the winter. Deer, coyotes, raptors, and many shorebirds and waterfowl can be viewed along the river. The BLM islands and the U.S. Fish and Wildlife Service refuge islands offer unique habitats to explore and are used by Canada Geese for nesting sites in the spring. To reach the Vernita Bridge, drive north of Richland on Highway 240 for approximately 30 miles to the bridge. The float down to Richland can be done in one or two days. Water levels fluctuate with releases from Wanapum Dam. Do not leave a boat unattended or untethered.

For more information: Contact the BLM Spokane District Office, East 4217 Main Avenue, Spokane, WA 99202; (509) 353-3144.

USGS topographic maps: Wooded Island, Savage Island, Hanford, Locke Island, Coyote Rapids, Vernita Bridge
BLM surface maps: Richland, Priest Rapids

COWICHE CREEK CANYON
hiking, wildlife observation

This small canyon is located just west of Yakima, along Cowiche Creek. There is an established hiking trail on an old railroad grade through the canyon. Old railroad bridges still cross the creek. Numerous species of birds can be viewed within the riparian habitat. The geology of the exposed basalt canyon is very interesting. Interpretive signs are located at each end of the canyon and trail guide brochures are available at the trailheads or from the BLM offices in Wenatchee or Spokane. The canyon makes an excellent half-day side trip, and the 3.2-mile walk is considered easy. To reach the lower trailhead, take 40th Avenue west out of Yakima. Turn left on Powerhouse Road. Another left on Cowiche Canyon Road leads you to the trailhead.

For more information: Contact the BLM Spokane District Office, East 4217 Main Avenue, Spokane, WA 99202; (509) 353-3144.
USGS topographic maps: Wiley City, Yakima West, Naches
BLM surface map: Yakima

DOUGLAS CREEK
mountain biking, hiking, camping, wildlife observation, fishing

Douglas Creek is a desert canyon with steep basalt cliffs and a well-defined riparian corridor featuring a trout stream. Many varieties of songbirds and raptors may be enjoyed here. The wildlife includes deer, porcupine, coyote, beaver, and more. An old railroad bed makes an excellent hiking trail. From Highway 28, 3.5 miles south of Rock Island Dam, turn northwest on Palisades Road to Douglas Creek Road. Drive north to the canyon. Douglas Creek Road traverses about half of the lower canyon, then becomes "H" Road and connects with State Highway 2 near Waterville.

For more information: Contact the BLM Spokane District Office, East 4217 Main Avenue, Spokane, WA 99202; (509) 353-3144.
USGS topographic maps: Palisades, Altown, Douglas
BLM surface maps: Wenatchee

FISHTRAP

hiking, mountain biking, cross-country skiing, boating, fishing, wildlife observation

Fishtrap is a 5,000-acre parcel of land with shoreline access to two large lakes and many small wetlands and pothole ponds. Diverse sage, marsh, Ponderosa pine, and hardwood thicket habitats offer good viewing opportunities for waterfowl raptors, songbirds, upland birds, deer, elk, and other animals. The area is closed to all motorized vehicles. This is a good winter cross-country skiing area. Access is from the Fishtrap exit off Interstate 90, thirty miles west of Spokane. From the freeway, drive south three miles to the area.

For more information: Contact the BLM Spokane District Office, East 4217 Main Avenue, Spokane, WA 99202; (509) 353-3144.
USGS topographic maps: Fishtrap Lake, Tyler
BLM surface maps: Spokane

GOOSE BUTTE

hiking, mountain biking, wildlife observation

A desert canyon with a seasonal stream, this region offers good off-season back-country exploring opportunities. The basalt cliffs are home to nesting raptors and other songbirds and waterfowl are abundant in the wet season. Deer, grouse, owls, rabbits, coyote, and other animals may be occasionally viewed. Six miles north of the Interstate 90 junction at the Tokio Weigh Station, access is via an old jeep trail which runs west off the Tokio-Harrington Highway (Hills Road). Motorized vehicles are not permitted beyond the gate, but parking is available near the Crab Creek Bridge. A BLM sign is on the cable gate, just north of the bridge. Adjacent private lands are marked—please respect private owner privacy and stay off posted lands.

For more information: Contact the BLM Spokane District Office, East 4217 Main Avenue, Spokane, WA 99202; (509) 353-3144.
USGS topographic maps: Harrington Southeast, Lamona
BLM surface maps: Ritzville

JUNIPER DUNES WILDERNESS

hiking, wildlife observation, wildflowers

This "pocket wilderness" of 8,000 acres offers a unique

combination of sand dunes and juniper trees that combine to make a special habitat area. The Dunes were designated a wilderness area in 1984. Wildflowers are spectacular in the spring. The area is recognized as a critical nesting habitat for a number of raptor species. Many other birds may also be viewed here. From Pasco, drive northeast on the Kahlotus Highway. The wilderness area lies 1.5 miles north of the highway between mile 15 and mile 18. Currently, access is only available over private lands and permission is required. Call the BLM office in Spokane before entering for the latest access information.

For more information: Contact the BLM Spokane District Office, East 4217 Main Avenue, Spokane, WA 99202; (509) 353-3144.
USGS topographic maps: Levy Southeast, Levy Southwest
BLM surface maps: Walla Walla

KETTLE RIVER
rafting, canoeing, camping, fishing, wildlife observation

The Kettle River flows into northeast Washington from Canada and has secondary highway access along most of its length. Most of the river is ideally suited for canoeing, with very little whitewater. In the summer, small sand beaches dot the shoreline. Fishing is for rainbow and brown trout. Eagles, osprey, kingfisher, and other birds populate the cottonwood groves; bighorn sheep can be seen on the canyon walls near the town of Curlew. There are both private and public access points to the river. Twenty miles north of Republic, on Highway 21, the river crosses at the town of Curlew. From there, the river road goes northwest (upriver) to Canada, and northeast (downriver). Inquire at the Curlew store for boating and fishing information.

For more information: Contact the BLM Spokane District Office, East 4217 Main Avenue, Spokane, WA 99202; (509) 353-3144.
USGS topographic maps: Vulcan Mountain, Curlew
BLM surface maps: Republic

LAKEVIEW RANCH/LAKEVIEW CREEK CANYON
hiking, mountain biking, camping, wildlife observation

One of the largest continuous parcels of native steppe habitat in the eastern Columbia Basin, this area offers excellent opportunities to observe and interpret the geology of the basin and to hike remote, scenic canyons. Wildlife includes raptors, upland birds, waterfowl, deer, and other animals. This is one of the last strongholds for the sage grouse in Washington. A number of primitive trails are open to mountain bike and hiking use. The ranch is located off State Highway 21, about six miles north of the town of Odessa. Maps are available from the BLM District Office and at the Odessa Community Visitor's Center.

For more information: Contact the BLM Spokane District Office, East 4217 Main Avenue, Spokane, WA 99202; (509) 353-3144.
USGS topographic maps: Pacific Lake, Sullivan Lake
BLM surface maps: Coulee Dam

METHOW RIVER
rafting, fishing, wildflowers

The Methow (pronounced Met'-how), located in Okanogan County, is a tributary of the Columbia River. It is a small river with some steep gradients and Class IV whitewater. Commercial rafting companies float the river in the spring and summer. Fishing is for resident rainbow trout and steelhead. Bald eagle, deer and other wildlife can be viewed along the river. The Methow is accessible via Highway 153 between Pateros and Twisp. There are public access points at various locations; check locally for the best access.

For more information: Contact the BLM Spokane District Office, East 4217 Main Avenue, Spokane, WA 99202; (509) 353-3144.
USGS topographic maps: Pateros, Methow, Twisp East, Twisp West
BLM surface maps: Twisp, Robinson Mountain

PEND OREILLE RIVER CANYON
rafting, canoeing, boating, fishing, hiking, wildlife observation

The Pend Oreille River Canyon runs north from the town of Metaline Falls to Boundary Dam on the Canadian border. This remote stretch of river meanders through a steep-walled limestone canyon, bordered by Forest Service and BLM land. The wildlife includes osprey, bald eagle, deer, elk, bighorn sheep, as well as a variety of other birdlife. Fishing is for both cold and warm-water species. Hiking is possible from both shores where roads and trails come down to the river. The lake behind Boundary Dam is popular for boating, but is never crowded. Streams and waterfalls dot the canyon walls in a few locations.

•**See also Best of the State, page 453**•
For more information: Contact the BLM Spokane District Office, East 4217 Main Avenue, Spokane, WA 99202; (509) 353-3144.

ROCK CREEK CANYON
hiking, backpacking, fishing, wildlife observation

A remote, narrow canyon located near Goldendale in Klickitat County. This a very wild and scenic area. Ponderosa pine and oak woodlands grow on the slopes with the creek creating a well-defined riparian zone. Fishing is for resident rainbow trout, although Coho salmon and steelhead do spawn in the lower stream. The lower canyon walls rise 1,000 feet above the creek and hiking into and out of the canyon may be strenuous. There are no established trails. There are good backpacking campsites along the creek. You must carry or treat all drinking water.

•**See also Best of the State, page 452**•
For more information: Contact the BLM Spokane District Office, East 4217 Main Avenue, Spokane, WA 99202; (509) 353-3144.

SADDLE MOUNTAIN
hiking, mountain biking, camping, off-road vehicle use, hang gliding

A steep escarpment, Saddle Mountain offers expansive vistas of the Columbia Basin, the Columbia River and the Crab Creek National Wildlife Refuge to the north. The sage-covered ridge is crisscrossed with primitive jeep roads and trails. The steep north slope is a good place to view raptors. The area is a popular rock hounding location, and is a good spot to see wildflowers in the spring. South of Interstate 90, drive 15 miles to Mattawa. Continue east of Mattawa one mile to "R" Road, and north into the western region. The eastern region is accessible through Wahluke Wildlife Area, 20 miles east of Mattawa.

For more information: Contact the BLM Spokane District Office, East 4217 Main Avenue, Spokane, WA 99202; (509) 353-3144.

USGS topographic maps: Beverly, Smyrna, Corfu
BLM surface maps: Priest Rapids

SPLIT ROCK RECREATION SITE
hiking, wildlife observation, fishing, boating

Drive along the Loomis-Oroville Road five miles north of Loomis. The best area for wildlife viewing is on the southeast shore of Palmer Lake. Bring your binoculars because it is possible to see mountain goats on nearby Grandview Mountain—one mile to the northwest across from the southeast shore of Palmer Lake. Around the lake, expect to see a wide variety of shorebirds, waterfowl, grebes, loons, and songbirds.

For more information: Contact the BLM Spokane District Office, East 4217 Main Avenue, Spokane, WA 99202; (509) 353-3144.
USGS topographic maps: Loomis, Nighthawk

WILSON CREEK CANYON
hiking, wildlife observation, wildflowers

A designated Watchable Wildlife/Wildflower Area, this little canyon is home to a number of songbirds, waterfowl and raptors—and features a well-developed riparian zone and a live desert stream. Deer, beaver, coyote and an occasional bobcat can be seen in the region. Historically, the canyon was used as an outlaw hideout during the late 1800s. The interpretive trail is located one-half mile south of the Lewis Bridge, and leads through a natural plant community to a canyon overlook. From the junction four miles west of Wilbur, drive south past the community of Govan to the end of the pavement (five miles), then continue west one mile to Lewis Bridge over Wilson Creek. The area lies downstream.

For more information: Contact the BLM Spokane District Office, East 4217 Main Avenue, Spokane, WA 99202; (509) 353-3144.
USGS topographic map: Almira Southeast
BLM surface maps: Coulee Dam

YAKIMA RIVER CANYON
hiking, canoeing, rafting, kayaking, wildlife observation, camping, fishing

Three recreation sites with primitive campgrounds are along the route: Umtanum Creek, Squaw Creek and Roza. Each has restrooms and boat launching facilities. Along the canyon, it is possible to see bighorn sheep, songbirds of many varieties and numerous raptors.

•**See also Best of the State, page 454**•

For more information: Contact the BLM Spokane District Office, East 4217 Main Avenue, Spokane, WA 99202; (509) 353-3144.

STATE INFORMATION OVERVIEW

SPOKANE DISTRICT OFFICE
East 4217 Main Avenue, Spokane, WA 99202; (509) 353-3144

WYOMING

(SEE MAP A)

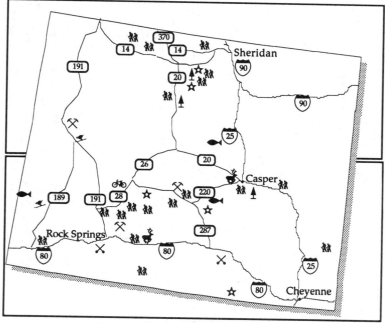

(SEE MAP B)

MAP A—WYOMING

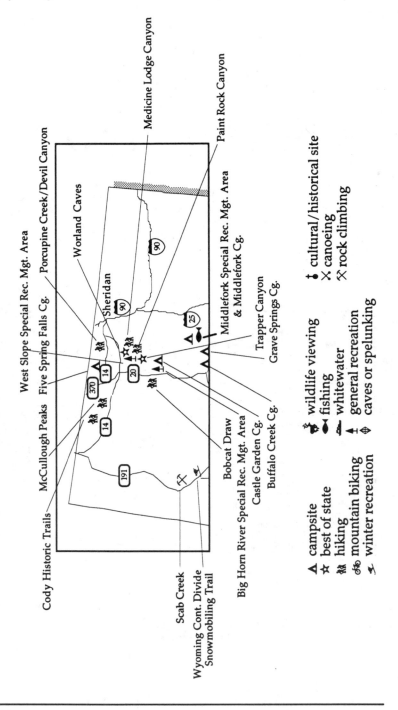

Medicine Lodge Canyon

Paint Rock Canyon

Porcupine Creek/Devil Canyon

West Slope Special Rec. Mgt. Area

Worland Caves

Five Spring Falls Cg.

Sheridan

Middlefork Special Rec. Mgt. Area
& Middlefork Cg.

McCullough Peaks

Cody Historic Trails

Trapper Canyon

Grave Springs Cg.

Bobcat Draw

Castle Garden Cg.

Buffalo Creek Cg.

Big Horn River Special Rec. Mgt. Area

Scab Creek

Wyoming Cont. Divide
Snowmobiling Trail

△ campsite
☆ best of state
鮏 hiking
☝ mountain biking
↙ winter recreation

🐾 wildlife viewing
🐟 fishing
↝ whitewater
↟ general recreation
⊕ caves or spelunking

† cultural/historical site
✕ canoeing
✕ rock climbing

MAP REFERENCES

CAMPGROUNDS

The following campgrounds are found in this area of Wyoming. Please call the BLM office listed following each campground's name for reservations and information. Contact information for each BLM office is on pages 501-502 for Wyoming.

Five Springs Falls Campground; Worland District Office
Castle Garden Campground; Worland District Office
Middle Fork Campground; Worland District Office
Grave Springs Campground; Casper District Office
Buffalo Creek Campground; Casper District Office

MAP B—WYOMING

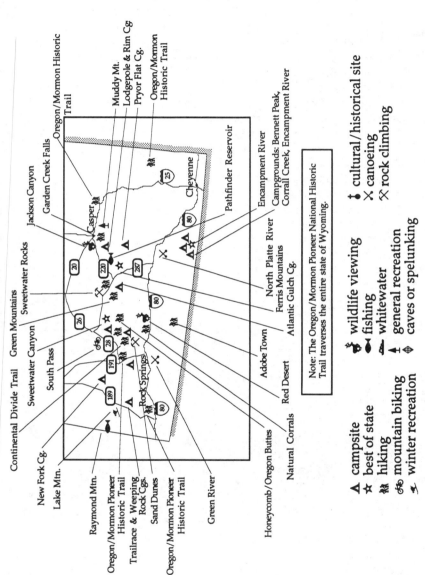

Continental Divide Trail Green Mountains
Sweetwater Rocks
Sweetwater Canyon
South Pass

Jackson Canyon
Garden Creek Falls
Oregon/Mormon Historic Trail
Muddy Mt.
Lodgepole & Rim Cg
Pryor Flat Cg.
Oregon/Mormon Historic Trail

Casper
Cheyenne

New Fork Cg.
Lake Mtn.
Raymond Mtn.
Oregon/Mormon Pioneer Historic Trail
Trailrace & Weeping Rock Cgs.
Sand Dunes
Oregon/Mormon Pioneer Historic Trail
Green River

Rock Springs

Honeycomb/Oregon Buttes
Natural Corrals

Red Desert
Adobe Town

Atlantic Gulch Cg.
Ferris Mountains
North Platte River

Pathfinder Reservoir

Encampment River
Campgrounds: Bennett Peak, Corrall Creek, Encampment River

Note: The Oregon/Mormon Pioneer National Historic Trail traverses the entire state of Wyoming.

▲ campsite
☆ best of state
🥾 hiking
🚲 mountain biking
⚶ winter recreation

🦌 wildlife viewing
🎣 fishing
⚓ whitewater
⚑ general recreation
⬦ caves or spelunking

✝ cultural/historical site
✕ canoeing
⚒ rock climbing

MAP REFERENCES

Adobe Town Wilderness Study Area—p. 492
Continental Divide National Scenic Trail—p. 482
Encampment River—p. 476-477
Ferris Mountains Wilderness Study Area—p. 478-479
Garden Creek Falls—p. 499
Green Mountains—p. 492
Green River—p. 493
Honeycomb and Oregon Buttes—p. 493
Jackson Canyon—p. 488
Lake Mountain—p. 493-494
Muddy Mountain—p. 499
Natural Corrals—p. 494
North Platte River—p. 497-498
Oregon/ Mormon Pioneer Historic Trail—p. 482-483
Pathfinder Reservoir—p. 499-500
Raymond Mountain—p. 495
Red Desert—p. 494-495
Sand Dunes Special Recreation Management Area—p. 495-496
South Pass Historic Mining Area—p. 497
Sweetwater Canyon—p. 500
Sweetwater Rocks—p. 500

CAMPGROUNDS

The following campgrounds are found in this area of Wyoming. Please call the BLM office listed following each campground's name for reservations and information. Contact information for each BLM office is on pages 501-502 for Wyoming.

Atlantic Gulch Campground; Rawlins District Office
Bennett Peak Campground; Rawlins District Office
Corral Creek Campground; Rawlins District Office
Encampment River Campground; Rawlins District Office
Lodgepole Campground; Casper District Office
New Fork Campground; Rock Springs District Office
Pryor Flat Campground; Rawlins District Office
Rim Campground; Casper District Office
Sweetwater Campground; Rock Springs District Office
Tailrace Campground; Rock Springs District Office
Weeping Rock Campgound; Rock Springs District Office

1

TRAPPER CANYON

Those who have braved the difficult terrain come away saying Trapper Canyon is one of the most spectacular and scenic canyons on the west slope of the Bighorn Mountain Range. It is little wonder, as the dramatic cliffs, rock spires, massive outcroppings, clear and cascading stream, and the wide variety of vegetation and wildlife have earned this canyon BLM's "most scenic" rating. Even the Department of Fish and Game rates the stream "a fishery of regional importance" because of the presence of brown, rainbow and cutthroat trout. Vegetation in and around the stream includes currant, gooseberry, grapevine, chokecherry, cottonwood, and aspen—at times so dense that passage may be impeded. When the berries are in season, keep a lookout for black bear who have sometimes been reported in the canyon. Those with a sharp eye for wildlife may spot bobcat, mountain lion, golden eagle, bald eagle, and peregrine falcon. Several hundred deer and elk also use the canyon as a wintering ground. This entire canyon system has been recommended for wilderness designation by the BLM.

HIKING

There is no developed trail system. Travel is by game trails and scrambling over rocks and loose talus slopes. The canyon is approximately 13 miles in length with several side canyons, most of them hanging, and offers the adventurous and experienced backpacker ample opportunity to fully enjoy a pure wilderness setting.

SPELUNKING

Great Expectations Cave, recognized as the third deepest cave within the United States, lies within the boundaries of Trapper Canyon Wilderness Study Area. This cave is very technical and risky to enter—do not explore without permits and experience, under any circumstances.

MANAGEMENT
BLM Worland District Office, 101 South 23rd, Worland, WY 82401; (307) 347-9871.

LOCATION
West of Interstate 90 and southwest of the city of Sheridan, just south of the Montana border.

GETTING THERE
Travel on the dirt access roads can be rough, muddy and challenging, four-wheel-drive vehicles are highly recommended. The point of access is located five miles southeast of the town of Shell and State Road 14. Black Mountain Road provides access. There are private holdings along the road and bordering the canyon area—do not trespass without express permission from the owner. Before entering, check with the BLM regarding legal and approved access points to the canyon.

CAMPING
Primitive camping is allowed anywhere within Trapper Canyon.

PERMITS
No permits are necessary for camping or backpacking. Seasonal campfire restrictions exist—check with the BLM office. Of special note is the entrance to the third deepest cave in the U.S., the Great Expectations Cave, which lies within the boundaries of Trapper Canyon. Permits for exploration are required and only issued to those who can prove experience in spelunking.

MAPS
USGS topographic maps: White Sulphur Springs, Bush Butte, Spanish Point, Black Mountain

ADDITIONAL INFORMATION
• *The Sierra Club Guide to the Natural Areas of Idaho, Montana, and Wyoming* by John and Jane Perry; published by Sierra Club, 730 Polk Street, San Francisco, CA 94109.
• *Wyoming Atlas and Gazetteer*, published by DeLorme Mapping, Main Street, Freeport, ME 04032; (800) 227-1656.

SEASON

Although the canyon is passable year-round, snow frequently blocks the use of necessary access roads between the months of December through April. The best time to visit is from May to October. Check with the BLM regarding current road conditions.

TIP: Apply a no-trace ethic everyday, everywhere.

BEST OF THE STATE

2

SWEETWATER CANYON/ LANDER RESOURCE AREA

This very wild canyon is a wilderness study area with excellent opportunities for fishing. Solitude and quiet abound. Geological formations are spectacular and bird life is abundant.

HIKING

Game trails wander throughout the canyon. Discernible trails follow the river—eight to nine miles each way through the canyon. Ticks and deer flies are prevalent during the summer—take appropriate precautions. Hiking is very rugged and not for the faint of heart. The reward, however, is that you are hiking where few have tread in a spectacular prairie canyon.

MANAGEMENT

BLM Lander Resource Area, P.O. Box 589, Lander, WY 82520; (307) 332-7822

LOCATION

South of Lander and near the southeast reaches of the Wind River Range.

GETTING THERE

From Atlantic City or Sweetwater Station, take the Hudson Atlantic City Road. The road is signed BLM 2302. There are a number of connecting trails, all heading south from 2302, but not passable by two-wheel-drive vehicles. If you choose to hike to the canyon, park your vehicle off to the side of 2302, anywhere that you are not obstructing traffic. There are places to leave four-wheel-drive vehicles near the canyon at the end of the access trails, but the canyon itself is closed to vehicular traffic. Wet conditions could make any of the roads impassable. Call the Lander Station first for detailed access and road condition information.

CAMPING

Camping is allowed anywhere within Sweetwater Canyon.

PERMITS

No permits are necessary.

MAPS

BLM surface maps: Lander, South Pass
USGS topographic maps: Lewiston Lakes, Radium Springs

ADDITIONAL INFORMATION

Wyoming Atlas and Gazetteer, published by DeLorme Mapping, Main Street, Freeport, ME 04032; (800) 227-1656.

SEASON

The season runs from July through September. Snow, high water or wet conditions can make access to the canyon area impossible—always check with the Lander BLM office before heading out.

TIP: Stay on the main trail even if it is wet or snow-covered. Leaving the trail to skirt these areas only creates another trail and point of erosion.

3
ENCAMPMENT RIVER

More of a large stream than a river, the Encampment River area is an awesome combination of rugged, unpopulated canyon country, framed by a variety of woodland and riparian settings. The BLM section provides a fitting four-mile introduction to the 16-mile-long route—the remaining miles belong to the Medicine Bow National Forest. Brook, brown and native trout ply the waterways, offering the angler a super fishing opportunity. Spending any less than two days in this area is a mistake as the rushing rapids, interspersed with tranquil waters, create an almost undeniable desire to kick up the feet and let time slip away amid a unique wilderness setting.

HIKING

In order to best experience the entire trail, a car shuttle is required. The hike begins at the BLM-managed Encampment Campground. The other vehicle will need to be left at Comissary Park on U.S. Forest Service Road 496, just off U.S. Forest Service Road 550 and Highway 70. Although the entire river is considered a blue ribbon trout stream, be aware that the first mile of the river, from the Encampment Campground, has no public access (a notorious problem throughout the state of Wyoming). This doesn't matter because the remaining 15 miles offer good access and fishing. Very few people venture along the entire route—your gain, their loss. This is really a superb wilderness trek. The first few miles are lined with cottonwood amid scrub and sage hillsides. The canyon will narrow quickly, becoming predominantly ruled by conifers and aspen. Sections of the canyon narrow into a gorge and are quite rocky, turning the stream into a roaring and tumbling imitation of a powerful river.

MANAGEMENT
•BLM Rawlins District Office, P.O. Box 670, Rawlins, WY 82302; (307) 324-7171.
•Hayden Ranger District, Medicine Bow National Forest, 204 West Ninth Street, Encampment, WY 82325; (307) 327-5481.

LOCATION
Approximately six miles south of the town of Encampment.

GETTING THERE
To get to the Encampment Campground and the Encampment River Trailhead, take Highway 70 for approximately two-tenths of a mile west of the town of Encampment. A BLM sign indicates the Encampment Campground—turn left on a dirt/gravel road suitable for all vehicles and drive two miles.

CAMPING
In addition to the U.S. Forest Service Lakeview Campground near Comissary Park, the BLM manages the Encampment Campground which serves as the trailhead for the Encampment River Trail. Primitive camping is allowed anywhere within the canyon, but keep in mind that the best sites are found within the first nine miles from the trailhead. Once into the narrow canyon, campsites become scarce and of poor quality.

PERMITS
No permits are necessary for hiking or camping.

MAPS
USGS topographic maps: Encampment, Dudley Creek
USFS maps: Medicine Bow National Forest

ADDITIONAL INFORMATION
• *The Hikers Guide to Wyoming,* by Bill Hunger, published by Falcon Press, P.O. Box 1718, Helena, MT 59624; (800) 582-2665.
• *Wyoming Atlas and Gazetteer,* published by DeLorme Mapping, Main Street, Freeport, ME 04032; (800) 227-1656.

SEASON
The season runs from May to November, depending on snow levels. Ticks are prevalent once the snow melts away; conduct frequent tick checks.

---

*TIP: Camp only in established
or previously used sites if available.*

4

FERRIS MOUNTAINS WILDERNESS STUDY AREA

This is a wilderness area beyond compare (no roads or even trails—it's all cross-country here). Access is practically nonexistent—a common problem throughout Wyoming. Peaks range from 8,000 to 10,000 feet, cut with deep canyons, crystal clear streams, wildflowers galore and sweetly scented pine forests. Wildlife is abundant here.

HIKING

This is not an area for the inexperienced backpacker or hiker. Solid orienteering and map reading skills are requisite. No trails exist in this region and hiking is essentially cross-country. Park your car, pick an area that looks inviting and head out. Just remember that you must have the awareness and navigational skills necessary to find your way back to your vehicle again. Water is abundant and of good quality, although you must treat it prior to drinking.

MANAGEMENT

BLM Rawlins District Office, 1300 Third Street, P.O. Box 670, Rawlins, WY 82302; (307) 324-7171.

LOCATION

Approximately 45 miles north of Rawlins.

GETTING THERE

The BLM currently recommends the following access, however it may change at any time so it is important that you contact the Rawlins District office to obtain current and accurate access information. From Rawlins, drive approximately 45 miles on Highway 287 which will bring you to a "blink and you'll pass right through it" town named Muddy Gap. From here, the Ferris Mountains are southeast. BLM road 3156 offers access. There are other access points off U.S. Forest Service roads, but you will need to inquire directly about them. Rain and snow make the routes impassable. Four-wheel-drive vehicles are an absolute necessity on any of the BLM roads in this region. Rain turns BLM dirt routes into impassable quagmires until the sun dries them—not a problem unless you are in the Ferris Mountain Area trying to get out.

CAMPING

Camping is allowed anywhere within the BLM Ferris Mountains Wilderness Study Area—private lands bound the region almost in its entirety. If you think that you may be on private land, even if it is not clearly signed, move on and don't camp.

PERMITS

No permits are necessary.

MAPS

USGS topographic maps: Spanish Mine, Youngs Pass, Muddy Gap
BLM surface maps: Bairoil

ADDITIONAL INFORMATION

• *Wyoming Atlas and Gazetteer*, published by DeLorme Mapping, Main Street, Freeport, ME 04032; (800) 227-1656.
• *The Hikers Guide to Wyoming*, by Bill Hunger, published by Falcon Press, P.O. Box 1718, Helena, MT 59624; (800) 582-2665.

SEASON

The season runs from May to November depending on snow levels.

TIP: Constantly stay alert for signs of your passing and erase them if possible.

5

HORSETHIEF CAVE

Horsethief Cave includes approximately 15 miles of known passage, much of which has been mapped. Most of the cave is dry, but wet formations (stalactites, stalagmites, and flowstones) are present in the cave. The cave itself displays extensive, diverse and beautiful cave formations. In fact, some formations represent some of the very best displays of mineralization found in any cold-climate cave in the U.S. Horsethief Cave is a "wild" cave, meaning no passage modifications have been undertaken and nothing has been added to or removed to lessen hazards or make the use of the cave any easier.

HIKING/SPELUNKING

The Horsethief Cave Underground National Recreation Trail is an unimproved primitive trail. Trail passageways vary in size from crawlways to rooms with thousands of square feet. Some sections of the trail require crawling and squeezing through constricted passageways—a daunting psychological task for some. Other portions of the trail are located in expansive rooms permitting individual exploration of the cave environment. The majority of the trail is dry and dusty and no attempts to improve or otherwise modify the trail are planned.

MANAGEMENT

BLM Cody Resource Area, 1714 Stampeed Avenue, Cody, WY 82414; (307) 587-2216.

LOCATION

On Little Mountain approximately 25 miles east of Lovell.

PERMITS

Permits to utilize the trail and enter the cave are available at no cost from the BLM in Cody. Use of the cave is controlled through a locked gate located immediately inside the cave entrance. Use of the cave is restricted to two groups with a maximum of eight per group, per day. Pets are not allowed inside the cave. Group leaders must demonstrate extensive cave exploration experience or have previous experience traveling in Horsethief Cave.

SEASON

This area is open all year, depending on the snow level and access road conditions—check with the BLM prior to heading out.

> *TIP: Pack out all that you bring in—*
> *and a little extra if you find it.*

1

WYOMING (GENERAL)

CONTINENTAL DIVIDE
NATIONAL SCENIC TRAIL
SPECIAL RECREATION MANAGEMENT AREA
hiking, backpacking, camping

Although this route was officially designated by Congress in 1978, it is not officially marked yet. This is because of the unusually restrictive laws prohibiting access to private lands which checkerboard the entire route, most obviously in the BLM-managed section between South Pass City and Medicine Bow National Forest. Although many hikers choose different routes, the best route through this section to date is as follows: Follow the Sweetwater River from South Pass City to the lower end of Sweetwater Canyon and then head east/southeast along the flank of Crooks and Green Mountains. From there, either head south along the high rims to Rawlins or go through the Ferris and Haystack Mountains to Rawlins. Once at Rawlins, the route heads southwest along the Atlantic Rim to Miller and Middlewood Hills and then to Medicine Bow National Forest. Potable water is scarce and a backpacker must carry plenty of reserves. Before crossing private land, you must secure the landowner's permission.

For more information: Contact the BLM Rawlins District Office, P.O. Box 670, 1300 North Third Street, Rawlins, WY 82301; (307) 324-7171.

OREGON / MORMON PIONEER
NATIONAL HISTORIC TRAILS
SPECIAL RECREATION MANAGEMENT AREA
horseback riding, hiking, mountain biking, historic sites, unique natural features, fishing

Without a doubt, the easiest way to view the Oregon/Mormon Pioneer National Historic Trail is by car. This is because of poor access to many sections of the trail that are private. Still, it is possible to view the trail by foot or mountain bike, but be ready to wade through a world of paper, including maps, landowner permission-to-pass requests, and detailed information regarding legal points of public access. The BLM will help all it can. Land ownership status maps are available from the BLM office in Wyoming. Specific resource offices can advise you of land ownership status and difficulties and provide recommendations about trail access.

For more information: Contact the BLM Wyoming State Office, 2515 Warren Avenue, P.O. Box 1828, Cheyenne, WY 82003; (307) 775-6BLM.

WYOMING CONTINENTAL DIVIDE SNOWMOBILING TRAIL

snowmobiling, cross-country skiing, snowshoeing, winter wildlife observation

The Wyoming Continental Divide Snowmobiling Trail extends from the south end of the Wind River Mountains at South Pass to the boundaries of Grand Teton National Park. Much of it passes through BLM lands. There are numerous other maintained "winter" trails throughout Wyoming. In fact, Wyoming has some of the most expansive and developed snowmobiling trails in the continental United States. Snowmobiling maps are available from the Wyoming Recreation Commission, 122 West 25th, Cheyenne, WY 82002; (307) 777-7695. Find out snow conditions around the state by calling (307) 777-6503.

For more information: Contact the BLM Wyoming State Office, 2515 Warren Avenue, P.O. Box 1828, Cheyenne, WY 82003; (307) 775-6BLM.

TIP: Respect public and private property including all trail signs and closure signs. Leave gates open or closed as you find them.

2

NORTHWESTERN WYOMING

BIG HORN RIVER SPECIAL RECREATION MANAGEMENT AREA
wildlife observation, camping, fishing (including spear gun fishing), float boating

Located 15 miles north of Thermopolis, the Bighorn River meanders through a cottonwood riparian area, agricultural lands and badlands. An especially scenic segment of the river is where it dissects the Sheep Mountain Anticline and Little Sheep Mountain. The state of Wyoming classifies this segment of the river as a Class I fishery, which indicates it is a fishery of national prominence. Large rainbow and brown trout may be fished within this section. Consistent public access to the river is a problem in many areas, so it is critical that you check with the BLM before heading out.

For more information: Contact the BLM Worland District Office, 101 South 23rd, Worland, WY 82401; (307) 347-9871.

CODY HISTORIC TRAILS STATE RECREATION MANAGEMENT AREA
hiking

The Cody Resource Area manages several significant historical trails including the Nez Perce, Bridger and the Red Lodge to Meeteetse Stage Route. The Nez Perce Trail has been designated a National Historic Trail. This trail is the route Chief Joseph and his tribe followed in 1877 during their attempt to escape to Canada rather than remain on their reservation. The Bridger Trail was used more heavily than the Bozeman Trail because the Sioux focused their efforts on stopping travel along the Bozeman. The Red Lodge to Meeteetse Stage Route was an important freight route in the 1800s. The route provided a vital link to the railroads, which did not enter into the area until much later. Hiking is the best way to explore these trails. Access to all parts of the trails is limited. There are some conflicting accounts as to where the actual trails originally existed.

For more information: Contact the BLM Cody Resource Area, 1714 Stampede Avenue, Cody, WY 82414; (307) 587-2216.

McCULLOUGH PEAKS
hiking, horseback riding

A dramatic and scenic badlands area that is heavily eroded and very colorful. Wild horse, mule deer and pronghorn live on the sparse vegetation. The golden eagle, prairie falcon, kestrel, red-tailed hawk, and great horned owl rule the skies. Access is five miles south of Powell via local roads. Wet conditions may make these roads impassable—check with the Worland District office for road information and directions before heading out.

For more information: Contact the BLM Worland District Office, 101 South 23rd, Worland, WY 82401; (307) 347-9871.
USGS topographic maps: Stone Barn and Camp (one map)

TRAPPER CANYON
hiking, backpacking, fishing, wildlife observation

Those who have braved the difficult terrain come away saying Trapper Canyon is one of the most spectacular and scenic canyons on the west slope of the Bighorn Mountain Range. It is little wonder, as the dramatic cliffs, rock spires, massive outcroppings, clear and cascading stream, and the wide variety of vegetation and wildlife have earned this canyon BLM's "most scenic" rating. Even the Department of Fish and Game rates the stream "a fishery of regional importance" because of the presence of brown, rainbow and cutthroat trout. Vegetation in and around the stream includes currant, gooseberry, grapevine, chokecherry, cottonwood, and aspen—at times so dense that passage may be impeded. When the berries are in season, keep a lookout for black bear who have sometimes been reported in the canyon. Those with a sharp eye for wildlife may spot bobcat, mountain lion, golden eagle, bald eagle, and peregrine falcon in the canyon. Several hundred deer and elk also use the canyon as a wintering ground. This entire canyon system has been recommended for wilderness designation by the BLM.

Wyoming

•See also Best of the State, page 472•
For more information: Contact the BLM Worland District Office, 101
South 23rd, Worland, WY 82401; (307) 347-9871.

PAINT ROCK CANYON
hiking, backpacking, mountain biking, fishing, wildlife
observation

You will best remember this area for its limestone cliffs,
towering above a pristine stream that offers good fishing.
Raptor and swallow activity is amazing. Hiking is easy and you
may camp anywhere along the canyon floor. It is important to
note that the first 1.7 miles of the hike are across private land
owned by the Hyatt Ranch. Public access to the canyon is
allowed only from April to September. Remember to close all
gates after passing through. April and May are perhaps the best
months to visit the canyon area, as summer is hot, filled with
deer flies and the grasses become very dry, turning your socks
into a walking seed sampler. To get there, take Highway 31
east from Worland toward the Bighorn Mountains and the
town of Hyattville. One-half mile north of town you will end
up on the Alkali/Cold Springs Road. Alkali turns to gravel and
heads north, but you will stay on paved Cold Springs Road to
a fork and where the pavement ends. Bear right on Hyatt Lane
to the signed parking area for Paint Rock.

For more information: Contact the BLM Worland District Office, P.O.
Box 119, 101 South 23rd Street, Worland, WY 82401; (307) 347-9871.
USGS topographic maps: Hyatt Ranch, Allen Draw, Lake Solitude
BLM surface maps: Worland, USFS Bighorn National Forest map

PORCUPINE CREEK / DEVIL CANYON
hiking, backpacking, mountain biking, fishing, historic sites,
wildlife observation

This area is located just northeast of the town of Lovell and
Bighorn Lake, near the Montana/Wyoming border. Porcupine
Creek flows for almost its entire length through the highly
scenic Devil Canyon—characterized by massive limestone rock
walls dropping steeply several hundred feet to the canyon
floor. According to the BLM, "few canyons in the region have
walls as high or as vertical, and few canyons are as undisturbed by the evidence of man." The canyon area is a critical

wintering habitat for bighorn sheep and is also noteworthy for the large number of raptor nests. Segments of the canyon have open sites and rock shelters that are listed on the National Register of Historic Places. Native Americans have shown increased interest in the region due to its geographic relationship with the Medicine Wheel and Spirit Mountain. Access is limited and should be first approved by calling the BLM office in Worland to obtain up-to-date information.

For more information: Contact the BLM Worland District Office, P.O. Box 119, 101 South 23rd Street, Worland, WY 82401; (307) 347-9871. **USGS topographic maps:** Medicine Wheel

WYOMING BY REGION

NORTHEASTERN WYOMING

BOBCAT DRAW
hiking, backpacking, wildlife observation

Wyoming is not famous for its badlands, and yet it probably should be. Bobcat Draw is an outstanding example of magical formations formed by the powers of erosion—arches, windows, hoodoos, mushrooms, and more. Colors are spectacular. Wildlife is limited, due to lack of available water, but pronghorn and wild horses may still be seen. Probably the best way to experience this region is to hike in a short way and set up a base camp from which to explore. Be sure to pack in all the water you will need as there is none available within Bobcat. This area is located west of Worland on State Road 431. Inquire at the Worland District office for more detailed and up-to-date access information.

For more information: Contact the BLM Worland District Office, P.O. Box 119, 101 South 23rd Street, Worland, WY 82401; (307) 347-9871. **USGS topographic map:** Dead Indian Hill, Dutch Nick Northwest

JACKSON CANYON
wildlife observation

Located approximately five miles southwest of Casper on State Road 220, Jackson Canyon serves as a roosting area for nearly 60 bald eagles from December through March. Although you cannot hike into the canyon because it is closed to public access to protect the eagles, the BLM and Audubon Society have collaborated to construct a birdwatching area at a signed turnoff just off the road. There are plaques to help identify raptors.

For more information: Contact the BLM Worland District Office, P.O. Box 119, 101 South 23rd Street, Worland, WY 82401; (307) 347-9871.

MEDICINE LODGE CANYON
hiking, backpacking, camping, fishing, wildlife observation, horseback riding

This 1,000-foot-deep canyon is spectacular and provides excellent access to the adjacent Bighorn National Forest. There is a streamside campground at the mouth of the canyon that is maintained by the Wyoming Recreation Commission. Medicine Lodge State Archaeological Site, which features many well-preserved petroglyphs, can also be accessed and enjoyed. The trail running through the canyon and up into the National Forest is named Dry Medicine Lodge Canyon and is the only maintained trail in the region. All other hiking is off-trail. Access into the Cloud Peak Wilderness makes this an attractive backpacking exploration area. Fishing is for rainbow, brown, brook, and cutthroat trout. Wildlife includes elk, deer, black bear, mountain lion, and cottontail rabbit. Wild turkey and pheasant are also seen. The area is closed from December 1 to June 1 to protect sensitive wintering wildlife.

To get there from Worland, take Highway 31 east toward the Bighorn Mountains and the town of Hyattville. One-half of a mile north of Hyattville you will end up on the Alkali/Cold Springs Road. Alkali turns to gravel and heads north, but you will stay on the paved Cold Springs Road for four miles to a sign indicating the Medicine Lodge Habitat Unit. From here continue approximately one and a half miles on the gravel road to a parking area.

For more information: Contact the BLM Worland District Office, P.O. Box 119, 101 South 23rd Street, Worland, WY 82401; (307) 347-9871.
USGS topographic maps: Allen Draw, Hyatt Ranch

MIDDLEFORK SPECIAL RECREATION MANAGEMENT AREA
spelunking, hiking, backpacking, fishing, camping

Made famous by the telling of the Butch Cassidy and the Hole-In-The-Wall Gang tales, this area is remote and rugged. The Hole-In-The-Wall is so named for its gap that provides a passable breach in the Red Wall, a 30-mile-long bright red sandstone cliff that rises 300 feet in some places and creates a physical barrier to passage. The other significant breach in the wall is created by the more visually stunning Middle Fork Canyon—carved by the eroding action of the Middle Fork of the Powder River. The west/east canyon runs up to 1,000 feet deep in some places and provides excellent opportunities for hiking, backpacking and fishing. Wildlife seen in the area include elk, bighorn sheep, mule deer, pronghorn, snowshoe hare, ruffed grouse, and wild turkey. The best season to visit is between May and September. The summer can get quite warm, but it isn't too uncomfortable. From Kaycee, take State Road 192 off Interstate 25. Four-wheel-drive vehicles are recommended and it is essential that you contact the local Casper District BLM office for detailed road conditions and access information. Those interested in spelunking will want to inquire about Outlaw Cave.

For more information: Contact the BLM Casper District Office, 1701 East E Street, Casper, WY 82601; (307) 261-7600.
USGS topographic maps: Gordon Creek

WEST SLOPE SPECIAL RECREATION MANAGEMENT AREA
hiking, backpacking, fishing, camping, snowmobiling, wildlife observation

Characterized by deep canyons that bisect the rolling and sometimes steep west slope of the Bighorn Mountains, the West Slope Special Recreation Management Area supports trout fisheries and a whole host of recreational opportunities. Five Springs Falls Campground, Middle Fork of the Powder

River Campground and several hiking trails are the developed recreational opportunities available.

For more information: Contact the BLM Worland District Office, 101 South 23rd, Worland, WY 82401; (307) 347-9871.

WORLAND CAVES SPECIAL RECREATION MANAGEMENT AREA
spelunking

The Worland District contains at least 40 known caves throughout the Bighorn Basin of north central Wyoming. More caves are certain to be discovered with time. The best known caves are Horsethief, Titan, Natural Trap, Spirit Mountain Cavern, Holey Sheep, Tres Charros, and the Great Expectation Cave System.

Horsethief Cave:

Horsethief Cave's underground trail, a 1.2-mile venture, was recently recognized as a National Recreation Trail, Wyoming's 14th such trail designation. It is an unusual designation, however, because this trail is entirely underground. Horsethief, located 25 miles east of Lovell, is perhaps best known for the length of its interior passages, its outstanding geological formations and its unique paleontological and archaeological resources. For obvious safety and impact reasons, visitors to the cave must first prove prior caving experience and then will be permitted entry by the BLM.

•See also Best of the State, page 480•

Titan Caverns:

Recently discovered, the caverns contain a very large room over 900 feet long and 60 feet wide. This is a significant cave, both for its magnificent and pristine formations and because many suspect a connection with Horsethief Cave will be eventually discovered.

Natural Trap:

Significant internationally for its paleontological resources which include the remains of a North American lion, a woolly mammoth and a Pleistocene camel. Access requires an 80-foot free rappel.

Spirit Mountain Caverns:

The caverns were discovered by a local spelunker in 1904 and became a national monument under an executive order signed by Teddy Roosevelt. It then became a commercial cave under a recreation and public purpose lease and finally reverted back to the BLM. Since the cave is close to the town of Cody, it sees a lot of novice cavers.

Holey Sheep Cave:

Discovered in 1988, the cave contains outstanding examples of rare minerals and unusual formations. For that reason, BLM is understandably being very strict in limiting access to this area.

Tres Charros and Great Expectations:

Both of these caves are critically important as part of the water recharge network for the Madison Aquifer.

I am deferring to BLM's request to specifically avoid giving directions to any of these caves to protect visitor safety and fragile cave resources. BLM will issue permits to anyone who wants to visit these caves as long as you can show sufficient prior spelunking experience. In some cases, BLM may be able to hook you up with a spelunking club who would be willing to "guide" you through a cave if you are a novice but show genuine interest.

For more information: Contact the BLM Worland District Office, 101 South 23rd, Worland, WY 82401; (307) 347-9871.

TIP: The most serious damage to a site occurs from innocent visitation. Staying on the trail will minimize the damage.

4

SOUTHWESTERN WYOMING

ADOBE TOWN WILDERNESS STUDY AREA
hiking, camping

Remote and rugged, this high desert plateau embodies the dramatic nature of badlands. Buttes and escarpments have been carved by wind and water into colorful and often contorted formations. Water is not available so pack all you will need; keep in mind that the summer heat can be oppressive. Getting there is creative at best—almost as much of an adventure as you are likely to have once there. Contact the BLM office for specific and detailed directions. Four-wheel-drive vehicles are required for driving on the BLM roads. However, rain will make the roads impassable—even with four-wheel-drive.

For more information: Contact the BLM Rawlins District Office, P.O. Box 670, 1300 North Third Street, Rawlins, WY 82301; (307) 324-7171.
USGS topographic maps: Kinney Rim
BLM surface maps: Kinney Rim, Baggs

GREEN MOUNTAINS
camping, hiking

Although the Cottonwood Campground is located here and there is a superb view to be enjoyed from on top of Wild Horse Lookout, this area has been severely scarred by undiscriminating clear-cutting, mining exploration and the building of the roads that were necessitated by all the vehicle traffic. Too bad—maybe it will recover someday. There are access trails from here that lead south to the Continental Divide and to the Continental Divide Trail. From Jeffrey City, drive six miles east on Highway 287 and then turn south onto Green Mountain Road.

For more information: Contact the BLM Rawlins District Office, P.O. Box 670, 1300 North Third Street, Rawlins, WY 82301; (307) 324-7171.

GREEN RIVER
fishing, camping, hiking, canoeing, wildlife observation

South from Fontenelle Reservoir to the Flaming Gorge National Recreation Area, the Green River offers tranquil waters on which to float and fish—ideal for the entire family. The only developed camping along the way is at Weeping Rock Campground which has tables and a vault toilet, but no potable water. All water is obtained from the river and must be treated before drinking. The river route floats through the Seedskadee National Wildlife Refuge which offers some of the finest birding opportunities in the state. Canoeists and rafters are likely to see moose, deer and antelope.

For more information: Contact the BLM Rock Springs District Office, P.O. Box 1869, Rock Springs, WY 82901; (307) 382-5350.

HONEYCOMB AND OREGON BUTTES
hiking, backpacking, camping, horseback riding

An excellent example of badlands topography with stunning vertical relief. Buttes rise sharply above the low sagebrush hills and greasewood flats. The area features cliffs and caves and offers a good habitat for pronghorn, mule deer, elk, bobcat and coyote. Numerous wild horses also frequent the area. Although there are a few springs and a number of small reservoirs built for livestock, pack all the water you will need, because the area is predominantly dry. Rock hounders will enjoy the opportunity to find agate, jade and petrified wood. From Atlantic City drive ten miles south on State Road 28. Then turn south on Oregon Buttes Road (County 445) and drive for approximately eight miles.

For more information: Contact the BLM Rock Springs District Office, P.O. Box 1869, Highway 191 North, Rock Springs, WY 82901; (307) 382-5350.

USGS topographic maps: Five Fingers Butte, Circle Bar Lake, Bob Jack Well, Continental Peak, Dickie Springs, John Hay Reservoir, Frayer Gap, Pacific Springs

LAKE MOUNTAIN
hiking, camping, fishing, horseback riding, cross-country skiing

This area features a mountainous terrain covered with aspen, Engelmann spruce and Douglas fir. Small meadows lush with wildflowers dot the landscape. Elevations range from 7,400 to 9,600 feet. Wildlife includes elk, deer, moose, black bear, beaver, pika, and ruffed grouse. Good quality streams offer excellent fishing opportunities. From La Barge, head south for one and a half miles on US 189. Then turn west onto County 315. County 315 parallels La Barge Creek and miles 12 to 18 represent the southwest boundary of Lake Mountain.

For more information: Contact the BLM Rock Springs District Office, P.O. Box 1869, Highway 191 North, Rock Springs, WY 82901; (307) 382-5350.

USGS topographic maps: Lake Mountain

NATURAL CORRALS
hiking, volcano tube scrambling, camping

Contrary to popular legend, Butch Cassidy didn't bury his loot here. But that's okay, because the ice caves amid the jumble of huge volcanic boulders is more than worth the time spent visiting. Wear old clothing, long pants and sleeves because volcanic rock is very abrasive. From Interstate 80 and Point of Rocks, head north and then east about eight miles on County Road 4-15 to the Jim Bridger Power Station. After two miles, turn west towards Superior at the Superior cut-off road. After another 3.5 miles, bear right at the fork. From here on, four-wheel-drive vehicles are recommended. After 2.5 miles, a faint track to the left will take you into the site.

For more information: Contact the BLM Rock Springs District Office, P.O. Box 1869, Highway 191 North, Rock Springs, WY 82901; (307) 382-5350.

BLM surface maps: Kinney Rim, Red Desert Basin

RED DESERT
wildlife observation, hiking, backpacking, camping, horseback riding

The Red Desert is a vast treeless area named for the brick-red soil that stretches as far as the eye can see in all directions. Light rainfall and oppressive summer temperatures make this a harsh place, yet it is worth a peek as it is the largest unfenced stretch of open land in the lower 48. In fact, some of the biggest herds of wild horses run free here, alongside herds of wild elk and one of the last remaining herds of wild bison.

The Red Desert is located in the Great Divide Basin west of Rawlins and north of Interstate 80.

For more information: Contact the BLM Rock Springs District Office, P.O. Box 1869, Highway 191 North, Rock Springs, WY 82901; (307) 382-5350.

BLM surface maps: Red Desert Basin

RAYMOND MOUNTAIN

hiking, backpacking, camping, fishing, horseback riding, cross-country skiing, rock climbing, birdwatching

Most who visit this area come for the fishing (Bonneville or Bear River cutthroat trout) or picnicking. For the hiker or backpacker, unless it is hunting season, the area will be largely unpeopled. Water is abundant, but must be purified. Numerous waterfowl are attracted to the area because of Huff Lake and area beaver ponds. Elk, moose and mule deer may be spotted in the region. Camping is allowed anywhere within the area. Raymond Mountain is located near the Wyoming/Idaho border between US 30 and US 89. I advise checking with the BLM for specific access information and road conditions before heading out.

For more information: Contact the BLM Rock Springs District Office, P.O. Box 1869, Highway 191 North, Rock Springs, WY 82901; (307) 382-5350.

USGS topographic maps: Salt Flat, Neugent Park, Big Park, Porcupine Creek

SAND DUNES SPECIAL RECREATION MANAGEMENT AREA

unique natural area, camping, rock climbing, hiking, historic site

This area is at the very heart of the largest active dune field in North America, with the dunes up to 200 feet and under constant change and flux—blown eastward by constant westerly winds. Good skills with a map and compass are essential, if you are to stay on course and really enjoy the five to six miles of hiking it takes to fully appreciate the area. Believe it or not, there are pools of water at the base of many of these dunes, some crystal clear and as deep as seven to eight feet. Mule deer and the area's only herd of desert elk inhabit the sand dunes. The Ord kangaroo rat, coyote, red fox, bobcat, and wild horse also call the moving sands home. The Boar's Tusk, a prominent volcanic plug shaped into a spire, is a favorite of local rock climbers. Shoshone petroglyphs also can be found nearby. From Rock Springs, drive 10 miles north on US 191. Turn right on Tri-Territory Road/County Road 4-17. At the intersection with County Road 4-16, turn left and continue on 4-16 approximately six miles to the site boundary on the right.

For more information: Contact the BLM Rock Springs District Office, P.O. Box 1869, Highway 191 North, Rock Springs, WY 82901; (307) 382-5350.

USGS topographic maps: Boar's Tusk, North Table Mountain, Tule Butte, Ox Yoke Springs, Essex Mountain

SCAB CREEK
SPECIAL RECREATION MANAGEMENT AREA
wildlife observation, hiking, backpacking, horseback riding, rock climbing, fishing, cross-country ski touring

Many visitors utilize this region as a doorstep to the nearby Bridger-Teton National Forest and Bridger Wilderness lake region. The National Outdoor Leadership School uses this area for winter activities. The terrain is characterized by steep and rocky granite outcrops which have been cut and sculpted by glaciers and streams. Off-trail hiking is possible, but very difficult. Orienteering skills and strong map-reading skills are necessary. There is a 2.5-mile maintained trail that receives very heavy use by those heading to the U.S. Forest Service area boundary. The abundant wildlife in this area includes elk, moose, mule deer, black bear, bobcat, mountain lion, coyote, badger, snowshoe hare, and wolverine. From Boulder and US 187, head east seven miles on State Road 353 and then north on County 23-122 and BLM 5423. The roads are dirt and require a high-clearance vehicle when dry, and a four-wheel-drive vehicle when wet.

For more information: Contact the BLM Rock Springs District Office, P.O. Box 1869, Highway 191 North, Rock Springs, WY 82901; (307) 382-5350.

USGS topographic maps: Scab Creek, Raid Lake

SOUTH PASS HISTORIC MINING AREA
SPECIAL RECREATION MANAGEMENT AREA
hiking, mountain biking, limited fishing, historic site

This area is located near Highway 28, approximately 30 miles south of Lander. The state's most notable gold rush began here in the late 1860s. The mining area contains the small town of Atlantic City and the remains of Miner's Delight, another early center of gold mining activity. Prospect pits and abandoned gold mines dot the area and although some small claims continue in operation today, no large scale mining has taken place for years. Amateur geologists will enjoy viewing some of the oldest rocks on the continent which lie exposed. Mule deer, pronghorn antelope and moose make up the most commonly seen wildlife population. There are two developed campgrounds located near Atlantic City. For a brief hike, a quiet fishing trip or a peaceful pedal, follow the trail that leads from South Pass City along Willow Creek.

For more information: Contact the BLM Lander Resource Area, 125 Sunflower Street, Lander, WY 82520; (307) 332-7822.
USGS topographic maps: Lander

WYOMING BY REGION

5

SOUTHEASTERN WYOMING

NORTH PLATTE RIVER
SPECIAL RECREATION MANAGEMENT AREA
wildlife observation, camping, hiking, fishing, canoeing, float boating

A quiet float along a tranquil river, this area offers excellent birding opportunities. The route is an historic one, previously used by Native Americans, explorers and trappers. The river meanders along both public and private lands. Red signs along the river mark the private lands. Blue signs indicate public land and public access points. Waterfowl, shorebirds, raptors, grouse, and numerous songbirds may be viewed. Wildlife includes mule deer, antelope, badger, beaver, muskrat, and rabbit—but keep a sharp eye out as they are reclusive.

This recreation area is located between the towns of Casper and Alcova alongside State Road 220.

For more information: Contact the BLM Casper District Office, 1701 East E Street, Casper, WY 82601; (307) 261-7600.
USGS topographic maps: Goose Egg, Bessemer Mountain, Alcova
Additional map: BLM North Platte River Leaflet

ENCAMPMENT RIVER
hiking, backpacking, fishing, wildlife observation

More of a large stream than a river, the Encampment River area is an awesome combination of rugged, unpopulated canyon country framed by a variety of woodland and riparian settings. The BLM section provides a fitting four-mile introduction to the 16-mile route—the remaining miles belong to the Medicine Bow National Forest. Brook, brown and native trout roam the waterways, offering the angler a super fishing opportunity for rainbow, brown and brook trout. Spending any less than two days in this area is a mistake as the rushing rapids, interspersed with tranquil waters, create an almost undeniable desire to kick up the feet and let time slip away amid a unique wilderness setting.

For more information: Contact the BLM Rawlins District Office, 1300 Third Street, P.O. Box 670, Rawlins, WY 82302; (307) 324-7171. Hayden Ranger District, Medicine Bow National Forest, 204 West Ninth Street, Encampment, WY 82325; (307) 327-5481.
BLM surface map: Saratoga

FERRIS MOUNTAINS
hiking, backpacking, wildlife observation, wildflowers

Although this is a wilderness area beyond compare (no roads or even trails—it's all cross-country here), access is practically nonexistent—a problem throughout Wyoming. The peaks range from 8,000 to 10,000 feet, and are cut with deep canyons, crystal clear streams, wildflowers galore and sweetly scented pine forests. Go for it, but you must absolutely contact the BLM first to gain accurate and up-to-date access information.

•**See also Best of the State, page 478**•
For more information: Contact the BLM Rawlins District Office, 1300 Third Street, P.O. Box 670, Rawlins, WY 82302; (307) 324-7171.

GARDEN CREEK FALLS
hiking

As long as you happen to be in the Casper area, a detour to the Garden Creek Falls is well worth the time and effort—especially in the spring when the falls truly resemble a cascade. Expect to find hordes of locals on weekends as this is a "hot" picnic and party spot. To get there from Interstate 25, turn south onto State Highway 258/Wyoming Boulevard. Drive around the southern reaches of Casper for approximately 6.5 miles to a stoplight at the intersection with Highway 251 and Casper Mountain Road. Follow Highway 251 south and uphill to Highway 252. Turn right and drive for three-tenths of a mile, keeping a sharp eye out for a blue Rotary Park sign indicating a road heading left to the parking area for Garden Creek Falls.

For more information: Contact the BLM Casper District Office, 1701 East E Street, Casper, WY 82601; (307) 261-7600.
USGS topographic maps: Casper
BLM surface maps: Casper

MUDDY MOUNTAIN
SPECIAL RECREATION MANAGEMENT AREA
hiking, backpacking, nature study, wildlife observation, snowmobiling, cross-country skiing, camping

Two campgrounds, a picnic area and good access make this an attractive recreational destination for anyone living in or visiting the Casper area. Cool in the summer and snowy in the winter, this region is a recreational playground. Located approximately 12 miles south of Casper on State Road 251. Muddy Mountain, within the recreation management area, is closed from the first major snowfall until June 1 to protect an elk calving area from disturbance, as well as to protect against possible road and trail damage.

For more information: Contact the BLM Casper District Office, 1701 East E Street, Casper, WY 82601; (307) 261-7600.
USGS topographic maps: Crimson Dawn

PATHFINDER RESERVOIR
camping, hiking, fishing, canoeing, boating, swimming

Fishing and birdwatching are the most popular activities in this region. Camping is allowed anywhere outside the signed

Pathfinder National Wildlife Refuge. Fishing is for brown, brook, and rainbow trout and walleye pike. Located on the North Platte River and linked to the Alcova Reservoir downstream by the "miracle mile" or more formally, Fremont Canyon. Miracle mile is so named because it is a trout fishery of outstanding quality. To get there, drive approximately 36 miles west on State Road 220 and then drive south on County Road 409 for eight miles.

For more information: Contact the BLM Casper District Office, 1701 East E Street, Casper, WY 82601; (307) 261-7600.

SWEETWATER CANYON
hiking, backpacking, fishing, wildlife observation

This canyon is a wilderness study area with excellent opportunities for fishing. Solitude and quiet abound amid an area that features remarkable geology.

For more information: Contact the BLM Lander Resource Area, P.O. Box 589, Lander, WY 82520; (307) 332-7822.

SWEETWATER ROCKS
hiking, backpacking, camping, rock climbing, rock hounding

Sweetwater Rocks is known around the U.S. as a super climbing spot, primarily because of the gigantic granite slabs, domes and spires. The terrain is rugged and mountainous—it is no wonder the National Outdoor Leadership School uses this area as a training site. Both Lankin Dome and McIntosh Peak are well-recognized climbing spots. If you are not going to be climbing, don't despair; the region is well suited for exploration on foot as well. In addition, the birding is excellent. However, access is challenging to say the least. Your best bet is to contact the BLM office for current access and road condition information before heading out. I recommend the following: From Jeffrey City, drive approximately seven miles east on US 287 and then head northeast on Agate Flat Road/BLM 2004—this road runs along the west edge of the region.

For more information: Contact the BLM Rawlins District Office, P.O. Box 670, 1300 North Third Street, Rawlins, WY 82301; (307) 324-7171.
USGS topographic maps: Rattlesnake Hills

STATE INFORMATION OVERVIEW

WYOMING STATE OFFICE
2515 Warren Avenue, P.O. Box 1828, Cheyenne, WY 82003; (307) 775-6BLM

CASPER DISTRICT OFFICE
1701 East E Street, Casper, WY 82601; (307) 261-7600

Platte River Resource Area, 815 Connie Street, Mills, WY 82644; (307) 261-5191

Buffalo Resource Area, 189 North Cedar, Buffalo, WY 82834; (307) 684-5586

Newcastle Resource Area, 1501 Highway 16 Bypass, Newcastle, WY 82701; (307) 746-4453

RAWLINS DISTRICT OFFICE
P.O. Box 670, 1300 North Third Street, Rawlins, WY 82301; (307) 324-7171

Great Divide Resource Area, 1719 Edinburgh, Rawlins, WY 82301; (307) 324-4841

Lander Resource Area, 125 Sunflower Street, Lander, WY 82520; (307) 332-7822

ROCK SPRINGS DISTRICT OFFICE
P.O. Box 1869, Highway 191 North, Rock Springs, WY 82901; (307) 382-5350

Green River Resource Area, 79 Winston Drive, Rock Springs, WY 82902; (307) 362-6422

Kemmerer Resource Area, P.O. Box 632, Kemmerer, WY 83101; (307) 877-3933

Pinedale Resource Area, 431 West Pine Street, Pinedale, WY 82941; (307) 367-4358

WORLAND DISTRICT OFFICE
P.O. Box 119, 101 South 23rd Street, Worland, WY 82401;
(307) 347-9871

Grass Creek Resource Area, P.0. Box 119, 101 South 23rd
Street, Worland, WY 82401; (307) 347-9871

Washakie Resource Area, P.0. Box 119, 101 South 23rd Street,
Worland, WY 82401; (307) 347-9871

Cody Resource Area, 1714 Stampede Avenue, Cody, WY
82414; (307) 587-2216

Index

Index

Index

A

APPENDICES

RECREATIONAL ACTIVITIES BY STATE

The following listings show major outdoor recreation activities in BLM lands according to activity and state. See the corresponding page numbers for more information on each activity.

WILDLIFE OBSERVATION

ALASKA
Denali Highway—p. 64-65
Gulkana National Wild and Scenic River—p. 66
Dalton Highway—p. 70
Steese Highway Conservation Area—p. 79
Seward Peninsula—p. 60, 69
Kasegaluk Lagoon—p. 80-81
Teshekpuk Lake—p. 81-82

ARIZONA
Betty's Kitchen—p. 117
Gila Box Riparian National Conservation Area—p. 94-96
Virgin River Canyon—p. 93
Paria Canyon/Vermillion Wilderness—p. 98-101
Aravaipa Canyon Wilderness—p. 118-119
Empire/Cienega Resource Conservation Area—p. 119
Burro Creek—p. 110-111

CALIFORNIA
Desert Tortoise Natural Area—p. 171-172
Cache Creek—p. 155
Carrizo Plain Natural Area—p. 140-141
Big Morongo Canyon Preserve—p. 170

COLORADO
Georgetown Bighorn Sheep Viewing Area—p. 205
Arkansas River—p. 219
Powderhorn Wilderness Study Area—p. 186-188
Rabbit Valley-Brewster Ridge—p. 205
Dolores River—p. 189-191

IDAHO
Wolf Lodge Bay—p. 246-247
Snake River Birds of Prey Area—p. 238-240
Snake River Plain—p. 240-243
Summit Lake—p. 313

MONTANA
Upper Missouri Wild and Scenic River—p. 270-272
Big Sheep Creek-Medicine Lodge Valley—p. 281-282
Howrey Island—p. 278-279

NEVADA
Brown Knoll—p. 322-323
Ely Elk Viewing Area—p. 310-311
Goshute Mountains—p. 303-304
Red Rock Canyon National Conservation Area—p. 304-306
Mahogany Creek—p. 313-314
Ash Springs—p. 322
Fish Lake Valley—p. 323

NEW MEXICO
El Malpais National Conservation Area—p. 336-338
Wild Rivers Recreation Area—p. 344-346
Gila River—p. 358-359
Organ Mountains—p. 342-344

OREGON
North Umpqua Wild and Scenic River—p. 381-382
Rogue Wild and Scenic River—p. 374-375
Leslie Gulch—p. 384-386
Yaquina Head Outstanding Natural Area—p. 394-395
Steens Mountain—p. 372-374
Dean Creek Elk Viewing Area—p. 388

HIKING/BACKPACKING

CALIFORNIA
Fort Sage Loop—p. 157
Afton Canyon—p. 169-170
Butte Creek Trail—p. 156-157
Bizz Johnson Trail—p. 136, 155
Pacific Crest Trail—p. 163
Fossil Falls—p. 174

COLORADO
San Luis Valley—p. 220
Upper Colorado River—p. 211
Gunnison Gorge—p. 198
Uncompahgre Plateau—p. 200-201

IDAHO
Mineral Ridge Trail—p. 246

MONTANA
Humbug Spires Wilderness Study Area—p. 283
Square Butte—p. 277-278
Bear Trap Canyon—p. 264-265
Garnet Recreation Trail System—p. 268-270

NEVADA
Red Rock Canyon National Conservation Area—p. 304-306
High Rock Canyon—p. 294-296
Pine Forest Range—p. 292-294
Desatoya-Clan Alpine Mountains—p. 298-299

NEW MEXICO
El Malpais National Conservation Area—p. 336-338
Wild Rivers National Recreation Area—p. 344-346
Baylor Pass National Recreation Trail—p. 343
Pine Tree National Recreation Trail—p. 343
Tent Rocks Area of Critical Environmental
          Concern—p. 355-357
Rio Grande Wild and Scenic River area—p. 354

OREGON

UTAH

WASHINGTON

WYOMING

MOUNTAIN BIKING

ALASKA
Tangle Lakes area—p. 61-63
Denali Highway—p. 64-65

ARIZONA
Black Hills Trail—p. 96-97
Empire Cienega Resource Conservation Area—p. 119

CALIFORNIA
Cache Creek—p. 155
Gene Chappie/Shasta—p. 157
Buckhorn Canyon—p. 155
Afton Canyon—p. 169-170
Cow Mountain—p. 156
Alabama Hills—p. 161-162
Spangler Hills—p. 178
King Range National Conservation Area—p. 138-140
Indian Valley/Walker Ridge—p. 157-158

COLORADO
Tabeguache Trail—p. 200-203
Rangely Loop Trail—p. 209
Yampa Valley Trail—p. 211
Alpine Loop—p. 212
Kokopelli's Trail—p. 203-204
Dolores River Canyon—p. 189

IDAHO
Marble Creek—p. 244
Quigley Canyon Trail—p. 235

MONTANA
Garnet Recreational Trail—p. 268-270

NEVADA
Red Rock Canyon National Conservation Area—p. 304-306
Black Rock Desert—p. 307-308
Pine Forest Range—p. 292-294
Wendover Spring—p. 303

NEW MEXICO
El Malpais National Conservation Area—p. 336-338
Tent Rocks—p. 355-357

OREGON
Hyatt Lake—p. 389-390
Klamath River—p. 383-384
North Umpqua Trail—p. 381-382

UTAH
Woolverine Loop Route—p. 416
Great Western Trail—p. 427
Kokopelli's Trail—p. 420, 435

WASHINGTON
Lakeview Ranch—p. 461
Fishtrap—p. 460
Saddle Mountain—p. 463-464
Douglas Creek—p. 459
Goose Butte—p. 460

WYOMING
Adobe Town Wilderness Study Area—p. 492

RAFTING/CANOEING/ KAYAKING

ALASKA

White Mountains National Recreation Area—p. 70-71
Birch Creek—p. 79
Delta River, Tangle Lakes—p. 65-66
Fortymile River—p. 79-80
Gulkana River, Tangle Lakes—p. 66-68
Squirrel River—p. 82-83
Teshekpuk Lake—p. 81-82
Kasegaluk Lagoon—p. 80-81

ARIZONA

Gila Box Riparian National Conservation Area—p. 94-96

CALIFORNIA

Eel River—p. 144-146
Trinity River—p. 146-147
South Yuba River—p. 168
Lower Kern River—p. 165
Upper Klamath River—p. 148-149
Sacramento River—p. 160
American River—p. 142-144
Tuolumne River—p. 150-151
Merced River—p. 165

COLORADO

Arkansas River—p. 219
Upper Colorado River—p. 211
Yampa Valley—p. 211
San Luis Valley—p. 220

IDAHO

Bruneau River—p. 232-234
Jarbidge River—p. 252
Salmon River—p. 236-238
Snake River—p. 240-241
Owyhee River—p. 229-230

MONTANA
Madison River—p. 264
Upper Missouri National Wild and Scenic River—p. 270-271

NEVADA
Owyhee River—p. 300-303

NEW MEXICO
Rio Grande Wild and Scenic River—p. 344-346
Rio Chama Wild and Scenic River—p. 353-354

OREGON
New River—p. 391
McKenzie River—p. 390
Klamath River—p. 383-384
John Day River—p. 399
Rogue River Canyon—p. 374-376
North Umpqua River—p. 381-382

UTAH
Westwater Canyon—p. 419-421
Desolation Canyon—p. 421-423
Dolores River—p. 419
San Juan River—p. 425-426
Labyrinth Canyon—p. 423-425

WASHINGTON
Pend Oreille River Canyon—p. 453-454
Kettle River—p. 461
Yakima River Canyon—p. 454-455
Methow River—p. 462
Palmer Lake—p. 464
Chopaka Lake—p. 457-458
Columbia River-Hanford Reach—p. 458-459
San Juan Islands—p. 456

WYOMING
North Platte River Special Recreation Area—p. 497-498
Upper Sweetwater River—p. 482
Encampment River—p. 476-477
Green River—p. 493
Bighorn River—p. 484

ROCK CLIMBING

ARIZONA
Baboquivari Peak—p. 122-123
Paiute Wilderness—p. 92-94

COLORADO
Penitente Canyon—p. 220-221

IDAHO
Silent City of Rocks National Reserve—p. 228-229
Twin Sisters—p. 228

MONTANA
Humbug Spires—p. 266-267

NEVADA
Mount Grafton—p. 318-319
Goshute Canyon—p. 316-317
Red Rock Canyon National Conservation Area—p. 304-306
South Egan Range—p. 328

NEW MEXICO
Organ Mountain—p. 342-344
Ignacio Chavez/Chamisa Wilderness Study Area—p. 350-351
Ojito Wilderness Study Area—p. 351

WYOMING
Sweetwater Rocks—p. 500

SPELUNKING

COLORADO
Deep Creek—p. 206

IDAHO
The Great Rift—p. 240-243

MONTANA
Pryor Mountain National Wild Horse Range—p. 279

NEVADA
Goshute Canyon—p. 316-317
South Egan Range—p. 328
Meadow Valley Range and Mormon Mountains—p. 325-326

NEW MEXICO
Fort Stanton Cave—p. 363
Chosa Draw—p. 363

OREGON
Christmas Valley—p. 395-396

UTAH
Gandy Mountain Cave—p. 429
Crystal Ball Cave—p. 429

WYOMING
Horsethief Cave—p. 480-481
Titan Caverns—p. 490
Natural Trap—p. 490
Spirit Mountain Caverns—p. 491
Holey Sheep Cave—p. 491
Tres Charros—p. 491
Great Expectations Cave System—p. 472

WINTER RECREATION/ CROSS COUNTY SKIING

ALASKA
Tangle Lakes area—p. 61-63
White Mountains National Recreation Area—p. 70-71
Kigluaik Mountains—p. 59-61

MONTANA
Garnet Recreation Trail System—p. 268-270

OREGON
Table Mountain Snow-Play Area—p. 390
Hyatt Lake—p. 389-390

ORDERING MAPS

A good map, or series of maps, is worth its weight in gold. Here's how to get the maps you'll need:

USFS MAPS
There is no single location for ordering Forest Service maps. By contacting state USFS offices, however, you will be able to obtain maps pertaining to the various national forests in each state. Many USFS lands abut BLM lands, so USFS maps may provide you with useful road and trail access information for traveling on BLM lands.

USGS TOPOGRAPHIC MAPS
You can obtain a USGS map catalog and all topographic maps for the western U.S. by mail from:

> Western Distribution Branch
> U.S. Geologic Survey
> Box 25286, Federal Center, Building 41
> Denver, CO 80225

In addition, many sporting goods stores, map centers and outdoor outfitters carry select USGS topographic maps pertaining to their region.

PRIVATE SOURCES FOR MAPS
•Trails Illustrated, P.O. Box 3610, Evergreen, CO 80439; (800) 962-1643.
•Map Link, 25 East Mason Street, Santa Barbara, CA 93101; (805) 965-4402.

BLM MAPS
The following pages show the Bureau of Land Management Surface Map Indexes for each state. Use them as a guide to order maps for areas that I have highlighted within this book, or to order maps for surrounding areas. When ordering maps, specify that you want the BLM surface management series with topographic relief. Map prices vary depending on map type and size, ranging from $3.50 to $5.00.

Order BLM maps by contacting each state's office. See the State Information Overview at the end of each chapter for the address and phone number of the main state office.

ARIZONA BLM MAPS

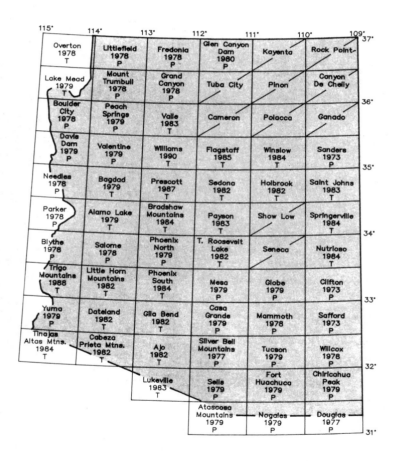

Overton 1978 T	Littlefield 1978 P	Fredonia 1978 P	Glen Canyon Dam 1980 P	Kayenta	Rock Point
Lake Mead 1979 T	Mount Trumbull 1978 P	Grand Canyon 1978 P	Tuba City	Pinon	Canyon De Chelly
Boulder City 1978 P	Peach Springs 1979 P	Valle 1983 T	Cameron	Polacca	Ganado
Davis Dam 1979 P	Valentine 1979 P	Williams 1990 T	Flagstaff 1985 T	Winslow 1984 T	Sanders 1973 P
Needles 1978 P	Bagdad 1979 T	Prescott 1987 T	Sedona 1982 T	Holbrook 1982 T	Saint Johns 1983 T
Parker 1978 P	Alamo Lake 1979 T	Bradshaw Mountains 1984 T	Payson 1983 T	Show Low	Springerville 1984 T
Blythe 1978 P	Salome 1978 P	Phoenix North 1979 P	T. Roosevelt Lake 1982 T	Seneca	Nutrioso 1984 T
Trigo Mountains 1988 T	Little Horn Mountains 1982 T	Phoenix South 1984 T	Mesa 1979 P	Globe 1979 P	Clifton 1973 P
Yuma 1979 P	Dateland 1982 T	Gila Bend 1982 T	Casa Grande 1979 P	Mammoth 1978 P	Safford 1973 P
Tinajas Altas Mtns. 1984 T	Cabeza Prieta Mtns. 1982 T	Ajo 1982 T	Silver Bell Mountains 1977 P	Tucson 1979 P	Willcox 1978 P
		Lukeville 1983 T	Sells 1979 P	Fort Huachuca 1979 P	Chiricahua Peak 1979 P
			Atascosa Mountains 1979 P	Nogales 1979 P	Douglas 1977 P

California BLM Maps

COLORADO BLM MAPS

108°	107°	106°	105°	104°	103°	102°
Canyon of Ladore 1988	Craig 1988	Walden 1985	Fort Collins 1988	Eaton 1986 S	Sterling 1978 P	Julesburg 1978 P
Rangely 1987	Meeker 1988	Steamboat Springs 1988	Estes Park 1986	Greeley 1986 S	Fort Morgan 1978 P	Wray 1986 S
Douglas Pass 1987	Glenwood Springs 1988	Vail 1985	Denver West 1986	Denver East 1986 S	Last Chance 1978 P	Bonny Reservoir 1978 P
Grand Junction 1985	Carbondale 1988	Leadville 1985	Bailey 1986	Castle Rock 1986 S	Limon 1985 S	Burlington 1982 S
Delta 1985	Paonia 1985	Gunnison 1986	Pikes Peak 1986	Colorado Springs 1985	Karval 1987 S	Cheyenne Wells 1987 S
Nucla 1985	Montrose 1986	Saguache 1988	Canon City 1988	Pueblo 1985	Las Animas 1977 S	Lamar 1982 P
Dove Creek 1986	Silverton 1986	Del Norte 1986	Blanca Peak 1986	Walsenburg 1986	La Junta 1986 S	Two Buttes Reservoir 1977 P
Cortez 1986	Durango 1986	Antonito 1987	Alamosa 1988	Trinidad 1988	Kim 1987 S	Springfield 1977 S,P

(latitudes along right side: 41°, 40°, 39°, 38°, 37°)

IDAHO BLM MAPS

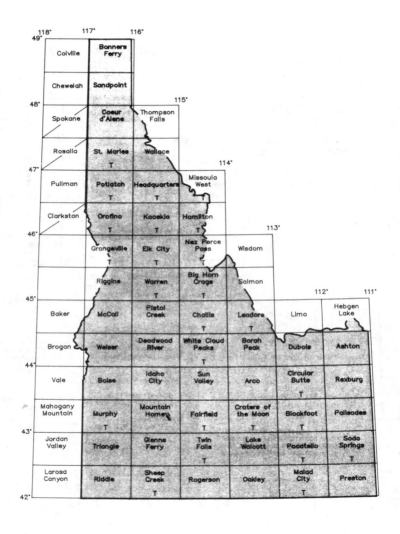

MONTANA BLM MAPS

Ophiem | Whitewater | Harlem | Havre | Chester | Sweetgrass Hills P | Cut Bank P | Saint Mary | Whitefish Range | Yak River | Bonner's Ferry

Glasgow | Malta | Dodson | Rocky Boy | Lonesome Lake P | Conrad P | Valier | Hungry Horse Reservoir | Kalispell | Libby | Sandpoint

Fort Peck Lake East | Fort Peck Lake West RAG | Zortman RAG | Winifred | Fort Benton P | Great Falls North P | Choteau | Swan Peak | Polson | Thompson Falls | Coeur D'Alene

Jordan | Sand Springs RAG | Winnett RAG | Lewistown | Belt P | Great Falls South P | Dearborn River P | Seely Lake | Plains | Wallace

Angela | Melstone | Musselshell | Big Snowy Mountains P | White Sulphur Springs P | Canyon Ferry Dam P | Elliston P | Missoula East | Missoula West | Headquarters

Foryeth | Hysham | Roundup | Harlowton P | Ringling P | Townsend P | Butte North P | Phillipsburg | Hamilton

Lame Deer | Hardin | Billings | Big Timber P | Livingston P | Bozeman P | Butte South P | Wisdom | Nez Perce

Birney | Lodge Grass | Bridger | Red Lodge P | Gardiner P | Ennis P | Dillon | Salmon | Leadore | Borah Peak

Sheridan | Burgess Junction | Powell | Cody | Yellowstone Park | Hebgen Lake P | Lima | Dubois | Ashton

NEVADA BLM MAPS

Vya 1979	Denio 1979	Quinn River Valley 1979	Bull Run Mountains 1978	Jarbidge Mountains 1979	Jackpot 1978
High Rock Canyon 1974	Jackson Mountains 1978	Osgood Mountains 1979	Tuscarora 1979	Double Mountains 1978	Wells 1979
Gerlach 1976	Eugene Mountains 1975	Winnemucca 1978	Battle Mountain 1975	Elko 1976	Wendover 1979
Kumiva Peak 1974	Lovelock 1978	Fish Creek Mountains 1978	Crescent Valley 1979	Ruby Lake 1978	Currie 1979
Reno 1975	Carson Sink 1974	Edwards Creek Valley 1975	Simpson Park Mtns. 1979	Newark Lake 1985	Kern Mountains 1976
Carson City 1975	Fallon 1978	Smith Creek Valley 1975	Summit Mountain 1978	Mount Hamilton 1979	Ely 1977
Smith Valley 1978	Walker Lake 1978	Ione Valley 1978	Mount Jefferson 1978	Duckwater 1978	Garrison 1979
Bridgeport 1975	Excelsior Mountains 1973	Tonopah 1978	Warm Springs 1978	Quinn Can. Range 1978	Wilson Cr. Range 1979
	Benton Range 1976	Goldfield 1978	Cactus Flat 1978	Timpahute Range 1977	Caliente 1978
		Last Chance Range 1978	Pahute Mesa 1979	Pahranagat Range 1978	Clover Mountains 1978
		Saline Valley 1976	Beatty 1978	Indian Springs 1979	Overton 1978
			Death Valley Jct. 1978	Las Vegas 1978	Lake Mead 1978
				Mesquite Lake 1979	Boulder City 1978
				Ivanpah 1979	Davis Dam 1979

NEW MEXICO BLM MAPS

Farmington	Navajo Reservoir	Chama	Wheeler Peak	Raton	Capulin Mountains
Toadlena	Chaco Canyon	Abiquiu	Taos	Springer	Clayton
Gallup	Chaco Mesa	Los Alamos	Santa Fe	Roy	Mosquero
Zuni	Grants	Albuquerque	Villanueva	Conchas Lake	Tucumcari
Fence Lake	Acoma Pueblo	Belen	Vaughn	Santa Rosa	The Caprock
Quemado	Magdalena	Socorro	Corona	Fort Sumner	Clovis
Tularosa Mountains	San Mateo Mountains	Oscura Mountains	Carrizozo	Salt Creek	Elida
Mogollon Mountains	Truth or Consequences	Tularosa	Ruidoso	Roswell	Tatum
Silver City	Hatch	White Sands	Alamogordo	Artesia	Hobbs
Lordsburg	Deming	Las Cruces	Crow Flats	Carlsbad	Jal
Animas	Columbus	El Paso			

Sanders
Clifton
Safford
Chiricahua Peak
Douglas
Alamo Hueco Mountains

37° 36° 35° 34° 33° 32° 31°
110° 109° 108° 107° 106° 105° 104° 103°

OREGON BLM MAPS

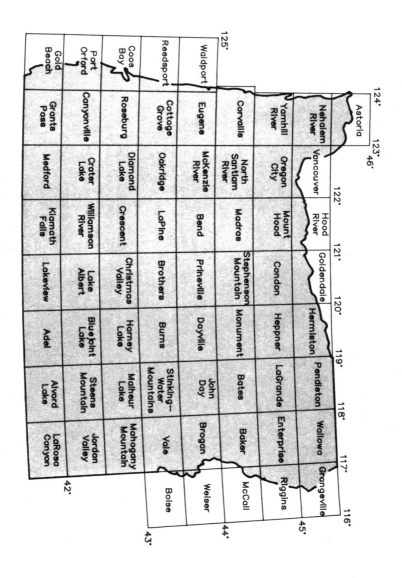

UTAH BLM MAPS

	115°	114°	113°	112°	111°	110°	109°
42°	Jackpot	Grouse Creek NT	Tremonton NT	Logan			
41°	Wells	Newfoundland Mountains	Promontory Peak NT	Ogden NT			
	Wendover	Bonneville	Tooele	Salt Lake City	Kings Peak	Dutch John	
40°	Currie	Wildcat Mountain	Rush Valley	Provo NT	Duschene	Vernal	
	Kern Mountains	Fish Springs	Lynndyl	Nephi	Price	Seep Ridge	
39°	Ely	Tule Valley	Delta	Manti	Huntington	West Water	
	Garrison	Wah Wah North	Richfield	Salina	San Rafael	Moab	
38°	Wilson Creek	Wah Wah South	Beaver	Loa	Hanksville	La Sal	
	Caliente	Cedar City	Panguitch	Escalante	Hite Crossing	Blanding	
37°	Clover Mountains	Saint George	Kanab	Smokey Mountain	Navajo Mountain	Bluff	

WASHINGTON BLM MAPS

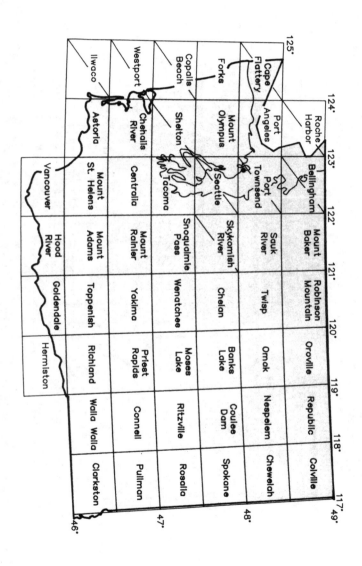

WYOMING BLM MAPS

111°	110°	109°	108°	107°	106°	105°	104°
Yellowstone National Park North	Cody	Powell	Burgess Junction	Sheridan	Recluse	Devil's Tower	45°
Yellowstone National Park South	Carter Mountain	Basin	Worland	Buffalo	Gillette	Sundance	
Jackson Lake	The Ramshorn	Thermopolis	Nowater Creek	Kaycee	Reno Junction	Newcastle	44°
Jackson	Gannett Peak	Riverton	Lysite	Midwest	Bill	Lance Creek	
Afton	Pinedale	Lander	Rattlesnake Hills	Casper	Douglas	Lusk	43°
Fontenelle Reservoir	Farson	South Pass	Bairoll	Shirley Basin	Laramie Peak	Torrington	
Kemmerer	Rock Springs	Red Desert Basin	Rawlins	Medicine Bow	Rock River	Chugwater	42°
Evanston	Firehole Canyon	Kinney Rim	Baggs	Saratoga	Laramie	Cheyenne	41°

The following are clubs, environmental organizations, and other state-wide affiliates that are active in trail and land preservation. Many of them are excellent sources of detailed trail and regional information, and some even offer maps and other published information.

HIKING AND OUTDOOR ORGANIZATIONS

ALASKA
Alaska Wilderness Guides Association, P.O. Box 141061, Anchorage, AK 99514; (907) 276-6634

ARIZONA
American Hiking Society Affiliates
•Central Arizona Backpackers Association, 5 South Pueblo Street Gilbert, AZ 85234
•Green Valley Hiking Club, 1601 West Placita Embate, Green Valley, AZ 85614
•Huachuca Hiking Club, P.O. Box 1256, Spokane, WA 99210

Arizona Wilderness Coalition, P.O. Box 60576, Phoenix, AZ 85082; (602) 254-9330

Arizona Rivers Coalition, 3601 North Seventh Avenue, Phoenix, AZ 85719; (602) 264-1823

CALIFORNIA
American Hiking Society Affiliates
•Berkeley Hiking Club, Box 147, Berkeley, CA 94701
•Coastal Conservancy, 1330 Broadway #1100, Oakland, CA 94612
•Contra Costa Hills Club, c/o YWCA, 1515 Webster #434, Oakland, CA 94612
•Diablo Hiking Club, 3424 Sentinel, Martinez, CA 94553
•Hayward Hiking Club, PO Box 367, Hayward, CA 94543
•Heritage Trails, 5301 Pine Hollow Road, Concord, CA 94521
•La Canada Flint Ridge Trail Council, P.O. Box 852, La Canada-Flint, CA 91022

Friends of the River, Fort Mason Center, Building C, San Francisco, CA 94123; (415) 771-0400

California Wilderness Coalition, 2655 Portage Bay East, Suite 5, Davis, CA 95616; (916) 758-0380

California Desert Protection League, 3550 West Sixth Street, Suite 323, Los Angeles, CA 90020

COLORADO
American Hiking Society Affiliate
• Colorado Mountain Club, 2530 West Alameda Avenue, Denver, CO 80219; (303) 922-8315

Colorado Environmental Coalition, 777 Grant Street, Suite 606, Denver, CO 80203; (303) 837-8701

High Country Citizens Alliance, Box 1066, Crested Butte, CO 81224; (303) 349-7104

Volunteers for Outdoor Colorado, 1410 Grant Street, Denver, CO 80203; (303) 830-7792

Wilderness Society, 777 Grant Street, #606, Denver, CO 80203; (303) 989-1175

IDAHO
Committee For Idaho's High Desert, P.O. Box 463, Boise, ID 83701

Idaho Sportsman's Coalition, Box 4264, Boise, ID 83711; (208) 336-7222

MONTANA
Montana Wilderness Associates, Box 635, Helena, MT 59624; (406) 443-7350

Friends of the Bitterroot, Box 422, Hamilton, MT 59840

NEVADA
Nevada Outdoor Recreation Association, P.O. Box 1245, Carson City, NV 89702; (702) 883-1169

NEW MEXICO
American Hiking Society Affiliates
•New Mexico Mountain Club, 119 40th Street NW, Albuquerque, NM 87105

New Mexico BLM Wilderness Coalition, P.O. Box 712, Placitas, NM 87043; (505) 867-3062

OREGON
American Hiking Society Affiliates
•Chemeketans, P.O. Box 864, Salem, OR 97308
•Desert Trail Association, Box 589, Burns, OR 97720
•Pacific Crest Trail Conference, 365 West 29th Avenue, Eugene, OR 97405

Oregon Natural Resources Council, 1050 Yeon Building, 522 Southwest Fifth Avenue, Portland, OR 97204; (503) 223-9001

UTAH
Southern Utah Wilderness Alliance, Box 518, Cedar City, UT 84721; (801) 586-8242

Utah Wilderness Coalition, P.O. Box 11446, Salt Lake City, UT 84147; (801) 532-5959

Wasatch Mountain Club, 888 South. 200 East, Salt Lake City, UT 84106; (801) 363-7150

WASHINGTON
American Hiking Society Affiliates
•Chinook Trail Association, P.O. Box 997, Vancouver, WA 98666
•Hobnailers Hiking Club, P.O. Box 1256, Spokane, WA 99210
•Washington Trails Association, 1305 Fourth Avenue, #512, Seattle, WA 98101

WYOMING
Wyoming Wildlife Federation, Box 106, Cheyenne, WY 82003

MOUNTAIN BICYCLING CLUBS

NATIONAL
International Mountain Bike Association, P.O. Box 412043, Los Angeles, CA 90410; (818) 792-8830

WOMBATS (Womens' Mountain Biking and Tea Society); P.O. Box 757, Fairfax, CA 94930; (510) 459-0980

National Off Road Mountain Bike Association, One Olympia Plaza, Colorado Springs, CO 80909; (719) 578-4717

ALASKA
Mountain Bikers of Alaska, 2900 Boniface Parkway #657, Anchorage, AK 99504; (907) 345-3960

ARIZONA
ORBA, 9542 East Duncan, Mesa, AZ 85207; (602) 984-6072

PIMA Trails Association, 5560 Paseo de la Tirada, Tucson, AZ 85715; (602) 577-2095

CALIFORNIA
Desert Off-Road Bicycle Group, 2150 Deborah, Palm Springs, CA 92262

Pasadena Mountain Bike Club, P.O. Box 6101, Altadena, CA 91001; (818) 794-3187

NEW MEXICO
Cruces Cactus Cyclists, 700 South Telshor #1012, Las Cruces, NM 88001; (505) 521-1686

OREGON
Disciples of Dirt, 2848 Greentree Way, Eugene, OR 97405; (503) 485-8929

PUMP, 2148 Northeast Schulyer, Portland, OR 97212; (503) 288-9627

WASHINGTON

Alki Bicycle Club, 2722 Alki Avenue S.W., Seattle, WA 98116; (206) 938-3322

Mountain Bike Specialists, 5625 University Way N.E., Seattle, WA 98105; (206) 527-4310

AMERICAN
DISCOVERY TRAIL

The American Discovery Trail, a brainchild of both the American Hiking Society and *Backpacker Magazine,* was turned from dream into reality on July 30, 1991 when the ADT scouting team completed a 14-month, 4,820-mile, coast-to-coast trek. (A significant portion of the hike crosses BLM lands across the West.) However, while the hike has been completed and legislation has been introduced to begin the process of designating this route as a National Scenic Trail, the real work is just beginning—creating a permanent corridor for the ADT.

As in the early days of the Appalachian Trail (it took nearly half a century to finish that trail), the ADT follows dirt roads and quiet byways. Trail supporters hope to get much of the trail moved off-road, which will require the help of local hiking clubs and others committed to seeing the ADT blazed officially across mountains, forests and prairies.

To that end, Foghorn Press and I are putting our money where our mouths are and donating a portion of the proceeds from the sale of *America's Secret Recreation Areas* to the American Discovery Trail. By purchasing this book, you have indirectly helped the American Hiking Society and all Americans realize the reality of a coast-to-coast trail. Want to do more? That's easy.

You can become an official part of the American Discovery Trail team by sending a $20 check (payable to the American Discovery Trail) to: American Discovery Trail, c/o American Hiking Society, P.O. Box 20160, Washington, DC 20077-0110. In return, you will receive official ADT updates, a subscription to *American Hiker* (the American Hiking Society's official publication), the American Hiking Society newsletter, and a free ADT decal.

NATIONAL TRAILS DAY

Scheduled to draw public attention to the National Trails System Act (celebrating its 25th anniversary on October 3, 1993), the first annual National Trails Day (NTD) is an attempt to unite all trail users, trail advocates, and the outdoor industry in a day of trails awareness nationwide.

"The goal of National Trails Day (the first one will be celebrated on June 5, 1993) is to make Americans more aware of the potential for developing and utilizing an interconnected and nationwide system of trails," states Bruce Ward, vice president of the American Hiking Society and outreach coordinator for REI in Denver, Colorado.

According to the American Hiking Society, 155 million people walk for pleasure; 93 million bicycle; 41 million hike; 43 million use trails for nature study, photography, small game hunting or primitive camping; 10 million ride horses on trails; five million backpack; and 11 million cross-country ski.

Through increased awareness and advocacy, it is hoped that a network of trails can be created nationwide that will provide all Americans access to local trails within 15 minutes of their homes. Cities such as Seattle, Miami, Missoula, Los Angeles, San Francisco and Portland, Maine have been active in creating such trail networks or greenbelts.

Getting involved with NTD is far more than just getting involved with a day of celebration, according to David Lillard, national director for NTD .

"I really see this as a kind of social revolution," says Lillard. "We are saying that trailways will bring together a wide range of community interests, including the needs of the community at large. By blurring the line between transportation and recreation, we are finding that trails are vital links between community facilities as well as between outdoor recreation areas."

The need for trails to become a critical part of a community's planning process is underscored by the fact that trail use is growing at an incredible rate. The U.S. Forest Service expects that day-hiking use will increase 93% over the next 50 years—incredible when you realize that presently, over 155 million Americans walk for pleasure.

The bottom line for ensuring long-term success instead of short-term sizzle, however, is the outdoor industry's and public's commitment to the national event and other similar events scheduled annually.

Kathleen Beamer, REI's public affairs director, sums up the importance of your participation this way: "(Public) involvement in trails and conservation ensures that places remain where people can escape to the outdoors and enjoy the solitude, challenge and beauty that makes this country so special."

The American Hiking Society, heavily behind the promotion and organization of this event, is ready to provide information about National Trails Day to everyone. Call (800) 972-8606.

What is the National Trails System Act?

Passed by Congress in 1968 to impart federal assistance to the Appalachian Trail and to help establish a national system of trails, the National Trails System Act provides for designation of approved trails as "national scenic trails" or "national historic trails." The Appalachian and Pacific Crest Trails were the first two trails to receive a "national scenic trail" designation.

The national scenic trail designation ensures continuous protected corridors for outdoor recreation. National historic trails recognize prominent past routes of exploration and military action. It is important to note that historic trails generally consist of remnant sites and segmented trails and are thereby not necessarily continuous. Although trails are protected by the government, land through which the trail travels may be either publicly or privately owned.

ACKNOWLEDGMENTS

There were literally hundreds of individuals without whom this book would not have been possible. I would like to take this opportunity to sincerely thank all who had a part in providing details and offering assistance to me. It is not possible to name everyone, so a collective thank-you will have to do. A special collective thank-you to all the dedicated recreation planners who took the time to review this text for accuracy and who provided information regarding specific recreation areas. BLM Recreation Specialists are a dedicated crew who rarely get the credit they deserve. I tip my hat to every one of you.

There are a few people who went well beyond the call of duty, patiently following up with me and enthusiastically describing areas that have been included within this book—even when I was screaming "Uncle!" and bandaging bleeding fingers from all the typing (just kidding.) I would like to recognize each of these people individually. My utmost gratitude and thanks goes out to: Kevin Carson, John Bristol, Suzzane Garcia, Chris Barns, Dwayne Sykes, John Bailey, Chuck Telford, Tracey Pharo, Lynn Clemons, Steve Dondero, Mel Ingeroi, Tommy Thompson, David Vickery, Susan Lynn, Beverly Gorny, Lou Jurs, Gary Yeager, Pat Entwistle, Rem Hawes, Stephanie Gilbert, Patricia Foulk, Barbara Perkins, Mark E. Golbach.

ABOUT THE AUTHOR

Michael Hodgson is a contributing editor of *Backpacker Magazine*, a weekly columnist for the *San Jose Mercury News*, technical editor for *Outdoor Retailer Magazine*, and adventure resource editor for *Adventure West Magazine*. He has also written for *Field and Stream*, *Pacific Northwest Magazine*, *Motorland Magazine*, and *Christian Science Monitor*.

Michael is the author of eight books on the outdoors, and has won numerous writing awards from the Outdoor Writers Association and Western Publications Association. He lives with his family in San Jose, California.

About the American Hiking Society

The American Hiking Society (AHS), is a nonprofit organization dedicated to expanding and improving the nation's hiking trails through education and advocacy. Since its inception in 1977, AHS has served as a major voice for its constituency, representing the interest of hikers and working to increase public awareness relating to trails issues. AHS testifies regularly before Congressional subcommittees, letting legislators know the concerns of hikers around the country. AHS also sponsors the *Volunteer Vacations Program* which sends dozens of volunteer trail workers to sites around the country to spend one to two weeks constructing or maintaining trails on federal lands.

In addition to publishing *American Hiker* magazine, AHS also publishes a member newsletter focusing on trails issues, a newsletter on the long distance trails network (in cooperation with the National Park Service), and a national directory of outdoor volunteer opportunities.

In a joint venture with *Backpacker* Magazine, AHS is seeking to establish the first east-west coast-to-coast hiking trail in America. As with the Appalachian and Pacific Crest Trails, the American Discovery Trail (ADT) will unite the hiking communities across the nation and offer the opportunity to walk across America.

For further information about the American Discovery Trail, contact National Coordinator, Reese Lukei at (800) 851-3442.

If you want to be a modern-day pathfinder and help break new trails, or maintain those that already exist on BLM land, contact the American Hiking Society and ask for information on their "Helping Out in the Outdoors" volunteer program. Contact: AHS, P.O. Box 20160, Washington, DC 20041. Or get in touch with the BLM office in your preferred state.

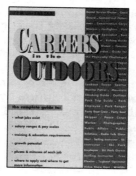